THE WORLD OF
ROTTWEILERS

THE WORLD OF
ROTTWEILERS

ANNA KATHERINE NICHOLAS

With a special chapter, "The Illustrated Standard,"
sponsored and produced by the American Rottweiler Club.

Title page: Ch. Birch Hill's Tank Commander, T.D., owned by Jane Wiedel, Stockton, Illinois.

Contents

About the Author

Since early childhood, Anna Katherine Nicholas has been involved with dogs. Her first pets were a Boston Terrier, an Airedale, and a German Shepherd Dog. Then, in 1925, came the first of the Pekingese, a gift from a friend who raised them. Now her home is shared with two Miniature Poodles and numerous Beagles.

Miss Nicholas is best known throughout the dog fancy as a writer and as a judge. Her first magazine article, published in *Dog News* magazine around 1930, was about Pekingese. This article was followed by a widely acclaimed breed column, "Peeking at the Pekingese," which appeared for at least two decades, originally in *Dogdom* and then, following the demise of that publication, in *Popular Dogs*. During the 1940's she was a Boxer columnist for *Pure-Bred Dogs/American Kennel Gazette* and for *Boxer Briefs*. More recently many of her articles, geared to interest fanciers of every breed, have appeared in *Popular Dogs, Pure-Bred Dogs/American Kennel Gazette, Show Dogs, Dog Fancy, The World of the Working Dog*, and for both the Canadian publications, *The Dog Fancier* and *Dogs in Canada*. Her *Dog World* column "Here, There and Everywhere" was the Dog Writers' Association of America winner of the Best Series in a Dog Magazine Award for 1979. Also a feature article of hers, "Faster Is Not Better," published in *Canine Chronicle*, received Honorable Mention on another occasion.

In 1970 Miss Nicholas won the Dog Writers' Association Award for the Best Technical Book of the Year with her *Nicholas Guide to Dog Judging*. In 1979 the revision of this book again won this award, the first time ever that a revision had been so honored by this organization. Other important awards that Miss Nicholas has gained as a dog writer over the years have been the Gaines "Fido" on two occasions and the *Kennel Review* "Winkies," also on two occasions, these both in the Dog Writer of the Year category.

It was during the 1930's that Miss Nicholas's first book, *The Pekingese*, appeared in print, published by the Judy Publishing Company. This book and its second edition sold out quickly and are now collector's items, as is her *The Skye Terrier Book*, which

Ch. Marlo's Rome Da Bratiana, C.D., bred and owned by Marlene and Robert Lore, Marlo's Rottweilers, Citrus Heights, California.

was published during the 1960's by the Skye Terrier Club of America.

During recent years, Miss Nicholas has been writing books consistently for T.F.H. Publications. Her T.F.H. titles include *Successful Dog Show Exhibiting, The Book of the Rottweiler, The Book of the Poodle, The Book of the Labrador Retriever, The Book of the English Springer Spaniel, The Book of the Golden Retriever, The Book of the German Shepherd Dog, The Book of the Shetland Sheepdog, The Book of the Miniature Schnauzer,* and *The World of Doberman Pinschers*. Plus, in the T.F.H. series, *The Maltese, The Keeshond, The Chow Chow, The Poodle, The Boxer, The Beagle, The Basset Hound, The Dachshund* (the latter three co-authored with Marcia A. Foy), *The German Pointer, The Collie, The Weimaraner, The Dalmatian, The Great Dane,* and numerous other titles. In a series of smaller T.F.H. books she has done *Rottweilers, Weimaraners,* and *Norwegian Elkhounds*. And she has done American chapters for two popular English books published in the U.S. by T.F.H., *The Staffordshire Bull Terrier* and *The Jack Russell Terrier*.

Miss Nicholas's association with T.F.H. began in the early 1970's when she co-authored for them five books with Joan Brearley. These are *The Wonderful World of Beagles and Beagling* (also honored by the Dog Writers Association), *This is the Bichon Frise, The Book of the Pekingese, The Book of the Boxer,* and *This is the Skye Terrier*.

Since 1934 Miss Nicholas has been a popular dog show judge, officiating at prestigious events throughout the United States and Canada. She is presently approved for all Hounds, all Terriers, all Toys and all Non-Sporting, plus all Pointers, English and Gordon Setters, Vizslas, Weimaraners and Wirehaired Pointing Griffons in the Sporting Group and Boxers and Dobermans in the Working Group. In 1970 she became only the third woman ever to have judged Best in Show at the famous Westminster Kennel Club event at Madison Square Garden in New York, where she has officiated as well on some sixteen other occasions over the years. She has also officiated at such events as Santa Barbara, Chicago International, Morris and Essex, Trenton, Westchester, etc., in the States and at the Sportsman's and the Metropolitan, among numerous others, in Canada, as well as specialty shows in several dozen breeds in both countries. She has judged in almost every state of the United States and in four of the Canadian provinces. Her dislike of air travel has caused her to refrain from acceptance of the constant invitations to officiate in more distant parts of the world.

Booth

Ch. Chaha vom Stienkopf, SchH. II, owned by Alan P. Kruse of Von der Kruse, Howell, Michigan. Numerous important German bloodlines are behind many of the dogs we see today in the United States.

CHAPTER ONE

Origin and the Early Days

Am. and Can. Ch. Rodsden's Kato v Donnaj, C.D.X., T.D., America's first Best-in-Show–winning Rottweiler, depicted here in the tradition of his ancestors, pulling a milk cart. This great dog was owned by Jan Marshall, Woodstock, Vermont.

Difficult though some people may find it to believe, the Rottweiler, rather than having originated in Germany, traces his roots back to the ancient Roman Empire. Several different types of dogs used for working purposes were known in ancient Rome, among them a short- or bristle-coated dog used primarily for herding. The resemblance between these dogs and our modern Rottweiler is striking, with only the most moderate changes in appearance having taken place through the years. These progenitors of the Rottweiler, although used as war dogs in battle, were used principally as drover dogs. We understand, too, that the Emperor Nero relied upon a number of them around his palace to discourage intruders.

How, then, did the breed come to be known as the Rottweiler? This came about through numbers of them remaining after arrival at Rottweil, in the Wurttemberg area of Germany, as they accompanied Roman troops through Europe, over the Alps via the St. Gothard Pass, and into this area of Southern Germany.

The city of Rottweil is the seat of the district for which it is named. Standing on a hill on the left bank of the Neckar River, it is centrally located in this lush agricultural area. Its name is said to have been acquired in about 700 A.D., when a Christian Church was erected on the land where formerly Roman baths had stood. Red tiles of an earlier Roman villa were unearthed during the excavation, causing the area to become known as "das Rote Wil" or "the red tile."

Due to its central location, Rottweil grew to become a trading center of importance— the marketplace to which farmers and cattlemen brought their produce for sale.

The dogs who had served the Roman troops so well during the invasion of Europe had no difficulty continuing their work in their new home. One of their principal values to the invading troops was herding and guarding the food supply; in those days, prior to food preservation and refrigeration, it was necessary that cattle travel with the troops "on the hoof" to provide food. It was the job of the drover dog to herd and guard the large herd against loss. Whatever other duties they may have fulfilled, the drover dogs were invaluable for the manner in which they performed this all-important task.

Those dogs who remained behind when the Romans left Germany made an easy transition in their new surroundings. Again there was a need for intelligent, strong working dogs of stamina and "lasting ability"—in this case, to herd the cattle being taken to market for sale. Additionally, the presence of these Rottweilers helped assure the safety of the traveling tradesmen, especially on the return journey when their cattle had been sold and their well-filled money bags occupied a position of safety tied to the collars of the big, black dogs. Thieves who might be encountered on the trail would hardly dare risk attempting to remove them.

Rottweil's popularity as a trading center expanded at a steady pace. Soon cultural interests flourished there, bringing numerous visitors. The merits of the butchers' dogs gradually generated interest among the transients as well as the local residents, and soon breeding of them was under way in an effort to improve and increase their type.

As interest in them grew, so did the desire of increasing numbers of people to own one of these splendid dogs. Then it was, in respect for their superiority over other types of drover dogs, that these impressive animals became known as Rottweilers, forever associating them in the minds of the public with the area where fullest appreciation of them began. It is the descendants of the original Roman drover dogs, as they were bred and developed by the Germans, who became the breed from then on known as the Rottweiler.

It did not take long for a competitive spirit to develop between Rottweiler owners in the "my dog's better than your dog" spirit. Owners tried to produce the best and finest looking in their area, and, even as today, one particularly pleasing in looks, temperament and working ability frequently sold for a sizeable price. Among their attributes as herding dogs was their calm, self-assured manner of working, avoiding any disturbances among the cattle as they were herded.

The second activity of the Rottweiler of that period was as a "cart dog." Fortunate, indeed, for the early welfare of the breed! For

the progress marked by the arrival of the railroad led to an entirely different method of transporting cattle, which did not include the services of a canine guardian.

Pulling of the milk carts was still needed, however, for a period of time, until the job became one for donkeys rather than dogs. This deprived the Rottweiler of both of his principal means of usefulness, leading to a decline in the breed's popularity. We are glad to note that some of those people who had been served so well by their canine friends remained loyal to their dogs, continuing to retain them as guards for their home and property.

Strangely, following the "quiet time" within the breed, when the great surge of renewed interest came, it did so in an entirely different area of Germany. We have been informed, on good authority, that in the year 1905 only one Rottweiler bitch could be located in all of Rottweil! At about this same time, however, the breed was "discovered" for police work. This amusing story has been told before, but in our opinion bears repeating. It has to do with a brawl one night in a waterfront saloon in Hamburg. Fourteen very drunken sailors, so we are told, were carrying on a dispute over an attractive member of the opposite sex. A passing policeman, who happened also to be a Rottweiler owner out walking his dog, arrived on the scene and felt obliged to take some action, which of course promptly made him the target of the mob and its wrath. But the Rottweiler upheld the honor of the police and became the hero of the situation when, in almost no time flat, several of the sailors were thrown to the ground by the weight of this dog; the others beat a hasty retreat from the scene.

It is interesting to read descriptions of the early Rottweiler as the breed took shape in Germany prior to the 20th Century. So far as general conformation and size and shape of head are concerned there is said to have been little change. The massive substance, aura of power, and self-assured confidence has remained through the years. But back in those days we find that two separate strains of Rottweiler were being developed, one larger and more muscular than the other. The big, muscular dogs were specifically for the work of

An early Rottweiler, Rudi Eulenspiegel of Mallion, representative of the famed German kennel Eulenspiegel.

drawing the carts. The smaller dogs, more agile and less bulky, were considered superior for herding. This difference was due to three considerations. First, the largest dogs were probably too heavily built for lasting power on the road; their extra weight might cause accidents in jumping; and their additional height could cause a tendency to nip the cattle on the shoulder or buttocks rather than on the hock, resulting in damaged stock which would be considered inferior and thus bring a smaller price at market.

These two sizes were bred as separate strains. Performance alone was important in the smaller dogs, with little concern for their looks. In fact this is the strain in which what we now consider "out of bounds" coloring existed. Such things as white collars, white chests, white spots or feet; or even red dogs with black stripes down their back, or light colored markings were recognized and accepted as Rottweilers, while the dogs of the larger strain were always scrupulously correct in the color and pattern we associate with the breed today. All of this suggests that the smaller strain was outcrossed thus permitting this variety of coloring to exist, while the larger dogs were the true Rottweilers, bred carefully within their own bloodlines.

BS'65, WS'65, Int. and Am. Ch. Erno von Wellesweiler, SchH. I was by BS'60, '61, '62, Int. and Am. Ch. Harras vom Sofienbush, SchH. I ex Alke vom Gomaringen, SchH II. Breeder, Karl Backes. Owner, Mrs. Bernard Freeman, Freeger Rottweilers, New York, New York.

CHAPTER TWO

The Rottweiler in Germany

Siegerin „Dora von Burgtobel", 27 644, Sch. H. 1
Züchter: Chr. Armbruster, Kirchheim/Teck

1952 Bundesiegerin Dora von Burgtobel, SchH. 1, is the bitch on whose bloodlines Von Arktos Rottweilers are founded. Photo courtesy of Judith Hassed.

The year was 1905. The location the Heidelberg Dog Show. The characters the two co-chairmen of this event, Albert Graf and Karl Knauf, who had been asked to select a splendid dog of unusual breeding and admirable character for the Honorary President of the Heidelberg Club. Critically examining the various canines on exhibit at the show, and conferring with a noted breeder who also contributed his opinion, it was decided that the most ideal of all dogs for the Honorary President would be a Rottweiler. At this point almost no information about the breed was available, not even in otherwise quite complete early histories of the dog.

The feeling arose that there should be a club developed for the standardization and protection of these fine animals. And so it came about that in Heidelberg two years later, on January 13, 1907, the original German Rottweiler Club (DRK) was founded, causing Heidelberg henceforth to be regarded as the true birthplace of the modern Rottweiler so admired and respected today.

Things often fail to run smoothly in specialty clubs, which proved almost immediately to be the case here. Within a matter of months a problem arose based on the expulsion of a member for what were considered to be gross infringements on the principles of good sportsmanship. Of course the offended member and friends promptly established a club of their own, (this, too, in Heidelberg), which was called the South German Rottweiler Club and began operations on April 26, 1907, slightly more than three months following the inception of the original organization. Unification of these two clubs proved to be impossible, so strong were the differences of opinion. It is small wonder that soon a *third* Rottweiler Club developed—the International Rottweiler Club (IRK), into which before long the already faltering South German Rottweiler Club quite speedily was absorbed.

It had already been determined, when the German Rottweiler Club was founded, that tremendous benefit would come to the breed could the interests and support of the police department be generated for these dogs. What could be better, now that the breed was, so to speak, "unemployed" since the loss of their use first as cattle dogs and then as cart dogs had passed into history, than their talents and tendencies as guard dogs and for police work be encouraged? It was not difficult to persuade the police in Hamburg that such an alliance might well prove mutually beneficial. Several dogs were recruited for the work; the first two were Max von der Stahlenberg (breed book No. 48) and Flock von Hamburg. The experiment proved highly successful, the Rottweilers working so impressively that in 1910 they became the fourth breed recognized by the German Police Dog Association. The German Rottweiler Club, of course, became affiliated with this Association.

In 1913, a movement was initiated towards unification of the German Rottweiler Club (DRK) and the International Rottweiler Club (IRK), to no avail at that time. Again, in 1920, efforts were resumed to bring this about, by which time evidently the disadvantages of "a house divided" had become generally apparent and the movement was successful. On July 3, 1921, a meeting at Gassel between the two groups resulted in ratification, on August 14th of that year, during a well attended general meeting in the establishment of the General German Rottweiler Club, more familiarly known as the ADRK. The Rottie Fancy obviously had "come of age" and its adherents were ready to join forces upholding the policies important to the best interests of their breed.

Both IRK and DRK kept Stud Books while going their separate ways, the DRK publishing just one volume while the IRK had put forth two. The one DRK volume included 286 dogs and 214 bitches. IRK's two volumes totalled 2340 listings, the second of which included 770 of entries from DRK.

Basically the listings were quite different in the Stud Books of these two organizations. Sieger Ralf vom Necker and the Strahlenburg dogs were dominant in the DRK, the Teck dogs in IRK. Historians tell us that IRK was striving for uniformity of type and conformation in the breed, while the DRK working qualities took precedence over conformation. We understand that when ADRK finally became a reality, there were faults with which to reckon within the breed. Lack of head type (a Pointer appearance) was not uncommon at that time; bad bites and steep hindquarters also were in need of correction, which took place with thoughtful breeding.

The Allgemeiner Deutscher Rottweiler Club, which is the correct full title of the ADRK in Germany, now is a member of the Verband fur das Deutsche Hundewesen (VDH) and the Federation Cynologique Internationale (FCI) and abides by their rules. In modern Germany there are numerous regional and local clubs, as is the case in the United States, all doing admirable work for their breed. ADRK is now located at Stuttgart. It has from the very beginning worked to keep its members and other interested parties informed regarding the correct maintenance, breeding and training of Rottweilers, standing up for the rights of dog owners and supporting all investigations into the history, psychology and maladies of the breed. Tests are carried on for the selection of Rottweiler dogs and bitches suitable for breeding, and performance trials are sponsored for all kinds of working dogs. Dog shows are also organized by ADRK at which Rottweilers are judged by breed specialists on type, general quality, and movement as outlined in the breed's standard. They present prizes to be awarded at these competitions, to which entries have come from all parts of the world as they are regarded with the highest esteem. Full records of breeding and performance are maintained and published annually. ADRK mediates with no charge in the sale and purchase of quality Rottweilers. It also publishes an informative, sizeable, generously illustrated magazine, subscription to which is included in membership.

The entire pattern of breeding dogs in Germany is quite different from dog breeding as we know it here. Such activities in that country, if the litters are to be registered, come under the auspices of ADRK's Head Breed Warden and of the Regional Supervisor in charge of the area, whose task it is to oversee all proposed breeding programs and the keeping and rearing of dogs. Obviously, the selection of people equipped to handle these posts intelligently is a serious one, and the requisites stringent. A solid background as a breeder, combined with long years of experience, is essential in preparation for the responsibilities involved in these positions.

It was in 1942 that the Koerung (selection for breeding suitability) became effective, announced by notice in the Stud Book that year that "Beginning in January 1944 only litters from dogs with Koerung or Zuchttauglichkeitspruefung can be registered."

A Koerung is obtained by bringing the dog or bitch before a judge who checks its appearance, condition, health, bearing, expression and conformation, the gait with which the dog moves, its temperament, and a study of the pedigree, upon which suitability for breeding is considered. Once a dog has been approved for breeding at the Koerung, his vital statistics then become a matter of record, published in the Stud Book. A permanent record of this sort is surely a tremendous help to future breeders, anxious to review the credentials behind their dogs or dogs they may be considering for purchase. Special comments and recommendations appear frequently, such as a particular dog being "correct for breeding with a well boned bitch but not for a lightly boned one," or whatever comment may be deemed helpful and pertinent.

A training degree is a further requisite for a Koerung, which must have been earned in advance, as well as good health, absence of hereditary faults; in addition, the dog must be an outstanding working dog.

The Zuchttauglichkeitspruefung, also regarded by the ADRK as necessary for responsible breeding, is a stern character test to eliminate from breeding dogs of weak fighting instinct and evidencing shyness or nervousness, lest such traits be passed along to future generations. To qualify, the dogs are required to actually be sharp and possess obvious fighting instinct; mere protectiveness is NOT sufficient. Only dogs or bitches who display no sign of nervousness or shyness will make it through this test, which calls for "iron nerves and the instinct of a fighter." Approval for this degree must be applied for at three year periods.

Approved dogs are to be mated only to approved bitches, and vice-versa. The penalty for ignoring this rule is severe, with suspension from the ADRK for the breeder and registration ineligibility for the litter very likely.

This fact is clearly stated on the pedigree form.

An Ahnentafel certificate, issued by ADRK, must accompany the Rottweiler being brought for Koerung testing. This consists of the dog's pedigree and other vital information. Two classes of Koerung may be issued: No. 1 which must be re-issued periodically; No. 2 which is permanent and remains effective throughout the dog's breeding years.

Possession of a *registered* kennel name is also a requisite for breeding dogs in Germany.

Breed Wardens or Breeding Supervisors must be permitted to inspect the premises where dogs to be used for breeding are kept. Should "errors" occur in the housing of the dogs, or within the breeding program itself, a warning is issued listing the complaints and the penalties should these unauthorized practices be allowed to continue. If corrections are *not* promptly made, the Breeding Supervisor reports the fact to the ADRK with immediate action taken against the breeder.

The following standard for the breed was prepared by the ADRK and is the German Standard for the Rottweiler. It was first adopted in Germany during the early 1900's, where the general type has remained practically unchanged over the years, as has breed character.

GENERAL APPEARANCE AND CHARACTER: The Rottweiler is a robust dog rather above the medium size, neither plump nor light, neither spindle-shanked nor like a Greyhound. His figure, which is short, compact, and strong in proportion, gives every indication not only of high intelligence but also of wonderful devotion, eagerness, and joy in work. A tractable dog with considerable power and stubborn endurance. His general appearance immediately proclaims him to be of determination and courage; his calm glance indicates his good humour and his unswerving fidelity. His nature exhibits no traces of disquietude, hastiness, or indecision. Treachery, maliciousness and falseness are entirely foreign to his nature.

HEAD: Of medium length; the skull broad between the ears and moderately arched in the line of forehead when viewed from the side. The frontal depression is well emphasized. The occipital point is well developed,

AHNENTAFEL FÜR DEN ROTTWEILER

aus Körungs~~und Leistungs~~zucht

Name des Hundes: **B r o n c o   vom Räuberfeld**   Geschlecht: **R ü d e**
Farbe: **schwarz/braun**   Wurftag: **03. Dezember 1978**   Wurfjahr in Buchstaben: **Neunzehnhundertachtundsiebzig**
Züchter des Hundes: **Gottfried Faßbender, Rothehausstr. 2 a, 5000 Köln 30**

Erläuterungen über den Wurf zu dem dieser Hund gehört

	Rüden	Hündinnen
Wurfstärke bei der Geburt	7	2
Totgeboren		
Verendet bis zur Eintragung	5	1
Zum Zuchtbuch gemeldet	2	1

Eingetragen in das Zuchtbuch des A D R K

Band: L **XII**   Nummer: **54 415**

Eintragungs- und Prüfungsbestätigung

Der hier beschriebene Rottweiler ist am **01. März 1979** in das Zuchtbuch des Allgemeinen Deutschen Rottweiler-Klub unter der Nr. **54 415** eingetragen worden.

Die Abstammungsangaben sind nachgeprüft und ihre Richtigkeit wird hiermit bestätigt.

Die Zuchtbuchstelle des ADRK

Züchter-Bestätigung

Für die Richtigkeit der Angaben an die Zuchtbuchstelle zur Ausfertigung dieser Urkunde bürgt als Züchter durch Unterschrift:

06. März 1979
Datum

(Unterschrift des Züchters)
(Ohne Unterschrift des Züchters nicht gültig)

Name: **Gottfried Faßbender**
Wohnort: **Rothehausstr. 2 a**
         5000   K ö l n   30

Eigentumswechsel

1) am **30.11.1979** an **Zorn, Günter**
in **5 Köln 90 Steinmetzstr. 17**

(Unterschrift des Verkäufers)

2) am **01.02.1983** an **Elisabeth Zorn**
in **5013 Elsdorf auf dem Driesch 3**

(Unterschrift des Verkäufers)

3) am **17. Mai 1983** an **Elaine Lubovich**
in **1045 Route 18 E. Brunswick**
New ... U.S.A.

Untersuchung auf HD

Datum: **3.12.79**   Tatowier-Nr.: ...
Unterschrift der Röntgenstelle: ...

Ergebnis der Röntgenauswertung:
Zucht- und körfähig
Zur Zucht geeignet
Zuchtverbot
Register-Nr.:
Unterschrift: **4169** | XX |

Ergebnis der Zuchttauglichkeitsprüfung

in **Blatzheim** am **05.04.1981**
Zuchttauglich ~~zur Zucht nicht geeignet~~
Körmeister oder Richter: **Friedrich Berger**
Bestätigung der Zuchtbuchstelle des ADRK
Porta Westfalica 4, den **14. April 1981**

1. Körung in ___ am ___

Für die Dauer von zwei Jahren angekört
(bis einschließlich ___)
Körmeister:
Bestätigung der Zuchtbuchstelle des ADRK
Porta Westfalica 4, den ___

2. Körung in ___ am ___

Auf Lebenszeit angekört
Körmeister:
Bestätigung der Zuchtbuchstelle des ADRK
Porta Westfalica 4, den ___

Eltern	Großeltern	Ur-Großeltern	Urur-Großeltern
1 Vater Benno vom Allgäuer Tor, 46 586 Körbericht: Mittelgroßer, gut aufgebauter Rüde. Richt. Breite u.Tiefe. Trocken, ruhig u.umgängl. Wesensstark. Sehr kräft. Kopf mit dunklem Auge u. seitw. anges. Ohr, dunkelbraune, nicht ganz klar abgegr.Abzeichen,derbes, kräftiges Haar, gesund., kräft.Scherengebiß, tiefgest. gute Brust u.Brusttiefe; feste Nerven, Kampftr., Mut u. Schärfe ausgepr., schußgleichgültig. Gekört bis EzA. Internationaler Champion-Schönheit. Bundessieger 1978. SchH III, FH Kein Hinweis für HD - körfähig.	**3** Dux vom Hungerbühl, 43 753 Körbericht: Mittelgroß, hervorragender Typ, Kopfform gut, Stirnfurche, Stop ausgepr.erwünscht, Auge dunkel, Ohr hoch/seitl.anges., klein, Oberkopf breit Winkelungen hervorrag., Abzeichen sehr gut, raumgreif.Traber; geschloss., fest trocken, außer dem etw.breit.Oberkopf keine Mängel;aufmerks., temperamentv. aufgew. selbst., Schutz-u.Kampffr.sehr gut,s.gut.Angriffsgeist,hieb-u.stockf. SchH I, HD frei - gekört **4** Evi vom Oberen Argental, 43 577 ZtPr.-Bericht: Mittelgroß, gut proport. Gebiß gut, typ.Kopf, Auge dunkel bis mittelbr.,Ohr sehr gut anges.u.getrag., Brand reichl.u.gut gez.,Vorhand u.Rücken gerade, Pfoten gut geknöch.,Hinterhand gut gest.u.gewink., frei u.leicht im Lauf;lebh.,aufmerks.,umgänglich, Schutz-u.Kampftr. sehr gut. SchH I, HD pos. - zuchttauglich.	**7** Kuno v.Butzensee, 40 415, SchH III **8** Britta v.Schloßberg, 39 075 **9** Dirk v.Ottenberg, 39 671, SchH I **10** Dina v.Oberen Argental, 41 308	**15** Wotan v.Filstalstrand, 37 422, SchH I **16** Edle v.Dürrbach, 38 079 **17** Alex v.Ludwigshafen/See, 37 409,SchH III,BS 1964 **18** Evi vom Kanzachtal, 36 339 **19** Astor v.Löwen,SHSB77 597 SchH II **20** Yonne v.Falkenstein-Schramberg, 36 732 **21** Cito v.Schloßberg, 39 888, SchH I **22** Alli v.Ludwigshafen/See, 37 413
2 Mutter Centa vom Dürschtal, 49 339 Körbericht: Kräftig, richtige Größe, rumpfig, tief und breit, kräftige Knochen, Kopfform gut, Schulter sollte besser anliegen, hintere Winkelung gut, Rücken gerade und fest bei guter Rückenübertragung, kleines, rückwärts angesetztes Ohr; feste Nerven, Kampftrieb, Mut und Schärfe ausgeprägt, schußgleichgültig. Gekört bis 22. Oktober 1980 SchH II Kein Hinweis für HD - körfähig.	**5** Donar vom Markgräflerland, 42 883 Körbericht: Mittelgroß, sehr ausgeglich. hervorrag.Verfass.,Gebäude o.Fehler, raumgreif.rationell.Gangw.,gute Gefügefestigk.,sehr kräft.Kopf, mittelbr. Auge, korrekt.,mittelschw.Ohr, Farbe u.Abz.ideal,knappes Scherengebiß;Mut u.Kampftr.ausgeprägt,mitt.Schärfe,lebhaft,aufmerks.,gutart.,feste Nerven. Gekört bis EzA., SchH III, FH, HD frei-körfähig. **6** Hexe vom Hiesfeld, 46 086 ZtPr.-Bericht: Mittelgroße,temperamentvolle Hündin, mittelgr.Ohr wird nicht immer korrekt getr.,braunes Auge,gute Lage der Schultern,Pfoten gut geschlossen, richt.Hinterhandwinkel.,durch Bänderriß gehemmt, fester gerader Rücken, stockhaarig,richt.Brand,vorn ausgreif. Schutz-u.Kampftr.ausreich.vorhanden. Kein Hinweis auf HD - körfähig.	**11** Alex v.Dobeltal,40 091 SchH II, Int.Champion-Schönheit, HD leicht positiv-körfähig. **12** Hetti v.Kursaal, 41 028 **13** Cuno v.d.Bönninghardt, 40 482, SchH III, HD frei - körfähig. **14** Carin v.Hiesfeld, 43 666, SchH I, HD positiv-zuchttaugl.	**23** Benno v.d.Michelsburg, 38 506 **24** Quinta v.Echterdingen, 37 153 **25** Blitz v.Schloß Westerwinkel, 37 642,SchH III,BS6? **26** Gerda v.Kursaal, 35 749 **27** Pio v.d.Solitude,39 419 SchH II **28** Bessi v.Westerwald, 37 930, SchH III **29** Armin v.d.Königshardt, 39 351,SchH III,LS 1970 **30** Britta v.Werrich,40 658 SchH I

although it does not in any way protude. The cheeks are well covered with muscle without being excessively so. The zygomatic arch is well pronounced.

The straight bridge of the nose is not very long. The length from the root to the tip is not longer than the upper part of the head (epicranium) from the occipital bone to the frontal depression.

The tip of the nose is well formed, rather broad than round, with comparatively large nostrils, and always black in color.

The flews are also black and firm; they fall gradually away towards the corners of the mouth which do not protrude excessively.

The teeth are strong, engaging one over the other like a scissors. The incisors grip in front of the lower jaw.

The medium sized eyes are of a dark brown color and expressive of good humour and self-confidence. The eyelids close down well.

The ears are small and triangular and stand away from each other as much as possible; they are set high and appear to give breadth to the upper part of the head; they are carried well forward and afford a good covering for the earhole.

The scalp is tightdrawn and sits well everywhere; at the most, it only forms folds when the dog is on the alert.

The neck is powerful, round and broad, with plenty of muscle and slightly arched line rising from the shoulders, fairly spare without any perceptible dewlap or superfluous skin.

FOREQUARTERS: show long, well set shoulders. The upper arm is well set, but yet not too close to the body. The lower arm is well developed, powerful and muscular. The fetlocks which are slightly "springy" are powerful and not too steeply set. The paws are round, very compact, and arched. The soles are very hard, the dark nails short and strong. The forelegs when viewed from all sides are straight and are not set too narrow.

TRUNK: Breast is roomy, broad and deep; rather round than oval. The back is straight and firm, rather short than long. The part in the region of the kidneys is short, powerful and deep; the flanks are very slightly drawn up. The buttocks are short and broad and do not fall away.

HINDQUARTERS: The upper parts of the thigh are short, broad, and well covered with muscle. The shanks are very long and very muscular above; they are sinewy below and powerful. The hocks have a good angle but not exaggerated, and still less steep. The paws are somewhat longer than those of the forelegs, but are very compact with strong toes and without dewclaws.

TAIL: (stumpy tail) is carried perpendicular as much as possible. It is short, set high, and prolongs the line of back in a perpendicular direction. The dog is often born with this stumpy tail, called "bob-tail." It is, however, to be subsequently docked if it is too long.

HAIR: is the so-called bristly hair, and is short, rough and strong. The underdown, which must be found on the neck and thighs, must on no account protrude from the outer hair. The hair is somewhat long on the fore and hind as well as on the tail. Otherwise it is rather short than long, sitting close and firm.

COLOR: is black with very distinct and dark markings on the cheeks, the muzzle, the breast, and the legs as well as over each eye; these markings are from mahogany brown to yellow in color. Small white markings on the chest and belly are not exactly faults but neither are they desirable.

SIZE: in the case of dogs, height at shoulder is from 24-27½ inches. In bitches from 22-26, always in good proportion.

Numerous faults are listed by the ADRK, ranging from dogs who are ineligible to compete at all, which includes those being monorchids or cryptorchids; having bad mouths; strongly marked reversal of sexual characteristics (doggy bitches and bitchy dogs); nervousness, cowardice or stupidity; long and curly coats or too smooth a coat with undercoat lacking.

Slightly less serious than the above faults are those which are considered to be "working faults" in that they affect the dog's usefulness and ability to work as well as appearance; and a number of what might be called "minor" faults.

Colonial Rottweiler Club Specialty, May 1962. Best of Breed, under judge Major B. Godsol, went to Arno v Kafluzu owned by Felicia Conover (now Luburich) and Gladys Swenson.

CHAPTER THREE

Rottweilers in the United States

Nixe vom Bayernland at age 18 weeks, Von Schwabing's newest edition from Germany. Owned by Roy and Fran Hiltermann, Warwick, Rhode Island.

Rottweilers evidently were virtually unknown as a breed in the United States until about the mid-1930's, although Jim Harwood did send us a reproduction of a photo of one, unidentified except for the information that it would be seen in dog shows in the New York area "in the future," which appeared originally, along with breed identification, in the June 1924 issue of *Dogdom* magazine. The photo is a headstudy of a noble looking dog. I am sure that it must have created interest at the time of first printing, and can still be seen in my earlier T.F.H. publication, *The Book of the Rottweiler*.

Beyond this one, the earliest references to Rottweilers in this country which we have found started during the 1930's. A bitch named Irma v Steinbach, who was American-bred and born in 1929, must have been among the earliest whelped in the United States. She was shown at Westminster at least once during the 1930's, was owned by Robert Sieber of Forest Hills, New York, as was a dog of that same period, which gives rise to the thought that possibly the Rottweiler pictured in *Dogdom* in 1924 may have been

owned by this gentleman, too. Or perhaps by Irma's breeder, J. Kocher, whose address is not included. Irma was sired by Franzl v d Kinzeg ex Zilly v d Steinbach. Mr. Sieber's dog, shown during the 1930's and referred to above, was named Prince and was bred as well as owned by Mr. Sieber, sired by Jank v d Steinbach ex Nora v d Landeck. These two were shown in New York both separately and in Brace Class competition.

Some of the earliest Rottweiler activity in the United States took place in California during the 1940's. Here it was that the first of the Rottweiler Specialty Clubs in this country was organized, known as the Rottweiler Club of America, founded in 1940, thanks to the interest and work of Noel Jones and Barbara Hoard Dillon.

A highly esteemed professional handler, Mr. Jones is credited with being the original individual to have introduced Rottweilers to the Pacific Coast, and he points with pride to the first two officially recognized champions having been of his breeding. In connection with the latter, it would seem that Rottweiler exhibitors got off to a somewhat stormy start, for the dog who actually earned the first American Kennel Club championship was deemed ineligible by that organization as the papers on this dog from Germany were still in the process of registration, and no permission had been obtained to show the dog in the interim. Mr. Jones was the handler of the dog, who was Astra von Weinsberger-Tal, purchased for W. M. Bruenig from Helen Heid. Champion or not, nothing can take away from this dog the fact that three five-point majors were won in rapid succession, earning for Astra a place of importance in Rottweiler history!

As a result of this misunderstanding, another splendid Rottweiler, Champion Zero, became officially the first A.K.C. recognized champion Rottweiler, (although actually the second) followed by Champion Cito v d Hohenzollern which Mr. Jones credits as having belonged to Mrs. Heid. These, then, were officially the first two A.K.C. champions of the breed.

Noel Jones's first Rottweiler was Cuna v d Schwartzen Eiche, who was sired by Herlinde v d Schwartzen Eiche, the first Rottweiler to gain a Utility Obedience and Tracking Degree in the United States. Mr. Eichler was a Rottie enthusiast from Wisconsin whose dogs contributed well to the breed.

Then, for Noel Jones, there was the outstanding dog who became Champion Kurt, the first Rottweiler to win a Working Group in California, which he did under the very knowledgeable eye of that esteemed Rottweiler enthusiast, Mrs. Geraldine Rockefeller Dodge. Mr. Jones speaks of this dog as having been "the best Rottweiler on the West Coast, who could win today in spite of our imports," adding that the dog was never dull, loved to "ham it up" and had lots of spirit so essential in a show dog. Mr. Jones could not afford to show this dog for himself, so he gave him as a gift to Harry Kramer, for whom he then handled him.

Noel Jones handled, or bred, or bred and handled, numerous other noted Rottweilers of the early California days.

Returning to the Rottweiler Club of America: it was in Mr. Jones's backyard that numerous early matches of this organization were held, sponsored by an active and enthusiastic group of members in the early days following the club's inception. Barbara Dillon became a charter member of the club; she and Mr. Jones and Nancy and Andrew Cooper are, we believe, the only ones of the original group still alive. This was intended to become the Parent Club for Rottweilers in the United States; but, as sometimes happens in dog clubs, a political situation is said to have taken place, leading to the ultimate destruction of the plan and its demise during the mid-1950's. As Barbara Dillon has told us, many of the original members were eliminated by a new clique which, with the membership "down to half a dozen or fewer people, then rotated the offices and would accept no applications to revive the Club." This put Rotties rather at a disadvantage with no Parent Club right at the time when the growth of the breed was really starting upward.

Barbara Hoard Dillon has been breeding Rottweilers in the United States longer than anyone else and is still active in the early 1980's. This lady, who is of German American descent (her father's parents were German born; her mother's family traces back to pre-American Revolutionary days) feels that she has roots in both places. Her interest in Rottweilers over the years has been tremendously beneficial to the breed from the very beginning of its growth in the United States right up to the present time, and will continue to influence the future through Panamint dogs and their descendants. Mrs. Dillon holds the longest consecutive membership of an American in the German Rottweiler Club (ADRK) and possibly the longest of *any* member outside of Germany. She and Mr. Pasanen of Finland are both the recipients of gold medals for this long-time interest. Additionally, Barbara Dillon holds the longest membership of any American in the Dutch Rottweiler Club and has been a member of the English Rottweiler Club since that organization's beginning.

But returning to the early U.S. Rotties: the foundation bitch for Panamint Kennels was acquired by Barbara Hoard Dillon in 1948, Zada's Zenda, bred by Nancy and Andrew Cooper, purchased by Barbara from Noel Jones. She also acquired the dog, Zuke, who was from the first litter bred by Noel Jones in 1947.

Panamint's first homebred litter was whelped in March 1952, sired by Champion Hannibal, and from the original bitch, Zenda.

Claus v Schildgen was acquired from W. F. and Mary Ann DeVore in 1952, then owner-handled by Barbara to his title. Kezia, from the first Panamint litter, bred to Claus, produced American and Canadian Champion Panamint Ragnarok.

Also in 1958 Emir v Kohlenhof, SchH. I, a German male came to visit frequently at Panamint, which practice continued over a period of several years. Ragnarok was bred to him in 1960, thus producing Champion Christal and American and Canadian Champion Panamint Antje.

Another member of the Rottweiler Fancy who has owned the breed over a lengthy period is Mrs. Margareta McIntyre, whose family had Rottweilers back in Sweden as long ago as 1935, and who has herself personally owned at least one of these dogs ever since then. Her first Rottie in America was acquired in 1950 but was never shown. In August of 1961, however, a splendid imported dog, Aviemore's Don Juan, was imported from Sweden by this fancier, and promptly proceeded to distinguish himself as a citizen of the United States. Don Juan was the first Rottweiler to become a Champion and Utility Dog here, sired six champions, and sired Mrs. McIntyre's first homebred litter.

It was with the purchase in November 1969 of Freeger's Ingela from Mrs. Bernard Freeman that Mrs. McIntyre considers she acquired her first real foundation bitch.

In 1945 the Rodsden Kennels acquired their first Rottweiler. At that time Rodsden was under the ownership of R. D. Rademacher and R. F. Klem; later, following Richard Klem's death in 1978, ownership transferred to P. G. Rademacher and Joan R. (Rademacher) Klem.

Feeling that in the early days American Rottweilers were becoming too closely bred owing to the lack of available breeding material, the owners of Rodsden determined to import some new bloodlines from abroad. The first of these was in 1961, when Richard

Klem's aunt agreed to bring back a Rottweiler from a trip she was making to Europe. The lovely four-month-old puppy, purchased from Jakob Kopf, President of the ADRK, became Champion Quelle v d Solitude, C.D. In 1963 she was Best of Opposite Sex at the Colonial Specialty, and she became the dam of Champion Rodsden's Felicia, who was the first bitch *ever* to take Best of Breed at a Rottweiler Specialty here, which she did at Colonial in 1965. Adding to all this, Felicia was sired by the first home-bred champion from this kennel, Champion Baron of Rodsden, C.D.

The next import acquired was Champion Bengo v Westfalenpark, C.D., who came to Rodsden as a youngster.

Then, in 1963, Bengo's sire joined him here, the 1960-'61 and '62 Bundessieger, Harras vom Sofienbusch, SchH. I. Although sparingly used at stud, this superb dog sired 12 American-bred champions. When bred to Quelle, in this one litter were Rodsden's Kaiser v d Harque, a Group-placing dog in Hawaii; Champion Rodsden's Kurt v d Harque, Ro-4, the first Rottweiler to place consistently in Pacific Coast Working Groups; and Champion Rodsden's Kluge v d Harque, C.D., Ro-50, the Top Producing stud dog in U.S. Rottweiler history until 1980 when he was surpassed by a later Rodsden import, Champion Dux vom Hungerbuhl, SchH. I, Ro-234.

Champion Afra vom Hasenacker, SchH. I, C.D., was brought to America at the same time as Harras, having been the Young Siegerin in Germany the previous year. Afra bred to a later import, Champion Falk vom Kursaal, SchH. I, produced Champion Rodsden's Lady Luck, C.D., Ro-60, dam of 12 OFA certified champions.

Champion Rodsden's Kluge v d Harque, C.D., Ro-50 was used for breeding on another of the Rodsden imports, littermate to Falk and to the 1966 Bundessiegerin, Flora vom Kursaal, she being Champion Franzl vom Kursaal. This made a notable contribution to Rottweiler history by producing the first two Best in Show Rottweilers in the United States, Champion Rodsden's Kato v Donnaj, C.D.X., T.D., Ro-37, the first to win Best in Show; and Champion Rodsden's

Duke du Trier, Ro-37, the first to win multiple Bests in Show. Also included in this litter was the second Rottweiler bitch to take Best of Breed at a Specialty, Champion Rodsden's Kirsten du Trier, C.D.

Still another dominant and successful import to Rodsden is a dog from the Netherlands, Champion Falco v h Brabantpark, Ro-286, the sire of more than 28 champions.

Judicious use of their imports, combined with their American-bred stock, has brought the Rodsden Kennels to a very prestigious postion, with a most imposing list of famous winners to their credit. Also, Rodsden dogs have distinguished themselves in other Rottweiler activities.

Here in the East, William Stahl, from New Jersey, was active over many of the early years as a breeder and exhibitor, helping to provide foundation stock to numerous kennels. One of his dogs, Rex von Stahl, was shown a good deal. The bitch, Missy von Stahl, sold to Felicia Luburich, became one of the early Srigo winners and completed her championship.

It is interesting that Rex von Stahl, who was bred by Hubert and Albert Riester, was sired by Joseph v Hohenzollern of Giralda ex Asta of Roberts Park, as Joseph was one of the Rottweilers owned by Mrs. Geraldine Rockefeller Dodge at Giralda Farms, Madison, New Jersey. Probably her most noted Rottie was Champion Krieger von Hohenreissach, born in 1953.

We could continue to tell you of many more early Rottweilers and their people. However, from the 1950's onward the years are very thoroughly covered in the following kennel stories.

Alastar

Alastar Rottweilers, Conroe, Texas, owned by Carole A. Anderson began in 1976 with a wonderful bitch, Panamint Ever A Lady, a daughter of German import, International Champion Jack vom Emstal, SchH. I, C.D. ex Champion Panamint Shasta Sage from the noted breeder Barbara Hoard Dillon of Panamint fame. Ever A Lady was shown some, pointed, but never finished. She was bred to Champion Nero von Schauer, C.D., in 1979, from which came the Top Producing Bitch,

Champion Alastar's Abbye vom Altar. That litter was co-bred by Carole Anderson with Edith Alphin.

Abbye has truly proven her worth and contributed much to her breed when, in her very first litter, she became the dam of Champion Alastar Come September owned by Katherine S. Cook and Champion Alastar Cherokee Chief owned by Bill and Ted Stewart. Then, in her second litter, she produced Champion Alastar Ebjales Von Roja owned by Lunita B. Frank. Both of these litters were sired by the same stud dog, Champion Millerhaus Benjamin of J-Dee.

The next step at Alastar was to acquire a nine-weeks-old male who grew up to become Champion Altar's Cujo vom Wald. Cujo was bred by Edward and Susan Griffin and purchased from Edith Alphin. He finished his championship at 19 months of age, then specialed a few months to gain 16 Bests of Breed and eight Group placements, including a first.

For her third litter, Abbye was bred to Cujo. This was a magical mating, to quote Carole Anderson, as it produced Alastar's "G" litter which included Champion Alastar's Gatsby von Cujo, better known as "Hawk." This splendid dog is owned by Brenda K. Jones. He finished his championship at only 12 months of age from the American-bred class, and along the way, from that same class, his wins included a Best of Breed over six top specials; then his first week out as a champion he went Group 4th. Following this, Hawk was put away for awhile to grow up; then at age 17 months, he returned to the ring with a Group placement his first weekend back. Within several shows he had acquired two Group firsts.

Abbye was again bred to Cujo, this time producing the "J" litter of six handsome pups. Five of these have gone to show homes, and at age eight months are looking very promising. One of them, Alastar's Jasmine v Cujo, was Winners Bitch at eight months from the puppy class.

Alastar has a lot of promising youngsters in the show ring as we write, these from Abbye, Cujo, and the Abbye-Ben daughters. And of course the breeding which produced Hawk will be repeated.

Ch. Altar's Cujo vom Wald taking Best of Breed and a Group placement at Brazoria in September 1983. Carole Anderson, owner, Alastar Rottweilers, Conroe, Texas. Agent-handler, Robert L. Vandiver.

Altar

Altar Rottweilers are owned by Edith Alphin at Fayetteville, North Carolina, a Doberman Pinscher breeder who, in 1975 decided that she would like to expand her kennel to include a second breed. Owing to the breed's handsome appearance and many outstanding qualities, the Alphins decided that the Rottweiler would be the breed they would add to their canine family, which they did with an eight-week-old puppy from Georgian Court Kennels, who was linebred on the noted Panamint Kennels breeding program. She became, in record time, Champion Georgian Court Bliss vom Altar, completing her championship before 11 months of age, with several Bests of Breed and Best of Opposite Sex from the classes, which put her in the No. 9 spot among Rottweiler bitches for 1976 in the United States.

A second bitch was then purchased, directly from Panamint, this one's dam being a littermate to the sire of the earlier puppy. The new bitch finished owner-handled to become a multi Best of Breed and Best of Opposite Sex winner. Her name, Champion Panamint Yonka v Altar.

In 1977 a third bitch was added, and owner-handled to become multi Best of Breed and Best of Opposite Sex winner Champion Gudrun von Anderson. Although shown only ten times in 1981 as a special, Gudrun was rated No. 17 Best of Breed bitch. She is Altar's leading producer to date, with seven championships to her credit, to which a couple more very likely soon will be added. Gudrun has the distinction of being the dam of three multiple Group winners:—her son, Altar's Gandolf vom Axel, among them, he going Best in Show in 1983. Axel was owner-handled to his championship and to his first Group 1st award—the start of some brilliant successes for him.

In 1978, following the disappointment of having two male puppies who did not turn out to be exactly what they wanted for their stud dog, Mrs. Alphin purchased what proved to be everything she had wanted in the form of a five-month-old puppy from Haserway Kennels. Champion Haserway's Freyr vom Altar was a champion at less than

a year old, then retired for a year to fully mature. When he returned to the show ring, he became a multiple Group winner, rated No. 6 Group placing Rottweiler for 1981, No. 11 Best of Breed, and in 1982 No. 9 Best of Breed winner. This excellent dog sired champions as well as pointed offspring from two of Altar's foundation bitches as well as outside bitches, and his progeny will be appearing in the ring about the time that this book is completed.

As we are working on this book, we have received the sad news from Edith Alphin that Freyr suffering from heart failure had to be put to sleep in April 1985. He is greatly missed by all who knew and loved him, and truly a tremendous loss to the breed.

Altar has completed titles on six Rottweilers purchased from other breeders and on ten homebreds since gaining their first title in 1976. Also they have bred two Canadian Champions, not included in the above count. Several also have earned obedience degrees.

Andan

Andan Rottweilers are owned by Mrs. Benjamin C. Tilghman, located at Centreville, Maryland. Early winners here included such dogs as American and Bermudian Champion Adler von Andan, C.D., by American and Canadian Champion Rodsden's Kato von Donnaj, C.D.X., T.D., ex Ehrenwache's Andernach. Adler was in the American Rottweiler Club Top Ten listing for 1975 and 1976, and he is a member of the Medallion Rottweiler Club's Hall of Fame Honor Roll. Also he was the first and still remains the only Rottweiler to have won an all-breed Best in Show at the Bermuda Kennel Club events, an honor which he gained in 1975. He won the Stud Dog Class and the Veteran Dog Class at the Colonial Rottweiler Club Specialty in 1977.

American and Bermudian Champion Andan Indy Pendence v Paulus, at eight years of age, won the Veteran's Bitch Class at her last show, the Colonial Rottweiler Club Specialty in 1983. In her day, Indy was a leading Top Winner show bitch, greatly admired for her sparkle and style. In 1977 she was No. 5 Rottweiler (*Working Dogs* magazine), the only bitch on the list; and in 1978 *Kennel Review* ranked her No. 10 on its list of Top Ten Rottweilers for that year.

Indy twice was Best of Opposite Sex at the Colonial Rottweiler Club Specialties (in 1977 and 1979), and she was Best of Opposite Sex at Westminster in 1978 and 1979. The American Rottweiler Club awarded her first place among Best of Breed winning bitches in 1977 and again in 1979. All told, Indy won 44 Bests of Breed and 38 Bests of Opposite Sex during her show career, quite a record for a bitch in those days! Indy was sired by Champion Axel von Schwanenschlag and Champion Amsel von Andan, C.D.

Champion Daba von Andan is a daughter of American and Bermudian Champion Adler von Andan, C.D., from Champion Andan Vesta von Paulus. In 1979, at 13 months old, she came from the classes to take a five-point major and Best of Breed over 11 specials in an entry of 46 at the Maryland Kennel Club under English breeder judge Mary MacPhail, handled by her breeder-owner, Mrs. Tilghman.

Mrs. Tilghman as co-owner, with Mrs. Charles R. Orr, of Andan Freiwillig von Paulus, is taking special interest in the career of this splendid young dog, of whom she also is co-breeder, the latter with Pauline Rakowski. Sired by American and Canadian Champion Rodsden's Elko Kastanienbaum, C.D.X., T.D., Canadian T.D. from Champion Andan Vesta von Paulus, he already has some exciting wins to his credit. Among them Best of Winners for a four-point major in the Colonial Rottweiler Club supported entry at Maryland Kennel Club in 1984, and a triumphant visit to Bermuda which netted him two Bests of Breed for five and four-point majors.

Recently Andan Kennels became Andan, Registered, denoting the fact that Mrs. Tilghman is, if anything, even more involved with the breed than formerly. The kennel is based on the bloodlines of Andan's foundation bitch, Ehrenwache's Andernach, a member of the Hall of Fame Honor Roll as dam of six champions; and those of American and Canadian Champion Rodsden's Kato v Donnaj, C.D.X., T.D., who was the first Rottweiler to go Best in Show in the United States.

Apache Hill

Apache Hill Rottweilers, at Abilene, Texas, are owned by Irene Castillo who had been a Miniature Schnauzer breeder for a number of years prior to the time that her heart was stolen by a Rottweiler. When that happened, Irene told her husband that they needed a large dog to guard their small ones. Champion Excalibur's B Apache War Song, C.D. soon found her way into the Castillo family, taking them quite by storm as she gained her C.D. at 11 months and her conformation championship at two years.

When Irene decided that she simply had to have another Rottie, Merrymoore's Pagan Ballyhoo, C.D. came to Texas. As Irene tells it, "She at first insisted she hadn't wanted to come, and would walk back to Georgia if necessary because it was one of those 90 degree days in February. Once we convinced her Texas weather wasn't so bad, she decided to stay and has been very glad she did. After all, someone else might not let her sleep on the bed."

"Hoo" had her C.D. by one year's age and has since done both breeder and owner proud in conformation with 11 points now to her title. Irene is looking forward to her first litter, and the C.D.X. ring.

Apache Hill stands behind their Rotties, furnishing written guarantees. All pet quality are sold on spay-neuter contracts. All puppies are raised in the house and are well on the way to being housebroken when they leave. The object here, as with so many conscientious Rottweiler breeders, is quality not quantity.

Beauhaven

Beauhaven Rottweilers, a fairly new kennel of this breed, is owned by Bob and Judy Beaupre at Aliquippa, Pennsylvania, fourteen miles from the Greater Pittsburgh Airport where both the Beaupres are employed by U.S. Air, Bob as a Captain and Judy as a flight attendant. The kennel, which is located at their home, consists of ten runs, a large puppy enclosure, and a built-in grooming area. It is climate-controlled at all times, and each of the dogs receives an equal share of house time with their owners.

The Beaupres chose this magnificent breed based on a mutual respect for the statuesque carriage and the outstanding temperament they have come to expect. The dogs they have purchased in collaboration with several co-owners have given them a solid foundation cemented with admiration of the breed, assuring that their efforts will remain intact as their interest in Rottweilers heightens.

Beauhaven's first bitch, Liebchen Von Vt. Yankee, is a Canadian Champion pointed in the United States. She was purchased in 1980 and is the dam of the Beaupres' first home bred, Beau's Alotta Dolly, who is sired by American and Canadian Champion Srigo's Flight of the Eagle. The second purchase, in 1981, was a dog who developed problems causing him to be neutered at a year of age. He is now a friend and companion in their household.

In April of 1983, the Beaupres purchased Srigo's Eagle All Over from Ms. Felicia Luburich of Srigo Kennels. "Wings" breezed to an owner-finished championship that summer.

Next came Degen Von Liebotschaner, co-owned with Dorothy and Mary Stringer of Hidden Meadow, in September of 1983. "Degen," totally owner-handled, received his championship in only four months, then began his specials career in 1985 with Best of Breed his first weekend out.

November 1984 brought the Beaupres a young bitch, Daverick's Carola V. Weihnacht, co-owned with Mr. and Mrs. Richard Gordon. She is just starting her show career as we write.

At present, three of the Beauhaven Rottweilers are working on their obedience titles. The two youngest bitches were placed in obedience classes pending the maturity the Beaupres realize is necessary for the conformation ring. This is another spectrum which serves to illustrate the versatility of the breed in all areas of owner-interest.

Currently a breeding plan is taking shape at Beauhaven, maintaining a line based on quality rather than quantity, the Beaupres limiting themselves to carefully studied aspects of which dogs fit into the guidelines they have set for themselves. This attitude of excellence

should carry this young kennel from its infancy to the achievement of its goal—the ultimate Rottweiler, an animal it is hoped future generations can reflect on with pride. To breed anything less, the Beaupres feel, is to cheat this majestic breed of its proper share of praise.

Beaverbrook

Beaverbrook Rottweilers, owned by Gary and Laura Brewton, are at Powell, Tennessee, which is on the outskirts of Knoxville. Laura, who has also been an exhibitor and a breeder of Irish Setters (from 1966 to 1978) acquired her first Rottweiler in 1974, Champion Rodsden's Nessus v h Brabant. Shortly thereafter the foundation bitch for Beaverbrook arrived, Champion Rodsden's Amber v Brabant (Champion Falco v h Brabantpark ex Champion Rodsden's Gay Lady, T.D.), who at the present time has produced nine champions, with others who are major pointed. She was named to the Top Producers List, Schlintz System, and to the Medallion Rottweiler Club Honor Roll in 1982. After producing four litters, Amber was retired and is still very much the grande dame at Beaverbrook.

The Brewtons have owned and/or bred 15 champions. Twelve of these are homebred. Currently in residence are five champion bitches and four youngsters to be shown. The quintet of champions are Amber, three of her daughters, and a granddaughter. Champion Beaverbrook Alexa v Iolkos (Champion Iolkos v Dammerwald, C.D. ex Amber) is the dam of three champions. Champion Beaverbrook Greta v Fable (American and Canadian Champion Trollegen's Fable ex Amber) has major pointed offspring starting in open classes in 1985. Champion Beaverbrook Chessi v Bruin (Champion Rodsden's Bruin v Hungerbuhl, C.D.X.—Amber) and Champion Beaverbrook Echo v Bruin (Champion Rodsden's Bruin v Hungerbuhl, C.D.X. ex Alexa) are the youngest of the champion girls. It is noteworthy that Echo finished her championship at 19 months of age, shown entirely from the Bred-by Exhibitor Class, with all majors, three five-point and one four-point, handled by Gary. Echo's dam, Alexa, finished at 15 months with six consecutive wins.

Laura has been a member of the Medallion Rottweiler Club for ten years (since the mid-1970's). She and Gary handle their own dogs, and Laura also handles professionally for others. She is currently specialing Champion Beaverbrook Eisen v Bruin for his owner, Jerry Gomer. Eisen was the 1983 American Rottweiler Club Best in Sweepstakes Puppy, following puppy class wins that same year at both the Colonial and the Medallion Specialties. As a two-year-old, Eisen already has numerous Group placements including Group 1st awards.

Other Beaverbrook champions prominent in the ring include Tom and Judy Hoover's Champion Beaverbrook Max v Huber (Fable and Amber), who is a multiple breed winner with several Group placements. Champion Beaverbrook Brenna v Fable (Fable ex Amber) was the No. 2 Rottweiler show bitch in 1982 and 1983—quite an accomplishment for that lovely bitch since she was absent from the ring the latter part of both years to produce two nice litters for her owner, Cat Klass. Additional champions bred by Gary and Laura are Champion Beaverbrook Becka v Fable (Edwards), Champion Beaverbrook Fable Triple Oak (Pearson), Champion Beaverbrook Falcon v Iolkas (Peppiatt), Champion Beaverbrook Styczen v Iolkos, C.D. (Romanowski), and Champion Beaverbrook Alex v Bruin (Cole and Rider).

In their 11-year involvement with Rottweilers, Gary and Laura have built their breeding program carefully, having produced only 12 litters by early 1985, with five of those litters still under two years of age. Many kennels become known for a famous stud. Gary and Laura chose not to acquire a stud. Instead they concentrated on their bitches, which have been sent to top producing studs throughout the country. The Brewtons consider the late Champion Rodsden's Bruin v Hungerbuhl, C.D.X., to have been a particularly important influence in their breeding program. In the fall of 1984, stud service was offered at Beaverbrook for the first time, when Laura began acting as agent for Mr. Gomer's Champion Beaverbrook Eisen v Bruin, a son of Bruin and Alexa.

Bergluft

Bergluft was established in 1962 by Mrs. Dorit S. Rogers of Sewickley, Pennsylvania, originally as a kennel for the breeding and showing of German Shepherd Dogs.

In 1967 the first of the Rottweilers, Champion Kuhlwald's Little Iodine, C.D., was acquired on a co-ownership at the age of ten weeks from Kuhlwald Kennels in Florida. She was one of the three foundation bitches of the Bergluft line. Little Iodine was raised, trained, and shown by Mrs. Rogers to her titles. She was bred only once, to Champion Axen vom Schwanenschlag, and produced the Kuhlwald "T" litter. These puppies were hand-raised by Mrs. Rogers. Four champions came from the mating; Champion Kuhlwalds Troll, Champion Kuhlwalds Tara, Champion Kuhlwalds Tobrina, and Champion Kuhlwalds Trakehner, the latter becoming foundation stud dog at Bergluft.

The second foundation bitch, Champion Drossel vom Molzberg, was purchased in 1968 at the age of six months from Molzberg Rottweilers of Tumwater, Washington. "Big Donka" matured into a very large and impressive bitch who was also owner-handled by Mrs. Rogers to her title. She was bred to Champion Axel vom Schwanenschlag and produced a litter of four champions, they being Champion Berglufts Cliff, Champion Berglufts Cai, Champion Berglufts Centa, and Champion Berglufts Carla who is owned by Mrs. Rogers.

Champion Drossel's second breeding was to Champion Kuhlwalds Trakehner, and the resulting litter was small. One bitch, Berglufts Elka, was sold to South America and was bred to produce one of the first litters of Rottweilers in Brazil.

In August of 1968, Mrs. Rogers purchased her third foundation bitch, Champion Danka vom Molzberg, a litter sister to Champion Drossel, at the age of nine months. Champion Danka was also owner-handled to her championship. She was bred only once, to Champion Kuhlwalds Trakehner, and that breeding produced Champion Berglufts Drauf and Champion Berglufts Dieter.

Champion Berglufts Carla was bred to Champion Radio Ranch's Axel von Notara.

CAPTIONS FOR PLATES 1-16

Plate 1

Ch. J-Mar's Glory B von Ansel, by Ch. Rodsden's Ansel Von Brabant ex J-Mar's Valentine Echoe, is owned by J-Mar's Rottweilers, Jerry and Margie Haralson, Harperville, Miss.

Plate 2

1. We especially like this lovely photo of Ch. Donnaj Green Mountain Boy winning the Working Group at Mason and Dixon in April 1983. Ross Petruzzo handling for owner, Anthony P. Attalla, Londonderry, N.H.

2. Am. and Can. Ch. Quick von Siegerhaus gained the title in both countries by age 15 months, always breeder-owner handled. By Ch. Birch Hill's Hasso Manteuffel, C.D.X., T.D. ex Ch. Meid von Siegerhaus. Thom and Carol Woodward, von Siegerhaus Rottweilers, Corning, Calif.

3. Ch. Imor von Stolzenfels, C.D., one of the many splendid Rottweilers owned by Dr. Evelyn Ellman, Augusta, Mich.

4. Ch. Georgian Court Bliss v Altar, was No. 9 Rottweiler Bitch for 1976 while still in the classes. A multi Best of Breed and Best of Opposite Sex winner. Owned by Edith Alphin, Altar Rottweilers, Fayetteville, N.C.

Plate 3

1. Ch. Rhomarks Axel v Lerchenfeld, C.D.X., T.D., received a very special gift from Bill and Kathy Candelario, a portrait painted by gifted artist Enid of Novato, Calif. Here is Axel posing with his portrait. Axel belongs to Ken and Hildegarde Griffin, Novato, Calif.

2. Tall, dark and handsome! Noblehaus Behexen, TT. Homebred and owned by Mark and Patricia Schwartz, West Nyack, N.Y. By Ch. Bergsgarden's Nero ex Ch. Noblehaus Ain't Misbehavin'.

3. Am. and Can. Ch. Marksman v Turick, multiple Best of Breed and Group-placing dog owned by Noblehaus Rottweilers, Mark and Patricia Schwartz, West Nyack, N.Y. Photo by Mark Schwartz.

4. The subject of this beautiful professional head-study is Bergluft's Fetz, owned by Sharon S. Statton, done at age four years. Photo courtesy of Dorit S. Rogers, Bergluft Kennels, Sewickley, Pa.

Plate 4

1. Marja Don Juan von Cannon, by Ch. Radio Ranch's D.J.V. Bethiel ex Ch. Marja Elka von Heidel, is owned by Marsh and Shepard Rappoport, handled by breeder Jacqueline Puglise, Farmingdale, N.Y. Winning at a Match Show as a baby.

2. Ronzyler's Anka Von Haiem, born in November 1984, by Rodsden's Strawlane Zephyr ex Tiboron da Bratiana was bred by Ron Fisher, Ronzwyler Rottweilers, Modesto, Calif., and is owned by Rottweilers Von Haiem, Jill Nakache, Kailua, Hawaii.

3. Ch. Vaelune's Dusky Francesca, English import, by English Ch. Vaelune Devethor ex Vaelune Dusky Contessa at North Western Ct. K.C. in 1982, Gerlinda Hockla handling for Anthony P. Attalla, Green Mountain Kennels, Londonderry, N.H.

4. Am. Ch. Tazmo's Taurus The Bull, T.T., owned by breeder Jack Tazzi, Dearborn, Mich., and J.J. Jay, Jan-Su's Rottweilers, Inkster, Mich. Suzanne Stewart handling.

5. Ch. Riegele's Astro von Eken owned by Ellen B. Walls, Riegele Farms, Hartly, Del.

6. Ch. Srigo's Heart of Gold owner-handled by Felicia Luburich, East Brunswick, N.J.

7. Am. and Can. Ch. Northwind's Helga, owned by P. Mowegue and J. Marshall, was sired by Mrs. Marshall's Ch. Rodsden's Kato v Donnaj, C.D.X., T.D. Helga produced five champions, four sired by Ch. Donnaj Vt. Yankee of Paulus, including the current "star," Anthony Attalla's Ch. Donnaj Green Mt. Boy (three times Best in Show winner).

8. Srigo's Loaded For Bear winning the Bred-By Exhibitor Class at the American Rottweiler Club National Specialty in 1985 under judge Barbara Dillon of Panamint fame. Felicia Luburich, breeder-owner, handling this splendid son of Int. Ch. Bronco v Rauberfelt, SchH 3, FH ex Srigo's Of Thee I Sing.

Plate 5

1. Von Gailingen's Ino Ikan Doit, Isadora Duzit and Izod Costalot seem to be saying "not us, Mom, we didn't do it." Three of the "young fry" at Catherine Thompson's Von Gailingen Kennels, Freehold, N.J.

2. Famous Best in Show winning bitch Ch. Pioneer's Beguiled at ten months' age. Bred and owned by Pioneer Rottweilers. Photo by Mark Schwartz.

3. The mature Berglufts Gustel at two years, who grew up to be a very handsomely headed dog. Dorit S. Rogers, owner, Sewickley, Pa.

4. Quincey von Stolzenfels, T.D.X., owned by Dr. Evelyn M. Ellman, von Stolzenfels Rottweilers, Augusta, Mich.

Plate 6

1. Ch. McCoy Von Meadow finishing his title win four majors at 13 months. This noted top-producing Rottweiler is behind the many notable champions owned by von Meadow Kennels, Donna Wormser, Ocala, Fla.

2. Blanka's Ambrosia Pandemonium, by Ch. Pandemonium's Caligula ex Ch. Blanka von Pandemonium, taking points at Wallkill K.C. in 1984. Owned by Eddie and Nancy Fong, Rye, N.Y.

3. Ch. Riegele's Greenhill Ima Maid, C.D., is owned by Nick and Lois Schwechtje, Greenhill Rottweilers, Broomall, Pa.

4. Am. and Can. Ch. Daverick's Alex vom Hasenkamp, C.D., ten months old, handled by his owner at the Colonial Rottweiler Club Specialty Show in 1982.

5. Ch. Falko vom Waldblick, SchH 1, by Dux v Kastanienbaum ex Frida v Hohen-Entringen. This magnificent dog, born in 1978, was imported and owned in this country by Mrs. Clara Hurley, Powderhorn Kennels, and Michael Grossman, Wencrest Kennels. Pictured in September 1980 at the Klubsieger Show where he was rated V 1.

6. The noted Ch. Altar's Gandolf vom Axel winning his first Best in Show. Handled by Gwendolyn Wolforth. David W. Lauster, owner, Naples, Fla.

7. Ch. Von Walber's Atom Smasher taking Winners Dog at Piedmont K.C. in February 1984. Owned by Sue Wales, Dexter, Mich.

8. Lindenwood's Anastasia, by Ch. Rodsden's Kane v Forstwald, C.D. ex Am. and Can. Ch. Bola von Meyerhoff, C.D., TT, bred and handled by Linda P. Michels. Owned by Virginia Malone and Eleanor Dufanny. Winning first in junior puppy bitches, 1982 Colonial Rottweiler Club Puppy Sweepstakes.

Plate 7

1. Dutchess of Highland Park owned by Brenda Grigsby, Wilhelmberg Rottweilers, Hasper, Tenn. Jasper is the dam of the only Rottweiler litter to produce six A.K.C. champions and one Canadian champion.

2. Ch. Windmaker's Arlo der Gremlin, by Ch. Lyn-Mar Acres Arras v Kinta ex Plaisence Irma, pictured at age 11 years. An outstanding sire and show dog, owned by Jim and Wanda White, Hickory, N.C.

3. Ch. Fangen v Arktos, C.D. photographed by M. Brandel. Owner, Judith H. Hassed, Von Arktos Rottweilers, Colorado Springs, Colo.

4. Rodsden's Lindenwood Hero owned by Roxanna and Jim McGovern, Port Crane, N.Y.

5. The imported English bitch, Thewina Summer Frolic, C.D., owned by Linda B. Griswold, Ravenwood Kennels, Michigan City, Ind.

6. Ch. Blitz von Gailingen, age one year in picture, owned by Vonpalisaden Rottweilers, Paramus, N.J.

7. Kristin von Arktos photographed by M. Brandel. Owner, Judith Hassed, Colorado Springs, Colo.

8. Lieba von Siegerhaus, left, and Schotzie von Siegerhaus at approximately ten months' age. Von Siegerhaus Rottweilers, Thom and Carol Woodward, Corning, Calif.

Plate 8
1. Srigo's Secret Weapon, a son of Felicia Luburich's great dog, Am., Can., and Int. Ch. Bronco v Rauberfeld, SchH. III, FH.

2. Handsome head-study of Carson's Jumping Jack Flash, by Birch Hill's Governor, C.D. ex Doroh's Hallelujah Tulla, U.D. Co-owned by Mary Lou Fiala and Carlos and Sandy Meijas, Washington, D.C.

3. Ch. The Chena Wilderness, handsome Rottweiler owned by Joann H. Turner, Wilderness Rottweilers, Anchorage, Alas.

4. Loneagle's Bravura v Seren, C.D., T.D. with friend Arlow of Loneagle, C.D.X., T.D., U.C.D. are owned by Matt and Jody Engle, Miami, Fla.

5. Ch. The Chena Wilderness at age two years. Owned by Joann Turner, Anchorage, Alas.

6. Big Oaks Lasko Bon Haiem at three and a half months age, pictured in Hawaiian quarantine. By Ch. Eiko vom Schwaiger Wappen, C.D.X., SchH. III, FH ex Ch. Beaverbrook Brenna von Fable II. Bred by Big Oaks Rottweilers, Powder Springs, Ga. Owned by Rottweilers von Haiem, Jill I. Odor-Nakache, Kailua, Hawaii.

Plate 9
1. Axelita von Meadow, by Top Producing Ch. Radio Ranch's Axel von Notara ex Top Producer Champion Margarita Von Meadow, was purchased from Donna Wormser and is owned by Rottweilers von Haiem, Kailua, Hawaii.

2. Am. and Can. Ch. Donnaj Vt. Yankee of Paulus, C.D.X., TT, owned by Jan Marshall, Donnaj Rottweilers, Woodstock, Vt. A crewel portrait by Chris Lewis.

3. Hexe vom Sachsen, sired by the great Dingo vom Schwaiger Wappen ex a Sachsen bitch. Hexe is currently owned by Heinz Miles of Ascothaus Rottweilers but is in the process of being purchased by Jill Nakache, Rottweilers von Haiem, Kailua, Hawaii.

4. Bomark's Allison an Beenen, C.D., TT, by Ch. El Toro von Stolzenfels ex Concord's von Adreana of CLF, is the foundation bitch at Beenen Rottweilers, owned by Donald and Lin Beenen, Lowell, Mich.

5. Ch. Jenny von Gruenerwald pictured at 12 years of age, August 6, 1985, celebrated her birthday with a trip to a formal professional photographer to bring us this picture. Dorothea Gruenerwald, owner, Colorado Springs, Colo.

6. Pionierhaus Ava Stolzenfels at 11 months. By 1983 KS Ch. Mirko vom Steinkopf, SchH. III, IPO III, FM ex Ch. Ute vom Mummler, C.D., T.D. Bred by von Stolzenfels and von Pionierhaus Rottweilers. Owned by von Pionierhaus, Jerry and Kay Watson, Pride, La.

Plate 10
1. Famed Rottweiler Ch. Oscar van het Brabantpark owned by Powderhorn/Wencrest Kennels, Hollywood, Calif.

2. Ch. Hexe v d Hoeve Cor Unum, C.D., another famous Rottweiler owned by Powderhorn/Wencrest Kennels.

3. Ch. Danny von Timmerman, noted winning Rottweiler owned by Powderhorn/Wencrest Kennels.

4. Ch. Artus vom Adelshof, SchH. III, famous Rottweiler owned by Alan P. Kruse, Von der Kruse Kennels, Howell, Mich.

5. American and Bermudian Ch. Andan Indy Pendence v Paulus at eight years old won the Veterans Class in her last show, the Colonial Rottweiler Club Specialty in 1983. A very famous and successful top winning show bitch of her day. Owned by Mrs. B.C. Tilghman, Andan Rottweilers, Centreville, Md.

6. Am., Dutch, and Luxembourg Ch. Quanto van het Brabantpark, bred by Mej. A. Huyskens, Holland, born in 1974, pictured at six years of age. Owned by Mrs. Clara Hurley and Michael S. Grossman, Powderhorn/Wencrest Rottweilers.

Plate 11
1. Lucas von Morgen Carroll at four months. Best Puppy at the Golden State Rottweiler Club Match Show in 1982. Owned by von Morgen Carroll Rottweilers, Ontario, Calif.

2. Powderhorn's Gero of Wencrest, C.D. Highest Scoring Rottweiler of the Day, Novice B, 192½, judge George Hyde, May 5, 1981, at the Kennel Club of Pasadena-Golden State Rottweiler Club 12th Annual Specialty. Trained and handled by Dawn Marshall, co-owner with Clara Hurley and Michael S. Grossman.

3. Lindenwood's Bouncer, TT, by Ch. Gasto vom Liebersbacherhof, C.D.X., T.D., SchH 1 ex Ch. Rodsden's Heiko v Forstwald, C.D., VB, TT. Breeders-owners, Linda P. and William L. Michels, Brunswick, Ohio. Pictured winning 9-12 month Puppy Dog Class at Colonial Rottweiler Club Specialty Puppy Sweepstakes 1984, shown by Junior Handler, Chandra Klem.

4. Ch. Frolic'n Darth Vader, C.D.X., T.D., TT winning Best of Breed at Sammamish Kennel Club under judge Mrs. Thelma vom Thaden. Owned by Frolic'n Kennels, Stephen and Charlotte Johnson and Linda Schuman, Redmond, Wash.

5. Ch. Pandemonium's Frauke, a frequent Best of Breed winner and Best of Opposite Sex at Westminster K.C. in both 1984 and 1985, exemplifies breed type in her striking head and compact, powerful body. Owned by Pandemonium Rottweilers, Valerie J. Cade, Goldens Bridge, N.Y.

6. Carado's Satin Classic at her first dog show, six months and a day old, going Winners Bitch under Mrs. M.L. Walton at the Guelph and District, owner-handled by Suzanne Stewart, Inkster, Mich., co-owned by Carol Kravets, Windsor, Ontario, Canada.

Plate 12

1. Von Der Kruse's Ch. Artus v Adelshof, SchH. III is one of the outstanding Rottweilers owned by Alan P. Kruse, Howell, Mich.

2. Ch. Riegele's Greenhill Ima Maid, C.D., granddaughter of Ch. Monika Maid of Denmark, at Trumbull County in 1982. Owned by Ellen B. Walls, Riegele Farms, Hartly, Del.

3. Powderhorn Mame of Wencrest, born Aug. 30, 1982, winning the 9-12 Puppy Bitch Class in an important Futurity. Owned by Powderhorn/Wencrest Rottweilers, Mrs. Clara S. Hurley and Mr. Michael S. Grossman, Hollywood, Calif.

4. Am. and Dom. Ch. Conny vom Niggelhoff, handsome young German import, son of a top German producer, who joined Anthony Attalla's Green Mountain Kennels, Londonderry, N.H., during 1984. Handled by Ross Petruzzo.

5. Ch. Torburhop's Patton Von Brawn winning under judge Robert Wills for Pamela Anderson, Wilton Manors, Fla.

6. Ch. Conny vom Nigglehof, German import, owned by Anthony P. Attalla, Green Mountain Kennels, Londonderry, N.H. By Brando vom Hause Neubrand ex Bessie vom Teinachtal. Ross Petruzzo handling.

7. Lindenwood's Bouncer, TT, by Ch. Gasto vom Liebersbacherhof, C.D.X., T.D., SchH 1 ex Ch. Rodsden's Heika v Forstwald, C.D., VB, TT. A homebred owned by Linda P. and William L. Michels, Brunswick, Ohio. Pictured winning the Bred-By Exhibitor Dog Class at the A.K.C. Centennial Show at age 16 months.

8. Ch. Bratiana's Micki von Follrath taking Winners Bitch, So. Oregon K.C. 1984. Michael and Beverly Johnson, Alameda, Calif.

Plate 13

1. Sisters winning on the same day. Left, Ch. Marlo's Inga v Follrath, C.D. (winner of *Dog World* Award, 1980) taking Best of Opposite Sex. Right, Ch. Marlo's Borgha Da Bratiana taking Winners Bitch. Breeders, Marlene and Robert Lore, Marlo's Rottweilers, Citrus Heights, Calif.

2. A good day at the dog show for von Siegerhaus "obedient" dogs! All four received a "leg" at Two Cities K.C., Oct. 1984. Left to right, Niyah von Siegerhaus, C.D. owner-handled by Evelyn Hertz. Reich von Siegerhaus, C.D. owner-handled by Carol Woodward. Pilar Ottawa von Siegerhaus, C.D., owner-handled by Pat Logue. And Medeah's Nadia von Siegerhaus, C.D. owner-handled by Charlotte Twinsham. Von Siegerhaus Rottweilers owned by Thom and Carol Woodward, Corning, Calif.

Plate 14

1. At the A.K.C. Centennial under judge J.D. Jones. Left, Ch. Doroh's Fantastic Serenade, Am. and Can. C.D.X., the dam, placed first in Veteran Bitch Class. Right, her daughter, Ch. Seren's Chantilly Lace, taking Winners Bitch for five points. Serenade is owned by P. and M. Piusz, handled by her breeder, Dorothy Wade. Lace was bred by P. and M. Piusz who co-own her with Linda Kowalski, and she is handled by Valerie Cade.

2. Alastar's Echo Natascha on the way to her title at Longview K.C. in 1983. Bred by Carole A. Anderson; owned by Lunita B. Frank and shown by Rita Chapman.

3. Marlene von Tengen, age two years, owned by Vonpalisaden Rottweilers, Paramus, N.J.

4. Ch. Margarita von Meadow, C.D., Top Producer, homebred and owned by Donna M. Wormser, Ocala, Fla. Winning Best of Breed at St. Petersburg in 1979.

5. Ch. Powderhorn's Joko of Wencrest, C.D. owned by Powderhorn/Wencrest Rottweilers, Mrs. Clara S. Hurley and Mr. Michael Grossman, Hollywood, Calif.

6. Powderhorn's Gina of Wencrest, C.D. making a good win for Powderhorn/Wencrest Rottweilers, Mrs. Clara Hurley and Michael S. Grossman.

7. Ch. Doroh's Jaegerin v Noblehaus at Bennington County in August 1983. Owned by Mark and Patricia Schwartz, Noblehaus Kennels, West Nyack, N.Y.

8. Ch. Contessa's C-Breeze V Jaro, by Ch. Rhomark's Axel V Lerchenfeld, C.D.X. ex Ch. Ansel's Contessa Von Ursa, owned by Donna M. LaQuatra, Beabear Rottweilers, High Springs, Fla.

Plate 15

1. Ch. Srigo's Eagle All Over, by Ch. Eiko v Schwaiger Wappen ex Ch. Srigo's Heart of Gold. Photo courtesy of breeder, Felicia Luburich, East Brunswick, N.J.

2. Epic's Adulteress, 1984 Sweepstakes winner, Colonial Rottweiler Club, at 13 months' age. Owned by Bob and Rose Hogan, by Ch. Birch Hill Governor ex Ch. Donnaj Happy Hooker. Bred by Bob Hogan and Jan Marshall.

3. Ch. Magnum McCoy Von Ursa on the way to his title. Donna LaQuatra, owner, Beabear Rottweilers, High Springs, Fla.

4. Ch. Trollegen's Aparri, C.D., owned by Powderhorn/Wencrest Rottweilers, Mrs. Clara S. Hurley and Mr. Michael S. Grossman, Hollywood, Calif.

5. Ch. Radio Ranch's Circuit Breaker, TT, by Am. and Can. Ch. Astro vom Chrisstenbrad ex Ch. Radio Ranch's Rox Island. Bred by Pam C. Brown, Circuit Breaker belongs to Gary Walker, Ojuara Rottweilers, Centereach, N.Y., who is handling.

6. Ch. Gudrun von Anderson, Top Producing Dam with seven champions, taking Best of Opposite Sex at Spartanburg K.C. in 1981. Carlos Rojas handling for Edith D. Alphin, Fayetteville, N.C.

7. Ch. Srigo's Viking Spirit, multi-Best of Breed and Group placing winner, by Panamint Seneca Chief ex Srigo's Honeybun. Owned by Felicia Luburich, Srigo Kennels, East Brunswick, N.J.

8. Ch. Delphi's Thetis Von Beabear, by Ch. Ansel's Cato Von Ursa ex Ch. Delphi Bitt'Amax, owned by Donna M. LaQuatra, Beabear Kennels. Here winning Best of Breed at West Volusia in Dec. 1984.

Plate 16

1. A brother-sister winning duo: *left,* Ch. Marlo's Rome Da Bratiana, C.D., taking Best of Breed; *right,* Champion Marlo's Inga v Follrath takes Best of Opposite Sex. Bred by Robert and Marlene Lore, Marlo's Rottweilers, Citrus Heights, Calif.

2. Three offspring of Ch. Starkhiem Duf Morgen Carroll. Taking Best of Breed, Ch. Maximilian Argus du Camelot. Winners Dog and Best of Winners, 4-points, Ch. Buccolas Kodiak von Duf. Winners Bitch, 4-points, Ch. Ein Min Huzzi von Rottdan. Von Morgen Carroll Rottweilers, Betty and Bill Carroll, Ontario, Calif.

3. Ch. Robil Marta von Donnaj *(left),* winning the Brood Bitch Class at the 1984 Colonial Rottweiler Club Specialty. Her offspring, pictured, are Ch. Brash Baer v Pioneer, C.D. *(center)* and the Best in Show winning bitch, Ch. Pioneer's Beguiled *(right).* The judge is Edeltraud Laurin. All three Rotties owned by Virginia Aceti and Sheryl Hedrick, Hollis, N.H.

PLATE 1

PLATE 2

1

2

3

4

PLATE 3

PLATE 4

B.K.C.
JULY 11, 1982
PUPPY WORKING GROUP 4TH
A BUSHMAN PHOTO

1

2

BEST OF OPPOSITE
NORTHWESTERN CONNECTICUT DOG CLUB
1982

3

BEST OF BREED
BRANTFORD & DISTRICT KENNEL CLUB

4

BEST OF BREED
GILBERT PHOTO

5

WINNERS
BURLINGTON COUNTY KENNEL CLUB
GILBERT PHOTO

6

BEST OF WINNERS
PHOTO Graham

7

BRED BY EXHIBITOR DOG
AMERICAN ROTTWEILER CLUB

8

PLATE 5

PLATE 6

PLATE 7

PLATE 8

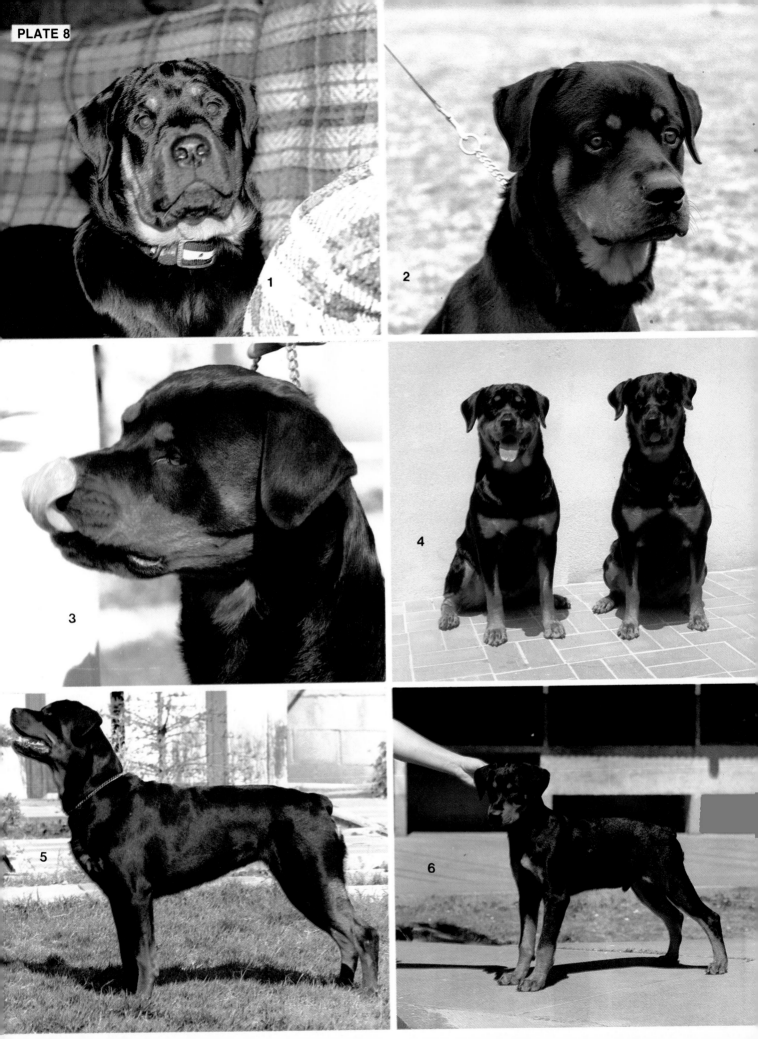

PLATE 9

PLATE 12

PLATE 13

PLATE 14

PLATE 15

PLATE 16

That mating produced Champion Berglufts Farra and Champion Berglufts Fee.

Champion Carla's second breeding was to Berglufts Donner, a strong linebreeding on Champion Axel vom Schwanenschlag and the Molzberg line. The resulting puppies were the Bergluft "G" litter, which included Champion Berglufts Gunda, Berglufts Grafin Grendal, C.D.X., T.D.X., ten points; and three other pointed littermates.

Champion Berglufts Fee was bred to American and Canadian Champion Srigo's Flight of the Eagle, American and Canadian C.D., which resulted in two pups, Berglufts Heiko and Berglufts Hasso, now two years old and carrying on the Bergluft line of substantial Rottweilers.

Mrs. Rogers takes pride in the fact that Bergluft continues to consistently produce the large, heavily boned Rottweilers of years ago. Her dogs are not offered at public stud, and her dedication to the Rottweiler breed means very selective breeding, only when placement in quality homes is assured.

Birch Hill

It was in 1970 when Jane F. Wiedel and her family, of Stockton, Illinois, purchased their first Rottweiler, a family pet named Taffy. Although Taffy was dysplastic, she earned her Companion Dog and Tracking Dog titles. An intelligent dog who enjoyed watching television, she quickly hooked Jane Wiedel on her breed.

Birch Hill Kennels began in 1971 with the purchase of a puppy from Rodsden Rottweilers, who later became Champion Rodsden's Willa v d Harque, U.D.T. She was the first female Rottweiler to hold all of the then available American Kennel Club titles, and she became one of Birch Hill's foundation bitches. Bred in partnership with Joan Klem, Willa had only eight puppies, but through her daughter, Champion Rodsden's Frolich Burga, C.D., T.D. came Champion Rodsden's Bruin v Hungerbuhl, C.D.X., the all-time leading Best in Show winner at time of writing with seven of them to his credit; and a top producer owned and bred by Jeffrey and Geraldine Kittner. Also in that litter was top producer (seven champions) Champion Rodsden's Birch Hill Bess, C.D., T.D., owned by

Jane Wiedel. Bruin's and Bess's sire was the influential import and top producer, Champion Dux vom Hungerbuhl, SchH. I.

Champion Rodsden's Gay Lady, T.D., was purchased as a puppy in 1974 on co-ownership with Joan Klem. Gay Lady was a top producer with eight champion offspring. Gay Lady, bred to the Dutch import, Champion Falco v h Brabantpark, produced the very influential and successful show and stud dog Champion Rodsden's Ansel v Brabant owned by Ruth and Harry O'Brien of Tennessee; and Laura Brewton's (Beaverbrook) foundation bitch, Champion Rodsden's Amber v Brabant. For Jane Wiedel herself, Gay produced American and Canadian Champion Rodsden's Birch Hill Hanna, C.D.X., T.D.; and, bred to Bruin she also presented Jane Wiedel with Champion Rodsden's Birch Hill Omega, C.D., T.D.

It was with Bess that the breeding program under the Birch Hill prefix began. Bess had small litters, and in her second of only one puppy, that one turned out to be American and Canadian Champion Birch Hill's Governor, C.D., owned by Mike and Debbie Conradt. Governor was sired by American and Canadian Champion Rodsden's Zarras v Brabant, C.D. An outstanding young dog, Governor is a multi-Specialty winner including Best in Show at the 1984 American Rottweiler Club National. He is also an all-breed Best in Show winner, and is the sire of numerous champions.

Bess was also bred to American and Canadian Champion Rodsden's Elko Kastenienbaum, C.D.X., T.D. thus producing Jane Wiedel's own American and Canadian Champion Birch Hill's Juno, T.D., who is the dam of three champions to date with others on the way. Juno was Winners Bitch at the 1980 Medallion Rottweiler Club Specialty as a puppy, and Best of Opposite Sex at the Colonial Rottweiler Club Specialty in 1982. A younger sister, American and Canadian Champion Birch Hill's Nanna v Brader, T.D. is Frank Brader's foundation bitch. Nanna was Best of Opposite Sex at the 1983 Medallion Rottweiler Club Specialty.

Hanna has produced five champions so far, with others on the way. Among them is Champion Birch Hill's Hasso Manteuffel,

C.D.X., T.D. owned by Vicki Wassenhove. Hasso's sire is Bruin. Hasso is a multi Specialty winner including Best in Show at the 1982 American Rottweiler Club National Specialty under German breeder-judge and breed warden Willi Faussner.

Omega has produced only one litter so far. She was bred to Elko and produced Champion Birch Hill's Fairview Quanna owned by Orval Thrasher; and American and Canadian Champion Birch Hill's Quincy, C.D., T.D. owned by Jane Wiedel. Quincy is a young dog who has already made his presence in the show ring felt with many breed and Group successes.

Hasso and Juno were bred to produce the next generation, Champion Birch Hill's Tank Commander, T.D. and Champion Birch Hills Twilla, T.D. owned by Jane Wiedel. Juno's third champion is by Best in Show winner, American and Canadian Champion Van Tieleman's Cisco, C.D. He is a Group winner, Champion Birch Hill's Ringmaster, owned by Shelley Voorhees.

There have been more than 30 champions and more than 30 obedience title holders bred at Birch Hill since 1973. As one can clearly see from the above account, the total dog is important, and Jane Wiedel's breeding Rottweilers have both conformation and obedience titles and OFA certified normal hips. Soundness of mind and body is of much importance. Along the way, she adds, she has been helped by many knowledgeable Rottweiler enthusiasts for which she is grateful.

Boulder House

Boulder House Rottweilers are owned by Mr. and Mrs. W. B. Lavender at Pioneertown, California, who are vigorously supporting the educational aspects of the continuing maintenance of the Rottweiler breed. They are attempting to reach the veteran fancier as well as the neophyte, to impress upon them the importance of the ethical approach.

The Lavenders believe that their greatest contribution thus far has been the newsletter of the Hi-Desert Rottweiler Club which they co-edit and produce. This newsletter, which is both interesting and informative, goes to every club from coast to coast for which the editors have addresses, and the Canadian

Rottweiler Club as well, on a newsletter exchange basis. The several copies I have seen are excellent.

The Boulder House Rottweilers are managed in accordance with their owners' principles. They are active advocates of selective, planned, intelligent breeding with iron-clad contracts in deference to both buyer and seller. Their fifteen acre compound was built as a labor of love. The Lavenders are members of the American Rottweiler Club, Medallion, and the Golden State in addition to the Hi-Desert Rottweiler Club of which they are founding members.

Champion Duke's Panzer von Bravo, TT, is the present young show "star" at Boulder House. "Boom Boom," as he is called, was entered in eight shows before his first birthday and undefeated in his class. He finished his championship within two months following his first points, at age 15 months, in wins which included twice Best of Breed from the classes, his wins coming under a variety of highly respected judges. Joanne Reed is Boom Boom's handler.

Brimstone

Brimstone Rottweilers are the result of Susan J. Suwinski, Ithaca, New York having been loaned a Rottie bitch for a year by a friend attending graduate school in a large city back in 1973. She was to be the family's farm watch dog and companion and she excelled so completely at both that when it came time to return her, nothing would do but that Susan have another Rottweiler. She was hooked on the breed's outgoing personality, coupled with common sense and protectiveness.

A pup then was purchased from Northwinds Kennel in Canada, who grew up to become Champion Northwind's Indigo, C.D., T.D., SchH. I. "Indy" did everything with such enthusiasm and heart, like taking Best of Winners at the Colonial Rottweiler Club Specialty in 1977 on a very warm day; earning her C.D. in three straight shows with scores of 195, 195½, and 187; her T.D. on the first try; and her Schutzhund I the first time out at 16 months, that she was truly a joy. Unfortunately she did not pass OFA certification, therefore was never bred.

As she worked with "Indy," Susan became more and more enthusiastic over the breed. So, feeling that she would like to become even further involved, and raise some Rottweilers herself, she again purchased from Canada a pup with a Northwinds background to train and show. She became Champion Balalaika of Ho-Rued-Ho, C.D., T.D., TT. She was trained also for Schutzhund, but did not manage to get her degree although she came within four points. She lacked "Indy's" fire and drive, but was reliable and a steady worker with wonderful temperament. It is she who became the foundation bitch of Brimstone Kennels.

Laika produced three litters with many fine offspring, two of whom have completed their titles, with many having TTs. Her youngest litter is just approaching two years as we write in May 1985. In her first litter came Champion Brimstone's Alexi, TT, who finished with three majors. From her second litter came Champion Brimstone's Bold Whisper, TT, co-owned with Pat Cyr, and Brimstone's Baron v Otto, C.D., SchH. I, VB, TT.

The emphasis at Brimstone is on correct Rottweiler temperament combined with quality, working ability and soundness. All pups are given a Puppy Aptitude Test at seven weeks to help determine the kind of household into which they best will fit. Susan also encourages all of her buyers to have their dogs tested at an ATTS test when they're mature, to help her monitor the basic temperament she is producing. She encourages training, both obedience and Schutzhund, with reputable trainers. In order to further encourage testing for physical soundness, she refunds fifty dollars when the dogs are x-rayed for hip dysplasia by OFA at two years. Susan also has continued to train all of her own dogs in Schutzhund as it is a very valuable tool in helping determine correct Rottweiler temperament. This, combined with Temperament Testing (TT), gives her, she feels, quite a clear picture of each dog's strength and weaknesses.

Brimstone at time of writing has produced only four litters, two of which are approaching two years of age. Susan now is beginning to expand her breeding program by purchasing several young bitches, closely related to her original bitches and one totally unrelated, all with strong backgrounds in physical and mental soundness combined with trainability and excellent breed type. She has also leased the outstanding bitch Champion Dachmar's Adah v d Barenhof, U.D.T., SchH. II to be bred in partnership with Dachmar Rottweilers who share the goal—breeding Rottweilers for working ability, quality and sound temperament.

Cersan

Cersan Rottweilers are at Syracuse, New York, where they are owned by Joseph N. Santaro, Marisa Santaro, and Alona Santaro, all very enthusiastic over this breed.

Young "star" of the kennel as we write (November 1985) is Champion Altar's Leo Vom Freyr, TT, Ro. 7475, known to his friends as "Rocco." This handsome dog finished in nine shows with three majors, and now in limited showing as a special has become a multi-Best of Breed winner. Expertly handled by Michael E. Scott, the future looks bright for this impressive young dog.

Cersan Rottweilers also co-own Windwalkers Antje Vom Mirko, by Champion Mirko Vom Steinkopf ex Champion Rodsden's Heika Vom Forstwald with Connie McLusky of LaFayette, New York.

Chutzpah

Dennis and Margaret Teague, owners of Chutzpah Rottweilers at Newcastle, California, acquired their first Rottie, Panamint Sultan v Rheintal, C.D.X., T.D., the "Chutzpah" for whom the kennel was named, in early 1975. He was to be strictly a pet, until his owners attended dog shows and in no time flat were "hooked" on Rottweilers and on showing. "Chutzpah" earned major points, but was never bred.

Next the Teagues acquired Champion Panamint Anytime Anywhere, C.D.X., T.D., a son of International Champion Jack vom Emstal, SchH. I, C.D., in 1976. "Jake," as he was known, was owner-handled to all his titles, and is still a great looking dog at age nine years. He has been bred very selectively, only once to Barbara Dillon's German import, Ella

Top: Ch. Rodsden's Gay Lady, T.D. taking Best of Breed at Fox River Valley K.C. in 1977. Owner-handled by Jane F. Wiedel, Stockton, Illinois. **Bottom:** Basko vom Aschafftal, C.D., T.D.X., SchH. II, AD, pointed, a Group placer, has one C.D.X. leg. Owned and trained by Dennis and Margaret Teague, Chutzpah. Imported by Barbara Dillon.

vom Weilheimer Stuckl. The only puppy from this litter to go to a show-working home was Panamint One More Time, C.D., T.D.X., SchH. I, AD.

The next Rottweiler arrival at Chutzpah Kennels was Panamint Ideal Impression, C.D.X., T.D.X., SchH. I, who also has one leg towards Utility. She earned her T.D., T.D.X. and Schutzhund I titles on the first attempts, and was owner-handled to all her titles. This splendid bitch has never been bred due to serious health problems despite her great working ability.

The original Rottweiler, Sultan, died at about the same time that Ella was bred to "Jake" (Anytime/Anywhere) of complications resulting from a bout with gastric torsion. Barbara Dillon then gave the Teagues a puppy from the Jake-Ella litter, this the one who grew up to become Panamint One More Time; she joined the Teague family when eight weeks old.

In 1981, Barbara Dillon imported a puppy for the Teagues, Basko vom Aschafftal, SchH. II, AD, C.D., T.D.X., known as Xanadu. This young dog has an outstanding pedigree, starting with his sire and dam, who are Fetz sur Klamm, SchH. III; and Dixi vom Elzbachtal, SchH. III, FH, IPO III respectively. Xanadu is described by Mrs. Teague as being extremely sound in both conformation and temperament and is producing these essential qualities in his puppies. He also had earned one C.D.X. leg, and recently began his conformation career by winning Best of Breed and a Group 4th placement.

Panamint One More Time was bred to Basko (Xanadu) in 1983, producing the Teagues' first (and to date only) homebred litter. The show puppies will soon be ready for the conformation ring as we write, and for the obedience rings. One already has earned a T.D. Several of them obviously have inherited Xanadu's natural tracking ability. The other puppies also have excellent temperaments, and have become centers of their families.

In 1982, the Teagues acquired Gabi vom Magdeberg, SchH. I, by Klubsieger Dingo vom Schwaiger Wappen, SchH. III. Gabi is described as a gorgeous bitch whose fortes are obedience and protection work. The Teagues

were so delighted with Gabi that they then imported two more puppies from the same dam, Klubsiegerin Babette vom Magdeberg, SchH. I. These latter two are Jorg vom Magdeberg, T.D. and Jenni vom Magdeberg, T.D. Jenni now is owned by Mrs. Fae Johnson.

The latest addition at Chutzpah as we write was Anuschka von der Haus Wick in 1984. She is from Gabi's littermate and sired by Cliff vom Waldhuck, SchH. III.

Since purchasing their first Rottweiler in 1975, the Teagues' primary interest has been to learn as much as possible about the breed, including bloodlines, working ability, training, conformation, etc. Since that time, they have earned four T.D.X. degrees, 10 T.D.s, three C.D.X.s, five C.D.s, one Schutzhund II, three Schutzhund I's and three ADs, plus one championship title. All training and handling for these titles has been done by the Teagues. In addition, Margaret provides instruction in tracking which has directly resulted in students earning 20+ TDs and six TDXs during the past five years.

Daverick

Daverick Rottweilers at Moorestown, New Jersey belong to Richard and Ricki Gordon, who acquired their first Rottweiler in 1975. She was Daverick's Traudel, by Alex v d Marienau ex Melsa Von Schauer, and she produced Daverick's Madchen von Degan, the dam of Daverick's "B", "C", and "D" litters.

The "A" litter at Daverick, whelped in 1981, turned out to be very special and exciting. This was when Richard and Ricki Gordon became involved with the breeding and showing of Rotties. Carla vom Hulsental was the dam of this litter, having been imported from Germany in 1979 by G. George Rogers. She was bred to another German import, the famous Champion Arras vom Hasenkamp and in this litter produced three outstanding winners whelped on July 11, 1981. These are Champion Daverick's Albert V Hasenkamp, American and Canadian Champion Daverick's Alex V Hasenkamp, C.D., and Champion Daverick's Acacia V Hasenkamp.

American and Canadian Champion Alex is the house dog at Daverick, who is presently training towards a tracking degree. Alex earned his C.D. at 17 months in three consecutive shows. In conformation, he took a five-point major at Westchester Kennel Club in 1983, then returned the following year to go Best of Breed there. He completed his championship during late 1983 at National Capital under judge Jim White. Now specialed only occasionally, he has multiple Best of Breed honors to his credit. At the American Kennel Club Centennial Show he was one of the four dogs pulled out in the final cut for the selection of Best of Breed. Alex is a wonderful family dog, though, so his owners prefer enjoying him at home rather than sending him out to be campaigned.

Albert, the litter brother to Alex, finished in good style also during 1983, gaining his title in ten shows with back-to-back four and five point majors at Suffolk and Westbury. He has been a successful contender as a special, has numerous Bests of Breed and a Group 2nd at Maryland Kennel Club in November 1984. Albert lives with Ricki Rogers's parents.

Delphi

The name Delphi is derived from Delphi, Greece, site of the temple and oracle of Apollo, the Greek god. Just as the Greeks of the Golden Age were engaged in an effort to express, through art and philosophy, examples of universal beauty, so are Al and Bonnie Wimberly committed to the art of breeding outstanding individuals of superior type, conformation, intelligence and disposition in the quest for living expressions which approach perfection.

Al and Bonnie Wimberly, owners of the Delphi Rottweilers at Havana, Florida, acquired their first Rottweiler in 1975 as a result of visiting friends who had just gotten a puppy, and then going to see the "parents" of the puppy where they learned that there was "just one puppy more." And then (you guessed it, I am sure) when they returned home that night, the Wimberlys were accompanied by the then small individual who substantially changed their lives: Jeepers Treu Argus, C.D. (Champion Joey von Kluge, C.D. ex Kuhlwald's Zee Zee) who remained their only Rottweiler for the next four years,

and their constant live-in companion in a two-bedroom apartment.

As with many things in their lives, the Wimberlys confess, if one something is just great, then another of the same has to be still greater. Thus began the search for a second Rottweiler.

Resulting was the purchase of a Champion Phaedra's Amax of Sunnyside daughter out of Hart's Kitten von Bravo Jill. She was to become Champion Delphi Bitt Amax when she finished in five shows on the 1982 Tar Heel Circuit with four, four, five and four point majors. Bitt has produced Champion Electra von Beabear; Delphi Briseis, C.D.; Delphi Hector, C.D.; Delphi Thetis von Beabear; Champion Delphi Teucer, C.D.X.; and she is the grandma of Delphi's first "home-grown" champion, Delphi Midas (by Ch. Ansel's Cato von Ursa ex Delphi Briseis, C.D.) who finished in a very respectable manner at age twenty-two months. Bitt Amax's first litter was sired by Jeepers Treu Argus, C.D., and all five dogs from that litter OFA certified with a good rating.

In 1983, Delphi purchased a finished champion bitch, Champion Troll Haus Beryl Von Ansel from Dr. and Mrs. Ross Love in Tupelo, Mississippi. Beryl has produced one litter of five by Delphi Theuseus, a son of Champion Ansel's Cato von Ursa out of Champion Delphi Bitt Amax—an excellent litter in both conformation and temperament.

Delphi has produced ten litters since they began in 1980 totaling 73 puppies. About 50 have been placed in family environments solely as companions. The others have been placed in experienced, serious show homes or have been kept by Delphi for future show and breeding purposes. Puppies generally, particularly the bitches, are co-owned by Delphi until age two years and OFA certified or until neutered.

Donnaj

Donnaj (pronounced Don-NARGE) Kennels started out as breeder-exhibitors of German Shepherd Dogs for ten years during the late 1950's and early 1960's. An allergy mandated the search for a shorter coated breed, and in 1968 the eight-weeks-old puppy who was to become the first Best in Show Rottweiler in the United States, future American and Canadian Champion Rodsden's Kato v Donnaj, C.D.X., T.D. came to live with Don and Janet Marshall and their three children at Woodstock, Vermont. Thus started the success story known as Donnaj Rottweilers!

Kato was bred by Laura Coonley and was sired by Champion Rodsden's Kluge v d Harque, C.D., the producer of twenty-seven champions. His dam was a German import, Champion Franzi vom Kursaal, the dam of seven champions, five of which were in Kato's litter.

In limited showing, owner-handled, over a five year period, Kato won 80 Bests of Breed, 29 Working Group placements, and Best in Show. In 1984 his great-great granddaughter, Champion Pioneer Beguiled, became the first *bitch* to go Best in Show, and the first Rottweiler to be breeder-owner-handled to that win, by Cheryl Hedrick and Virginia Aceti. Although he produced only ten litters, from which the puppies were sold mostly to pet homes, Kato sired five champions and six of his daughters became the foundation of successful kennels.

The second Rottweiler at Donnaj became American and Canadian Champion Donnaj Vt. Yankee of Paulus, C.D.X., TT. Yankee was sired by a German import, Champion Axel vom Schwanenschlag out of Champion Amsel von Andan, who was a Kato daughter bred by Pauline Rakowski. There were four champions in the litter.

Yankee, Jan Marshall tells us, is the *only* Rottweiler to have won four Specialty Shows and an all-breed Best in Show. He was in the top three of the breed (based on Group wins) over a four year period during which he was mostly owner-handled. Yank also earned a High in Trial at the Colonial Rottweiler Club Specialty, as his grandsire, Kato, had done before him!

Yankee will long be remembered as a sire of leading show dogs. Up to mid-1985 36 of his offspring had become American champions. These include 14 with Group placements, and three American Best in Show winners, the latter being Champion Donnaj Green Mtn. Boy with three Bests in Show, Champion Alina's Adelbear of Wesley, three

Bests in Show, and Champion Krugerand von Meadow. The first two winners are out of Kato daughters. Also winning Best in Show honors are American, Canadian, Bermudian and Venezuelan Champion Maxmillion Schwartzgruen in Canada and American, Canadian, Bermudian, Puerto Rican and Venezuelan Champion Powsells Song of Deborah, litter sister to Green Mtn. Boy, in Venezuela.

In the past, Donnaj has co-owned two bitches and owned none. Champion Northwind's Helga produced Champions Donnaj Bennington, Champion Donnaj Green Mtn. Boy, Champion Donnaj Happy Hooker, Powsell's Classic Brute, and Powsell's Song of Deborah. Happy Hooker, a Yankee daughter co-owned with Bob Hogan, has four pointed offspring from her first litter at under two years' age.

The first bitch now owned at Donnaj is Donnaj Balled of Seren, ten points, a Yankee daughter whose first litter will soon be born at Donnaj.

All Donnaj Rottweilers are raised in the Marshalls' home and are a part of the family. Sometimes there are five or six Rottweilers under foot, most often including the latest puppy hopeful. The current hopeful as we are working on this book is Donnaj Very Special, a Happy Hooker pup from her second litter. He was so named as he arrived two weeks before Yankee's death and helped Jan bear his loss at what must have been a very sad time for her.

Other successful youngsters raised at Donnaj include Champion Donnaj Crusader in Ohio, Champion Donnaj Herr I Am, C.D., TT, co-owned with Bob Hogan in Rhode Island, and Donnaj Diplomat in New York.

Jan Marshall is a charter member of the American Rottweiler Club, and since then has been a director or officer for all but two years. She has been active on the Illustrated Standard Committee, Chairman of the Committee on Principles and Practices, and is Chairman of the Publications Committee. She is also a founding member of the Woodstock Kennel Club (1956) and is their delegate to the American Kennel Club. She has taught obedience classes and been the club's obedience chairman for more than ten years.

Dschungel

Dschungel Kennels are owned by Glenn Goreski at Wallington, New Jersey. This is the home of Champion Castor von Palisaden, by Champion Erich von Paulus ex Marlene von Tengen, who has done some very nice winning handled by Kathleen Kilcoyne, a partner in the kennel. Castor, born in 1981, completed his title with three majors, including Best of Winners at a supported 4-point entry at Ramapo Kennel Club, within a three month period and with limited showing. Along the way he gained a Best of Opposite Sex on one occasion, and a Group 1st from the classes. Now out as a special he has Best of Breed victories to his credit.

The kennel also includes a nine-year-old Rodsden dog and five bitches. Tops among the latter as we write is Champion Greenbriar Pinch Hitter, who was Winners Bitch at the Westminster Kennel Club in 1984 at ten months of age. The others include a nine-year-old matron of Merrymoore lines, and her daughters.

Among the puppies, hopes are high over two representing a repeat of the breeding which produced Champion Baron Von Kalhenback who completed title at 17 months. These are by Champion Castor von Palisaden ex Gerta von Goreski and they are eight months old as we write.

Eureka

Eureka Kennels are the result of a lifetime interest in dogs on the part of owners Meredith and James Millard, Parker, Colorado.

Rottweilers attracted their attention during the mid-1970's, leading to their acquisition of the first two Rottie bitches owned by them. Sad to report, both were lost in a tragic accident. Following this, the Millards decided to move to the country and at the same time began their search for the best bloodlines they could acquire on which to base a breeding program.

The puppy who became Champion Peril's Blackhawk von Meadow joined their family at age eight weeks, when her education towards becoming a companion and show dog started. She also became the foundation bitch and the beginning of Eureka Rottweilers. This lovely bitch has now produced several quality litters which are beginning to make their presence felt in the show ring and on the Schutzhund fields. Eureka's Bewitching Elvira and Eureka's Princess Czarina had the honor of winning Best Brace in Show at the Colorado Springs Kennel Club Dog Show before they had even reached the age of ten months.

Of equal importance to showing and keeping good conformation in their lines, the Millards are also attending to the working heritage of their dogs by actively training for and participating in Schutzhund activities.

Freeger

Freeger Rottweilers are owned by Mrs. Bernard Freeman of New York City, who is widely known and admired as a pioneer in the breed here in the United States, author of a splendid book about it, owner and breeder of outstandingly representative dogs, and a multiple breed judge of tremendous popularity.

Mrs. Freeman has never been one to campaign her dogs to any extent. Prior to her becoming a judge, she took pleasure in personally handling them through to their championships, seldom using a professional handler, but when on occasion doing so, she herself accompanied the dog to the show.

Several very notable dogs are among those belonging to Mrs. Freeman. For example, the great Champion D'Artagnan of Canidom, C.D., who won 19 consecutive Bests of Breed in cities from Massachusetts to Florida and from New York to California, including Eastern, Westminster, Westchester, Ladies Dog Club, National Capital, Philadelphia, Chicago International and Miami, owner-handled in all but five of these events. His kennel mate, American and Canadian Champion Friska vom Kursaal was Best of Opposite Sex to him on a substantial number of occasions.

It is interesting to note that D'Artagnan and Friska carry the OFA numbers RO 1 and RO 2, which identifies them as having been the first and second Rottweiler to have been given these tests, since Mrs. Freeman was among the earliest to approve and appreciate the importance of this certification.

To speak a bit further about Friska vom Kursaal, she was an imported daughter of BS, WS, International Champion and American Champion Erno vom Wellesweiler from BS,

Am. and Can. Ch. Priska vom Kursaal, RO 2, by BS, WS, Int. Ch. and Am. Ch. Erno vom Wellesweiler, SchH. I ex BS, Sch.S, Int. Ch. Assy vom Zipfelbach, Sch II, was bred by Richard Schmidgall. Mrs. Bernard Freeman, owner, Freeger Kennels, New York, N.Y.

SchS., International Champion Assy vom Zipfelbach, SchH. II. Her sire, Erno, was another of Mrs. Freeman's imports who came over in the mid-1960's after an impressive European career during which, in 1965, he had become Bundeseiger and World Seiger and an International Champion.

Champion Freeger's Electra, C.D. was sired by D'Artagnan from Friska, bred by Mrs. Freeman who then became co-owner with Mrs. Gisela Nightinggale.

Champion Freeger's Noah, C.D., Canadian C.D., was bred by Mrs. Freeman and Richard Iadarola, by Champion Caro vom Zimmerplatz ex Champion Freeger's Juno, C.D., and later co-owned by Mrs. Freeman with Miss Joan Laskey.

American and Canadian Champion Groll vom Haus Schottroy American and Canadian C.D. was born March 4, 1975, bred by Theo. Oymann in West Germany. By Champion Chris vom Wildberger, SchH. II ex KS Afra vom Haus Schottroy, SchH. I.

Frolic'n

Frolic'n Acres Kennel is owned and operated by Charlotte and Stephen Johnson and Linda Schuman, located at Redmond, Washington. It has always been the goal of Frolic'n Kennel to produce, own and exhibit the all-around Rottweiler. These fanciers have participated with their dogs in various Rottweiler activities including conformation, obedience at all levels, Schutzhund tracking, carting and temperament testing. In addition they have produced dogs who are now working as cattle dogs, retrieving bird dogs, and police dogs.

Breeding is on a very limited basis with a watchful eye on quality, and great attention to temperament, conformation, and intelligence. Feeling strongly that quality of life and family bond is of primary importance to this breed, great emphasis is placed, when permitting puppies to go to new owners, that these factors take precedence over career and future fame.

Frolic'n Rottweilers have included such outstanding individuals as American and Canadian Champion Nobel v Falkenberg, C.D., by Champion Dieter Vom Konigsberg C.D. ex Champion Panamint Elka v Hohenwald, who was purchased as a puppy from Barbara

Hoard Dillon. Nobel was an outstanding Rottweiler in many ways. He was the first of the cart dogs owned by the Johnsons and Linda Schuman, thus did not have the advantage of their later experiences in this area. Nonetheless, he was willing to overlook all the preliminaries, and when put in harness and hooked up to the cart, he took to it as though it had been a daily activity all his life. He pulled it in the correct Rottweiler manner—with pride and confidence.

Nobel was also worked by his owners in the show ring, his career in conformation being limited to the Northwest. Even with limited showing he gained national ranking for several years. His owners chose not to campaign him extensively despite several offers because, first and foremost, he was, to them, a friend from whom they did not want to be separated.

Also bred on a limited basis, Nobel contributed toward the improvement of his breed. From his last litter, four brothers quickly completed championships, three of the four going on to Group placements and obedience degrees. Two of his sons went to Canada where they were ranked nationally, one in conformation, the other in obedience. These two were instrumental in helping Frolic'n become the Top Producing Kennel in Canada for 1982, following its No. 3 position in 1981.

American, Bermudian, Canadian, Mexican and International CACIB Champion Jack vom Emstal, American and Canadian C.D., Mexican PC, ADRK Schutzhund I was imported from Germany by Frolic'n Kennel with the help of Barbara Hoard Dillon. All of Jack's titles except the Schutzhund I were earned almost exclusively owner-handled, including the remaining CACIB certificate and the CACIT certificate needed to complete his FCI International Championship title.

In speaking of Jack, his owners comment that many people do not understand the time and love that goes into helping a foreign born and raised Rottweiler adjust to new language, food, climate and customs. Much goes into developing the loving and trusting devotion that Jack possessed. In tribute to this dog, they add "Our efforts were rewarded manyfold."

Top: Ch. D'Artagnan of Canidom, C.D., owned by Mrs. Bernard Freeman, Freeger Kennels, N.Y., co-breeder with Canidom Kennels. Stuart S. "Bud" Sliney handling. **Bottom:** Ch. Freeger's Noah, C.D., Can. C.D., at 11 months of age, was bred by Mrs. B. Freeman and Miss Joan Laskey. Handled by Mrs. Freeman, who also co-owns with Richard Iadarola.

Both Jack and Nobel were shown at the same time. Had either of them been shown without competition from their housemate, the show careers of both would have been more impressive. As it was, they shared the glory of being the best. Jack was No. 2 in conformation in Canada at the age of seven years; and the next year, when eight years old, he became No. 1 on the Canadian rankings. He received Group placements in four countries and held obedience titles in them, too. He also loved cart work, and was deeply hurt when the cart was pulled by any other dog, but equally proud when it became his turn.

Nobel and Jack, handled by Charlotte, teamed up to become the first Rottweilers to win Best Brace in Show in Canada in January 1976. They repeated this victory in the United States at the Seattle Kennel Club Dog Show during that same month, then in February did it again at Portland Kennel Club. At the Golden Gate Kennel Club, February 1, 1981, Jack with his daughter and two grandsons made up the first Rottweiler Team of common ownership to win the title of Best Team in Show. Jack contributed greatly to the continued quality of Rottweilers today.

American, Canadian, Mexican Champion and 1978 World Siegerin Uschi Vom Hause Henseler, C.D., ADRK SchH. I, Producer of Merit and holder of three CACIB certificates was imported from Germany. Her Schutzhund I degree was earned in Germany, but her other titles were earned after coming here, owner-handled, with considerable ease. The World Siegerin title was earned in Mexico City. Of her, her owners comment "You could not have asked for a more devoted friend and protector."

American, Canadian and Mexican Champion Panamint Rani v d Sandhaufen, C.D., was owner-handled to all of her titles. She was awarded four CACIB certificates, but was not old enough at that time to compete for the CACIT. Rani was also a Producer of Merit. She was the dam of the litter by Nobel referred to as having produced four champions, this litter having also included two pointed bitches. Rani is still a much loved member of the Frolic'n family.

Kandy von der Sandhauffen was purchased as an adult, and there are many things she would rather do than show. Regardless of her lack of enthusiasm for the show ring, she possessed outstanding conformation. Her quality has carried through in her offspring, making her a Producer of Merit.

Champion Arras Vom Schloss Stutensee, C.D.X., T.D., TT, SchH. III, IPO, III, FH, AD, and Gekort Bis EzA, was imported from Germany in 1982, already having earned his SchH. III, FH, AD, and a High in Trial. He also brought with him the coveted Gekort Bis EzA. This dog is a very self-confident and loving Rottweiler who quickly adapted to living in the house with the others at Frolic'n. Arras earned all of the additional titles listed above except as noted plus his American Championship here in the United States owner-handled. He also earned a SchH. III High in Trial under a noted German ADRK judge.

Champion Sundance Kid, C.D., American and Canadian T.D., earned the latter degree at the first American Rottweiler Club Tracking Test when only nine months of age, after which he went on to earn his C.D. and his championship.

Stephen Johnson organized and chaired the first American Rottweiler Club Carting Extravaganza, in which seven carts participated, each one unique and pulled by one or more Rottweilers. The event was enjoyed as much by the participants as it was by the spectators. Frolic'n Kennels had three entries, all designed and built by themselves. The single cart was modeled after an Alpine cart and pulled by one dog. The other two were scaled down replicas of antique fire fighting apparatus. The hose and ladder apparatus was pulled by a team of two Rottweilers, the steam pumper by a triple hitch pulling three abreast. These carts have been entered in parades several times and have won many honors.

Goldmoor

Goldmoor Rottweilers are owned by Marge and Comman Gold at Concord, North Carolina.

Active in Rottweilers since the late 1970's, the Golds were for more than 26 years previous to that time breeders and exhibitors of

CAPTIONS FOR PLATES 17-32

Plate 17

1. One dog's family! Some of the children of Ch. Axel v Lerchenfeld, C.D.X., T.D., representing their sire, relaxing at the Sacramento K.C. dog show in 1984. *Left to right* (upper row): Rocky v Axel, 16 month male owned by Lori Cook, Alamo, Calif., was second in American-bred Class; Ch. Marlo's Sohn v. Axel, C.D., T.D. was Winners Dog and Best of Winners, completing his championship for owners Terry and Penny Dodds, Novato, Calif.; Marlo's Snowfire v Axel, C.D., two and a half year old female, sister to Sohn, owned by Beth McGaw, Stockton, Calif., completed her C.D. that day and was High in Trial; Bay Acres Heidi v Axel, six months, owned by Jeanne Jackson, Tenn., placed in junior puppy class; Rassentreau C-Maestro v Jaro, 10-month-old-male, won the senior puppy class and is also owned by Jeanne Jackson; Fidelis Mann of Peace, 16-month-old male owned by John and Kristy Peixoto, Castro Valley, Calif., won his American-bred Class; and Bay Acres Jena v Axel, sister to Heidi, owned by Ed and Linda Dennis, competed in Open Bitches. Sohn was Group 3rd at Golden Gate K.C. in 1985; Maestro is pointed and a Group 1st winner in Tennessee; and Mann has points towards his title, owner-handled. Photo courtesy of the Griffins.

2. Colonial Rottweiler Club Sweepstakes, May 1979. *Left to right:* Srigo's I Am Invincible, Best in Sweeps; Srigo's Incredible Is The Word, 2nd in 12-18 months class; Srigo's Heart of Gold, 3rd in 12-18 months class; and Srigo's Joy To The World, also among the winners. Srigo Rottweilers are owned by Felicia Luburich, East Brunswick, N.J.

Plate 18

1. Note the impeccable topline and movement that helped Ch. Brash Baer von Pioneer, C.D. to finish his championship in 12 shows, win multiple Bests of Breed, and Group placements owner-breeder-handled by Kandy Galotti and Sheryl Hedrick. Bred by Pioneer Rottweilers.

2. Ch. Cabot v Arktos owned by Barb and Don Fors of Des Moines, Iowa. By Ch. Nick v Silahopp ex Dagna v.d. Eichen. Pictured at Waterloo K.C. in 1976.

3. Ch. Gator's Ruffian Von Ursa, by Ch. Rodsden's Ansel v Brabant ex Ch. RC's Gator Bel Von Meadow, at age 13 months winning a first prize in the 1982 Medallion Rottweiler Club Futurity Sweepstakes as Champion Bitch. Owned by Tom and Chris Stenftenagel, High Springs, Fla.

4. Ch. Donar v d Hoeve Cor Unum, C.D., receiving his Award of Merit from the Medallion Rottweiler Club in 1984. This great dog is owned by Powderhorn/Wencrest Rottweilers, Hollywood, Calif. Mrs. Clara S. Hurley and Mr. Michael S. Grossman.

5. Ch. Degan von Liebotschaner taking Best of Winners on the way to his title in 1984. Owned by Beauhaven Rottweilers, Bob and Judy Beaupre, Aliquippa, Pa.

6. Ronzwyler's Anka von Haiem, by Rodsden's Strawlane Zephyr, (who is a son of Ch. Rodsden's Zarras von Brabant ex Ch. Strawlane's Abra) from a linebred Bratiana dam. Pictured three days after coming out of quarantine. Owned by Rottweilers von Haiem, photo courtesy of Jill Nakache.

7. Winning 1st in the Brace Class at Colonial Rottweiler Club Specialty in 1985, Von Gailingen's Leading Lady and Von Gailingen's Lofty Ideals, by Ch. Arras v Hasenkamp ex Am. and Can. Ch. Von Gailingen's Dassie Did It, U.D.T., Canadian C.D. Breeder-owner-handled by Catherine M. Thompson, Von Gailingen, Freehold, N.J.

8. Ch. Fraulein Gretchen von Fox, Demon von Fox, and Madchen Greta von Fox. Photo courtesy of Ellen Monica Towarnicki, Philadelphia, Pa.

Plate 19

1. Ch. Marja's Obsidians Pegasus, handsome young son of Best in Show Ch. Donnaj Green Mountain Boy ex Ch. Marja Elka von Heidel, here pictured winning a Group placement under judge Robert S. Forsyth, handled by Mrs. Terry Lazzaro Hundt for owners Jacqueline and Mary Puglise, Marja Rottweilers, Farmingville, N.Y.

2. Ch. Rodsden's Pandora v Forstwald, handled by Bill Burrel, taking a 5-point major for owner Frank J. Fiorella, Boxford, Mass.

3. Powderhorn's Letz of Wencrest winning Best Junior Puppy, Medallion Rottweiler Club Futurity, June 1982. Owned by Powderhorn/Wencrest Rottweilers, Mrs. Clara S. Hurley and Michael S. Grossman, Hollywood, Calif.

4. Liebchen von Vt. Yankee is owned by Beauhaven Kennels, Bob and Judy Beaupre, Aliquippa, Pa.

5. Ch. Katryn the Great Von Ursa, C.D.X., owned by Pamela Anderson, Zornhaus Rottweilers, Wilton Manors, Fla.

6. Ch. Srigo's Eagle All Over finishing his championship with his owner handling at New Castle K.C. in 1983. Bob and Judy Beaupre, Beauhaven Rottweilers.

7. Ch. Altar's Loyal Lindsay v Freya, multiple Best of Breed and Best of Opposite Sex winner. Handled by Carlos Rojas for Edith Alphin, Fayetteville, N.C.

8. Ch. Ansel's Cato Von Ursa, by Ch. Rodsden's Ansel V Brabant ex Ch. RC's Gator Bel Von Meadow, T.T. Owned by Donna M. LaQuatra, Beabear Rottweilers.

Plate 20

1. The English import Thewina Summer Ferrymaster, C.D.X., has produced some very handsome children with a flair for obedience. This handsome and talented dog belongs to Linda B. Griswold, Ravenwood Kennels, Michigan City, Ind.

2. Panzer von Siegerhaus, handsome young Rottweiler owned by Thomas and Carol Woodward, Corning, Calif.

3. Ch. Alastar Come September, bred by Carole A. Anderson and owned by Katherine S. Cook, completed title at age 21 months winning many Bests of Opposite Sex over specials as a class bitch. Born Sept. 22, 1981.

4. Graudstark's Quatro Tempo at age five months. This lovely puppy grew up to become the Top Producing foundation bitch of Pandemonium Kennels. Valerie J. Cade, Goldens Bridge, N.Y.

Plate 21

1. Ch. Mirko vom Steinkopf, C.D., SchH. III, IPO III, FH, owned by Dr. and Mrs. Richard Wayburn, Irmo, S.C., noted Specialty and all-breed Best in Show winner. This photo loaned to us by one of his admirers, Margie Haralson, Harperville, Miss.

2. Am. and Can. Ch. Jacqueline Da Bratiana, C.D., at age eight years. Dam of six show champions and six offspring with obedience degrees, she proudly heads the Marlo Rottweilers owned by Marlene Lore, Citrus Heights, Calif.

3. Ch. Doroh's Fantastic Serenade, Am. and Can. C.D.X., owned by Peter and Marilyn Piusz, Johnstown, N.Y.

4. Noblehaus Chewbacca at 14 months, Sept. 1984. One of the many splendid Rottweilers owned by Noblehaus Kennels, Mark and Patricia Schwartz, West Nyack, N.Y.

Plate 22

1. Ravenwood Queen's Request at 14 months. English-bred bitch by the imported Thewina Summer Ferrymaster, C.D.X.

ex Thewina Stormraven, C.D. Owned by Ravenwood Rottweilers, Linda B. Griswold, Michigan City, Ind.

2. Dux vom Rauchfang, SchH. III, FH, GEKORT. Sired by Ch. Benno vom Allgauer Tor, SchH. III, FH and out of a Rauchfang bitch. Dux belongs to David Dellessiegues of von Steinbeckland Rottweilers. Dux has consistently placed during a three-year period at major European shows, including the Eiffle Shows where he won twice the Bundessiegerschaus, the Europasiegerschaus, the Weltsiegerschaus, etc. Photo courtesty of Jill Nakache, Rottweilers von Haiem, Hawaii.

3. Am. and Can. Ch. Wotan Zwei von Sonnenhaus, C.D. owned by von Siegerhaus Rottweilers, Thomas and Carol Woodward, Corning, Calif.

4. Taber Gold von Stolzenfels, C.D., 28 months old, weighing in at 97 pounds. Dr. Evelyn Ellmans, von Stolzenfels, Augusta, Mich.

5. Enjoying their toys! Puppies by Ch. Alexandrus G. Roadway ex Strudel von Trostheim. Von Morgen Carroll Rottweilers, Ontario, Calif.

6. Von Bruka Jaguar at age three months. Owned by Windwalker Kennels, Port Crane, N.Y.

7. Bonnie Jo von Beenen owned by Don Beenen, Lowell, Mich.

8. Ch. Riegele's Astro von Eken at play with his tire, a favorite "toy" with Rottweilers. Owned by Riegele Rottweilers, Ellen B. Walls, Hartly, Del.

Plate 23
1. Ch. Rhomark's Frau Helga taking Winners Bitch and Best of Winners at Wine Country K.C., April 1984, judge Robert S. Forsyth. Mike Stone handling for owners George and Ann Goring.

2. Ch. Kuhlwald's Little Iodine, C.D. shown and handled by Dorit S. Rogers for her championship and C.D. Pictured winning her third "leg" for C.D. degree. *An important note:* this bitch is the granddam of Champion Radio Ranch's Axel v Notara, the No. 1 producing sire in Rottweiler history! Photo courtesy of Mrs. Rogers.

3. Ch. Peril's Blackhawk von Meadow taking a 4-point major towards title. Meredith and Jim Millard, owners, Eureka Rottweilers, Parker, Colo.

4. Ch. Excalibur's B Apache War Song, C.D. taking Best of Opposite Sex at Abilene K.C. for owner Irene Castillo, Abilene, Texas.

Plate 24
1. Anke Becker von Beenen, C.D., owned by Lin Beenen, handled here by co-breeder Don Beenen, taking Winners Bitch and Best of Opposite Sex at Monroe Kennel Club, Sept. 1984. Daughter of Can. Ch. Fairvalley's Kluge ex Bomark's Allison An Beenen, C.D.

2. Marlo's Black Maverick, C.D. taking Winners Dog handled by his owner, Liz Stein. Bred by Robert and Marlene Lore, Citrus Heights, Calif.

3. Ch. Baron von Kalhenback finished title at age 17 months. Owned by Glenn Goreski, Dschungel Rottweilers, Wallington, N.J.

4. Ch. Donnaj Green Mountain Boy wins the Colonial Rottweiler Specialty in 1984. Ross Petruzzo handling for Anthony P. Attalla, Londonderry, N.H.

5. Ch. Fangen von Arktos, C.D., by Ch. Dann v Arktos, C.D. ex Antje v Arktos, C.D. is the only American-bred Rottweiler with

multiple V ratings in Europe, including V-I Excellent. Bred and owned by Judith H. Hassed, Colorado Springs, Colo.

6. Maja von Stolzenfels, by Ch. Dolf Fuller von Stolzenfels, C.D.X. from Ch. Czarina von Stolzenfels, C.D. Owned by Valery McCreedy of New Mexico, bred by Dr. Evelyn M. Ellman, Maja has 12 points towards the title as we are writing.

7. Ch. Pioneer's Das Bedazzled, here taking Winners Bitch at the 1985 American Rottweiler Club National Specialty. By Am., Can., and Int. Ch. Bronco v Rauberfeld, SchH. III, FH ex Ch. Robil Marta von Donnaj (dam of five champions and three C.D. titlists), 1st in Brood Bitch at the 1984 Colonial Rottweiler Club Specialty, and on the Medallion Rottweiler Club Honor Roll.

8. Ch. Alpha Alexandros G. Roadway, multiple Group winning and placing son of Int. Ch. Jack vom Emstahl, C.D.X. from Champion Starkheim's Catinka G. Roadway. Owned by von Morgen Carroll Kennels, Bill and Betty Carroll, Ontario, Calif.

Plate 25
1. Ch. Cora v Hartumer Busch owned by Powderhorn/Wencrest Kennels, Hollywood, Calif.

2. Lady Ruger, C.D.X., Wilderness Rottweilers' foundation bitch. Pictured at age five years. Owned by Joann H. Turner, Anchorage, Alas.

3. Goldmoor's Kodiak v. Marquis at eight weeks. Owned by Kevin and Paula Ray, Huntington, W. Va.

4. Bob von Haus Beenen at three months. Owned by Lin Beenen and Cindy Carter, bred by Don and Lin Beenen, Lowell, Mich.

5. Aust. Ch. Rotvel Uberbeiten and Hartzog Kennels "A" litter. Owned by Mrs. C. Wakeham, Koonawarra, N.S.W., Australia.

6. "Let's get going"! Madchen Greta von Fox, Ch. Fraulein Gretchen von Fox and Demon von Fox all settled in the car and ready to start on a trip. Photo courtesy of Ellen Monica Towarnicki, Philadelphia, Pa.

7. Ch. Jiggs von Kruse owned by Alan Kruse, Howell, Mich.

8. Head study of Am. and Can. Ch. Daverick's Alex vom Hasenkamp, C.D., at age three years. By Alex vom Hasenkamp (Germany) ex Carla von Hulsental (Germany) owned by Rick Rogers Gordon, Mooreston, N.J.

Plate 26
1. Ch. Ute vom Mummler, C.D. T.D. is sired by the 1977 Europe Sieger, Int. Ch. Ives Eulenspiegel, SchH. III, and is owned by von Stolzenhaus and Pionierhaus Rottweilers, Pride, La.

2. Von Gailingen's Joie De Vivre, by Ks. Ch. Condor zur Klamm, SchH. III, FH ex Am. and Can. Ch. Von Gailingen's Dassie Did It, U.D.T., Can. C.D. Catherine M. Thompson, owner, Freehold, N.J.

3. All nine-week-old puppies look adorable! This one is from the von Gruenerwald Kennels, Colorado Springs, Colo.

4. Erdelied Zebest at eight weeks. Daughter of top producer Ch. Graudstark's Luger, C.D. ex Ch. Daba von Andan. Bred and owned by Surely Rawlings, Coral Gables, Fla.

5. Dutchess of Highland Park in an informal moment. Owned by Brenda Grigsby, Wilhelmberg Rottweilers, Jasper, Tenn.

6. Ch. Brimstone Bold Whisper, TT, owned by Brimstone Kennels, Ithaca, N.Y. and Pat Cyr.

Plate 27

1. Ch. Delphi Midas, by Ch. Ansel's Cato von Ursa ex Delphi Briseis, C.D., finishing at age 22 months, becoming the first "homegrown" champion produced by Delphi Rottweilers. Handled by Charles O'Hara for owners Al and Bonnie Wimberly, Havana, Fla.

2. Big Oaks Kila Von Haiem at age four and a half months. By Ch. Big Oaks Bogart Vom Brenna ex Ch. Troll House Bandit. Bred by Cat Klass and Jay Meissner. Owned by Jill I. Odor-Nakache, Kailua, Hawaii.

3. Jaeger Vonpalisaden at age nine months taking Best of Winners at Mohawk Valley in 1985. Owned by Joan Maggio.

4. Am. and Can. Ch. Hasso Vom Steigstrassle, C.D., handled by Dawn Honaker, winning Best of Breed at Carroll K.C. 1984 for owner Michael R. Helmann, Arlington Heights, Ill.

5. Ch. Degan Von Liebotschonor on the way to his title in 1984, Butler Kennel Club. Owners, Beauhaven Kennels, Bob and Judy Beaupre, Aliquippa, Pa. Bob Beaupre handling.

6. Am., Can., and Int. Ch. Bronco v Rauberfeld, SchH. III, FH, HD minus. Owned by Felicia Luburich, Srigo Rottweilers, East Brunswick, N.J.

Plate 28

1. Ch. Beaverbrook Chessi v Bruin, by Ch. Rodsden's Bruin v Hungerbuhl, C.D.X. ex Ch. Rodsden's Amber v Brabant. Breeder-owner-handler, Laura Brewton, Powell, Tenn.

2. Ch. Beaverbrook Eisen v Bruin, by Ch. Rodsden's Bruin v Hungerbuhl, C.D.X. - Ch. Beaverbrook Alexa v Iolkos, winning Best of Breed at Thronateeska K.C. in October 1984. Laura Brewton, owner, Powell, Tenn.

3. Am. and Can. Ch. Nicholas von Siegerhaus, C.D. taking Best of Breed at Wine Country under Robert S. Forsyth on the way to Group 1st, April 1984. Thom and Carol Woodward, Von Siegerhaus Rottweilers, Corning, Calif.

4. Ch. Radio Ranch's Ebony Gold Bar, by Am. and Can. Ch. Astro v Chrisstenbrad ex Ch. Radio Ranch's Gypsey v Notara. Breeder, Vina Bechard. Owned by Marge Gold, Goldmoor Kennels, Concord, N.C. Winner of *Dog World* Award of Canine Distinction for completing championship on one weekend with three 5-point majors and Best of Breed over excellent specials.

5. Taber Gold von Stolzenfels, C.D., pointed towards championship. Owned by Dr. Evelyn M. Ellman, Augusta, Mich.

6. Ch. Holly's Pimora von Stolzenfels, C.D. By Imor von Stolzenfels, C.D. ex German import Holly von der Grünen Grenze. Dr. Evelyn M. Ellman, von Stolzenfels, Augusta, Mich.

7. Ch. Tara von Stolzenfels winning Best of Breed at Oakland County 1983. Completed title with just three majors, the final one under judge Henry H. Stoecker at the prestigious Detroit Kennel Club. Owned by Adolph and Beverly Wacker. Agent, Debbie Herrell.

8. Ch. Donnaj Green Mountain Boy, outstanding winning Rottweiler, taking the Working Group at Mohawk Valley in 1983, handled by Ross Petruzzo for owner Anthony P. Attalla, Green Mountain Kennels, Londonderry, N.H.

Plate 29

1. Ch. Altar's Gandolf vom Axel winning his very first Group placement as a special, on this occasion owner-handled by David W. Lauster, Naples, Fla.

2. Ch. RC's Lexia Von Ursa, T.T., by Ch. Rodsden's Ansel V Brabant ex Ch. RC's Gator Bel Von Meadow, T.T. Owned by Donna M. LaQuatra, Beabear Rottweilers, High Springs, Fla.

3. Ch. Kaiserelli Puko Von Schleper winning the Working Group at Ft. Lauderdale Dog Club, December 1984. Owned by Donna LaQuatra, High Springs, Fla.

4. Ch. J-Mar's Glory B von Ansel taking Group 4th under Mrs. Muriel Freeman at Fort Bend K.C. in October 1983. Jerry and Margie Haralson, owners, Harperville, Miss.

5. Ch. Gator's Ruffian Von Ursa, by Ch. Rodsden's Ansel v Brabant ex Ch. RC's Gator Bel von Meadow. Owned by Tom and Chris Stenftenagel, Stenften Farm, High Springs, Fla.

6. Ch. Rodsden's Ansel v Brabant, famous and magnificent Rottweiler owned by Harold and Ruth O'Brien, O-Haus Rottweilers, Mt. Juliet, Tenn.

7. Ch. Delphi's Electra Von Beabear, by Ch. Ansel's Cato Von Ursa ex Ch. Delphi Bitt'Amax. A littermate to Ch. Delphi Thetis Von Beabear. Donna LaQuatra, owner, High Springs, Fla.

8. Ch. Delphi Bitt' Amax, by Ch. Phaedra's Amax of Sunnyside ex Hart's Kitten von Bravo Jill. Handled by Charles O'Hara, she finished in five shows on the 1982 Tar Heel Circuit for owners Al and Bonnie Wimberly, Havana, Fla.

Plate 30

1. Ch. Pandemonium's Faust owned by Valerie J. Cade and Robert Lena, Goldens Bridge, N.Y. Best of Breed, Westbury K.A. in 1984.

2. Headstudy of Ravenwood Lord MacBeth, both parents English imports, owned by Ravenwood Rottweilers, Linda B. Griswold, Michigan City, Ind.

3. Liebchen von Vt. Yankee already ruling the house at three months old. Beauhaven Kennels, Bob and Judy Beaupre, Aliquippa, Pa.

4. This beautiful head-study is of Ch. Katryn the Great Von Ursa and Ch. Torburhop's Patton Von Brawn from a portrait by their artist-owner Pamela Zorn Anderson.

5. Srigo's Hoist the Flag and Srigo's Josie, two of the handsome Rottweilers from Srigo Kennels, Felicia Luburich, East Brunswick, N.J. Photographed by the lake, summer 1983.

6. This is Eros, handsome son of Ch. Dolf Fuller von Stolzenfels, C.D., owned by Jack and Dr. Evelyn Ellman, von Stolzenfels Kennels, Augusta, Mich.

Plate 31

1. Ch. Rodsden's Pandora v Forstwald taking Best of Winners from the American-bred Class for a 5-point major at South Windsor K.C. in 1983. Handled by Bill Burrell for owner Frank J. Fiorella, Boxford, Mass.

2. Ch. Cedar Knolls Alexis, by Ch. Freeger's Nebuchadnezzar ex Ch. Frauke Vom Haus Schottroy, owner-handled by Judith Uggiano to take Winners at Tuxedo Park in 1981 under judge Robert Wills.

3. Ch. Daverick's Acacia V Hasenkamp rounds out the trio of champions from Daverick's "A" litter. By Ch. Arras vom Hasenkamp ex Carla vom Hulsental. Owned by G. George Rogers, Richard and Ricki Rogers, Cinnaminson, N.J.

4. V1 rated Karol v Georgshof, SchH. III, FH Gekort. HD free. Sire of Winners Bitch from the Bred-By Exhibitor Class at the 1984 American Rottweiler Club National Specialty Show. Felicia Luburich, owner, Srigo Kennels, East Brunswick, N.J.

5. Ch. Altar's Dasi Mae vom Freyr winning points towards the title at Union County in 1984, handled by Carlos Rojas for Edith D. Alphin, Altar Rottweilers, Fayetteville, N.C.

6. Ch. Donnaj Vt. Yankee of Paulus, C.D.X., TT, owned by Jan Marshall, Donnaj Rottweilers, Woodstock, Vt.

Plate 32
1. Ch. Srigo's Eagle All Over taking Best of Winners at Tuxedo K.C. in 1983 en route to his title under noted all-breed authority Ed Dixon who is the judge. Owned and handled by Bob Beaupre and by Judy Beaupre, Beauhaven Rotties, Aliquippa, Pa.

2. Ilse von Harsa taking Best in Match at 15 weeks of age, Russian River K.C., October 1983. Owners, Keith and Charlotte Twineham, Union City, Calif.

3. Am., Ber., and Can. Ch. Srigo The Jig Is Up, Reserve Winners Dog at the Colonial Rottweiler Club Specialty. Best in Show in Bermuda. Felicia Luburich, owner, East Brunswick, N.J.

4. Athena Vom Oldenwald, C.D., who has seven points towards U.S.A. Championship, was the first Rottweiler at Tula's Kennels, owned by Tula Demas, San Bernardino, Calif. Taking Winners Bitch for a 5-point major at Rogue Valley 1984, handled by Mike Shea.

BIRCH HILL ROTTWEILERS
PEDIGREE

Litter Reg. No. _____

Individual Reg. No. **WF 352412**

Registered Name of Dog: **CH. BIRCH HILL'S TANK COMMANDER, T.D.** — RO-7385-T (Good)

Date Whelped __January 22, 1983__ Sex __Male__

Breeder __Jane F. Wiedel__ Address __4400 S. Eden Rd., Stockton, IL 61085__

Owner __Jane F. Wiedel__ Address __815-598-3159__

PARENTS	GRANDPARENTS	GREAT-GRANDPARENTS	GREAT-GREAT-GRANDPARENTS
SIRE: CH. Birch Hill's Hasso Manteuffel, CDXTD WE 344268 RO-2678 BIS-1981 MRC BOB-1982 GSRC BIS-1982 ARC Specialties	CH. Rodsden's Bruin v Hungerbuhl, CDX WD 375753 RO-1189	CH. Dux vom Hungerbuhl, WC18804 SchH 1 RO-234	Kuno vom Butzensee, SchH 3 40 415
			Britta vom Schlossberg 39 075
		CH. Rodsden's Frolich Burga, CDTD WC589812 RO-649	CH. Max v d Hobertsburg 44 896 RO-320
			CH. Rodsden's Willa vd Harque, WB854722 RO-321 UDT
	A/C CH. Rodsden's Birch Hill Hanna, CDXTD WD 653282 RO-1543	CH. Falco vh Brabantpark WC162229 RO-286	CH. Erno von Wellesweiler, 39 499 RO-5 SchH 1
			Dutch CH. Burga vh Brabantpark NHSB366489 HD Free, Utrecht
		CH. Rodsden's Gay Lady, TD WC635810 RO-647	CH. Rodsden's Ikon vd Harque, WC81494 RO-355 CD
			CH. Rodsden's Lady Luck, CD WB262642 RO-60
DAM: A/C CH. Birch Hill's Juno, CDTD WE 449506 RO-2968 WB-1980 MRC BOS-1982 CRC Specialties	A/C CH. Rodsden's Elko Kastanienbaum, CDXTD WD 694350 RO-1448	Int. CH. Elko vom Kastanienbaum, 46 340 SchH 1 HD Free, Utrecht	Elko vom Kaiserberg, SchH 1 44 352
			Gitta vom Bucheneck, SchH 1 44 776 HD Free, Utrecht
		CH. Gundi vom Reichenbachle 48 086 RO-846	Berno vom Albtal, SchH 3,FH 42 673
			Antje v d Wegscheide 41 225
	CH. Rodsden's Birch Hill Bess, CDTD WD 363207 RO-1174	CH. Dux vom Hungerbuhl, WC18804 SchH 1 RO-234	Kuno vom Butzensee, SchH 3 40 415
			Britta vom Schlossberg 39 075
		CH. Rodsden's Frolich Burga, CDTD WC589812 RO-649	CH. Max vd Hobertsburg WC308208 RO-320
			CH. Rodsden's Willa vd Harque, WB854722 RO-321 UDT

PLATE 17

1

2

PLATE 18

PLATE 19

PLATE 20

PLATE 21

1

2

3

4

PLATE 22

PLATE 23

PLATE 24

PLATE 25

PLATE 26

PLATE 27

1

18

BEST OF
WINNERS
ACADIANA
KENNEL CLUB
FALL 1984
PHOTO BY
L. SOSA

2

4

BEST OF
BREED
CARROLL
KENNEL CLUB
1984
ASHBEY

BEST OF
WINNERS
MOHAWK VALLEY
KENNEL CLUB
1985
ASHBEY

3

5

WINNERS
BUTLER
KENNEL CLUB
SEPT. 1984

6

CLUB

HARKINS

PLATE 28

PLATE 29

PLATE 30

BEST OF
BREED
WESTBURY
KENNEL ASSN.
1984
ASHBEY

PLATE 31

BEST OF
WINNERS
SOUTH WINDSOR
KENNEL CLUB
1983
1   ASHBEY

WINNERS
TUXEDO PARK
KENNEL CLUB
1981

2

4

3

5

WINNERS
UNION COUNTY
KENNEL CLUB INC

6

GROUP
FIRST

GUST 1979
ASHBEY

PLATE 32

German Shepherd Dogs and Pembroke Welsh Corgis.

After losing the last of their German Shepherds, the Golds decided that they would like to have a Rottweiler, at which time they purchased nine-week-old Radio Ranch's Ebony Gold Bar. Five months later they also acquired seven-week-old Radio Ranch's Ten of Goldmoor. Both completed their championships prior to reaching three years of age; and Gold Bar was winner of the *Dog World* Award of Canine Distinction for the speed with which the title was attained.

The Golds breed only OFA clear stock and limit their breedings to one a year. Their oldest homebred, Goldmoor's Robin Hood, is started on a promising show career, while others from the second litter are doing well at the puppy match shows.

Greenhill

Greenhill Rottweilers are owned by Nick and Lois Schwechtje at Broomall, Pennsylvania. This is the home of Champion Riegele's Greenhill Ima Maid, C.D., who finished her championship in less than four months of local showing with a non-professional handler, and obtained her C.D. at the same time, handled in obedience by Lois Schwechtje. These achievements were accomplished while she was less than two years of age. Between her first points and finishing, this splendid bitch was Reserve Winners at two minor and four major shows, and had one minor and one major Reserve from the puppy class with Lois handling her. She won back-to-back majors, was Best of Winners four times and Best of Opposite Sex five times, was specialed a few times, and was Best of Opposite Sex at majors, including Trenton Kennel Club under Mr. Heido Ito, international judge from Japan for whom an entry of 111 Rottweilers had assembled.

Lois Schwechtje has been active in the dog show world since 1966, in the earlier days as an exhibitor of German Shepherds in both show and obedience. Then she acquired her first Rottweiler in 1978. She is very proud of her lovely Ch. Riegele's Greenhill Ima Maid, who is known as "Tory," born September 25, 1980, and is a daughter of American and Canadian Champion's Rodsden's Ander v h Brabant ex Champion Riegele's Erin Maid, and was bred by E. and H. Walls, Riegele Kennels.

Tory is noted for her sound temperament and correct type. Her owner is a hard-working member of the Colonial Rottweiler Club for whom she has done the "Newsletter" for more than two years. She also belongs to the American Rottweiler Club, the Delaware County Kennel Club (since 1966, was their Secretary for many years, then "chaired" various committees, and is now on the Board), the Philadelphia Dog Training Club, and the Pennsylvania Federation of Dog Clubs. She also likes judging at match shows.

Green Mountain

Green Mountain Rottweilers were established at Londonderry, New Hampshire, by Anthony P. Attalla, who had obtained his first show dog, a Doberman Pinscher, in 1970. For about five years he participated in breeding and showing Dobermans. Although he did enjoy his Dobes, he wanted, as he puts it, "a little bit more from the breed that wasn't there," so he decided to go to "the source of the breed, the Rottweiler."

After two years of looking, talking to breeders, visiting kennels, and searching for the right "look," Mr. Attalla finally decided on Donnaj Kennels, and selected ten-week-old Donnaj Green Mountain Boy. The rest is history!

This puppy grew up to become American and Canadian Champion Donnaj Green Mountain Boy, born December 18, 1977, son of American and Canadian Champion Donnaj Vt. Yankee of Paulus, C.D.X. from Champion Northwind's Helga (Canada).

"Brock" has set records that will be difficult to beat. He received the American Rottweiler Club "Top Dog" award for two consecutive years, 1982 and 1983, by leading both Top Ten Dogs and Top Ten Group categories, in 1983 defeating more dogs in Group competition than any Rottweiler before his time. His lifetime records consist of the following:

Three times Best in Show

300 Bests of Breed—Rottweiler record

100 Group placements—Rottweiler record

Top Rottweiler 1982 and 1983

Set record for Best of Breed wins in a single year, 100

Defeated record number of Rottweilers in a single year, 2,332

Set record for Group placements in single year, 55

Set record for number of dogs defeated by a Rottweiler in single year

Only Rottweiler ever to place in the Group at Westminster

"Brock" has proven himself a quality sire as well as a truly great show dog, and his champion progeny are making their presence felt in the show ring.

Without question "Brock's" phenomenal show record has helped to open the door for other members of the breed to receive serious consideration from the Group and Best in Show judges in all parts of the country. "Nothing succeeds like success" has very truthfully been said on many occasions and "Brock's" success has pointed out to many the admirable qualities of his breed. "Brock" has been presented in the show ring most efficiently by his handler, Ross Petruzzo.

The Griffins

Ken and Hildegarde Griffin are comparitive newcomers to owning Rottweilers—people who truly went about things the right way when they decided that this was the breed for them, and who consequently are reaping the rewards in pleasure now. The source of this pleasure is Champion Rhomarks Axel v Lerchenweld, CDX, T.D., who is their only Rottweiler and through whom they have enjoyed many facets of dog ownership.

Axel was selected with the greatest of care. Hildegarde Griffin points out, "I knew his dam and sire, and was given the privilege of the pick of the litter. What I liked best about my new puppy was his stable temperament. He has an excellent disposition and he is exceptionally smart. At the same time, he has sort of a great humor and is so loving, sharing toys and bones willingly. He loves company (he thinks they all come to visit him). He is a true companion and beloved member of our household. In the show ring, Axel excels and loves the approval of the crowd. He is very animated, and one can put him in just about any situation and Axel is enjoying himself (mostly getting very merry)."

So much for Axel, the family dog! Just one of the ways in which he excels. Axel gained his championship in 1981 in just ten shows with four majors among his wins. In 1982 he became the first California-born Rottweiler to win an all-breed Best in Show, and the tenth of his breed to gain the Best in an all-breed event. He was No. 1 Group Winning Rottweiler in 1982, defeating 8292 working dogs; and the same year he became No. 2 Rottweiler Breed Winner with 1279 points. For 1982 and 1983 he was an American Rottweiler Club Top Ten Dog.

Axel scored with equal success in obedience. Owner-trained and handled, he won six legs in seven American Kennel Club sanctioned trials during 1983; then in 1984 added the C.D.X. degree when he earned three legs in five trials. In March 1985, again owner-trained and handled, he added a Tracking Dog degree. Presently, in early 1985, he and his owner are working together for the Utility title, and having much fun doing so along the way.

Axel has been used at stud and had his first offspring around 1982. To date he has sired nine litters. In both line breedings and outcross breedings he has produced well, with very uniform litters. The Griffins say, "We have turned away many bitches, not being interested in producing just puppies, but rather in keeping up the Rottweiler standard and improving the breed." Some of his offspring are already doing well in the show ring, with important wins and championship titles.

Haus Trezilians

Haus Trezilians Rottweilers are owned by Douglas K. Loving of Richmond, Virginia, whose kennel is headed by the splendid and wellknown dog, Rowehaus A. Erwin Rommel, son of Champion Adi von der Lowenau ex Ada vom Platz.

Rommel is well known on the dog show circuits where he is earning his championship under Sidney Lamont's capable handling. But he is also noted as an actor, having been hired by MGM Studios to play the part of an estate protection dog in the CBS Miniseries "George

Washington." Rommel's job was to bark and to guard Benedict Arnold's home. He is shown in the film at about the time Arnold was discovered as a traitor. In his scene, it is Rommel's job to bark and attempt to prevent George Washington and his aides from approaching General Arnold's home. As Washington draws near, Rommel is given a hand signal to stop barking, and then allows Barry Bostwick (portraying George Washington) to pet him. Barry Bostwick was very nearly hurt when he disregarded Doug Loving's instructions and made challenging eye contact with the dog. As it turned out, Rommel only took off the actor's wig! Other cast members included David Dukes, Jacquelyn Smith (of Charlie's Angels fame), Patty Duke Astin and Lloyd Bridges.

Rommel got this job due to his own and his owner's participation in the Schutzhund sport. The Rottweiler was chosen due to his having had the highest probability of having been around as a breed in colonial days; and because he was the only controllable protection trained dog in the area with the exception of Doberman Pinschers and German Shepherd Dogs.

Hidden Meadow

Hidden Meadow Rottweilers are owned by Mary and Dorothy Stringer at Burlington, New Jersey, who, although they do not have kennel or breeder status, so they modestly tell us, have had the pleasure and good fortune of owning two exceptional male Rottweilers over the past 12 years who have made positive contributions to the Fancy.

The first is Champion Kokas K's Degan von Berga, C.D., T.D., who lived from April 4, 1975 to September 20, 1982. He is listed as an American Rottweiler Club GOLD SIRE Producer. In a total of 35 litters, he sired 19 breed champions, three Utility Dog titled offspring, one Tracking Dog, and four who earned C.D. degrees.

This handsome dog was truly royally bred, having been a son of Champion Lyn-Mar Acres Arras von Kinto (Top Producer) ex Burga von Isarstrand.

The second is German import Champion Arras vom Hasenkamp, who was whelped November 26, 1978 and came to the United States at eight months of age. He was a Top Producer in 1983, seeing five of his offspring finish their breed championships. Five of his get also have C.D. degrees to date, one of which captured the *Dog World* Award of Canine Distinction for earning the C.D. title in three consecutive trials scoring better than 195 in each, with an average score of 198.

Arras is by Flavio vom Dammerwald, Schutzhund III, EzA, ex Blanka v d Schachtschleuse, SchH. I.

Jan Su

Jan-Su's Rottweilers are owned by Suzanne Stewart and J. J. Jay at Inkster, Michigan, who acquired their first Rottie in September 1981. He was so stubborn that his new owners promptly named him Bull, short for Tazmo's Taurus the Bull, son of Champion Sciroco's Mac Arthur Park (Champion Ero v d Mauth C.D.—Champion Northwind's Jasmine) from Crookhaus Buffy von Trojanov (Sir Arco Supreme—Chesara Dark Elsa), bred by Rodger L. Crooks and Jack Tazzi. Bull's show career started at age nine months, and by age two and a half years, Bull had completed both his American and Canadian championships. Due to a knee injury, Bull now has been retired. As Sue says, "He enjoys just lying around and being a wonderful pet and beloved friend." Bull is co-owned by Jack Tazzi of Dearborn, Michigan, and J. J. Jay of Inkster, Michigan.

September 1982 rolled around, and the feeling grew that the time had come to acquire a playmate for Bull. Carado's Commander Cody came to Jan-Su from a litter of six pups at age nine weeks. His first shows at age six months brought many blue ribbons, and his first points were won at age seven months. He finished his Canadian championship at age 17 months, followed shortly thereafter with his title in the United States. From September 1984 through December 1984, Cody took eleven Bests of Breed and two Group 3rd placements to finish as No. 3 Rottweiler in Canada for 1984. The first quarter of 1985 has him winning nine Bests of Breed, including the prestigious Detroit Kennel Club, and a Group 2nd placement at the Seaway Kennel Club in Thorold, Ontario. Cody is owned by Suzanne Stewart. He is by

Champion Bulli v Meyerhoff ex Inga von Tannenwald.

By January 1985 it was felt that it would be nice to add a little girl Rottie to round out the kennel. Carado's Satin Classic has warmed the hearts of everyone. She is a daughter of American and Canadian Champion Ebony Acres Yankee Alliance (Champion Donnaj VT Yankee of Paulus, C.D.X.—Champion Radio Ranch's Gypsy v Notara C.D.) from Carado's Satin Sidney (Champion Bulli v Meyerhof—Inga v Tannenwald TT). Her maternal great grandparents are Champion Ero von der Mauth C.D., Champion Northwind's Inka, Champion Radio Ranch's Axel v Notara and Champion Rue De Rennes.

At age six months and a day, Satin Classic went Winners Bitch, Best of Opposite Sex, and Best Puppy in Breed under breeder-judge Mrs. M. L. Walton. In her other six shows she has taken numerous awards, including another Winners Bitch, and five times has been Best Puppy in breed. She is co-owned by Suzanne Stewart and Carol Kravetz.

J-Mar

J-Mar Rottweilers are owned by Jerry and Margie Haralson, and located at Harpersville, Mississippi.

The Haralsons have been "in Rottweilers" since 1974, during which time they have chosen to breed only two litters, both carefully planned and well thought out.

The first of these was by Champion Rodsden's Ansel v Brabant from their lovely bitch J-Mar's Valentine Echoe, and was born June 13, 1980. Three champions were included in these puppies, a bitch and two dogs. The boys became Champion J-Mar's Theodore Roosevelt, "Teddy," and Champion J-Mar's General Luger Von Russell, "General." It was the bitch, however, who was destined for special fame. She became Champion J-Mar's Glory B V Ansel in March 1982 with four majors, then went on to a brief but highly successful career as a special. By the end of four months in specials competition, Glory B had become No. 8 bitch in the 1982 Top Ten Rottweiler Bitch ratings. Then from January to December of 1983, Glory B went on to No. 1 Rottweiler Bitch and No. 2 among all Rottweilers for that year (dogs and bitches) owing

to her defeat of 1537 in breed competition.

At the present time, Glory B has five Group 1st placements from a total of 20 Bests of Breed and an impressive total of 80 times Best of Opposite Sex ribbons at the young age of five years, proudly owner-handled all the way. Glory B is the only Rottweiler bitch to have received a Group placement from that highly respected breeder-judge Mrs. Muriel Freeman. She has broken all previous records for a Rottweiler bitch having defeated more members of her breed than any other Rottie bitch in history.

Now at home with her brothers and puppies, Glory is carefully observing the rearing of her puppies, the second litter her owners have bred, these sired by the famous Specialty and all-breed Best in Show winner Champion Mirko vom Steinkopf, C.D., SchH. III, IPO III, FH. Like her own mother, Glory B seems destined to become an outstanding producer, and hopes are high for these promising youngsters.

Nor is Glory herself through with the shows. We understand that she will be back in competition again, too, to hopefully add a few additional honors to those she has already attained.

Michael and Beverly Johnson

Champion Bratiana's Micki von Follrath was born on June 10, 1983 in San Francisco, California. When she was five weeks old, she was purchased by Michael and Beverly Johnson of Alameda, and from that day on she has been a source of pleasure to her owners both as a show and family companion bitch. Her breeders were Sirpa and Thomas Scallan, her parents J.B.'s Alphonso da Bratiana and Bratiana's Jessica, both of whom were sired by Champion Bratiana's Gus de Michaela, the sire of 11 champions.

Micki's show career began when she was just six months old at the Golden Gate Kennel Club Dog Show, when she placed in a class of 15 puppies. On that occasion, her award was the only fourth prize she has ever received; from then on there have been many high class awards. At her third show, still in junior puppies, she went on to Reserve Winners Bitch to a 4-point major. From senior puppies she won two three-point majors, taking Best of Winners and Best of Opposite Sex both times. Micki was Winners Bitch seven times for a total of 19 points and her championship which she completed at just two days past her 15th month birthday.

As a special Micki has continued to do well, even though she started her career there when only 15 months of age. Now fully matured, she is on her way again and will also try obedience. She is the Johnsons' only Rottweiler at the time of writing, sharing their home and affections with her great companion and playmate Barclay, who is a Cocker Spaniel.

Laran

Laran Rottweilers are the result of an interest in dogs by Larry and Alice Lee of Franklin, Indiana, which started in 1970 with the purchase of their first Doberman. The association with Dobermans continued until 1981, strictly in the obedience field.

In June of 1981, following much thought and consideration, the decision was reached by the Lees to purchase a Rottweiler. This was Lee's Ebony Emperor who joined the family that summer and to date has earned his C.D. and is now ready to go for the C.D.X.

Initially the Lees had been interested in obedience only. However, they found that showing in some conformation matches was fun, and they decided to try becoming involved in that aspect, too.

In August 1983 they purchased two puppies, littermates, by American and Canadian Champion Rodsden's Elko Kastanienbaum, C.D.X., T.D., Canadian C.D., ex Champion Michelob Von Applegat. The male, Champion Baron Elko Von Dealcrest, finished his championship at the age of 20 months, while his litter sister, Champion Baroness Elka Von Dealcrest, completed hers at the age of 16 months. Both are ready and will be shown for their C.D.s, and a promising future for both of them is looked forward to by their owners.

At the Medallion Rottweiler Club Specialty in June 1984, the Lees met Dieter and Ursel Hoffman from West Germany. Their bitch, Gitte von der Bergschmiede, SchH. I, was about to be bred to Falko Von Der Tente, SchH. III, who was the 1984 ADRK Klub Sieger. The Lees had the good fortune to obtain a puppy bitch, Eike Vom Klosterdiek, from this litter, which they feel will prove a tremendous asset.

Lindenwood

Lindenwood Rottweilers are owned by Linda and Bill Michels, Brunswick, Ohio, who acquired their first Rottweiler in 1978 with the help of Pat Hickman Clark of Northwinds fame. This was an eight-week-old Dutch import who became Canadian Champion Astor, C.D., TT. Astor was sired by Astor von Landgraben, SchH. III, FH, who has sired many top working and conformation dogs in Germany, including the famous International Champion Ives Eulenspiegel, SchH. III. As a show dog he started out with a bang at age 18 months, when he was exhibited five times in Canada, taking Best of Breed on all five occasions (twice over specials) owner-handled by Linda Michels to earn his Canadian championship. He earned his American and his Canadian C.D. degrees in three shows each. He was x-rayed shortly afterwards, was unfortunately found to have hip dysplasia, was neutered, and never shown in conformation in the United States. "Thor," as he is known to his friends, lives the good life of the family pet, even down to having his own wading pool in which to relax and as an escape from summer heat.

In 1979 the Michels acquired an eight-week-old bitch puppy from Ruth Meyer in Canada. This youngster was sired by Top Producer American and Canadian Champion Ero von der Mauth, American and Canadian C.D., TT, ex Canadian Champion Northwind's Inka, the latter from the highly successful Champion Igor von Schauer—American and Canadian Champion Northwind's Danka, American and Canadian C.D., breeding. This puppy grew up to become American and Canadian Champion Bola von Meyerhoff, C.D., TT, who was the foundation bitch for Lindenwood Rottweilers and a multi-Best of Breed winner in both the United States and Canada. During 1981 she was bred to Champion Rodsden's Kane v Forstwald, C.D., which was a linebreeding on the Northwind's

85

"D" litter. From this came Champion Lindenwood's Anaconda, C.D., TT, who finished with three majors and had several Best of Opposite Sex wins over specials. The three bitch puppies from that Lindenwood "A" litter were shown at the 1982 Colonial Rottweiler Club Specialty with considerable success, bringing home first prize, third and fourth in the regular 6- to 9-month puppy bitch class plus first in that class in the Sweepstakes. This was Bola's only litter.

In 1982 the Michels acquired a seventeen-month-old bitch from the famous Champion Rodsden's Kane v Forstwald, C.D. ex Champion Rodsden's Roma von Brabant breeding who became Champion Rodsden's Heika v Forstwald, C.D., VB, TT. Heika finished her championship with four majors, then was bred to Champion Gasto vom Liebersbacherhof, C.D.X., T.D., SchH. I for the first time in 1983 and for the second time the following year. This produced the Lindenwood's "B" and Rodsden's Lindenwood "L" litters. The "B" litter is just eighteen months old as we write, but shows lots of promise. The Michels kept Lindenwood's Bouncer, TT, who was first in 9- to 12-month puppy dogs at the 1984 Colonial Rottweiler Club Specialty Sweepstakes, second in 9- to 12-month puppy dogs at both the Futurity and regular classes of the Medallion Rottweiler Club Specialty, and first in Bred-by Exhibitor at the A.K.C. Centennial Show.

Besides "Bouncer," Lindenwood has another promising youngster at home. Rodsden's Hallelujah. She is by Champion Gasto vom Liebersbacherhof, C.D.X., T.D., SchH. I ex Champion Lindenwood's Anaconda, C.D., TT.

The Michels both enjoy obedience, tracking, Schutzhund, carting, and conformation training. They put a premium on quality in temperament as well as type and soundness, and have become very much involved with temperament testing of puppies and adults.

Little Flower
Little Flower Rottweilers belong to Frank and Val Fiorella at Boxford, Massachusetts, whose interests include numerous breeds since the kennel was started in 1966 with Collies and Samoyeds. Since then there have been Doberman Pinschers, Rhodesian Ridgebacks and Chinese Shar-Peis, with the principal breeds there now having become Rottweilers and Shar-Peis.

The first of the Little Flower Rottweilers was purchased from a little-known (at the time) kennel, owned by Anthony Attalla, which has now become one of the breed's best known since the arrival on the show scene of their Champion Donnaj Green Mountain Boy. The Fiorellas purchased a daughter of this dog who became Champion Green Mountains Flora, who has proven to be a superstar in her own right. Flora is the first American-bred Rottweiler bitch to have earned the International Championship from the F.C.I. Her list of titles is imposing to say the least, including American, Canadian, Dominican, Puerto Rican, and Mexican championships, Champion of the Americas, International Champion (FCI), and, pending confirmation World Champion. As her owner comments, "She may prove to be the most titled Rottweiler in America."

Additionally, this splendid bitch has earned a Puerto Rican C.D., and T.D. and TT degrees in Mexico. She was on the American Rottweiler Club Top Ten Bitches for 1982, is a member of the Medallion Rottweiler Club Hall of Fame, has earned the *Dog World* Award Of Merit, and was Best Foreign Dog in Show, Puerto Rico 1982.

The next Rottweiler bitch purchased by the Fiorellas was Champion Rodsden Pandora v Forstwald from the Rodsden Kennels. This bitch descends directly from two of the first three Rotties registered with the American Kennel Club, Jon v.d. Steinlach and Stina v Felsenmeer. She has gained championships in America, Canada, the Dominican Republic, and Champion of the Americas along with four CACIB points towards her International Championship.

The Fiorellas also own dogs with Susan Rademacher, Tony Attella, and Arthur Twis.

The Little Flower breeding program has been carefully thought out and planned for the next ten years in hopes of creating a line that will be competitive anywhere in the world.

Loneagle

Loneagle Rottweilers, owned by Matt and Jody Engel of Miami, Florida, acquired their first Rottweiler companion in 1980, after much reading and research. The Engels' first Rottweiler was Arrow of Lone Eagle, C.D.X., T.D., U.C.D., by Champion Mc-Coy von Meadow ex Champion Orlando von Ocala. In a very short show career, Arrow was always in the ribbons and would have been a great foundation for Loneagle but unfortunately she did not receive normal hip evaluation from OFA and was spayed. Arrow is, however, a terrific obedience dog and is now preparing for Schutzhund competition.

The next addition to Loneagle was Loneagles Bravura von Seren, C.D., T.C., by Champion Donnaj Vt Yankee of Paulus, C.D.X. ex Champion Doroh's Fantastic Serenade, C.D.X. "Brava," too, proved to be a good working dog, acquiring her C.D. at the age of only 12 months and by completing a picture-perfect track record at the age of only 22 months for her TD. OFA results this time indicated normal hip status and Brava is now competing in the breed classes, always owner-handler-trained to all her wins. Shown on only a few occasions to date, she has been in the ribbons 90% of the time and has received both of her major wins, and now needs only single points to finish her championship.

All of Loneagle's accomplishments have been owner-handled, which adds to the fun and enjoyment of owning such great companions. Brava is now preparing for an upcoming breeding which will be the first litter produced by Loneagle Rottweilers—an event to which the Engels are looking forward with keenest anticipation. As they comment, "Good things are worth waiting for."
At the time of writing, the Engels are also proud of the fact that the American Rottweiler Club has recognized Jody's strong support of the breed by nominating her to the Board of Directors and the position of Club Secretary. The next few years look to be very exciting for Loneagle Rottweilers and their enthusiastic owners.

Marja

Marja Rottweilers are owned by Jacqueline and Mary Puglise and located at Farmingville, Long Island, New York.

This has always been a dog-oriented family. The first Rottweiler owned by them was acquired in 1966. This was Hilda, a two-day-old orphaned puppy raised by Miss Puglise.

In 1977 the first show Rottweiler came to the Puglises. This was the bitch Champion Marja Elka von Heidel, from Merrymore's Pastis ex Tara von Nadriches. Elka became the foundation bitch at Marja, finishing her championship in short order and earning a position among the Top Bitches in the country during 1978, 1979 and 1980. Among her exciting awards was that of Best of Opposite Sex at the Westminster Kennel Club in 1980.

Elka was bred to Best in Show winning Champion Donnaj Green Mountain Boy during 1980, and a very impressive litter of quality pups was the result. Particularly outstanding is Champion Marja's Obsidians Pegasus, presently making his mark as a show dog and as a sire.

Marlo's

Marlo's Rottweilers are owned by Marlene A. Lore, who is strictly a hobby breeder and located at Citrus Heights, California.

Marlene acquired her first Rottweiler, who is also her foundation bitch, in 1976 from a well-known and respected breeder, Jonathan Bratt of San Francisco, California. Marlene well recalls the hours she spent researching Rottweilers at the public library, speaking with various prominent breeders, and looking for a line of truly excellent breed type prior to deciding from whom to make this important purchase. She then selected American and Canadian Champion Jacqueline Da Bratiana, C.D., who certainly proved to be a wise choice, having to date produced six champions and six offspring with working titles.

All four of Marlene Lore's personal Rottweilers live in the home with her as part of the family. Showing in conformation, working in obedience, and protection is a sport she enjoys; plus breeding a litter occasionally (once a year at most) is a pleasurable hobby for her, opening many avenues of friendships with other people who own, love and work with Rotties she has bred.

To date she is the breeder of Champions Marlo's Inga von Follrath, C.D. (*Dog World Award* winner in 1980), Marlo's Falk v Apache Heart, Marlo's Choctaw Chief, Marlo's Rome De Bratiana, C.D. (owner-handled in bred-by exhibitor to championship), Marlo's Borgha Da Bratiana, Marlo's Sohn v Axel, C.D., T.D., and, with points towards the title, Marlo's Black Maverick, C.D. and Marlo's Snowfire v Axel, C.D.

The foundation bitch here, American and Canadian Champion Jacqueline Da Bratiana, C.D., is a daughter of Champion Panamint Seneca Chief (Champion Fals vom Kursaal, Germany, ex Champion Panamint Cheyenne Autumn) from Katrina of Cassiopeia (Champion Frederick von Alfenheim—Cassiopeia De Bratiana).

Jacqueline has twice taken the Best Brood Bitch award at the prestigious West Coast Golden Gate Kennel Club Show in San Francisco—a handsome and beautifully bred bitch who has proven her worth in many areas.

Marquis

Kevin and Paula Ray of Huntington, West Virginia, purchased their first Rottweiler, a bitch, in February 1982. She was whelped December 10, 1981, a daughter of Champion Bethel Farms' Apollo and Champion Radio Ranch's Angus Barhund. She grew up to become American and Canadian Champion Locatah's Avant-Garde, C.D.X., but is better known as "Morgan." Both her championships and her C.D.X. degree were completed within a ten-week period of showing during the fall of 1983. She went on to a number of Best of Opposite Sex awards in very limited showing as a special in 1984.

Morgan completed her Canadian championship in two weekends, going Winners Bitch in three out of four shows. This performance garnered her recognition as the 19th ranked Rottweiler in Canada including both males and females. She whelped her first litter in October 1984, and is now back into training for her Utility Degree. She is a member of the Medallion Rottweiler Club Honor Roll, and winner of *Dog World* Magazine's "Award of Canine Distinction."

The Rays' second bitch, from Rodsden's Kennel, was obtained in June 1983, Rodsden's Christa V. Brader, C.D.X. She is by Champion Gasto Vom Liebersbacherhof, C.D.X., T.D. and Champion Rodsden's Hella v. Forstwald, T.D.

In June 1984 the Rays purchased their first male, Goldmoor's Kodiak V. Marquis, whose parents are Champion Radio Ranch's Ebony Gold Bar and Champion Radio Ranch's Ten of Goldmoor.

In February 1985, American and Canadian Champion Kreger's Nero Hercules Heamac joined the Marquis family, he by Champion Nero Von Schauer, C.D. and Torburhop's Brigitt Kreger, co-owned with Bill and Judy Stine of Grafton, Ohio. "Herc," the sire of the Rays' first litter, is a multi-Best of Breed and group placer in both the United States and Canada. According to the publication *Dogs In Canada*, he was the third-ranked Rottweiler in 1982. He was the No. 3 ranked Rottweiler there in 1983 and 1984.

Although the Rays have been involved in this fine breed for a short time, they have established a firm foundation for their kennel based on several outstanding lines. This will ensure their ability to produce Rottweilers who will be capable of competing in both the conformation and the obedience rings of the future.

Noblehaus

Noblehaus Rottweilers are owned by Pat and Mark Schwartz of West Nyack, New York. Their first Rottweiler, Amie of Northwinds, was acquired from Patricia Hickman Clark in 1974. Amie never distinguished herself by becoming a champion and was never used for breeding, but became a dog hero by saving Mark's life from a would-be mugger.

The Schwartzes' second dog came from Graudstark Kennels, owned by Judith Johnson. He became Champion Graudstark's Luger, C.D., TT, and he was sired by Champion Radio Ranch's Axel v Notara ex Shearwater's Pyewacket. Luger distinguished himself in the show ring as a multi-Best of Breed and Group placing dog, but the Schwartzes are particularly proud of him as a producer.

In very limited breeding, Luger has sired 13 champions and six Companion Dog degree recipients. Four of his offspring are multi-Group placers and winners, including the first all-breed Best in Show Rottweiler bitch, Champion Pioneer's Beguiled (Luger ex Champion Robil's Marta v Donnaj). Luger is following in the pawprints of his ancestors, as he has four generations of Best in Show producers in his pedigree.

Noblehaus embarked on its breeding program in 1979 when the Schwartzes leased Northwind's Kindred Spirit, out of the famous Northwind's "K" litter, and bred her to their own Luger. This produced Champion Noblehaus Ain't Misbehavin', TT, who was breeder-owner-handled by Mark to her title, finishing in ten shows with three majors. "Bee" now is starting to make her own record as a producer. From her first litter of four pups, by Champion Bergsgarden's Nero, she produced Champion Noblehaus Beretta, who finished his championship with ease, going Best of Breed from the classes over top specials along the way. The highlight, and an exciting one indeed, of Beretta's career to date was when he was chosen Winners Dog and Best of Winners at the American Kennel Club Centennial Show in 1984 for a 5-point major. Also from this litter, Noblehaus Behexen, TT, is major pointed and well on her way towards the title.

Another of the Noblehaus winners is Champion Doroh's Jaegerin v Noblehaus, purchased from Dorothy Wade at seven weeks' age, who finished her championship with three majors including a win from puppy class, and is currently working towards a C.D.

Noblehaus looks forward to the future as there are several promising youngsters on the horizon. One of them, Noblehaus Executor (American and Canadian Champion Birch Hill's Governor, American and Canadian C.D. ex Champion Noblehaus Ain't Misbehavin', TT) was Best Puppy in Match at four months of age under Pamela C. Brown of Radio Ranch fame.

Noblehaus is not a kennel in the true sense of the word. Only one or two litters are bred here each year, and all of the dogs live in the Schwartzes' home as family members.

O-Haus

O-Haus Rottweilers are owned by Harold and Ruth O'Brien at Mt. Juliet, Tennessee. The O'Briens are not large breeders, but are striving for quality by using only sound, healthy, OFA certified breeding stock. They comment that they would like to see their breed NOT grow so fast in numbers as quality can often suffer under those circumstances.

Top dog at this kennel is Champion Rodsden's Ansel v Brabant, who was campaigned for between two and three years. A son of Champion Falco v h Brabantpark ex Champion Rodsden's Gay Lady, C.D., this splendid Rottie scored such victories as No. 5 Rottweiler in 1978, No. 2 in 1979, and to culminate it all, No. 1 Rottweiler in the United States in 1981.

As of December 1984, Ansel had sired 39 American Champions, one Canadian Champion, and many with obedience degrees. He was the Top Producing Rottweiler in 1982, 1983 and 1984. His progency include the No. 1 American Rottweiler Club bitch for 1983, Champion J-Mar's Glory B von Ansel; and of the No. 1 American Rottweiler bitch for 1982, Champion RC's Magnum Force. Also No. 4 and No. 8 that year.

Now retired from the show ring, Ansel continues to produce outstanding youngsters.

The O'Briens also own O-Haus Trouble, who is now being owner-handled in the ring. Just over three years old and soon to be bred, she has some good wins to her credit in keen competition.

Then there is O-Haus Master von Ansel, an American Champion at 15 months of age, a Canadian Champion at 18 months. Master is an Ansel son from a litter in which six have finished championship. An impressive dog who should contribute greatly to the breed.

Ojuara

Ojuara Rottweilers at Centereach, New York, are owned by Betty and Gary Walker who became involved with the breed during the mid-1970's.

The first, and foundation, bitch here is the lovely Champion Radio Ranch's Circuit Breaker, T.T. "C.B." completed her championship owner-handled, with some exciting wins including a Best of Breed from the classes over specials. She is sired by American and Canadian Champion Astro vom Chrisstenbrad ex Champion Radio Ranch's Rox Island Line, a daughter of the Top Producing Rottweiler bitch in the history of the breed, Champion Radio Ranch's Axel von Notara.

The Walkers are strictly hobby breeders, producing only one or two litters each year, striving for quality rather than for quantity. They take pride and pleasure in training and showing their own dogs and are doing so successfully in the conformation and obedience rings with their home-bred Rottweilers. Although actively breeding only since the early 1980's, the Walkers are producing some excellent stock backed by the finest bloodlines—surely the ingredients for a kennel destined for importance in the breed.

Pandemonium

Pandemonium Rottweilers, now located at Goldens Bridge, New York, where they moved in January 1985, have met with great success within a comparatively short period of time. To quote her own words, owner Valerie J. Cade, "never thought that the purchase of an active, bouncing bitch puppy of an obscure and then difficult-to-locate breed known as Rottweilers would lead to Pandemonium Rottweilers becoming the top producing show kennel on the East Coast." This was certainly not her intent at the time! However, and again we quote, "if you are fortunate to have come across one of the unique and wonderful temperaments of a truly good Rottweiler, the breed will be first in your heart the rest of your life."

Champion Graudstark's Pandemonium, TT, was purchased at age eight weeks from Graudstark Kennels. Later Valerie decided that Pandemonium would make an appropriate name for her breeding hobby as there is never a dull moment with a Rottweiler around, and they are certainly NOT easy dogs to breed.

Graudstark's Quatro Tempo, also acquired from Graudstark, was also of paramount importance to the success of Pandemonium's future breeding program. An extraordinarily large, typey bitch whose dam was imported from Finland, "Tempo" made the notable contribution of two Specialty winners and a number of other offspring of magnificent type and soundness.

Since 1979, Pandemonium has finished 14 dogs, all of their own breeding, including the following Specialty winners:—Champion Pandemonium Balzac v Bautzer, TT, Winners Dog at the 1981 Colonial Rottweiler Club Specialty, judged by Robert Moore; Champion Pandemonium's Ciastus, C.D., TT, Winners Dog at the 1981 American Rottweiler Club Specialty, judge J. C. Parker, Reserve Winners Dog at the Colonial Rottweiler Club's 1981 Specialty; and Best in Match at Colonial's 1981 Specialty Match Show; Pandemonium's Knockout, Winners Bitch at the 1984 American Rottweiler Club Specialty, judge Muriel Freeman; and Champion Pandemonium's Laredo v Blanka, Reserve Winners Dog at the 1985 American Rottweiler Club Specialty, judge Barbara Dillon.

Graudstark's Quarto Tempo is the dam of two of these above dogs and granddam of another.

Young "stars" at this kennel include Champion Pandemonium's Frauke, a consistent Best of Breed winning bitch who was, as well, Best of Opposite Sex at the Westminster Kennel Club in both 1984 and 1985. She is a litter sister to Champion Pandemonium's Faust, TT, who has gained several Group placements in limited showing.

Champion Pandemonium's Jiko of Falklin is another young dog bred at this kennel to whom Valerie Cade points with pride. Now living with his owners in Southern California, he is already winner of first in a Working Group despite very limited showing to date. Valerie Cade has surely done extremely well with her Rotties within a very short time span, all the more notable as she had no previous background "in dogs" when she purchased that first Rottweiler beyond her great love of animals in general. Now that she has experienced it, the pressure is on to continue to produce excellence through controlled breeding which seems to be the acid test of one's true mettle. With very few exceptions, most of the Pandemonium Rottweilers have been breeder-owner-handled, which Valerie comments has been an education in itself.

On May 4, 1985, Champion Graudstark's Pandemonium died suddenly and unexpectedly, this the day of the Colonial Specialty. Her loss is deeply mourned as the namesake of Pandemonium Rottweilers and as the producer of great ones. Our sympathy to Valerie, whom we know feels the loss keenly and by whom "Panda" will never be forgotten.

Pioneer

Pioneer Rottweilers belong to Virginia Aceti and Sheryl Hedrick at Hollis, New Hampshire. They are both members of the Colonial and Medallion Rottweiler Clubs as well as the American Rottweiler Club.

Their foundation bitch, Champion Robil Marta von Donnaj, is a daughter of American and Canadian Champion Donnaj Vt. Yankee of Paulus, C.D.X., TT, three time Colonial Rottweiler Club Specialty Best in Show winner and an all-breed Best in Show winner as well as a top producing sire. Marta, who is known as "Brick," was acquired as a puppy in 1979, and while she was never shown as a special, she is making her mark as a top-producing dam, and in 1984 won first place in the Brood Bitch Class at the Colonial Rottweiler Club Specialty.

Brick is the dam of Pioneer's "B" litter, sired by Champion Graudstark's Luger, C.D., TT, which includes Champion Brash Baer von Pioneer, C.D. "Baer" finished his championship breeder-co-owner handled by Sheryl in only 12 shows, with four majors, at 18 months of age. In very limited showing as a special, handled by Sheryl or his owner Kathy Galotti, Baer is already a multi-Best of Breed winner and Group placer. Another litter brother, Champion Pioneer's Brute Force, C.D., was handled to his championship and C.D. by owner Ted Galotti. Baer and Brutus are also shown as a Brace, and have won multiple Brace Group 1sts and are among the few Rottweiler braces who have won Best Brace in Show. A litter sister, Pioneer's Black Shadow v Bullock, owned by Martha Clancy, is major-pointed and will soon be the fourth champion from this litter.

The "star" of the "B" litter, however, is "Gillie," more formally Champion Pioneer's Beguiled, who made Rottweiler history on August 5, 1984 when she won Best in Show at the Wampanoag Kennel Club event under judge Don Bradley, thus becoming the first bitch in the history of the breed ever to do so. Gillie is also the first Rottweiler bitch to win multiple Group 1sts and she is the first Rottweiler ever to have been breeder-owner handled to an all-breed Best in Show. Her accomplishments have earned her automatic entry into the Medallion Rottweiler Club Hall of Fame. Specialed for only five months on a limited basis in 1984, Gillie ended the year with 19 Bests of Opposite Sex, including the American Kennel Club Centennial Show under judge J. D. Jones; eight Bests of Breed; one Group 2nd, two Group 1sts, and a Best in Show. She is No. 7 bitch, American Rottweiler Club System, for 1984, and is the only bitch in the Top Twenty Group System, American Rottweiler Club, for 1984. Gillie is surely a breeder's dream come true!

Another Brick daughter, Pioneer's Das Bedazzled, sired by the 1982 German Klubsieger, Champion Bronco vom Rauberfeld, SchH. III, FH, has just started her show career at 15 months by taking Winners Bitch, Best of Winners, and Best of Opposite Sex over specials from the Bred-by Exhibitor Class, this at only her second show! "Dassie's" litter brother, Pioneer's Drillmaster Cherich, co-owned with Richard and Cheryl Corbett, is working in Obedience and Schutzhund before starting his show career shortly. Pups from later litters are just starting work in Obedience and Tracking.

Sheryl and Virginia now are beginning the second generation of their breeding program at Pioneer, and their goals are to maintain the soundness and quality which they were fortunate enough to produce in the first generation.

At Pioneer there are no kennels. All of the dogs are house dogs and are part of their owners' daily lives. The puppies are whelped and raised in the home, well socialized and temperament tested. Every effort is made to place them in homes where they can live up to their full potential as show or working dogs and, most importantly, in the true sense of the word, working dogs.

Powderhorn/Wencrest

Powderhorn/Wencrest Rottweilers are owned by Mrs. Clara Hurley and Michael S. Grossman at Hollywood, California, where lives a most impressive collection of outstanding Rottweilers.

Powderhorn is the name of Clara Hurley's ranch at Arroyo Grande on the central coast of California. Her kennel carries the name as does her publishing company which translates and publishes literature about the Rottweiler from all over the world.

Mrs. Hurley's first Rottweilers in 1966 were the personality every breeder loves— even tempered, strong and willing companions. Unfortunately, even though they earned C.D. titles and championships, and a Best of Opposite Sex at a Specialty, they were all stricken with hip dysplasia.

That sad factor has been a major influence in the determined breeding practices of Powderhorn Rottweilers.

In 1969 as a delegate to the organizational meeting of the International Federation of Rottweiler Friends (IFR) in Essen, Germany, Clara Hurley met and worked with the leading Rottweiler breeders of the world. The advantages of adopting a serious program to match the German Standard for dogs in America was clearly of merit. She determined, with the help of Herr Friedrich Berger, Chief Breed Warden of the German Rottweiler Club, to learn as much as she could and to utilize that learning to enhance the breed in America.

Mrs. Hurley learned to speak, write and translate German. For 14 years she and Herr Berger carefully went over his data and shared experiences about Rottweiler genetics and breeding. She contacted the authors and publishers of most of the world's literature about Rottweilers, and created the Powderhorn Press to bring this material, in English, to American readers.

As a result of her experience with hip dysplasic (HD) Rottweilers and armed with her confidence in the German Standard (FCI Standard), Mrs. Hurley campaigned with the Rottweiler Clubs in America to adopt a policy to curb HD. The only candle in the darkness of this disease was the discovery that a genetic, hereditary factor may be a cause of it.

The new policy, in short, if on x-ray the animal is not free of hip dysplasia as certified by the Orthopedic Foundation for Animals (O.F.A.), don't breed it. "The battle was bitter," to quote Mrs. Hurley, but in August 1968 the Golden State Rottweiler Club in California courageously began the experiment. Soon the Colonial Rottweiler Club and the Medallion Rottweiler Club joined the ranks and stand firmly committed to that policy to this day.

Clara Hurley began and maintains the most comprehensive compilation of statistics concerning HD in the breeding stock of American Rottweilers. Her Rottweiler Registry and Biodex of HD-free stock is of great assistance to serious breeders in the United States.

Powderhorn Rottweilers acquired Champion Trollegen's Aparri, C.D. (Best of Opposite Sex at the Golden State Rottweiler Club Specialty in 1975 and 1977) as a four-month-old puppy in 1979. Bred to Champion Falco v h Brabantpark, from Holland, "Darri" produced Champion Powderhorn's Abel, C.D.; Powderhorn's Astra, C.D.; and Powderhorn's Ajax. From her next mating, with Champion Dux v Hungerbuhl, SchH. I, a German import, came the Powderhorn "B" litter: Brodar, Black Maria and Banja. "Darri" was a Top Ten Bitch for 1976.

Mrs. Hurley feels strongly (as do the majority who truly know and love the breed) that a Rottweiler does best when regularly socialized from his earliest days in a home setting. Left caged in a multi-kennel situation, uneven temperament can destroy an otherwise fine prospect. To have sufficient animals to form a broad enough base to support a quality breeding program, more than one household is required. Thus a partnership was founded. Powderhorn/Wencrest (P & W) with Michael S. Grossman, Wencrest Rottweilers, who owned Champion Gatstuberget's Eskil Jari, C.D., a son of Champion Dux v Hungerburh, SchH I. Eskil was a successful show dog, the sire of four champions, and eight obedience-titled Rottweilers, and in the Top Ten for the years 1976, 1977 and 1978.

To Powderhorn/Wencrest from Holland came the Dutch and Belgian Champion Oscar v h Brabantpark at five years of age. This

CAPTIONS FOR PLATES 33-48

Plate 33

Ch. Quanto van het Brabantpark, owned by Powderhorn/Wencrest Kennels, Hollywood, Calif.

Plate 34

1. Ch. Pioneer's Brute Force, C.D. winning his first major on the way to his title. Bred by Pioneer Rottweilers, Virginia Aceti and Sheryl Hedrick, Hollis, N.H.

2. Ch. Srigo's You've Now Seen Yameen taking 2nd in the Puppy Sweepstakes under a German judge, then 2nd in the Puppy Class under a Dutch judge at the American Rottweiler Club Specialty in California; 2nd in Puppy Class the following day at the Western Rottweiler Breeders Association supported entry under a leading American judge. This bitch is now a champion and she is a granddaughter of Champion Srigo's Elyssian Fields. Bred, owned and handled by Felicia Luburich, East Brunswick, N.J.

3. Janko von Tengen, SchH 1, age eight years, is major pointed in the U.S., V-rated KSZ/Germany Ztgl. Owned by Vonpalisaden Rottweilers, Paramus, N.J.

4. Ch. The Cheno Wilderness, by Am. and Can. Ch. Hasserway's Rommel Victor ex Lady Ruger, C.D.X., finished in California competition at 17 months. Her brothers dominated the Alaska shows in 1984. Joann H. Turner, owner, The Wilderness Rottweilers, Anchorage, Alas.

5. Ch. Berglufts Farra at nine and a half months. Owned by Jack and Mary Raifsnider, bred by Dorit S. Rogers, Sewickly, Pa.

6. Am., Can., and Mex. Ch. Burley von Morgen Carroll scoring one of his Best of Breed wins. Owned by von Morgen Carroll Rottweilers, Ontario, Calif.

7. The noted Ch. Blitz von Gailingen winning Best of Breed at K.C. of Philadelphia in 1977 Vonpalisaden Rottweilers, Paramus, N.J.

8. Powderhorn's Jeze of Wencrest at 11 months taking points towards championship. Owned by Powderhorn/Wencrest Rottweilers, Mrs. Clara S. Hurley and Mr. Michael Grossman, Hollywood, Calif.

Plate 35

1. Berglufts Fetz showing off his strong topline and excellent chest. Bred by Dorit S. Rogers, Bergluft Rotties, Sewickley, Pa. Owned by Sharon S. Statton.

2. This unusual looking dog is a Dutch Rottweiler WITH TAIL, seen at a dog show in Holland, June 1984. Photo courtesy of Powderhorn/Wencrest Rottweilers, Hollywood, Calif.

3. Head-study of Ch. Monika Maid of Denmark, foundation bitch at Ellen Walls's Riegele Farms, Hartly, Del.

4. Am. and Can. Ch. Von Gailingen's Dream Come True, C.D., owned by Laura Kirshman.

5. Ch. Frolic'n Darth Vader, by Am. and Can. Ch. Panamint Nobel v Falkenburg, C.D. ex Am., Can., and Mex. Ch. Panamint Rani vd Sandhaufen, C.D., owned by Frolic'n Rottweilers, Charlotte and Stephen Johnson and Linda Schuman, Redmond, Wash.

6. An informal pose of Am. and Can. Ch. Razdy's Abraham, a Group winner, homebred and owned by Judith Uggiano, Razdy Kennels, Bridgewater, N.J.

7. Ch. Graudstark's Pandemonium, Ch. Pandemonium Balzac v Bautzen, and Ch. Graudstark's Quatro Tempo, all owned by Pandemonium Kennels, Valerie J. Cade, Goldens Bridge, N.Y. Pandemonium and Tempo are the two foundation bitches behind the Pandemonium Rottweilers.

8. Jeepers Treu Argus, C.D. *(left)*, Delphi's first Rottweiler at age eight years with his look-alike sire, Ch. Joey von Kluge, C.D., age ten years. Joey is retired from the Tallahassee, Florida, Police Department, K-9 Division and has 57 felony arrests to his credit. Son Jeepers continues his daily caretaker and babysitting farm chores at Delphi and is the constant companion of Al and Bonnie Wimberly, Havana, Fla.

Plate 36

1. Noblehaus "E" litter owned by Mark and Patricia Schwartz, West Nyack, N.Y.

2. Fourteen week old puppy bitch sired by Ch. Beaverbrook Eisen v Bruin. Owners, Laura and Gary Brewton, Powell, Tenn.

3. Seren's Crystal Calliope, C.D. at four months. Owned by Seren Rottweilers, Peter and Marilyn Piusz, Johnstown, N.Y.

4. Aust. Ch. Retohr Regnans is the first Rottweiler owned by Retohr Kennels, Mrs. C. Wakeham, owner, Loonawarra, N.S.W., Australia.

5. Von Dorow puppy, by Am. and Can. Ch. Tulake's Apollo ex Ch. Merrymoore's Imp von Dorow, owned by Nancy C. Estes, Midland, Tex.

6. Nero vom Lowenrau, SchH. 1, is among the German imports owned by Alan P. Kruse, Howell, Mich.

7. This very interesting picture is of a long-haired Rottweiler bitch at four years old. Owned by Powderhorn/Wencrest Rottweilers, Mrs. Clara S. Hurley and Mr. Michael S. Grossman, Hollywood, Calif.

8. Ravenwood Premier Applause, C.D., by Thewina Summer Ferrymaster, C.D. ex Champion Ravenwood Nightmare, C.D. Owned by Ravenwood Kennels, Linda B. Griswold, Michigan City, Ind.

Plate 37

1. Pioneer's Black Shadow v Bullock, by Ch. Graudstark's Luger, C.D., TT ex Ch. Robil Marta von Donnaj, owned by Martha Clancy and just starting her show career going Winners Bitch under judge Chester Collier and handled by Bill Burrell.

2. Am. and Can. Ch. Tramonte's Baby Face Nelson taking Best of Breed at Richland County, August 1981. Owned by Jack S. Tramonte, Akron, Ohio.

3. Ch. Starkheim Duf Morgen Carroll, by Am., Mex., and Can. Ch. Burley von Morgen Carroll ex Ch. Bee Matilda vom Haus Kalbas. Owned by von Morgen Carroll Rottweilers, Ontario, Calif.

4. Ch. Berit v Alemannenhof, SchH.1, FH, owned by Powderhorn/Wencrest Rottweilers, Hollywood, Calif.

5. Ch. Brahsh Der Volmund Genosse, by Ch. Windmaker's Arlo Der Gremlin ex Black and Beautiful, a most promising young dog owned by Steve and Tannice Gladden, N. Wilkesboro, N.C. He will be starting his Specials career in 1985.

6. Am. and Can. Ch. Krugaran von Meadow, bred by Donna M. Wormser, Ocala, Fla. Owned by Anne Walker. No. 3 Rottweiler Dog in U.S. for 1983. Pictured here taking Best in Show over an entry of 1700 dogs at Atlanta K.C. in 1983.

7. Ch. Powderhorn's Jora of Wencrest, C.D. taking Best of Winners at Valley Forge K.C. in 1982. Powderhorn/Wencrest Kennels, Hollywood, Calif.

8. Ch. Miss Ellie von Meadow, C.D., T.D., a Top Producer who finished title with five Bests of Opposite Sex and was 1983 No. 3 Rottweiler Bitch in the U.S. Bred by Donna M. Wormser; owned by Betty Crumpton. Here taking Best of Winners at mid-Kentucky in 1981.

Plate 38

1. Bodo vom Stuffelkopf, the sire of Ch. Kuhlwalds Little Iodine, C.D., owned by Paul and Norma Harris, Kuhlwald Kennels, Fla.

2. Ch. Frolic'n Darth Vader as a puppy of tremendous show potential. Owned by Frolic'n Rottweilers, Charlotte and Stephen Johnson and Linda Schuman, Redmond, Wash.

3. "Tall, dark and handsome", Kavick vom Chutzpah, owned by Jean Benkowski, Omro, Wis. Bred by Dennis and Margaret Teague, Penryn, Calif.

4. Pandemonium's C'est Si Bonne in 1982. Owned by Valerie J. Cade and Donna Trafton-Woods, Goldens Bridge, N.Y.

Plate 39

1. Ch. Marlo's Rome Da Bratiana, C.D., owner-handled by his breeder to his championship from the Bred-by Exhibitor Class. Rome is a multiple Best of Breed and Group winner. Breeders-owners, Robert and Marlene Lore, Marlo's Rottweilers.

2. Tramonte's Baby Face Hannibal, Am. and Can. C.D., is a son of Ch. Tramonte's Baby Face Nelson. Here pictured winning Highest Scoring Rottweiler at Western Pennsylvania in March 1983, judge Irma Dixon. Owned by Jack W. and Sally H. Papp, Akron, Ohio.

3. Ch. Altar's Leo Vom Freyr, TT, by Ch. Haserway's Freyr Von Altar ex Ch. Gudrun Von Anderson, finished title in nine shows with three majors. In limited showing as a special and is a multi Best of Breed winner. Pictured taking the breed at Troy K.C. in 1985, handled by Michael Scott for owner Joseph N. Santaro, Cersan Rottweilers, Syracuse, N.Y.

4. Ch. Artus Adelshof, SchH. III, rated "V" in Germany, with his handler, Brian Sill. Owned by Alan P. Kruse, Howell, Mich.

Plate 40

1. Powderhorn's Kegg of Wencrest, eight-week-old show prospect puppy owned by Powderhorn/Wencrest Rottweilers, Hollywood, Calif.

2. From Beenen's "A" litter, owned by Don and Lin Beenen, Lowell, Mich.

3. Frohlich von Stolzenfels and puppies in San Juan, Puerto Rico.

4. "C'mon, let's play" is what Scharf Elko von Regenbogen is quite obviously saying to his friend the pig. Note small stick in Scharf's mouth, which he is using in an effort to get the pig to chase him. He finally succeeds, but the pictures did not turn out clear enough for use. Norma Dikeman, owner, Westfield, N.J.

5. The Green Mountain Sled Team, Green Mountain's "Little Bubba" in the lead, owned by Anthony P. Attalla, Londonderry, N.H.

6. Three sisters from three repeat breedings of Ch. Rodsden's Ansel v Brabant ex Ch. RC's Gator Bel Von Meadow. From youngest to oldest, left to right, Ch. Gator's Ruffian Von Ursa, Ch. RC's Lexia Von Ursa, and Ch. RC's Magnum Force Von Ursa, T.T. Photo courtesy of Chris Stenftenagel, High Springs, Fla.

7. Rex vom Kastanienbaum, SchH. III, "V" rated, Korung winner owned by Alan P. Kruse, Howell, Mich.

8. Scharf Elko von Regenbogen, TT, C.D., VB, by Ch. Rodsden's Elko Kastanienbaum, C.D.X., T.D. ex Tamara's Brandywine, owned by Norma Dikeman, Westfield, N.Y.

Plate 41

1. Ch. Apache v Arktos at 15 months. By Ch. Dann v Arktos ex Christa v Arktos. Owned by Judith H. Hassed, Colorado Springs, Colo.

2. Multiple breed winner and multiple Group placer, Ch. Excaliber's Atlas von Ament, born May 1981 by Ch. Bulli Von Meyerhoff ex Ch. X-Thedora von Gruenerwald. Owned by Adolf and Anna Ament and Joseph Hedl. Bred by the Aments and Dorothea Gruenerwald.

3. Ch. Alastar Cherokee Chief taking Best of Breed at Acadiana K.C. in 1984 under judge Bob Ligon. Bred by Carole A. Anderson and owned by Bill and Ted Stewart.

4. Ch. Daverick's Alex v Hasenkamp, C.D. on the way to his title at Westchester K.C. in 1983. One of the "A" litter at Daverick Rottweilers, three of which finished during 1983. Owned by G. George Rogers, Richard and Ricki Rogers Gordon, Cinnaminson, N.J.

5. The climax of a truly historic day in Rottweiler history. Ch. Mirko vom Steinkopf, C.D., SchH.III, IPO III, FH goes on from winning Best of Breed in the 1985 Colonial Rottweiler Club Specialty Show to take the all-breed Best in Show award at Bucks County K.C. May 1985, the first time the winner of the Colonial Specialty has been honored by the Best of Breed win at the all-breed Club hosting its show. The judge of this memorable event is Mr. William L. Kendrick, center, and Dr. Josephine Deubler, Bucks County Chairman, is presenting the trophy. Mirko is handled by Jeff Brucker for owners Mr. and Mrs. Richard Wayburn, Waxel's Rottweilers, Irmo, S.C.

6. Am. and Can. Ch. Tramonte's Baby Face Nelson completing his Canadian Championship at the Rottweiler Club of Canada Specialty judged by Betty Baxter of England. Handled by Sally H. Papp for owner Jack S. Tramonte, Akron, Ohio.

7. Ch. Bella of Limehouse, herself a Top Producer, is the dam of many more Top Producers including Ch. R.C.'s Gator von Meadow who in July of 1983 was the No. 1 Top Producer of all breeds according to Canine Chronicle figures. Owned by Donna Wormser, Ocala, Fla.

8. Ch. R-Bar's Fantom von Ansel, by Ch. Rodsden's Ansel v Brabant ex Ch. R-Bar's Frieda vom Lott, was winner of the 1983 Medallion Rottweiler Club Specialty Show. Bred by Diana Durrance. Owned by Robert and Jeanne Gray.

Plate 42

1. Can., Am., and Ber. Ch. Srigo's The Jig Is Up was Reserve Winners Dog at the Colonial Rottweiler Club Specialty Show in 1980. Srigo Rottweilers, Felicia Luburich, East Brunswick, N.J.

2. Ch. Srigo's Zoom v Kurtz, C.D., by Ch. Lyn Mar Acres Arras v Kinta ex Ch. Srigo's Madchen v Kurtz, well-known conformation winner. Also an obedience "star" who was High In Trial at the Colonial Rottweiler Club Match in 1977 and that held by the American Rottweiler Club in 1978. Dam of Srigo's Imitation of Life, Best in Match at the American Rottweiler Club's National Specialty Match in 1978. Felicia Luburich, breeder-owner, Srigo Kennels.

3. This English import is Thewina Summer Ferrymaster, C.D.X. "Eros" went Highest Scoring Rottweiler for all three trials to gain his C.D. title. A truly excellent obedience dog owned by Ravenwood Rottweilers, Linda B. Griswold, Michigan City, Ind.

4. Powderhorn Koch of Wencrest with Papillon friend. This

handsome Rottie, and the Pap, belong to Thomas and Doris Baldwin, Pleasant Hill, Calif. Koch was bred by Clara Hurley and Mike Grossman.

5. Two of the handsome Rottweilers owned by Irene Castillo, Apache Hill Kennels, Abilene, Texas. Top, Apache Hill Midnight Warrior. Bottom, Apache Hill's Sunis Halo. Pictured at four months' age.

6. Ursula von Stolzenfels, sister to Ch. Ursus von Stolzenfels, owned by Dr. Evelyn M. Ellman, Augusta, Mich.

Plate 43

1. Handsome headstudy of Loneagle's Bravura v Seren, C.D., T.D. owned by Matt and Jody Engel, Miami, Fla.

2. Ch. Doroh's Jaegerin v Noblehaus at seven weeks. Mark and Patricia Schwartz, West Nyack, N.Y.

3. Grief vom Steinkopf, SchH. I, rated "V" in Germany, imported and owned by Alan P. Kruse, Howell, Mich.

4. Ch. Brimstone Bold Whisper, TT, owned by Brimstone Kennels and Pat Cyr.

5. Ch. Arras vom Hasenkamp, German import who came to the U.S. in 1979 when eight months of age. Owned by Mary and Dorothy Stringer, Hidden Meadow, Burlington, N.J.

6. Ch. The Cheno Wilderness at six months. Owned by Joann H. Turner, Anchorage, Alas.

Plate 44

1. Morgen, at age four months. By Ch. Starkheim Duf Morgen Carroll ex Lady Ruger. Owned by Joann H. Turner, Anchorage, Alas.

2. Headstudy of Ch. Razdy's Akimo Grande who was bred by Judith Uggiano and is owned by her with D. Hendershot.

3. Ch. Magnum McCoy Von Ursa, by Ch. McCoy Von Meadow, C.D. ex Ch. RC's Magnum Force Von Ursa, T.T. Owned by Donna LaQuatra and Lloyd Dockter.

4. Ch. Merrymoore's Imp von Dorow owned by Nancy C. Estes, Midland, Texas.

Plate 45

1. Rowehaus A. Erwin Rommel, pictured with Thea D. Miller from the television miniseries "George Washington." Owned by Douglas K. Loving, Richmond, Va.

2. Ch. Romark's Axel v Lerchenfeld, C.D.X., T.D., owned by Ken and Hildegard Griffin, Novato, Calif., with his favorite handler and friend, Robert Hanley.

3. Ch. Duke's Panzer von Bravo, TT in the Fall of 1984 on the way to the championship which he completed at age 15 months in 11 shows. Handled by Joanne Reed for owners W.B. and Patricia Lavender, Pioneertown, Calif.

4. Ch. Kuhlward's Little Iodine, C.D. owned by Dorit S. Rogers and pictured with her son.

Plate 46

1. Ch. Beaverbrook Echo v Bruin, daughter of Ch. Rodsden's Bruin v Hungerbuhl, C.D.X. ex Champion Beaverbrook Alexa v Iolkos. Bred, owned, and handled by Laura Brewton, Powell, Tenn.

2. Ch. Alastar Gatsby von Cujo winning Best Puppy, age seven months, at Blue Bonnet Rottweiler Club Specialty Match judged by Dorothea Gruenerwald. Owned and handled by Brenda K. Jones

3. Ch. Beaverbrook Echo v Bruin, daughter of Ch. Rodsden's Bruin v Hungerbuhl, C.D.X., from Champion Beaverbrook Alexa v Iolkos. Bred, owned and handled by Laura Brewton, Beaverbrook Rottweilers, Powell, Tenn.

4. Merrymoore's Pagan Ballyhoo, C.D. owned by Irene Castillo, Abilene, Texas, taking Best of Opposite Sex at Trinity Valley 1985, owner-handled.

5. Can. and Am. Ch. Srigo's Flight of the Eagle, Can. and Am. C.D. is an all-breed Best in Show winner bred by Felicia Luburich, East Brunswick, N.J. Owned and handled by Mr. Art Rihel.

6. Ch. Adora von Meadow, C.D., homebred representing five generations of OFA parentage. Owner, Donna M. Wormser, Blue Meadow Farms, Ocala, Fla.

7. Ch. Merrymoore's Imp von Dorow taking points en route to the title. Owned by Nancy C. Estes, Von Dorow Kennels, Midland, Texas.

8. Ch. Mirko v Steinkopf, C.D., SchH.III, IPO III, FH, here is winning Best of Breed at the 1985 Colonial Rottweiler Club Specialty under judge Mrs. Muriel Freeman, handled by Jeff Brucker for owners Mr. and Mrs. Richard Wayburn, Waxel's Rottweilers, Irmo, S.C.

Plate 47

1. Blackgold's Bruno Bear J, sired by Ch. Trollegen's Drumson, C.D. ex Champion Stablemates Diamond Bear, here is taking points towards his title in 1981. Owned by Louis and Jamie Peterson, Hawaii.

2. Ch. Marja Elka von Heidel, daughter of Merrymore's Pastis ex Tara von Nadriches, owned by Jacqueline Puglise, Marja Kennels, Farmingdale, N.Y. Handled here by Ross Petruzzo. In limited showing, this elegant bitch has ranked among the Top Ten Rottweilers for three straight years, 1979, 1980 and 1981.

3. Am. and Can. Ch. Razdy's Abraham winning a Group 1st from the classes to complete his championship at age 16 months under judge Peggy Adamson. Previously that day he had won the breed over seven specials under judge Victor Clemente. Sid Lamont handling at Ox Ridge K.C. in September 1984 for breeder-owner Judith Uggiano, Bridgewater, N.J.

4. Srigo's Risky Business, by Am., Can., and Int. Ch. Bronco v Rauberfeld, SchH. III, FH, is winning in the U.S. and Canada. Ms. Felicia Luburich, owner, Srigo Kennels, East Brunswick, N.J. Sid Lamont handling.

5. Ch. Razdy's Akimo Grande winning at the Colonial Rottweiler Club Specialty in 1985 under judge Mrs. Margareta McIntyre (Winners Dog) and then going on to Best of Winners under Mrs. Bernard Freeman, two outstanding authorities on this breed, thus completing his championship owner-handled. Bred by Judith Uggiano, co-owner with D. Hendershot.

6. Erdelied Zephyr v Maremitch winning 3-point major from puppy class. By Ch. Graudstark's Luger, C.D. ex Ch. Daba von Andan. Owned by Mary Forte; bred, co-owned, and handled by Surely Rawlings, Coral Gables, Fla.

7. Donnaj Dictator at eight months old. By Ch. Birch Hill's Governor, C.D. ex Ch. Donnaj Happy Hooker. Earned his C.D. at 11 months in three shows. Was pointed before 16 months. Owned by Pamela Anderson, Zornhaus Rottweilers, Wilton Manors, Fla.

8. Ch. Razdy's Amelia Earhart winning Group 3rd from the classes under judge L. Goldworm at 18 months of age. Han-

dled by Sid Lamont for breeder-owner Judith Uggiano, Bridgewater, N.J.

Plate 48

1. The German import, Bronco v Rauberfeld, owner-handled by Felicia Luburich, East Brunswick, N.J.

2. Two handsome Rottweilers from Altar Kennels. Ch. Altar's Dasi Mae vom Freyr completing his title. The Group winning Ch. Altar's Gunner of Woodland going Best of Breed. Edith Alphin, owner, Fayetteville, N.C.

3. Ch. Erdelied Astraea, C.D. pictured with her sire Ch. Donnaj Vt. Yankee of Paulus, C.D.X. Two outstandingly excellent representatives of the Rottweiler breed. "Star", *left,* owner-handled by Surely Rawlings. "Yank", *right,* owner-handled by Janet Marshall.

DONNAJ

Litter Reg. No. _____

WD-139569
Individual Reg. No.

Pedigree of

CH. DONNAJ VT YANKEE OF PAULUS C.DX RO-964-T ⌐. ⌐.
Registered Name of Dog

Date Whelped _____ July 4, 1975 _____ Sex _____ Male

Breeder _____ Pauline Rakowski _____ Address _____ Middletown, N.J.

Owner _____ Jan Marshall _____ Address _____ Woodstock, Vt.

WORKING ROTTWEILERS WITH BRAINS AND BEAUTY

PARENTS	GRANDPARENTS	GREAT-GRANDPARENTS	GREAT-GREAT-GRANDPARENTS
SIRE:	Furst von der Villa Daheim, SchH 1	Axel v Simonskaul, SchH3	Kuno vom Weidbach, SchH 1
			Alli vom Elemenau, SchH 1
Ch. Axel vom Schwanenschlag		Blanka v Itzelbach, SchH 1	Int. Ch. Lord v Blankenhorn SchH 2
			Flori vom Kanzachtal
RO-166	Cora Vom Crevingsberg	Quinn von der Schwarzwiese, SchH1	Eddi v d Hobertsberg
			Olli von der Schwarzwiese
		Britta von der Zuflucht	Quinto von der Solitude, SchH1
			Dolly von der Hardt
DAM:	Am. Can. Ch. Rodsden's Kato v Donnaj, CDX, TD	Ch. Rodsden's Kluge v d Harque, C.D. RO-50	Int. Ch. & BS, Ch. Harras vom Sofienbusch, SchH 1
			Ch. Quelle v d Solitude, C.D.
Ch. Amsel von Andan, C.D.	RO-37	Ch. Franzi v Kursaal	Wotan vom Filstalstrand, SchH 1
			BS Assy vom Zipfelbach SchH 1
RO-300	Ehrenwache's Andernach	Fetz vom Oelberg, SchH 2 RO-25	Hektor von der Solitude
			Dora v d Brotzingergasse
	RO-111	Rodsden's Ubermutig Karla, C.D.	Ch. Rodsden's Kluge v d Harque C.D. RO-50
			Ch. Afra v Hasenacker, SchH 1, C.D.

96

PLATE 33

PLATE 34

BEST OF
WINNERS

NORTHWESTERN
CONNECTICUT
DOG CLUB

1983

ASHBEY

1

2

3

BEST OF
OPPOSITE SEX

4

5

6

7

BEST OF
BREED

THE KENNEL CLUB
OF PHILADELPHIA

DECEMBER 1977

ASHBEY

8

PLATE 35

PLATE 36

PLATE 37

1

WINNERS
MIDDLESEX COUNTY
KENNEL CLUB
1984
ASHBEY

2

BEST OF BREED
OR VARIETY
RICHLAND CTY
KENNEL CLUB SHOW

3

4

BEST OF
OPPOSITE SEX
GREATER DAYTONA
DOG FANCIERS ASSN
JANUARY 1983

5

BEST OF
WINNERS
SALISBURY N.C.
KENNEL CLUB
MAY 1984

6

BEST IN SHOW
ATLANTA
KENNEL CLUB
OCTOBER 1983
PHOTO BY SABRINA

7

BEST OF WINNERS
VALLEY FORGE
KENNEL CLUB
JOE C   SEPT 1982

8

BEST OF
OPPOSITE SEX

BEST OF
WINNERS
MID-KENTUCKY
KENNEL CLUB

PLATE 38

1

PLATE 39

2

3

4

PLATE 40

1

PLATE 41

2

BEST OF BREED
OR VARIETY
INGHAM COUNTY
KENNEL CLUB

3

BEST OF
BREED
ACADIANA
KENNEL CLUB
SPRING 1984
PHOTO BY
L. SOSA

4

BEST OF
WINNERS
WESTCHESTER
KENNEL CLUB
1983

5

BUCKS COUNTY K.C.
BEST IN SHOW

6

Rottweiler Club
OF CANADA
BEST OF
WINNERS
1980

7

BEST OF
WINNERS

8

GMC

BEST OF
WINNERS
TENNESSEE VALLEY
KENNEL CLUB

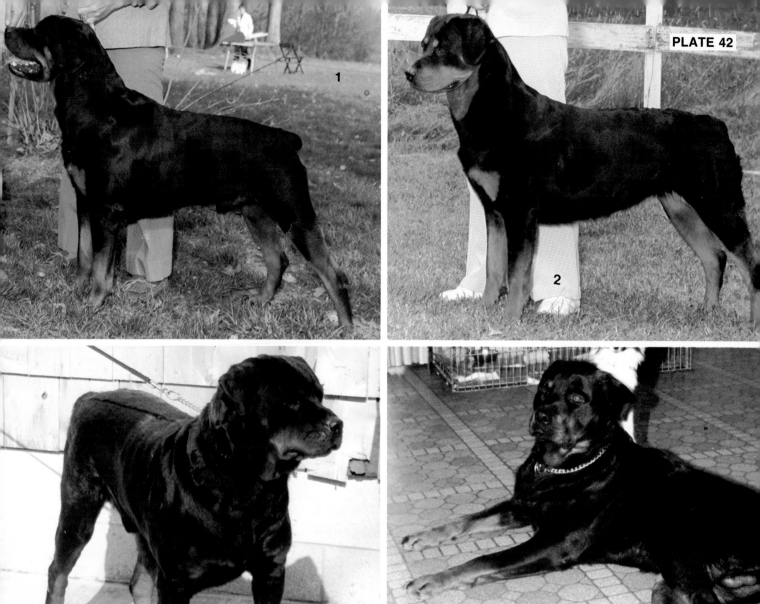

PLATE 42

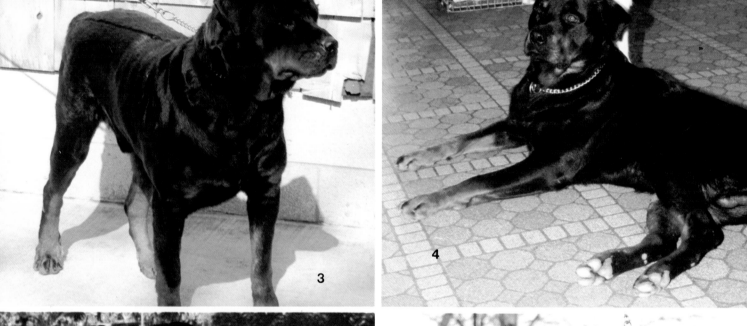

PLATE 43

PLATE 44

PLATE 45

PLATE 46

PLATE 47

PLATE 48

dog's outstanding characteristics brought his American championship and during the one year in which he was shown he was declared Best in Show, received first in four Working Groups, 12 other Group placements, and 54 times was Best of Breed, adding up to his becoming the No. 1 Rottweiler in the United States for the year 1979. As a Top Producer with ten champions and eight obedience titled offspring, he is a major influence in Rottweilers of the American West.

An Oscar son, Powderhorn's Fetz of Wencrest, was exported to Australia, arriving there at just under three years of age. Fetz's progeny consistently place in the ribbons and earned his Australian owners, Pat and George Hall, the coveted Breeders of the Day Award in 1984 at the Rottweiler Championship Show, judged by Germany's Chief Breed Warden, Herr Wilhelm Faussner.

Champion Taba v d Leizersianden was imported from Holland and Ilona v Haus Schottroy from Germany also in 1978. Taba is the dam of three champions, six obedience titled offspring, and a Top Ten Bitch for the year 1978. Ilona is the dam of four champions and four obedience titled offspring.

Dutch and Luxembourg Champion Quanto v h Brabantpark was a full brother to Oscar from a repeat breeding, who came to Powderhorn/Wencrest in his fifth year. Although he was shown for only six months, retired due to injury, he earned his American championship, first in five Working Groups, five additional Group placements, and had 26 Bests of Breed. He was No. 3 Rottweiler in the country for the entire year of 1980. To date he has sired six champions and obedience titled offspring.

A current Powderhorn/Wencrest sire of distinction is Champion Donar v d Hoeve Cor Unum, C.D., imported from Holland. Donar, along with Oscar and Quanto, has become Powderhorn/Wencrest's third Specialty winner and is also a Medallion Rottweiler Club Award of Merit Rottweiler and a multi-Group placer.

A 1983 import from Germany is Champion Falko v Waldblick, SchH I. Champion Danny v Timmerman, an outstanding son of Oscar; and Champion Powderhorn's Joko of Wencrest, C.D., a promising son of Quanto, round out the stud force at Powderhorn/Wencrest.

The brood bitches there are Champion Hexe v d Hoeve Cor Unum, C.D., imported from Holland; Janka v Duracher Tobel; Champion Berit v Alemannenhof, SchH I, FH; Cora v Hartumer Busch; Vesta v Rodehof (all of these from Germany); Powderhorn's Fimi of Wencrest; Champion Powderhorn's Gwen of Wencrest; Powderhorn's Loki of Wencrest; and Powderhorn's Oreo of Wencrest, C.D.

Ravenwood

Ravenwood Kennels were established by Leonard and Linda Griswold at Michigan City, Indiana, in 1970, originally as an Alaskan Malamute kennel. Rottweilers were added in 1974, along with the slogan "Special Dogs for Special People"—for Rottweilers are truly very special dogs.

Dagna Von Artkos, C.D., the foundation bitch Rottweiler, proved to be an excellent obedience and conformation dog, but an untimely tangle with a car left her rear leg unable to stand any great stress. Dagna proved, however, to be a good producer of bone, substance, and a great temperament. Not wanting to lose the dual purposes of the breed (conformation-working), a search was on by the Griswolds for additional bloodlines. Temperament was of high concern as Ravenwood puppies often go into homes with small children where they grow into family companions and guards. England proved to have what the Griswolds were seeking—an eager obedience attitude with an outstanding phenotype and genotype. All of the English Rottweilers imported by Ravenwood are from the highly accomplished Thewina Kennels, who are credited with several times "Top Obedience Rottweiler," a "top dual purpose Rottweiler," and of course English champions, which are very difficult to attain. At present, Ravenwood is the largest breeding kennel of English Rottweilers, based on importations direct from Great Britain to North America.

The Ravenwood obedience dogs have done well in the obedience ring. Thewina Summer Ferrymaster, C.D.X., went "highest scoring Rottweiler" all three shows for his C.D. title, as have his progeny. Following in the paw-prints of his half-brother, Thewina Dance Master, C.D., has also three "Highest Scoring Rottweiler" obedience trials to his credit, all gained before the age of 15 months.

In the conformation ring, Thewina Sundevil, C.D., finished his championship at 13 months, and he, too, completed his C.D. by going "Highest Scoring Rottweiler."

Since Rottweilers are working dogs, Ravenwood has not been content with only A.K.C. titles, but as members of the Chicago Schutzhund Club, strive to attain the maximum potential from each dog in tracking, obedience, and manwork by obtaining the difficult Schutzhund titles.

Linda Griswold is the only United States member of England's Midland Rottweiler Club.

Surely Rawlings

Surely Rawlings of Coral Gables, Florida, acquired her first show quality Rottweiler from Joanna Sawyer. Her name is Champion Erdelied Astraea, C.D., better known as "Star." This lovely bitch became an outstanding winner-owner-handled, far beyond Surely's fondest hopes. At age 10½ months she won Grand Prize Futurity at the Medallion Rottweiler Club's first Futurity in the United States for Rotties. She also won her large puppy class the next day under the breed warden from Germany. "Star" finished her championship in seven shows with all majors and earned her Companion Dog title simultaneously, qualifying with class placements in three consecutive trials.

"Star" began 1980 as a special and gained numerous Best of Breed and Group placements. She was ranked No. 1 Rottweiler bitch according to the American Rottweiler Club ratings. In 1981, with limited showing, she finished as No. 3, again gathering Bests of Breed and Group placements. "Star" was always owner-handled. How sad that so lovely a bitch was never bred, but this was impossible as she had hip dysplasia.

Surely's next purchase was a show quality male from Dorothy Wade, Doroh Kennels. He is Champion Doroh's Janus Erdelied, C.D., who finished his championship within

13 shows and also went on to become a multiple Best of Breed and Group placement winner. He is a son of the top producer American and Canadian Champion Rodsden's Elko Kastanienbaum, C.D.X., T.D., RO and Champion Doroh's Grand Escapade RO. Janus is from a litter of four champions, the other three being Champion Doroh's Just A Whim, Champion Doroh's Jaegrin v Noblehaus, and Champion Doroh's Just Grand T.D. The latter, Just Grand, was handled by her co-owner, Veronica Wade, to numerous wins in both Junior Showmanship and regular classes, the most notable win having been Best of Opposite Sex at the Colonial Rottweiler Club under Mrs. Joan Klem; and Best of Breed at the American Rottweiler Club Specialty under J. D. Jones. This is the first time that a bitch has won a National Specialty and an Independent Specialty Best of Breed.

Surely Rawlings has now gone into professional handling and has finished many dogs of all breeds. She campaigned the 1984 Top Rottweiler bitch, Champion Sunnysides Royal von Meadow, C.D., to best bitch at the Colonial Rottweiler Specialty, the American Rottweiler Specialty, and the Medallion Rottweiler Specialty—the first time that any one Rottweiler has won at all three of these Specialties in the same year, Surely notes. As a handler, she is very critical about what she will show, especially in Rottweilers. Her feeling is that too many handlers are showing lesser quality and in these days of the incredible popularity rise in the breed it is particularly important to make certain that only the best are campaigned and bred for the protection of the future of the breed.

Razdy's

Razdy's Rottweilers are owned by Judith Uggiano of Bridgewater, New Jersey, who has been into this breed since 1975. It was in 1979, after careful thought and study, that she selected and purchased the foundation bitch behind her breeding program, Champion Cedar Knolls Alexis, whom she then owner-handled to championship. This lovely bitch produced two litters for a total of thirteen puppies, of which six now have completed their American Championship and hold a total of ten Champion and Obedience titles between them. Two more should have become American Champions by the time you are reading this book, while two others as we write are entering the ring headed, hopefully, for C.D. degrees.

The breeder, Judith Uggiano, kept five of Alexis' offspring for her own kennel; and co-owns another. These are Champion Cedar Knolls Born Free, C.D.; Champion Razdy's Arazz-Matazz, C.D.; Razdy's A Second Chance (close to finishing as we write); Champion Razdy's Amelia Earhart; Champion Razdy's Akemo-Grande; and Champion Razdy's Abraham.

Amelia Earhart was shown eight times, three times going Best of Opposite Sex, twice Best of Breed, and a Group 3rd placement, all from the classes and over specials.

Akemo-Grande, co-owned with D. Hendershot, won Best Puppy at the Professional Handlers Association Super Match in September 1983 under Harry Issacs; Best Puppy at the Long Island Rottweiler Club Match under Jan Marshall; Winners Dog and Best of Winners at the 1985 Colonial Rottweiler Club Specialty under Mrs. McIntyre and Mrs. Freeman respectively.

Abraham finished both his American and his Canadian titles by the time he had reached 17 months age. Three times he was Best of Winners, three times Best of Breed, and a Group 1st under Peggy Adamson to complete his American Championship with a total of 22 points. The next day he was moved up to specials, winning Best of Breed and a Group second. One month later he campaigned in Canada, going through to Best of Breed each day, returning home a Canadian Champion. He is now being used at stud, and will return to the ring as a special during 1986.

The Razdy foundation bitch now has been spayed, but Judith Uggiano has high hopes for these fine offspring to continue well with the bloodlines of their dam. One daughter, Champion Cedar Knolls Born Free, C.D., has her first litter now going on eight months' age as we write, and these puppies indicate that she is carrying on her dam's tradition of producing outstanding quality.

The Uggianos consider their Rottweilers to be part of their family, and all puppies are raised in this manner until sold. Three years ago they turned a spare bedroom into a permanent whelping room, so now they are easily able to give "special care to special puppies for special people."

R-Bar's

R-Bar's Rottweilers at Bowling Green, Florida, are owned by Diana Durrance who has been breeding and showing Rotties since the mid-1970's, working on a limited basis as a breeder of one or two litters annually.

Foundation bitch at this kennel is Champion R-Bar's Frieda vom Lott, daughter of Champion Axel vom Schwanenschlag ex Champion Happy von Gruenerwald. This bitch has produced the impressive number of eight champions for her owner, with four additional pointed offspring and numerous obedience titles sired by Champion Rodsden's Ansel v Brabant.

One of the best-known youngsters from these parents is the winner of Best of Breed at the 1983 Medallion Rottweiler Club Specialty Show, Champion R-Bar's Fantom von Ansel, who is owned by Robert and Jeanne Gray and handled by Jeffrey Lynn Brucker.

Riegele

Riegele Rottweilers at Hartly, Delaware, have been in existence since Christmas 1971 when future champion Monika Maid of Denmark arrived at her new home as a nine-week-old puppy. Over the following 14 years, Riegele Farms, owned by Ellen B. Walls, has produced many quality Rottweilers who became breed champions themselves and obedience-tracking titled dogs as well. Most of them stemmed from Monika.

In 1975, the Top Bitch (American Rottweiler Club Award) was Champion Riegele's Agreta Maid. She was amateur owner-handled all the way. Her littermate, Champion Riegele's Astro von Eken, at age 11+ years, still staunchly defends the Walls' farm.

The foundation bitch, Champion Monika Maid of Denmark, was by Champion Denmark's Ehrin von der Keil ex Champion Shar von Roehr of Denmark, C.D. Monika's offspring, Champion Riegele's Agreta Maid and Champion Riegele's Astro von Eken, were sired by Champion Dux von Hungerbuhl.

Another lovely bitch belonging to the Walls, Champion Riegele's Greenhill Ima Maid, C.D. was sired by Champion Rodsden's Ander v.h. Brabant from Champion Riegele's Erin Maid.

The Riegele kennel consists of house dogs, with breeding on only a limited basis. Mrs. Walls' goal in her breeding program is to produce a sound of mind and body, typey Rottweiler who is raised correctly and will make an excellent family dog, someone's best friend. Matching the right dog with the right owner is paramount in the placing of any Riegele Farm Rottweilers going to new homes. How well this works out has been put into words in a letter she recently received telling her that "Today I lost my best friend. He was everything I ever expected a Rottweiler to be. The only time he ever failed me was dying too soon." This is the type of relationship between dog and owner which warms a breeder's heart!

Arthur L. Rihel

Arthur L. Rihel is well known to the Rottweiler Fancy as the owner of the widely admired Amerian and Canadian Champion Srigo's Flight of the Eagle, American and Canadian C.D., who was born on May 10, 1977. Bred by Srigo Kennels, and sired by Champion Kokas K's Degen von Burga, C.D., T.D., Eagle lost no time in becoming outstanding, and a leading winner among Rottweilers. Both his American Championship and his American C.D. had been completed by the time he reached age 14 months. His Canadian Championship and C.D. had been garnered by the time he was 22 months old.

As the record shows, Eagle was, in 1980, the first Rottweiler to go Best in Show in Canada. Here in the United States, he was ranked No. 7 in 1979 and No. 8 in 1980. He has multiple Group wins in both the United States and Canada.

Eagle is a well balanced dog, powerful in appearance and movement. This fine male was shown on a limited basis, and was exclusively owner-handled. Mr. Rihel is from Butler, Pennsylvania.

Seren

Seren Rottweilers are owned by Peter and Marilyn Piusz at Johnstown, New York, who began their careers as Rottweiler enthusiasts quite by accident. Their house was broken into, making them decide that they needed a dog for protection, so they read and studied all the dog books, then decided that dog should be a Rottweiler.

This turned out to be Mondberg's Bulger V Beier, C.D.X., Canadian C.D., who was purchased purely as a pet with no intention of showing him. Neither Peter nor Marilyn ever had been to a dog show and had no desire to go, even though they had both been brought up with dogs. However, the acquisition of "Rowdy" in 1975, with a contract agreeing to obedience training for him, followed by his excellent work, encouraged them to show him. And so off the three of them went to the first dog show. As so frequently happens under those circumstances, they loved it, and have been enjoying the shows ever since.

The second purchase was a show bitch in 1977, Champion Doroh's Fantastic Serenade, American and Canadian C.D.X. and she has formed the background of their kennel (named in her honor, SEREN) with her four litters.

Presently the household consists of Serenade as well as three of her offspring; Seren's Crystal Calliope, C.D.; Seren's Dancin' Dynamo, and Seren's Dancin' Drummer. Also a bitch was purchased in 1984, Seren's Nightwood Bit of Magic, who is by American and Canadian Champion Donnaj Vt. Yankee of Paulus, C.D.X. from Champion Nightwoods Betta Von Maita. She is out of the next-to-last litter sired by Yankee, having been whelped in 1984.

In addition to the five dogs living at home with them, Peter and Marilyn Piusz also co-own six of Seren's offspring. Also they co-own a bitch, Blanka's Peril V Pandemonium with Janice Berg and James McLaughlin. She was whelped July 31, 1984, bred by Valerie Cade and Bodo Fischer and is by Arri Von Der Hembachbrucke, German import, out of Champion Blanka Von Pandemonium.

All of the dogs at Seren live in the house and co-exist beautifully with young three-year-old Stephen Piusz. In fact the three youngest dogs, Marilyn tells us, are his best friends; they play for hours together in the house and outdoors.

Following is a rundown on the Seren Rottweilers and their accomplishments.

Mondberg's Bulger V Beier, 8/10/75-4/21/84, was by Waco of Ledgefarm ex Champion Britz von Andan, bred by Ruth Parker, Monberg Haus Rottweilers. "Rowdy" completed his C.D. at age one year, in three consecutive shows with scores of 195½, 194 and 192½ from the Novice A. class. He was No. 10 Obedience Rottweiler in 1976, and earned his Canadian C.D. in 1977 with 195½, 196 and 194½. His C.D.X. was earned in 1980. He had a problem with arthritis in his shoulder due to an injury, so he never went any further.

Champion Doroh's Fantastic Serenade, American and Canadian C.D.X., was born May 29, 1977, a daughter of Champion Rodsden's Axel v h Brabant out of Champion Doroh's Enchantress v Eberle, C.D. She was bred by Dorothy A. Wade, Doroh Rottweilers.

"Seren" started her show career by going 2nd in the 9-to-12-month puppy bitch class at the 1978 Colonial Rottweiler Club Specialty. She was not shown again until she was three years old, except to attend the first New England Rottweiler Fanciers Match in 1980, where she won Best in Match. Returning to the ring, she finished quickly with two Bests of Breed and four Bests of Opposite Sex from the classes along the way, handled by Mel Goldman. In limited showing as a special she has 13 Bests of Opposite Sex to her credit. In 1982 at the Independent Breeders Association for Rottweilers Match judged by ADRK judge Herr Teschke she received a V rating. She was second in the Brood Bitch Class at the 1983 American Rottweiler Club Specialty and at the 1984 Colonial Rottweiler Club Specialty Shows. She won the Veteran's Bitch Class at the American Kennel Club Centennial, the first time she was shown in the class and unfortunately also the last as she was discovered to have pyometria the following week and was spayed. She was pointed in Canada, but never got back there to finish her title.

"Seren" earned her American C.D. in a four show weekend with scores of 192½,

190, 195, and another 195. This was her first time ever in the obedience ring, including matches. Her Canadian C.D. was earned with an average score of 190 including a third place. She earned her Canadian C.D.X. next with a first and two second place awards, then her American C.D.X. with one third place award. Her C.D.s were earned at five years of age; her C.D.X. at age six years. She is presently being trained towards her U.D. and if that becomes a reality, she may well be the oldest Rottweiler to have ever achieved that title, as she will be eight years old in May 1985.

"Seren" is a member of the Medallion Rottweiler Club's Hall of Fame and has been nominated for the American Rottweiler Club's Bronze Production Award.

"Seren's" four litters were sired by, "A", American and Canadian Champion Donnaj Vt. Yankee of Paulus, C.D., as was her "B" litter. For her "C" litter the sire selected was American and Canadian Champion Rodsden's Elko Kastanienbaum, C.D.X., T.D., Canadian C.D., while her "D" litter was by American and Canadian Champion Altar's Gatsby v Radio Ranch. It is on the offspring of these breedings, and their descendants, that the Seren Rottweiler breeding program is continuing.

Peter and Marilyn Piusz are members of the American Rottweiler Club, the Colonial Rottweiler Club, the Medallion Rottweiler Club, and they are charter members of the New England Rottweiler Friends. They breed for conformation but are equally, if not more, concerned over temperament and working ability, and thus take particular pride in the "Seren's" working kids.

Srigo

The background for Srigo Rottweilers was set in 1948, when Felicia Luburich was but twelve years old and the first litter listing her as breeder was born. These puppies were Dobermans, the breed which preceded Rottweilers in Felicia's interest. At age 18 years she acquired another Doberman from a noted breeder in New Jersey. Then later, in the fifties, she personally whelped a litter for the first time, again a Dobe. During these years every word about dogs which Felicia could find to read was eagerly devoured. How fortunate that Rottweilers were written of in one of these books!

Srigo Rottweilers are located at East Brunswick, New Jersey. Felicia's first of the breed, a grown bitch for which she had waited, was acquired in 1955, the year during which Felicia also joined the Colonial Rottweiler Club and the Allgemeiner Deutsche Rottweiler Klub (ADRK). The new Rottie bitch was Reidstadt's Helissend, whose first litter of only one puppy went to her previous owner, but who in her second litter produced Champion Srigo's Bernard v Dervis and Srigo's Bernice v Heller who had already one major when she unfortunately broke a foot.

For her second bitch, Felicia acquired the well known Missy v Stahl, who was a consistent entrant in many Eastern dog shows of that period. Missy came to Felicia in 1961 after belonging to two previous owners, and Felicia made her a champion despite a large scar on her leg which had resulted from a bad heartworm treatment.

The "A" and the "C" litters at Srigo were from the same parents, the sire Champion Dervis v Weyershof, the dam Champion Missy v Stahl. Champion Srigo's Amai v Missle had been in the first litter; the "C" litter included Champion Srigo's Creshenda v Missle and Srigo's Constance v Missle. The latter in her only litter, which was sired by Champion Arno v Kafluzu, produced of eight puppies, four dogs, four bitches. Among the latter were Champion Srigo's Econnie v Lorac, C.D., Champion Srigo's Eshenda v Lorac, and Champion Srigo's Missle Again. These three bitches were completely dominant at the important shows throughout their careers in the ring.

Champion Missy v Stahl was also the dam of Srigo's "D" litter, this time bred to Champion Arno v Kafluzu. In it was Champion Srigo's Diensta v Missle (who became the granddam of Champion Srigo's Watch My Smoke) and Champion Srigo's Darla v Missle who never produced.

Champion Arno v Kafluzu, sire of Missy's "D" litter, was acquired by Mrs. Luburich from Gladys Swenson. At the first show in which he had ever competed, a Colonial Rottweiler Club Specialty, he provided Felicia with one of those never to be forgotten days when he went clear through to Best of Breed, owner-handled by her on a loose lead with no stacking, under Major Godsol in the process of which he defeated several leading champions and professional handlers. To top it off, his daughter was Winners Bitch and Best of Opposite Sex on this same occasion.

Periodically Felicia Luburich has brought fine dogs from Europe to combine with her already established bloodlines. Casper v d Lowehau, a son of Champion Harras v Sofienbusch came over at about the same time as Arno joined the kennel, or slightly later, and three of Srigo's finest bitches were bred to him. Of Casper, Felicia has written "On the whole, the temperaments of his puppies were too intense and too sharp, particularly the males, but also some of the bitches. And it passed through to the next generation. When his daughters were bred to sharp dogs, the resulting progeny were a liability. I therefore sold him feeling that dogs not manageable in a household are not the essence of the Rottweiler for all practical purposes."

Casper left his mark of quality on Srigo, however, as the sire of Srigo's Hester von dem Walde who was Reserve Winners Bitch at a Colonial Specialty prior to her untimely death; and also as the sire of Srigo's Honeybun who, bred to Champion Srigo's Garner v Zaghin, became the dam of the very important and admired Champion Srigo's Opportunity and How and also of the handsome Champion Srigo's Viking Spirit.

The "M" litter was Srigo's next of notable importance. Sired by German Bundessieger and American Champion Erno v Wellesweiler from Champion Srigo's Econnie v Lorac, C.D., the puppies included the two who became Champion Srigo's Merno v Kurtz and the tremendously important Champion Srigo's Madchen v Kurtz. The latter started in the show ring at age eight months and throughout her lifetime was either Best of Breed or Best of Opposite Sex on 90 per cent of her appearances, which included first in the Puppy Bitch Class when she made her debut at the Colonial Rottweiler Club Specialty; Winners Bitch and Best of Opposite Sex there the following year under judge Peter Knoop; Best of Opposite Sex a year later under judge

Robert Wills; then Best of Breed the year following that under judge Eleanor Evers. Two years later she returned in the Veteran's Class from which she placed Best of Opposite Sex to Champion Srigo's Viking's Spirit's Best of Breed under Barbara Hoard Dillon.

Viking had an exciting career in the ring, and sired two nice litters for his owner. Champion Srigo's Big Opportunity and Champion Srigo's Billet Doux were from the second of these, their dam Champion Srigo's Xclusive v Kurtz.

There have been a great many outstanding Rottweilers produced at Srigo Kennels in addition to those already mentioned. For instance the super litter from Champion Srigo's Zoom v Kurtz, C.D. sired by Champion Kokas K's Degan v Burge, C.D., T.D. included Srigo's Incredible Is The Word, Imitation of Life, and I Am Invincible. And the "J" litter which included Champion Srigo's The Jig Is Up and Champion Srigo's Joy To The World.

Champion Srigo's Watch My Smoke was the American Rottweiler Club's Top Winning Bitch for 1973. Champion Srigo's Elyssian Fields was another in the "breeder's dream come true" category. And then the fabulous litter by Champion Kokas K's Degan v Durga, C.D. included Champion Srigo's Flim Flam Man, Champions Srigo's Front Runner, and the famed American and Canadian Champion Srigo's Flight of the Eagle, American and Canadian C.D., now a Best in Show winner and a steady winner from the beginning, in the Top Ten while being campaigned, always owner-handled by Mr. Art Rihel.

An extremely important acquisition at Srigo Kennels during the early 1980's was the German import who became American, Canadian, International Champion Bronco v Rauberfeld, SchH. III, FH, who was Best of Breed at the 1983 Colonial Rottweiler Club Specialty Show. In addition to his notable show successes, Bronco is proving his worth as a sire. One of his youngsters, just starting out as we write this chapter, is Srigo's Loaded For Bear who won the important Bred-by Exhibitor Class at the 1985 American Rottweiler Club National Specialty.

Then the V1 rated Karol v Georgshof, SchH III, FH, Gekort, has also joined the Rotties at Srigo. He is the sire of the Winners

Bitch from Bred-by Exhibitor at the 1984 American Rottweiler Club Specialty. Both he and Bronco will undoubtedly have spectacular influence on future generations at Srigo as time progresses.

Recently Felicia has cut back a bit on exhibiting due to commitments at home in her breeding and boarding kennel, which causes the showing aspect of Srigo's current history to have become rather sketchy during the past few years. Since finishing Champion Srigo's Heart of Gold and American and Canadian, and Bermudian Champion Srigo's The Jig Is Up, she has been concentrating on building her collateral and outside blood with which to combine her own earlier stock to achieve a broader genetic base with which to carry on her breeding program. To accomplish this, she has done very selective importing from Germany. Her first two of these importations were the last producing of the immortal Bulli v Hungerbuhl; V Karol v Georgshopf, SchH III, FH, Gekort; and Froni v Silberwald, Weltsiegerin '75 and '79, Swiss Siegerin '79, International Champion, 20 times V1 and 13 CACIB, she the dam of Clubsiegerin Babette von Magdeberg.

Karol produced two litters for Srigo, from which one puppy was kept, Srigo's Quail Feathers. He produced five litters from outside bitches, one of which was Winners Bitch from the Bred-by Exhibitor Class at the 1984 American Rottweiler Club National Specialty.

Later Felicia imported two outstanding bitches, neither of which ever produced a live puppy. Subsequently she brought over four other bitches; Cora v Kressbach, who descends from Benno v Allgauer Tor and Ives Eulenspiegel, who was bred before leaving to BS, CS, WS Nergo v Schloss Reitheim, from which came Srigo's Only At Dawn and Srigo's Only At Midnight; Lissy v Schloss Ickern (principally v. Dammerwald lines and to be bred to Srigo's Loaded For Bear; Imke v Dammerwald; and Cinfy v Eisplatz, an Arras daughter who has already whelped a splendid litter in the United States. From Imke, Felicia has kept Srigo's Silken Cord, and she also looks forward to a great future for her brother, Srigo's Secret Weapon, who has already started off well in limited showing.

Following is Felicia's account of her acquisition of the great American, Canadian, International Champion Bronco c Rauberfeld, SchH III, FC. Of him Felicia says:—"This dog is the male counterpart of Champion Srigo's Madchen v Kurtz. They are fully the same type, and he excels over her only in having more stifle let-down and in movement. On Madchen's behalf it is only fair to say that she has excellent movement, but Bronco's movement goes beyond anything I have ever known in a Rottweiler. I saw him for the first time at the 1982 ADRK Clubsieger Show. He was Best of Breed at that prestigious event. At that time I let it be known that I was interested in an outstanding male. That December I was offered another dog, and declined, 'not my type.' I was glad that I had waited, for in March I received a call that Bronco was for sale, and to 'come now and bring cash.' Which I did, and came home with Bronco. This dog is everything anyone could want in a dog. He is surely a male Rottweiler with a Schutzhund III degree—such things should not be taken lightly. But nonetheless he is a very loving dog with a marvelous sense of humor, very affectionate, and now that he no longer is Schutzhund trialed he is very friendly in any relaxed setting. He is a sensible and proficient stud dog who has outstanding ability to produce Rottweilers of exceptionally high quality, many of whom have inherited his movement to a great extent. It is not surprising, but gratifying, that he is able to do this. Both his sire and dam are Gekort bis Eza (breeding approved for life) and also both are SchH,III and HD Minus. This makes him Kor und Leistung Zucht, which is the highest designation of suitability for breeding rated by the ADRK. In any one year there are but a handful of breedings which would qualify for this designation. For instance, in 1980 there were 312 litters of Rottweilers registered in Germany. Of these 181 are Einfache Zuct. (the dam has no degree, only the sire). GZ is Gebrauchhund Zucht, and there were 80 of these breedings. KZ is Korzucht, when both breeding partners are Angekort, of which breedings there were two. LZ is Leistungzucht, which means that both parents and all four grandparents have training degrees, of which there were 47. KLZ, or Kor und Leistungzucht, is when both parents and all four grandparents have training degrees, of which there were two."

Bronco's show record in Europe was outstanding. In 27 times shown in Gebrauchshund Class, which is the only class from which Best Male, Best Female and Best of Breed are chosen, he was V 1 on 17 occasions, V on four occasions, V 2 on six occasions, V 3 on three occasions, V 4 on two occasions; and V 6 once. In other words, he was never less than V. Additionally he was CACIB three times and awarded his International Championship, three times Best in Show all breeds, and Club Seiger and Best of Breed at the 1982 ADRK Sieger Show.

Upon arrival in the United States during March 1983, Bronco launched his career by going Best of Breed at the Colonial Rottweiler Club Specialty under judge Joan Klem. At the American Rottweiler Club National he was 2nd in Open. He then took Best of Breed at the Super Match under Harry Isaacs, and was not shown again until 1984. His championship here was gained under the most respected of breeder judges. Then on to Canada for more honors and another title.

Now Bronco progeny are starting to make their presence felt, and those for which to watch include Champion Jay Moore's St. Bartholemew (from the first outside stud service to Bronco), Srigo's Loaded For Bear, Wyreglen's Archangel, Srigo's Risky Business, Bestafeka's Raven v Circe, and Champion Pioneer's Das Bedazzled.

Commenting on the breed in general, Felicia Luburich notes "I feel the two biggest faults in the breed at this moment are bad toplines and poor movement. The next fault, one which can become a real problem, is a pink mouth. Since the prohibition of awarding V ratings in Germany to Rottweilers with pink mouths, many of them have been exported to America."

Bronco's sperm is now being collected in a sperm bank for use in future years. During his lifetime, he will be bred to many of Srigo's finest bitches; and made available to those outside breeders whose bitches qualify.

Stenften Farm

Stenften Farm Rottweilers are at High Springs, Florida, where they are owned by Tom and Chris Stenftenagel.

This kennel is the home of Champion Gator's Ruffian Von Ursa, outstanding son of Champion Rodsden's Ansel v Brabant ex Champion RC's Gator Bel Von Meadow, TT.

Ruffian's sire, Ansel, was the Top Producing Rottweiler Sire for 1982, 1983 and 1984, having sired 39 champions until the present time. Her dam, Gator, was Top Producing Rottweiler bitch in 1981, 1982, 1983 and 1984. Her total being fifteen champions to date, thus making Gator the No. 2 Top Producing Bitch in the history of the breed.

Ruffian herself lives up well to her heritage, having attained her championship with all majors. She was also the Medallion Rottweiler Club Champion Bitch at their Futurity Sweepstakes in 1982 at only 13 months of age.

A "young hopeful" presently at this kennel is from a Ruffian litter sired by her grandsire, Champion Radio Ranch's Axel v Notara, who is the all-time Top Producing Rottweiler. The puppy looks truly exciting, and the Stenftenagels have high hopes for its future in the show ring when fully matured.

Tramonte

Tramonte Rottweilers belong to Jack S. Tramonte, Akron, Ohio, whose famous winner, American and Canadian Champion Tramonte's Baby Face Nelson, was purchased as a puppy from Dorothy Davis because he did, indeed, have a "baby face."

Nelson finished his American championship in six months with limited showing. He then went off to Canada with his friend and handler, Sally Papp, and at the Barrie Kennel Club Shows in 1980 he finished his Canadian championship by going Best of Winners at the National Rottweiler Club of Canada Specialty under the noted judge from England, Betty Baxter.

Nelson is proving an outstanding producer as well as an excellent show dog, passing on his superior head and temperament to his many puppies.

One of Nelson's sons, Tramonte's Baby Face Hannibal, American and Canadian C.D. is enjoying a distinguished career in obedience competition.

Tula's

Tula's Rottweilers began in the late 1970's at San Bernardino, California, when Tula Demas purchased Athena Vom Oldenwald, C.D., who was seven points towards her American show championship (including a five-point major) and has produced one litter. For this she was bred to Champion Brahm Vom Oldenwald, C.D., and produced Champion Tula's Golden Nugget.

Nugget has already made an exciting record, starting with Best of Opposite Sex from the classes her first time in the ring at 16 months of age with Mike Shea handling. Three weeks later she won a four-point major in Arizona, then three weeks after that she went Best of Winners and Best of Opposite Sex at the Philadelphia K.C. on Centennial weekend, judged by Stanley Saltzman. Four days later she returned home to California to complete her championship on the "Turkey Circuit" with two more four-point majors, gaining her title at the age of 18 months. Nugget has been shown in breed seven times by Mike Shea, and has six Bests of Opposite Sex awards (two of them from the classes) to her credit, including the prestigious Beverly Hills K.C. event. Additionally Nugget is a Mexican champion.

Nugget comes from the Vom Odenwald line which goes back into the Kursaal line. Nugget's granddam is American and Canadian Champion Kitty Vom Kursaal, top winning bitch over two years. Kitty's grandsire is BSG Blitz Vom Schloss Westerwinkel. Athena's grandsire on her sire's side is BSG Karol von Wellesweiler who also is descended from Blitz.

With these two excellent bitches as the background, Tula Demas has hopes for a bright future in the Rottweiler world. It is her ambition to breed an entire litter of quality winning and working Rottweilers, one which we are sure she will attain as time progresses.

Vom Pionierhaus

Rottweilers vom Pionierhaus, owned by Jerry and Kay Watson of Pride, Louisiana, is a small kennel that has been in existence since 1975. It is a kennel devoted to the working aspect of the Rottweiler as well as the conformation of the dog. Champion Bandetta von Stolzenfels, U.D.T., owned, trained and shown exclusively by Kay Watson is one of the few Rotties to have attained all of the degrees offered by the American Kennel Club at the time she was in competition.

Champion Ute vom Mummler, C.D., T.D., co-owned with the Jack Ellmans of von Stolzenfels, is the foundation bitch at Pionierhaus. She is a daughter of the 1977 Europa Sieger International Champion Ives Eulenspiegel, SchH. III, and she was bred to the 1983 Klub Sieger Champion Mirko vom Steinkopf which produced the first litter at Pionierhaus. Mirko, interestingly, is a grandson of Ives through the world-renowned Dingo vom Schwaiger Wappen. Although the puppies from this litter are too young for serious competition at the time we are writing, several have done quite nicely in the matches. Also four of the pups are actively engaged in training for the Schutzhund sport and are showing great potential.

Silas Eulenspiegel, T.D., a young male imported as a pup from the famed Eulenspiegel kennel of Marieanne Bruns is showing great aptitude as a top working dog, along with being of splendid breed type and with an outstanding pedigree. With the advent of a newly formed Schutzhund Club in the area, it should not take Silas long to achieve his Schutzhund I.

Von Arktos

Von Arktos Rottweilers were established in 1972 as a small breeding kennel founded on the produce of Panamint Dagna von der Eichen, who was linebred on the 1952 Bundesiegerin, Dora vom Burgtobel, Schutzhund I, a bitch of outstanding quality. All of the residents of this kennel trace back to her.

Judith Hassed owns von Arktos, located at Colorado Springs, Colorado. Her breeding program started with Dagma, who during her lifetime was mated to three different males, resulting in a total of 27 puppies. Of these, 14 are title holders with an aggregate total of 21 titles, all earned by owner-trainers and handlers. Dagna has received the Silver Production Award from the American Rottweiler Club, and is also classed as a Producer of Merit by the club. She has the *Dog World* Award for Breeding Excellence.

Of Dagna's puppies, one male and four bitches were retained as a breeding nucleus. These were bred and further puppies retained and bred back, always within the family. Judith Hassed is now in the fourth generation of this close linebreeding. The program was begun as an experiment designed to conserve the old lines for the future. Most second and third generation bitches were retained by the home kennel.

Von Arktos Rottweilers are typically cart dogs, possessing natural substance, bone and muscle with fluid, correct gait. They are strong trotters possessing a high degree of trainability with very pleasing personalities. The virtues of the old time Rottweiler are still demonstrated in this line, including proper character.

The first homebred sire at this kennel was a son of Dagna, Champion Dann von Arktos, C.D. He was sired by Champion Nick von Silahopp. Never offered at public stud, all 30 of his puppies were whelped at Von Arktos, five of them champions with a total of eight titles. Dann is the first Rottweiler in the mid-West to have finished his title entirely from the Bred-by Exhibitor Class, and was the co-winner in 1977 of the MacKenzie obedience trophy offered by the Western Rottweiler Owners. He has nine Bests of Breed and a Group placement in very limited exposure, all owner-handled, the most recent in 1982 at the age of eight years over other specials. He is the planned sire for two litters in 1985 at the age of 11 years.

Dann's son, Champion Fangen von Arktos, C.D., won a Best Puppy in Match at the early age of four and a half months, and is the only American-bred Rottweiler, his owner tells us, with "V" rating in Europe, including V-1 Excellent. He also finished his American title owner-handled from Bred-by Exhibitor.

The future sire will be Quantum von Arktos, who will be shown when fully mature.

Of the four Dagna daughters retained for breeding, there are two who have become American Rottweiler Club Producers of Merit, one of whom is also a *Dog World* Award winner. Her name is Christa von Arktos, and she produced 16 puppies, all of excellent quality. Three are now champions and there are two with obedience degrees.

Christa's daughter, Kristin von Arktos, is the current brood bitch and is also proving an excellent producer. She has had outstanding litters by both Champion Dann and Champion Fangen.

The second American Rottweiler Club Producer of Merit owned by Von Arktos, and out of Dagna, was Antje von Arktos, who produced one litter of five males which included Champion Fangen.

The next step in the Von Arktos breeding program will be location of a suitable outcross male for the next generation. Judith Hassed comments:—"It will be difficult to find one which represents both the qualities of the old-time Rottweiler and has a compatible pedigree. However, I believe that the finest quality Rottweilers are now in the United States, and I am confident that I will find the one that I want."

Von Balingen

Von Balingen Rottweilers are at Naples, Florida, where they are owned by David W. Lauster who was born in 1954, at Balingen, a tiny hamlet about 15 kilometers from Rottweil (hence the selection of his kennel name). He remembers as a boy occasionally seeing these magnificent dogs, and wanting one. Somehow that was never possible.

In 1968 the Lausters moved to the United States, and after graduating from college in 1976 David met his wife. From the beginning of their courtship he told her that someday when he had a home of his own he would have a Rottweiler. They were married in 1978 and in 1981 started looking for a dog. David at this point had never owned any kind of dog. They read books and made phone calls but were unable to locate an available Rottweiler puppy. One breeder would refer them to another, then finally they met someone who mentioned a lady by the name of Edith Alphin. David called, told her he wanted a

puppy, that he had no intention of showing, but did have two requirements; a pretty head and a sweet temperament. She told David that she had no puppies, but did have a six-month-old male by Champion Radio Ranch's Axel V. Notara whom she had initially intended to keep. She told him too that the youngster had what he wanted, but she did not know if he'd ever grow out of his awkward all legs and elbows appearance. "He's definitely a show quality puppy," she said, "and I won't sell him for less than one thousand dollars."

That is quite a price for a young couple just getting started to pay for a dog, and probably would have turned off many in similar circumstances, but the Lausters had saved some money, and David's father and mother-in-law had given them some, so they did have five hundred dollars, and David borrowed another five hundred dollars on his Visa card and sent along to Edith Alphin a certified check for his puppy.

When the "puppy" stepped out of his airline crate, all 72 pounds of him, and laid his head on David's wife's shoulder, there was no question but that he was staying! She was the one who had said, on seeing her first Rottweiler, "If you think I'm going to have one of those ugly monsters galloping around in my house, you can start looking for another wife." Perhaps the young Rottie sensed that she was the one he had to win over!

At two years of age, this gangly, clumsy puppy started looking pretty nice. Knowledgeable friends encouraged David to show him, but David explained that he was "just my boy." Finally, however, the friends prevailed to the point that David attended some "conformation classes" at the local dog club, and entered him at a show in Ft. Pierce. They came home with reserve in a 5-point major entry. They were delighted, and thought the ribbon was real pretty. The next Saturday they came home with a purple and gold ribbon after taking Best of Breed over five specials for a five-point major! They skipped the following week, then went to another show where they gained their second major, three points, with a Best of Winners. The following Saturday two more points were added with Best of Winners, and the next week again

Best of Winners, this time for the final five points. And so it was that the gangly, awkward puppy became the handsome matured Rottweiler, Champion Altar's Gandolf Von Axel.

Two months later, the shows started again, so the Lausters and Gandolf took a week's vacation and a trip to south Georgia. Under Phil March they won Group 2nd; under Bob Moore, Group 1st. And people started telling the Lausters, "This dog deserves a professional handler." Gwendolyn Wolforth was selected, and the Lausters feel that they could not possibly have made a better choice. The first week out with her, Gandolf took a Group 2nd one day and a Best in Show in Fort Myers.

So began the show career of the Rottweiler puppy with the pretty head and the sweet temperament. In 1983 he was No. 9 in Group placing Rottweilers. In 1984 he was No. 4, and so far in 1985, after only ten shows at the time of writing, he's running a close second. Gandolf is a son of Champion Radio Ranch's Axel V. Notara. His dam is Champion Gudrun Von Anderson, daughter of Champion Panamint's Seneca Chief and Susan Von Anderson.

Gandolf's breedings are carefully arranged, with the result that to date he has only six litters on the ground, the oldest of which is one and a half years old. He himself was born on April 3, 1981 and he came to the Lausters in early October of that same year. The Lausters also have a bitch named Lexa from entirely different breeding. She ended up not certifying, so is entirely a pet, both Gandolf's and the Lausters'.

In true Rottweiler fashion, Gandolf is never more than a few feet away from his owners when they are home, and at night sleeps on the floor by their bed.

Von Beenen

Von Beenen Rottweilers at Lowell, Michigan, are owned by Don and Lin Beenen who founded their kennel on the bitch Bomark's Allison von Beenen, C.D., TT, who is a granddaughter of one of Evelyn Ellman's foundation bitches, Champion Cosi von Steigstraasle. Allison has produced one champion to date and one C.D. titlist who has, as well, both her majors.

Champion Alec von Beenen, C.D., finished his championship at the age of 19 months with all majors. His first appearance in the ring was at the Medallion Rottweiler Club Specialty where he was Reserve Winners Dog from the junior puppy class. He is owned by Dr. Royce and Marilyn Poel.

Anke Becker von Beenen, C.D., has ten points including both majors, and is out in 1985 to complete her conformation championship. She will be bred later on to a carefully selected stud whose lines are complementary to her own.

The "B" litter at Beenen is less than a year old as we write and includes several especially promising puppies. The sire is the late Champion Rodsden's Bruin v Hungerbuhl, C.D.X., who won more Best in Show honors than any other Rottweiler and has more than 50 titled offspring to his credit. The Beenens are hoping to add a few to this number!

Von der Kruse

Von der Kruse Rottweilers are owned by Alan P. Kruse of Howell, Michigan, an hour west of Detroit. In the early 1970's Mr. Kruse and his family first became interested in this breed, and since then have established a kennel well-known for quality. The kennel is rather a "family project," with Alan's wife, Karen, handling all of the correspondence and inquiries; and, as her parents say, "the wheels would not turn were it not for Jennifer—the Kruses' 15-year-old daughter who has been helping since age four years."

It is interesting to note that Alan Kruse's father, a communications specialist during World War II, was in charge of communications at Germany's Nuremberg Trials in 1945. Among his duties, incidentally was to serve as escort for a young correspondent named Walter Cronkite.

It was during the trials that the senior Mr. Kruse met a French interpreter whom he soon married. And it was during the trials that he obtained his first Rottweiler, who returned with the newlyweds, Alan Kruse's parents, when they came home to the United States.

CAPTIONS FOR PLATES 49-64

Plate 49

1. *Left to right:* Ch. Noblehaus Ain't Misbehavin', Ch. Graudstark's Luger, C.D., TT, Ch. Doroh's Jaegerin v Noblehaus, and Amie of Northwinds. Noblehaus Rottweilers owned by Mark and Patricia Schwartz, West Nyack, N.Y. Photo by Mark Schwartz.

2. Am. and Bda. Ch. Von Gailingen's Dark Delight, U.D.T., Bermuda C.D.X., Canadian C.D. and Am. and Can. Ch. Von Gailingen's Dassie Did It, U.D.T., Can. C.D. Two of the outstanding Rottweilers owned by Catherine M. Thompson, Freehold, N.J.

Plate 50

1. Daverick's Dina v Stratford, six months old, peers wistfully through the fence. Owned by Daverick Rottweilers, Ricki and Richard Gordon, Moorestown, N.J.

2. Heiko von Stolzenfels, C.D. Owned by Dr. Evelyn M. Ellman and Stan Horn, Augusta, Mich.

3. Anke Becker von Beenen at four months. Owned and bred by Lin Beenen, Lowell, Mich.

4. Pioneer's Das Bedazzled at 16 months, by 1982 Ksg. Ch. Bronco vom Rauberfeld, SchH III, FD ex Ch. Robil Marta von Donnaj, is a homebred owned by Pioneer Rottweilers, Hollis, N.H.

5. Ch. Von Gailingen's Welkerhaus Cia in May 1978 at age 24 months. Owned by Rita A. Walker, Oak Ridge, N.C.

6. Janko von Tengen, SchH 1, age seven years. Owned by Vonpalisaden Rottweilers, Paramus, N.J.

7. Seven-week-old Berglufts Heiko asleep on his water bowl. Bergluft Rottweilers belong to Dorit S. Rogers, Sewickley, Pa.

8. Can. Ch. Astor, Am. and Can. C.D., TT, by Astor vom Landgraben, SchH.III ex Tosca, enjoying his favorite place — his own wading pool! This Dutch import, bred by A.J. Hulsman, belongs to William L. Michels and Mable G. Petty.

Plate 51

1. Ch. Taba v d Keizerslanden owned by Powderhorn/Wencrest Rottweilers, Mrs. Clara S. Hurley and Mr. Michael S. Grossman, Hollywood, Calif.

2. Ch. Czarina von Stolzenfels, C.D., owned by Jack P. and Dr. Evelyn M. Ellman, von Stolzenfels, Augusta, Mich.

3. Ch. Bratiana's Micki von Follrath completed her title in 1984 for proud owners Michael F. and Beverly J. Johnson.

4. Ch. Doroh's Fantastic Serenade, American and Canadian C.D.X. on the way to her title in 1980. Bred by Dorothy Wade, handled by Mel Goldman, owned by Peter and Marilyn Piusz, Johnstown, N.Y.

5. Ch. Noblehaus Ain't Misbehavin', TT, by Ch. Graudstark's Luger, C.D., TT ex Northwinds Kindred Spirit. Homebred owned by Mark and Patricia Schwartz, Noblehaus Kennels, West Nyack, N.Y.

6. Ch. Noblehaus Beretta winning the breed at Newton K.C. 1984. Owned by Mark and Patricia Schwartz.

7. Am., Can., Int. Ch. Bronco v Rauberfeld, SchH. III, FH, H.D. minus O.F.A. here winning Best of Breed at the Colonial Rottweiler Club Specialty in 1983, owner-handled by Felicia Luburich, Srigo Kennels.

8. Ch. Rodsden's Heika V Forstwald, C.D., VB, TT, was leased from Linda and Bill Michels by James and Roxanna McGivern for their first litter at Windwalker Rottweilers, Port Crane, NY.

Plate 52

1. Lutz von Siegerhaus in April 1980 at four months' age. Owned by von Siegerhaus Rottweilers, Thomas and Carol Woodward, Corning, Calif.

2. Srigo's Josie loves being photographed. Here she is at Lake Michigan looking pretty for the camera. Ms. Felicia Luburich, Srigo Rottweilers, East Brunswick, N.J.

3. This lovely portrait is of Ch. Srigo's I Am Invincible, T.D. Bred by Felicia Luburich from her "I" litter at Srigo Kennels, this magnificent Rottweiler is by Champion Kokas K's Degan v Burge, C.D., T.D. ex Ch. Srigo's Zoom v Kurtz, C.D.

4. Panamint One More Time, C.D., T.D.X., SchH 1 pictured at age eight weeks. Owned and trained by Dennis and Margaret Teague, Newcastle, Calif.

5. Some of the Rottweilers owned by Judith Uggiano, Bridgewater, N.J. — the dam with two daughters and a son. *Left to right,* Ch. Cedar Knolls Alexis, Ch. Razdy's Arazz-Matazz, C.D., Am. and Can. Ch. Razdy's Abraham, and Ch. Cedar Knoll's Born Free, C.D.

6. *Left to right,* Xanadu's Bronson Jos v Altar, age one year; May-Mars Brooks Dawg v Joy, age one year; and Ch. The Chena Wilderness, age one and a half. All are owned by Joann H. Turner, Wilderness Rottweilers, Anchorage, Alas.

Plate 53

1. Four-day-old baby Rottweiler, Beau's Alotta Dolly, lies close to her mother's watchful eye. Beauhaven Rottweilers, Bob and Judy Beaupre, Aliquippa, Pa.

2. Ch. Altar's Gandolf vom Axel on his third birthday. Owned by David W. Lauster, Naples, Fla.

3. Vesta von Rodehof owned by Powderhorn/Wencrest Rottweilers, Mrs. Clara Hurley and Mr. Michael S. Grossman, Hollywood, Calif.

4. Ch. Noblehaus Ain't Misbehavin' at 12 months. Mark and Patricia Schwartz, owners, West Nyack, N.Y.

5. Ch. Graudstark's Pandemonium and her son, Ch. Pandemonium's Balzac v Bautzen, TT, in 1979, the latter four months old. Pandemonium Rottweilers, Goldens Bridge, N.Y.

6. Judy Hoover with an armful of Beaverbrook puppies, five weeks old, sired by Ch. Rodsden's Kane v Forstwald. Owned by Laura and Gary Brewton, Beaverbrook Rottweilers, Powell, Tenn.

Plate 54

1. Bestafka's Raven v. Circe, bred and owned by Marlene Messinio, shown taking 1st in 9-12 Month Puppy Bitch Sweepstakes at the American Rottweiler Club National Specialty in 1985. By Am., Can., Int. Ch. Bronco v Rauberfeld, SchH.III, FH ex a daughter of Srigo's Challenge v Caduses, son of Ch. Srigo's Xclaim v Kurtz, Winners Bitch at a Colonial Rottweiler Club Specialty during the 1970's.

2. Lindenwood's Aggi, by Ch. Rodsden's Kane v Forstwald, C.D. ex Am. and Can. Ch. Bola von Meyerhoff, C.D., TT, was bred by Linda P. Michels, co-owner with James S. Petty. Handler, Cindy Jo Brown. Aggi here is winning the 6-9 month puppy class at the 1982 Colonial Rottweiler Club Specialty Show. Her littermates, Lindenwood's Anastasia and Lindenwood's Anaconda, were 3rd and 4th that day in a very big class.

3. American Rottweiler Club Specialty 1979. Best of Breed, Sciroco's Nashua of Royson, handled by breeder Josef Hedl. Best of Opposite Sex, Doonsbury's Myria Angeline, handled by owner Shirley Rose. Judge Jeannie Tunstill. Photo courtesy of Elizabeth Miller.

4. Am. and Can. Ch. Daverick's Alex vom Hasenkamp, C.D., handled by Walter Kuberski for owners Ricki and Richard

Gordon, Daverick Rottweilers, Moorestown, N.J. Winning Best of Breed under judge Virginia Hampton at Penn Ridge K.C. 1984.

5. This is the historic occasion when Ch. Pioneer's Beguiled became the first Rottweiler bitch to win all-breed Best in Show and the first Rottweiler of either sex to have won this award breeder-owner-handled. Bred and owned by Virginia Aceti and Sheryl Hedrick. Handled by Sheryl. This is the Wampanaug K.C. event on August 5, 1984. The judge was Don Bradley.

6. Ch. Seren's Chantilly Lace taking Winners Bitch from the American-bred Class at the A.K.C. Centennial Dog Show. Valerie Cade handling for breeder-owner Piusz and co-owner Linda Kowalski, Johnstown, N.Y.

7. Ch. Pandemonium's Balzac v Bautzen, TT, taking Winners Dog at the Colonial Rottweiler Club Specialty in 1981, handled by Gerlinde Hockla for owner Valerie J. Cade, Golden's Bridge, N.Y.

8. Ch. Excaliber's Aarich von Ament, born May 19, 1981, by Ch. Bulli Von Meyerhoff ex Ch. X-Thedore von Gruenerwald. Owned by Janet and John Swayze, bred by Adolf and Anna Ament and Dorothea Gruenerwald.

Plate 55
1. Ch. Srigo's Eagle All Over, handsome winning Rottweiler dog belonging to Beauhaven Rottweilers, Bob and Judy Beaupre, Aliquippa, Pa.

2. Ch. Donnaj Vt. Yankee of Paulus, C.D.X., TT, winning Best in Show, handled here by Mel Goldman for owner Jan Marshall, Donnaj Rottweilers, Woodstock, Vt.

3. This handsome Rottweiler is Am. and Can. Ch. Marksman von Turick owned by Lee Whittier, Woodstock, Vt. Here taking Best of Breed at Wachusett in 1982.

4. Multiple breed winner and Producer of Merit, Ch. Bulli Von Meyerhoff (March 28, 1979—April 14, 1984) by Am. and Can. Ch. Ero von der Mauth ex Canadian Champion Northwind's Inka, owned by Adolf and Anna Amont, bred by Ruth Meyer. Handled here by Jay Richardson to Best of Breed at Janesville, Wis. Photo courtesy of Dorothea Gruenerwald.

5. Ch. The Chena Wilderness at age nine months in October 1983. Owned by Joann H. Turner, Wilderness Rottweilers, Anchorage, Alas.

6. Andan Freiwillig von Paulus taking Best of Winners for a 4-point major in Colonial Rottweiler Club Supported Entry, Maryland K.C., Nov. 1984, under Finnish judge Hans Lehtinen. Owner-handled by Mrs. Charles R. Orr, bred by Mrs. Benjamin Tilghman and Pauline Rakowski.

7. Bucmar's Apollo Regere, C.D.X., in 1982. Bred by Jane Claus and Harold Claus, Jr. By Ch. Radio Ranch's X-tra Special ex Ebony Acres Onyx Amber. Apollo is shown here to a 5-point win. A splendid Rottie owned by Bruce Mau, Hawaii.

8. Best Brace in Show, Colorado Springs K.C. Dog *on left,* Eureka's Princess Czarina; *on right,* Eureka's Bewitching Elvira, owned by Meredith and James Millard, Eureka Kennels, Parker, Colorado. Mrs. Edd Bivin judged.

Plate 56
1. Ch. Pandemonium's Ciastus, C.D., TT, taking Winners Dog at the 1981 American Rottweiler Club Specialty Show. Valerie J. Cade, owner, Golden's Bridge, N.Y.

2. Am. and Can. Ch. Birch Hill's Juno, C.D., T.D. taking Best of Opposite Sex at the Colonial Rottweiler Club Specialty in May 1982. Cynthia Meyer handling for owner Jane F. Wiedel, Stockton, Ill.

3. Ch. Green Mountain's Athena, daughter of Ch. Donnaj Green Mountain Boy, handled by Gerlinda Hockla for Anthony P. Attalla, Green Mountain Kennels, Londenderry, N.H. Gaining points towards her title.

4. Ch. Wilderness Brand, by Am. and Can. Ch. Haserways Rommel Victor ex Lady Ruger, C.D.X., completed his championship with three 5-point majors and one Group 3rd. Owned by Joann H. Turner, Wilderness Rottweilers, Anchorage, Alas.

5. Ronzwyler Anka Von Haiem was Hawaii's No. 1 Puppy Bitch in 1985. Shown taking first prize and Best Puppy at the West Oahu Kennel Club Show on July 14, 1985. Bred by Ron Fisher of Modesto, Calif. Owned by Rottweilers von Haiem, Jill I. Odor-Nakache, Kailua, Hawaii.

6. Ch. Artus v Adelshof, SchH. III, winning Best of Breed at Westminster in 1985 under Mrs. Bernard Freeman for owner Alan P. Kruse, Howell, Mich.

7. This is the first team of Rottweilers to go Best in Show with all dogs owned by the same owners. *Left to right:* Am., Can., Bda., Mex., and Int. Ch. Jack Vom Emstal, Am. and Can. C.D., Mex P.C., ADRK SchH1; Am., Can., and Mex. Ch. Panamint Rani v d Sandhaufen, C.D.; Ch. Frolic'n Darth Vader, C.D.X., T.D., TT; and Ch. Frolic'n Grand Muff Tarkin, C.D. Owned by Frolic'n Rottweilers, Charlotte and Stephen Johnson and Linda Schuman, Redmond, Wash.

8. Ch. Baroness Elka von Dealcrest taking Best of Opposite Sex, Northeastern Indiana K.C., February 1985. Full sister to Ch. Baron Elko von Dealcrest, both owned by Larry and Alice Lee, Laran Rottweilers, Franklin, Ind.

Plate 57
1. Ch. Altar's Cujo v Wald placing Group 4th at Brazos Valley K.C. in 1984. Handled by Beau Galle for owner Carole A. Anderson, Alastar Rottweilers, Conroe, Tex.

2. Ojuara's Boy I'm It von Altree winning Bred-by Exhibitor Class at the Colonial Specialty in 1984 judged by Mrs. Margaret Walton. Gary Walker handling for himself, Betty Walker and Al D'Anna who co-own this fine young dog.

3. Ch. Monika Maid of Denmark, the first Rottweiler belonging to Ellen B. Walls, Riegele Farms, Hartly, Del.

4. Ch. Rhomarks Axel v. Lerchenfeld placing in the Working Group at Redwood Empire in 1984 under judge Glen Sommers. Retired from the show ring at age five years on this occasion, Axel then went on to concentrate on obedience and tracking. Owned by Ken and Hildegarde Griffin, Novato, Calif.

5. Winning a quality Working Group under noted judge Doris Wilson is the handsome Am. and Can. Ch. Srigo's Flight of The Eagle, American and Canadian C.D., owned by Arthur L. Rihel, Butler, Pa.

6. Ch. Alec von Beenen, C.D., by Canadian Ch. Fairvalley's Kluse ex Bomark's Allison an Beenen, C.D. handled here by Jim Berger to Best of Winners at Ann Arbor in April 1984. This young special is owned by Dr. Royce and Marilyn Poel, and was bred by Don and Lyn Beenen, Lowell, Mich.

7. Ch. Green Mts. Flora, lovely bitch owned by Frank J. Fiorella, Boxford, Mass., taking Best of Breed, handled by Bill Burrell, at Riverhead K.C. 1982.

8. Am. and Can. Ch. Bola von Meyerhoff, C.D., TT, by Am. and Can. Ch. Ero von der Mauth, Am. and Can. C.D., TT, ex Can. Ch. Northwind's Inka. Breeder, Ruth Meyer. Owner, Linda P. Michels, Brunswick, Ohio. Winning Best of Breed here over nine top Canadian and American specials from the classes, owner-handled, at Barrie Kennel Club, Canada, in August 1980.

Plate 58

1. Ch. Kokas K's Degen v Burga, C.D., T.D., is the sire of two Best in Show dogs: Ch. Srigo's Flight of the Eagle and Ch. Srigo's The Jig Is Up. Srigo Rottweilers, Felicia Luburich, owner, East Brunswick, N.J.

2. Ch. Pioneer's Beguiled at ten months, who grew up to become the breed's first all-breed Best in Show bitch in the United States. Bred and owned by Pioneer Rottweilers, Virginia Aceti and Sheryl Hedrick, Hollis, N.H.

3. Ch. Northwind's Indigo, C.D., T.D., SchH. 1, foundation bitch for Brimstone Rottweilers, was Best of Winners at the Colonial Rottweiler Club Specialty in 1977. Susan J. Suwinski, owner, Ithaca, N.Y.

4. Alastar's Fade To Black, by Ch. Altar's Gaither von Axen ex Panamint Ever A Lady. Bred by Carole A. Anderson, owned by Joseph Owens, born March 7, 1983. In the snow on January 12, 1985.

Plate 59

1. Am. and Can Ch. Von Gailingen's Dassie Did It, U.D.T., Can. C.D., owned by Mrs. Catherine Thompson, Freehold, N.J.

2. Ch. Pandemonium's Laredo v Blanka is owned by Valerie J. Cade and Mary Ellen Laycock, Goldens Bridge, N.Y.

3. Am. and Can. Ch. Birch Hill's Quincy, C.D., T.D. owned by Jane Wiedel, Stockton, Ill.

4. "Love is a dog named Klodo." Dorit S. Rogers hugs her old friend, age ten years. A beautiful study of the affection which exists between a Rottweiler and his special person! Bergluft Kennels, Sewickley, Pa.

5. Mondberg's Bulger v Beier, C.D.X. owned by Peter Piusz, Johnstown, N.Y.

6. Two English imports brought to America as part of their foundation stock by Ravenwood Kennels, Linda B. Griswold, Michigan City, Ind. Sitting, the dog, Thewina Stormtrooper, top dual purpose Rottweiler in England 1984. Standing, the bitch, Caprido Operetta From Thewina, who is an English Champion.

Plate 60

1. Ch. Ursus von Stolzenfels, "Bulli" to his friends, by Ch. Eiko Vom Schwaiger Wappen, C.D.X., SchH 1 ex Kola von Stolzenfels-Huff is owned by Erika Beqaj, Richmond Hill, N.Y. Winning Best of Breed at Suffolk County Kennel Club Dog Show 1984.

2. Xanadu's Bronson Jos v Altar, by Ch. Altar's Gaiter vom Axel ex Georgian Court Gaylee, taking Reserve Winners from the puppy class, Alaska K.C. 1984. Joann H. Turner, owner, Wilderness Rottweilers, Anchorage, Alaska.

3. Ch. Srigo's Elyssian Fields won her first major from the puppy class at Colonial Rottweiler Club Specialty 1977. By Ch. Jack v Emstal, C.D. ex Ch. Srigo's Xclusive v Kurtz. Srigo Rottweilers, Felicia Luburich, East Brunswick, N.J.

4. The late outstanding Ch. Haserways Freyr v Altar, by Ch. Rex of Old Acres ex Ch. Brady-Haserway v Haus Kalbas, famous Group winner with many outstanding honors to his credit, was the foundation stud dog at Altar Kennels. Co-owned by Kacky Evans with Edith M. Althin, Fayetteville, N.C. Carlos Rojas, handler.

5. Blaise von Lann was bred by Linda A. Binnie and born August 12, 1983. She is pictured with her handler, Jerry Kaplan, as she takes points towards her championship, now nearing completion as we write. Owned by Steven M. Lettick, Hamden, Ct.

6. Way-Mar's Brooks Dawg V Jos at age 17 months. Winning at Alaska K.C. Dog Show, Jan. 6, 1985. By Ch. Bratianas Rommel v Laurich ex Ch. and OTCH Way Mar's Disco Dawg. Joann H. Turner, owner, Anchorage, Alaska.

7. Am. and Can. Ch. Elka von Siegerhaus, C.D. was Best of Breed in the Western Rottweiler Owners Supported Entry in 1984, handled by Thomas Woodward for himself and co-owner Carol Woodward, von Siegerhaus Rottweilers, Corning, Calif.

8. Ch. Altar's Gandolf vom Axel, noted Best in Show winner owned by Edith D. Alphin, Altar Rottweilers, Fayetteville, N.C.

Plate 61

1. Ch. Alina's Adelbear of Wesley, owned by Linda and Leo Minisce and handled by Bob Hogan to three Best in Show wins, including the largest entry Best in Show won by a Rott to this time. Sired by Yankee, in this picture he is winning Best in Show at the same event that his great-grandsire, Kato, won the breed's FIRST Best in Show in the U.S. Photo courtesy of Jan Marshall.

2. Green Mountain's Sir Michael, winning Best of Breed at Wachusett K.C. in 1985, handled by Carol Petruzzo for Anthony P. Attalla, Green Mountain Kennels, Londonderry, N.H.

3. Am. and Can. Ch. Lakotah's Avant-Garde, C.D.X. is owned by Kevin and Paula Ray, Huntington, W. Va.

4. Wilderness Black Turk at age two years, taking a 5-point major at Alaska K.C., 1985. Owned by Mark and Silvia Whaley, bred by Joann Turner, Wilderness Rottweilers, Anchorage, Alas.

5. Ch. Ukiah von Gruenerwald, dam of Butkus von Gruenerwald, a fifth generation of the von Gruenerwald breeding program. Dorothea Gruenerwald, owner, Colorado Springs, Col.

6. Ch. Daba von Andan taking Best of Winners at Greater Miami in 1982, handled here by C.L. Rawlings. Bred, owned, and usually handled by Mrs. Benjamin C. Tilghman, Centreville, Md.

7. Can. Ch. Majorhausen's Beaumark, Can. C.D., owned by Akamai Guard Dogs, Hawaii and Neil O'Connor, and bred by Jacques Major. Sired by the late Ch. Donnaj Vt. Yankee of Paulus ex Can. Ch. Northwind's Juno, Can. C.D.X., SchH 1, TT. Pictured winning a Best of Breed under judge Mrs. Dolly Ward. Photo courtesy of Jill Nakache, Rottweilers von Haiem.

8. Am. and Can. Ch. Carado's Commander Cody, T.T. taking Best of Breed at Detroit K.C. in March 1985. Owner-handled by Suzanne Stewart, Jan-Su Rottweilers, Inkster, Mich.

Plate 62

1. Baroness Vom Herta, by Am. and Can. Ch. Hasso vom Steigstrassle, C.D. ex Bianca von der Waldschule at the Medallion Rottweiler Club 1984 Futurity. Dick McKenney handling for owners Michael R. Helmann and Carol Helmann, Arlington Heights, Ill.

2. Can. Ch. Trollegens Yanka at 13 months. By Moran Kralicky Sneznik (imported from Czechoslovakia) ex Am. and Can. Ch. Van Tieleman's Charly Girl. Owned by Marie Kanera, Langley, B.C., Canada.

3. Am. and Can. Ch. Birch Hill's Governor, Am. and Can. C.D., owner-handled by Michael Conradt taking Best of Breed at the Medallion Rottweiler Club Specialty in June 1983. Dany Canino, judge Mrs. Joan Klem presenting trophy. Photo courtesy of Jane Wiedel.

4. Ch. Alfredo II Protettore, or "Fredo" to his friends, pictured

winning the Working Group at Bryn Mawr Kennel Club, June 1985, handled by Jeffrey Brucker. "Fredo" is owned by Frank D. Zaffere, III, River Forest, Ill., and is a son of Ch. Rodsden's Ansel v Brabant and grandson of Ch. Haserway's Polar Bear. This splendid dog started his show career in 1983, winning the Group from the Open Dog Class his first two times in the ring, finishing title within one month with five majors. Since that time he has many Best of Breed wins and multiple Group honors in stiffest Eastern competition.

Plate 63

1. Pionierhaus Ans Stolzenhaus, sired by 1983 KS Ch. Mirko vom Steinkopf, SchH.III, IPO III, FH ex Ch. Ute vom Mummler, C.D. Owned by Rottweilers vom Pionierhaus, Jerry and Kay Watson, Pride, La. Co-bred by von Pionierhaus and von Stolzenfels Kennels.

2. Ch. Riegele's Greenhill Ima Maid at age four and a half years is by Am. and Can. Ch. Rodsden's Ander van het Brabant ex Ch. Riegele's Erin Maid. Owned by Nick and Lois Schwechtje, Greenhill Rottweilers, Broomall, Pa.

3. Am. and Can. Ch. Donnaj Vt. Yankee of Paulus, C.D.X., TT, July 1975—May 1984. Owned by Mrs. Jan Marshall, Donnaj Rottweilers, Woodstock, Vt. "Yank" is an immortal in the breed for his personality, his show record, and his quality as

a sire.

4. Panzer von Stolzenfels, son of Ch. Imor von Stolzenfels, C.D. From von Stolzenfels Rottweilers, Dr. Evelyn M. Ellman, Augusta, Mich.

Plate 64

1. Ch. Sunnysides Royal von Meadow, No. 1 Rottweiler Bitch in the United States for 1984, the only bitch ever to have won all three Specialties: those of the American Rottweiler Club, Medallion Rottweiler Club and Colonial Rottweiler Club. Owned by Donna Wormser, Blue Meadow Farms, Ocala, Fla.

2. Ch. Graudstark's Luger, C.D., TT enjoying "flying." Owned by Noblehaus Rottweilers, Mark and Patricia Schwartz, West Nyack, N.Y. Photo by Mark Schwartz.

3. Bob Barber and Ch. Von Walbers Atom Smasher, the latter at one year old. By Ch. Hintz von Michelsberg ex Torburhof's Gunda von Brawn, Bob is the son of Sue Wales, owner of Von Walber's Rottweilers, Dexter, Mich.

4. "Brock" saying "please." Ch. Donnaj Green Mountain Boy, owned by Anthony P. Attalla, one of the breed's foremost winners.

			WE449506
Litter Reg. No.	**PEDIGREE**		**Individual Reg. No.**

A/C CH. Birch Hill's Juno, TD, CD   RO-2968

Registered Name of Dog

Date Whelped __September 16, 1979__   Sex __Female__

Breeder __Jane F. Wiedel__   Address __4400 S. Eden Rd., Stockton, IL 61085__

Owner __Jane F. Wiedel__   Address

PARENTS	GRANDPARENTS	GREAT-GRANDPARENTS	GREAT-GREAT-GRANDPARENTS
SIRE: A/C CH. Rodsden's Elko Kastanienbaum, A/C CD, Amer. CDXTD WD 694350 RO-1448	International CH. Elko vom Kastanienbaum, SchH 1 46 340 HD Free, Utrecht	Elko vom Kaiserberg, 44 352 SchH 1	Hasso vom Oelberg, SchH 3 39 223
			Anni vom Kaiserberg 42 306
		Gitta vom Bucheneck, 44 776 SchH 1 HD Free, Utrecht	Furst vd Villa Daheim, SchH 1 42 204
			Indra Vom Schloss Westerwinkel, 40 758 SchH 1
	CH. Gundi vom Reichenbachle 48 086 HD Free, Utrecht RO-846	Berno vom Albtal, 42 673 SchH 3, FH	Hasso vom Oelberg, SchH 3 39 223
			Heidi vom Durrbach 38 916
		Antje von der Wegscheide 41 225	Quick vd Solitude, SchH 3, FH 38 608 HD Free, Utrecht
			Anka von der Kurmark 37 832
DAM: CH. Rodsden's Birch Hill Bess, CDTD WD 363207 RO-1174	CH. Dux vom Hungerbuhl, SchH 1 WC 018804 RO-234	Kuno vom Butzensee, SchH 3 40 415	Wotan v Filstalstrand, SchH 1 37 422
			Edel vom Durrbach 38 079
		Britta vom Schlossberg 39 075	Alex v Ludwigshafen/See, SchH 3 37 409
			Evi vom Kanzachtal 36 339
	CH. Rodsden's Frolich Burga, CDTD WC 589812 RO-649	CH. Max von der Hobertsburg WC 308208 RO-320	Caro vom Kupferdach, SchH 3 41 065
			Adda vom Dahl, SchH 3 41 299
		CH. Rodsden's Willa vd Harque, UDT WB 854722 RO-321	CH. Rodsden's Kluge vd Harque, WA553102 RO-50 CD
			Rodsden's Gypsy WB046987 RO-54

PLATE 49

PLATE 50

PLATE 51

PLATE 52

PLATE 53

PLATE 54

1

9-12 MONTH
BITCH
SWEEPSTAKES
AMERICAN
ROTTWEILER CLUB
1985

2

FIRST
BUCKS COUNTY
KENNEL CLUB
1982
GILBERT PHOTO

3

AMERICAN
ROTTWEILER CLUB
JUNE 24 1979
BEST OF BREED
BEST OF OPPOSITE SEX
JUDGE
JEANNIE TUNSTILL

4

BEST OF
BREED OR VARIETY
PENN RIDGE
KENNEL CLUB
1984
LEASH TO LENS PHOTO
BY GILBERT

5

WAMPANOAG KC
BEST IN SHOW

6

WINNERS
A.K.C. CENTENNIAL
RITTER PHOTO
BY KATHY

7

WINNERS DOG
TRENTON KENNEL CLUB INC
MAY 3 1981
PHOTO BY CHUCK GOODMAN

8

BEST OF
WINNERS
CUDAHY
KENNEL CLUB
AUG.
1983
BOOTH PHOTO

PLATE 55

PLATE 56

PLATE 57

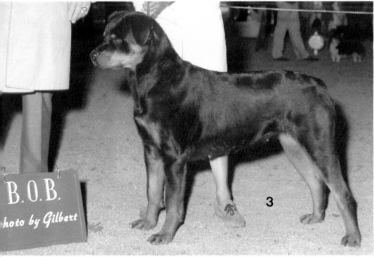

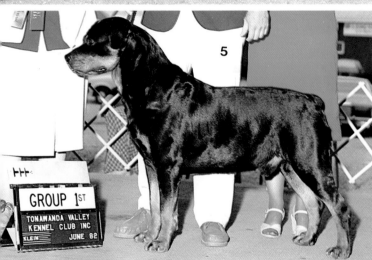

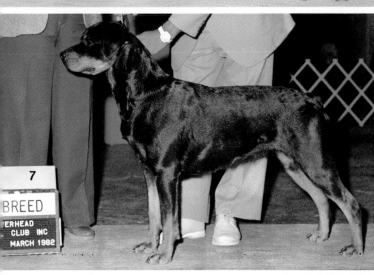

PLATE 58

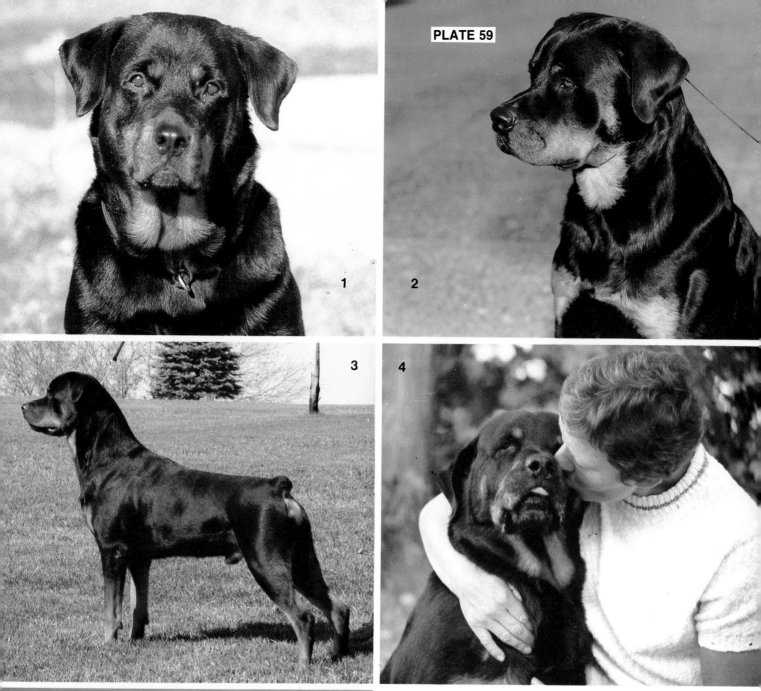

PLATE 59

1

2

3

4

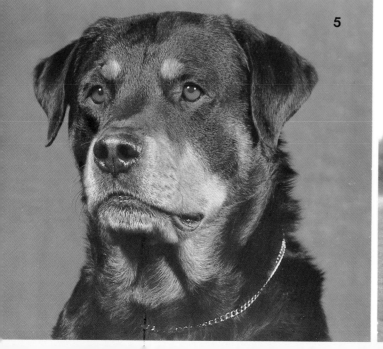

5

6

PLATE 60

PLATE 61

PLATE 62

PLATE 63

PLATE 64

In 1971, when Alan Kruse himself started out to breed the best Rottweilers possible in the United States, the breed was still not too generally well-known. Having grown up with members of this breed, Alan was well aware that the intelligence, loyalty and working ability of these dogs made the breed one of very superior desirability.

For the past two and a half years as we write, Alan Kruse has been importing some very outstanding dogs from Germany including, in 1981 a male "Korung" Rottweiler. "Korung" is the term for the exhaustive German evaluation of superior Rottweilers. A dog can qualify for this ONLY with the approval of the German breed warden, and the tests involved take two years' time to complete.

More recently another Korung rated Rottie, this a female, has joined this kennel, and Mr. Kruse has imported others as well.

Foundation matron at Von der Kruses was Champion Olga von Gruenerwald, from Dorothea Gruenerwald's famous kennel. Olga was a daughter of Champion Donar v.d. Neckarstroom ex Champion Jenni von Gruenerwald.

Von Dorow

Von Dorow is another comparative newcomer to the ranks of Rottweiler breeding kennels which would seem to be destined for a bright future. Owned by Nancy C. Estes and situated at Midland, Texas, this kennel was already well-known as home of the Beaconsfield Bassets since 1975 when, in 1981 after many years' interest in the breed, Ms. Estes obtained a foundation bitch for her Rotties. This was in the form of a nine-week-old puppy bitch from Shelly Moore's Merrymoore Kennel, who grew up to become Champion Merrymoore's Imp von Dorow. The von Dorow suffix is the maiden name of Ms. Estes's maternal grandmother.

Imp finished her championship in June of 1984 with two Bests of Breed and five Bests of Opposite Sex from the classes, and was specialed only during the latter part of 1984, winning four Bests of Breed over dog specials, 1 Group 1V and nineteen Bests of Opposite Sex, qualifying her for the American Rottweiler Club Top Ten Bitches for 1984. Imp will be trained in obedience in 1985 and will also be specialed on a limited basis. To date she has been shown once in 1985, owner-handled, five and a half weeks after whelping her first litter, when she won Best of Breed under Mrs. Edna Travinek.

Thus far, Ms. Estes has bred one Rottweiler litter, Imp to American and Canadian Champion Tulake's Apollo, which produced seven bitches and two dogs in January 1985. Due to the time limitations imposed by being involved in two breeds, she plans to continue a limited breeding program, linebreeding on Merrymoore or outcrossing to lines complimentary to Merrymoore. As well as breeding for show, she intends to breed for working ability and to have one or more dogs from each future litter trained for Schutzhund or police work.

Von Fox Rottweilers

Von Fox Rottweilers are owned by Maria and Marvin Fox and located in Philadelphia, Pennsylvania. The foundation bitch here is Demon von Fox who is the dam of this kennel's first two litters, by Zum Verkauf's Eric Behalter and Champion Bethel Farm's Apollo respectively. Demon, herself, born in October 1979, is a daughter of Titanium von Lester ex Magneto von Lester and was bred by Ken Lester. She descends from Lyn Mar Acres, Srigo, and imported German bloodlines.

Demon's first litter produced Champion Fraulein Gretchen von Fox who finished her championship at 23 months of age in very limited showing.

The younger litter includes the bitch Fraulein Cinder von Fox, C.D., who completed her obedience title in three shows consecutively and at only 14 months' age. And also Madchen Greta von Fox, owned by Ellen Monica Towarnicki, beginning her show career as we write, under Alan Levine's handling and starting as well in training for her C.D.

Currently Champion Fraulein Gretchen von Fox is training in obedience and tracking work, hoping to add those titles to her show championship. Also she will be bred during 1985, a new litter to which the Fox family is looking forward with keenest anticipation.

Von Gailingen

The Von Gailingen Rottweilers belong to Catherine M. Thompson of Freehold, New Jersey, whose kennel slogan is "Puppies with a future." Judging by her success as a breeder, there can be no doubt of this fact, as Mrs. Thompson's Rottweilers have distinguished themselves by producing exceptional quality right from the beginning.

Cathy Thompson's family always had dogs—Toy Manchester Terriers as house pets and Irish Water Spaniels as hunting dogs. A good deal of her youth was spent training and showing horses, which she still raises and shows occasionally. Then in 1969 she purchased her first Rottweiler, a breed in which she had been interested for several years. This first Rottweiler was owner-handled by Mrs. Thompson to her bench championship and her companion dog degree in obedience. Her name was Champion Natascha vom Hohenreissach, C.D. She was by Champion Fago von Hohenreissach and out of a German import bitch, Catja von Friedrichsberg.

Champion Natascha was bred to the German import Champion Dux von Hungerbuhl, SchH I. This was Natascha's only litter and all the pups were sold. Then, says Cathy Thompson, "seven months later I was privileged to buy back one of the bitch puppies, Anka von Gailingen."

Anka promptly took over as the primary brood bitch and show gal, doing both entirely in an admirable manner. She was the Top Producing Bitch, *Kennel Review System*, for the breed in 1977. Anka had four litters by three different studs, all of which were from the same male line: two grandsons and a son of Champion Ferdinand von Dachsweil. Like her dam, Natascha had been before her, Anka was owner-handled to her championship, which she scored in a spectacular manner including a five point major at Baltimore (Maryland Kennel Club) where she was Winners Bitch, Best of Winners, and Best of Opposite Sex over specials under the German judge, Frederick Berger, Head Breed Warden for the ADRK (German Rottweiler Club). She was Winners Bitch at Westminster under Peggy Adamson for another point, took a five point major under Robert Wills at Tidewater Kennel Club, and finished with a four point

major at Virginia Kennel Club under Robert Salomon—all of this from the Bred-by Exhibitor Class.

Littermates of Anka in the Von Gailingen "A" litter included Champion Axel von Gailingen, C.D., a dog; Alfie von Gailingen, C.D., a dog; Ampa von Gailingen, a bitch with major points when she was killed by a car; and Ampa von Gailingen, a bitch who has produced champions.

Anka's first litter, the Von Gailingen "B" litter, was sired by the Champion Ferdinand von Dachsweil grandson, Champion Hintz von Michelburg, top producer in 1977 and 1978. Hintz was by Champion Lyn-Mar Acres Atlas v Kinta and out of Hylamar's Heidi. Included in it were the following dogs: Champion Bokar von Gailingen, C.D.; Champion Blitz von Gailingen, a Top Ten Placer; Champion Braunswen von Gailingen; and Baer von Gailingen, pointed.

Anka's second litter was the von Gailingen "C" litter. This litter was sired by the Ferdinand son, Champion Igor von Schauer, a Group winner and Top Producer. This time Anka produced Champion von Gailingen's Chancellor, a champion producing dog; Champion von Gailingen's Carry On, also a dog; Champion Von Gailingen's Welkerhaus Cia, C.D., a Group placing Top Ten bitch who was also a Top Producer; Champion Von Gailingen's Witzend Caper, a multiple champion producing bitch; and the major pointed dog, Von Gailingen's Commandant.

The Von Gailingen "D" and "E" litters were both out of Anka and were sired by the Top Producer Champion Srigo's Zarras v Kurtz, who is by the Top Producing son of Ferdinand, Champion Lyn-Mar Acres Arras v Kinta and out of the Top Producing super show bitch Champion Srigo's Madchen v Kurtz. Heading the "D" list is American and Canadian Champion Von Gailingen's Dassie Did It, U.D.T., Canadian C.D., who is the fifth Champion—U.D.T. Rottweiler bitch and the first Champion—U.D.T. Rottweiler who was breeder-owner trained. American and Bermudian Champion Von Gailingen's Dark Delight, U.D.T., Bermuda C.D.X., Canadian C.D. is the first C.D.X. Rottweiler in Bermuda, the 1983 American Rottweiler

Club Top Obedience Dog, and Highest Scoring Dog in Trial at the 1984 American Rottweiler Club National Specialty. Also in the "D" litter are Champion Von Gailingen's Dream Come True, C.D. and Von Gailingen's Decidedly, C.D., both bitches. The dog, Von Gailingen's Determined, C.D., was Highest Scoring Dog in Match at the 1980 National Specialty Match, and first in Novice A at the 1981 National Specialty. Dassie and Dark Delight have won the Brace Class at the Colonial Rottweiler Club Specialty in 1979 and 1980, the American Rottweiler Club Specialty in 1979. From the "E" litter there is the pointed bitch, Von Gailingen's Elfin Magic C.D.X.

Dassie and Dee (Dark Delight) have taken over the brood bitch responsibilities. The only puppy to have made it to the show ring thus far is now Champion Von Gailingen's Finest Hour, a Group placing dog from the classes over specials. He is by Champion Von Gailingen's Chancellor and out of American and Canadian Champion Von Gailingen's Dassie Did It, U.D.T., Canadian C.D. Dee's daughter, Von Gailingen's Heaven Sent, won the Novice B Class at the 1983 National Specialty. A second daughter, Von Gailingen's the Katz Meow, won a Best in Match at an all-breed match.

Mrs. Thompson remains very active in obedience, being the Training Director for Bayshore Companion Dog Club. She is also hard at work for the breed as a whole serving on the Board of Directors of the American Rottweiler Club, having served two terms as the Club President. Cathy is the American Rottweiler Club statistician and was instrumental in formulating the club's system for Production Awards.

Von Gruenerwald

Von Gruenerwald Rottweilers are owned by Bill and Dorothea Gruenerwald at Colorado Springs, Colorado. Their story of involvement with the Rottweiler breed began in 1959 when they acquired their first bitch, Abingdon Aphrodite. She was primarily their companion-friend, shown only once in the Chicago area. "Aphra" was by Champion Arras vom Stadhaus ex Champion Dagmar von Schildgen.

When bred to the outstanding German import, Bundessieger Champion Harras vom Sofienbusch, SchH I, in 1964, the mating produced only one lovely female puppy. This hand-raised puppy, Champion Lorelei, was to become the Gruenerwalds' foundation bitch, typifying strong topline, correct temperament, flawless movement, and sound hips.

The motivating moment to become totally involved with Rottweilers nineteen years ago (1966) was the realization that Lorelei was, indeed, something special. Shown by her good friend Ann Maurer, "Lori" finished easily in five shows including three majors.

The chance opportunity to acquire a German imported puppy in 1964 proved to be a happy coincidence. Nick vom Silahopp had been sired by another Bundessieger, Blitz vom Schloss Westerwinkel, Schutzhund III. The combination of these two famous bloodlines was the beginning of the Gruenerwald line.

Nick and Lori's first litter of eight produced four champions: Champion Carla von Gruenerwald, Champion Cache von Gruenerwald, Champion Conrad von Gruenerwald, and Champion Colin von Gruenerwald. Two repeat breedings in 1967 and 1969 produced Champion Drusus von Gruenerwald and Champion Eloise von Gruenerwald. Champion Nick vom Silahopp was used at stud on a limited basis, siring an additional seven champions.

Champion Cache von Gruenerwald, used at stud only twice, was the sire of Champion Rich von Rickthofen, C.D.X., and American and Canadian Champion Ivan von Gruenerwald.

Troll vom Hook, a five year old German import, was introduced into the Gruenerwald breeding program in 1971. Troll carried the qualities of large bone and strong heads in his pedigree, which by then had become the signature of the Gruenerwald dogs. He was bred twice to Champion Eloise von Gruenerwald, producing Champion Fates Chance von Gruenerwald, Champion Hannalore von Gruenerwald, and litter-sister Champion Happy von Gruenerwald.

Champion Eloise von Gruenerwald was bred for a third and last time to German import Champion Dieter von Gruenerwald,

C.D. This proved to be her most outstanding litter. Out of five puppies four became titled: Jaeger von Gruenerwald, C.D., Champion Juno von Gruenerwald, Champion Jenni von Gruenerwald, and Champion Jiggs von Gruenerwald, C.D.X.

Troll vom Hook was also bred to a granddaughter of Nick and Lorelei, Alexis von Kongslien. A litter of four males produced Champion Goliath von Gruenerwald and American and Canadian Champion Grimm von Gruenerwald. A third male was pointed. Bred to outside bitches, Troll vom Hook sired an additional six champions and, in 1974, was named Top Producer by *Kennel Review*. Despite the fact that when acquired he was past his prime for conformation competition, his contribution to the breed was invaluable.

In 1974, Champion Goliath von Gruenerwald was bred to Gina vom Ingenhof, a German import. This litter produced Champion Maxa Bear von Gruenerwald, C.D., and Champion Marlee Bear von Gruenerwald, C.D. Champion Marlee Bear went on to fame as the foundation bitch of Weissenburg Kennels, producing six champion offspring. Gina finished her championship and C.D. title when owned by Andrea Vrana.

Champion Hannalore von Gruenerwald was bred to Champion Starkrest's Polo-R in 1976. Their first two-puppy litter produced Champion Noralei von Gruenerwald and Neela Namora von Gruenerwald, C.D. A repeat breeding produced Champion Pfeffer von Gruenerwald.

On July 4, 1976, Champion Jenni von Gruenerwald whelped a litter sired by Dutch import Champion Donar vom Neckarstroom. This litter produced Champion Olga von Gruenerwald, who was to become the foundation bitch of Von Kruse Kennels. Olaf, a pointed litter brother, was bred to a daughter of American and Canadian Champion Ivan von Gruenerwald, producing Champion Ukiah von Gruenerwald, the dam of Butkus.

Champion Noralei von Gruenerwald bred to Champion Centurion's Che Von Der Barr produced Champion X-Theodora von Gruenerwald. After completing her championship, "Megan" was shown by Janet Swayze to multiple Best of Breed and Best of Opposite Sex

awards and was rated No. 5 Rottweiler bitch in 1983, American Rottweiler Club System. At the Janesville-Beloit Kennel Club Dog Show in 1983, she went 4th in Working Group, handled by Janet.

Champion Bulli von Meyerhoff ex Champion X-Theodora von Gruenerwald produced Champion Excaliber's Atlas Von Ament and Champion Excalibur's Aarich Von Ament, bred by Adolph and Anna Ament and Dorothea Gruenerwald.

A litter-brother, Xavier von Gruenerwald, after siring the "B" litter in 1982, was exported to Brazil where he is at stud. A promising young daughter of his, "Rio," is back home at the Gruenerwalds waiting to be shown.

In 1985, three Rottweilers owned by Dorothea Gruenerwald received recognition for their contribution to the breed. The American Rottweiler Club's Production Awards for outstanding accomplishments by progeny, which are described in detail elsewhere in this book, were presented to: Champion Eloise von Gruenerwald (Bronze), Champion Gina vom Ingenhof, C.D. (Bronze), and Champion Nick vom Silahopp (Silver). Never deviating from the Standard in size, and striving to produce consistency in type, temperament, and movement has been a long-time goal of the owners of these famous dogs.

Total commitment to Rottweilers for more than twenty years has not been limited alone to the breeding of twenty-seven champions. Mrs. Gruenerwald has personally finished six of her own dogs. She has given generously of her time and effort in serving as President of the American Rottweiler Club, 1975-1977; as Director, 1977-1979, and 1982-1984; and as Vice-President, 1985-1986. She was the American Rottweiler Club breed columnist for the *American Kennel Gazette—Pure-Bred Dogs* from April-December 1976 and again from 1981-1983. Besides being the Editor-Publisher of *ARK*, the Club's bi-monthly newsletter, Mrs. Gruenerwald is Chairman of the Illustrated Standard Committee and initiated the American Rottweiler Club's publication of three *Rottweiler Pictorials*, published in 1976, 1978 and 1982.

Top left: 1966-1985! In this picture judge Derek Rayne is awarding Best of Winners to Future Ch. Lorelei von Gruener-wald, owned by Bill and Dorothea Gruenerwald, for a 4-point major with the record (then and at that show) class entry of 27 at Oakland Kennel Club. Ann Maurer, handler. **Top right:** Nineteen years later Derek Rayne awards Best of Winners and then Best of Breed over two specials to Butkus von Gruenerwald at Greeley, Colorado in May 1985. Butkus was sired by Xavier von Gruenerwald and is linebred on Ch. Nick vom Silahopp ex Ch. Lorelei. Butkus represents the *sixth* homebred generation of von Gruenerwald breeding. Owned by Jeff Howard, he has been owner- and amateur-handled, with seven Bests of Breed to date. Majors being almost non-existent in Colorado, Jeff and Butkus drove 14 hours to Tulsa, Oklahoma in hopes of winning his first of them, which he did there under Muriel Freeman. **Bottom:** Ch. Nick vom Silahoff, recipient of the American Rottweiler Club Silver Production Award. Owned by Dorothea Gruenerwald, Colorado Springs, Colorado.

Top left: Troll vom Hook, a German import owned by Dorothea Gruenerwald, Colorado Springs, Colorado. **Top right:** Carrie von Gruenerwald in 1967 with an Irish Setter friend. Dorothea Gruenerwald, owner. **Bottom:** Ch. Happy von Gruenerwald finishing her championship in Oct. 1979. Handled by Jeffrey Brucker and owned by Ellen Lott, Happy was an Eloise daughter.

In 1982, Dorothea Gruenerwald was elected Secretary-Treasurer of the International Federation for Rottweiler Friends (I.F.R.) held in West Germany, and subsequently played a prominent role in organizing the lectures and official Meeting of the Sixth I.F.R. Congress held in the U.S. in May 1985.

As for the future, judging of Rottweilers in several fun and sanctioned matches in 1984 and 1985 is the beginning of another challenge—an American Kennel Club judges license. To quote Mrs. Gruenerwald, "There will always be a Rottweiler in our home. Champion Jenni is now twelve years of age. Champion Noralei is over nine years old, and we have two youngsters ready for the show ring."

Von Meadow

Von Meadow Kennels, owned by Donna M. Wormser at Ocala, Florida, have certainly made a spectacular record breeding Rotties since the mid-1970's. In 1984 this kennel was breeder of the No. 1 Rottweiler Bitch in the United States, Champion Sunnysides Royal von Meadow. Among her distinguished accomplishments was that of being the only bitch ever in the history of Rottweilers to have won all three Specialties under three different judges. These were the American Rottweiler Club, the Medallion Rottweiler Club, and the Colonial Rottweiler Club Specialties.

Royal is a home-bred, making her success even more fun. She is a daughter of Champion McCoy von Meadow, C.D., T.D. RO out of Champion Reza vom Hause Schumann RO.

In 1984, the Wormsers' von Meadow dogs made their owners the No. 1 Breeders for Top Dogs in the United States. This included the No. 1 Bitch in the United States and also another bitch in the Top Ten, Elka von Meadow. In 1983 von Meadow's owners had also been the No. 1 Rottweiler breeders in the United States of Top Ten dogs, three of theirs having been included that year: Champion Krugerend von Meadow, Champion Miss Ellie von Meadow, and Champion Sunnysides Royal von Meadow. Also in 1983 the Wormsers were the No. 1 Breeders of Top

Producers in the United States, which also includes their male, Champion McCoy von Meadow. Donna Wormser comments that they "consider ourselves very fortunate in that we are No. 1 Breeders in the United States for percentage of OFA champion offspring," which she mainly attributes to the fact that most of their bloodlines are five generations of clear hips.

The Wormsers never breed a Rottweiler having a show disqualification. They try to do obedience with most of their Rottweilers, feeling that this training makes them a much better dog. Rottweilers are very brilliant and intelligent, and since the Wormsers keep more than one as house dogs, they feel that the obedience does make them obey better and the living with them more enjoyable.

The Wormsers have made trips to Germany a couple of times annually during the past several years, and feel that they can breed better bitches here than are being offered in that country. But of course the desire for "new blood" always enters into anyone's breeding program. Thus she has shipped bitches of her own to Germany for breeding to the leading producers there, but to date has had little luck in doing so.

The Wormsers do not believe in attack training Rotties since the breed is naturally protective. They endeavor to get an obedience degree on each dog, then show it in conformation.

Another dog whom Donna Wormser mentions with pride is their homebred Champion R.C.'s Gator von Meadow, who in July 1983 was awarded the title of "Top Producing Female of All Breeds." As she says, "I only wish it were not so hard to breed another one just like her."

Hard perhaps, but certainly not unattainable to people whose breeding record has been so outstanding!

Von Medeah

Von Medeah Rottweilers were founded in 1973 with the purchase of their foundation bitch, Wunderhund Medeah, from whose name the kennel name was derived. Keith and Charlotte Twineham own these Rottweilers, who are located at Union City, California.

Misty whelped only one litter, bred to a cornerstone of the breed on the West Coast, Champion Panamint Seneca Chief. Among her puppies were future Champion Kane von Medeah and future Champion Karly Von Medeah, C.D., the latter noteworthy as the American Rottweiler Club's No. 2 Conformation Bitch in 1980.

Karly, during her show career, earned approximately 35 Best of Opposite Sex placements and two Bests of Breed, one only five weeks after whelping her first litter; and one of the Best of Opposite Sex awards from the Veteran Bitch Class. Karly has offspring currently in show competition.

In addition to conformation, the Twinehams have been active over the years in obedience, with many of their dogs having earned obedience degrees. Most noteworthy of their obedience winners was Medeah's Shane De Michaele, C.D., who was the Top Rottweiler Obedience Dog of the Year in 1979. Shane achieved his C.D. with one of the highest average set of scores ever earned by a Rottweiler. He also served as ringbearer at his owners' wedding.

The Twinehams continue today in both conformation and obedience with their latest youngster, Ilsa von Harsa, C.D. She was the Highest Scoring Rottweiler at the American Kennel Club Centennial Show to finish her degree. She is maturing nicely and also starting now to do well in the conformation ring.

Von Morgen Carroll

Von Morgen Carroll Kennels, Ontario, California, had its beginning back in 1968 when Bill and Betty Carroll purchased their first of the breed, Inga von Chrisma Carroll. Bred to Champion Gibralter of Casterline, she produced the Carrolls' first champion, Brinker von Morgen Carroll, and Tanya von Morgen, the latter later becoming dam of American, Mexican and Canadian Champion Burley von Morgen Carroll, C.D. who was Top Rottweiler in conformation competition for two years straight.

Champion Bee Matilda vom Haus Kalbas was bred to Burley, thus producing Champion Starkheim Duf Morgen Carroll who has sired 15 champions to date. This dog, too, has a splendid winning record, having placed in the Top Ten Dogs in conformation for three consecutive years.

Joining Duffy at stud at von Morgen Carroll is his nephew, Champion Alexandros G. Roadway, a son of International Champion Jack vom Emstahl, C.D.X. ex Champion Starkheim's Catinka G. Roadway.

All of the studs and brood bitches at von Morgen Carroll are of outstanding quality and soundness with desired temperament.

Vonpalisaden

The name Vonpalisaden was established in 1971 and it is used since in context with publishing, consulting, information retrieving, translating of canine documents, etc. It also became known as a Rottweiler breeding line, Vonpalisaden Rottweilers, since its first litter, "A" was whelped in the United States.

The owners have been active in canine fields for many years, both in Europe and in the United States. Dr. Dagmar Hodinar is a biomedical scientist, a teacher, author, and lecturer who speaks and writes in several languages. She focused her research on international aspects of canine activities, e.g., showing, training, breeding, etc., and she is especially involved with the Rottweiler breed. As a founding member of the North American Working Dog Association (NASA), she helped to introduce the Schutzhund sport to the North American continent. The owners of Vonpalisaden Rottweilers are members of the United States Rottweiler Clubs and of the ADRK (Allgemeiner Deutscher Rottweiler Klub) and they are adhering not only to the A.K.C. standard of the breed; their activities are also guided by the more rigorous international standard and breeding regulations for the Rottweiler.

The bloodlines of Vonpalisaden dogs are based on German and American breeding lines of Von Hungerbuhl, represented by Champion Blitz von Gailingen, U.S. Top Ten Rottweiler in 1978/79, a grandson of Champion Dux von Hungerbuhl, SchH I, CACIB, Gek; and Janko von Tengen, SchH, major pointed in the United States, a Best of Breed winner, V rated at German shows, who is a grandson of International Champion Bulli von Hungerbuhl, SchH II, KS, Gek. EzA. These two sires have a great depth of conformation and personality in their pedigrees and reproduce reliably their desirable traits.

Another outstanding import has been added, Pit von der Klosterhardt, SchH III, FH, AD, VB, WH, based on well-known North German utility lines von Dammerwald and von der Klosterhardt, known for dogs highly competitive in top performance trials. Pit's ancestry includes a high performer, Brando V. Poppelsdorfer Schloss, SchH III, the personal dog of the late West German chancellor, Dr. K. Adenauer.

Vonpalisaden females can be traced to oldest and most famous German breeders, representing a balance of reliable producers (Gek. EzA) and working individuals with numerous Schutzhund titles, participants in top German performance trials. Cilbel's Ascha Vonpalisaden, granddaughter of International Champion Karol von Wellesweiler, SchH, BS, KS, Gek, EzA, daughter of Champion Blitz von Gailingen, produced several offspring with C.D. and C.D.X. degrees from her breeding to Janko von Tengen, SchH I. Ascha is also the dam of Happy Vonpalisaden, Best of Opposite Sex and pointed at age seven months. Ondra von Tengen, pointed, is the daughter of the most decorated German Rottweiler of all time, International Champion Nero von Schloss Rietheimm SchH III, FH, Gek, EzA, several times BS, KS, WS, ES, participant of several top performance trials. Her breeding to Champion Blitz von Gailingen produced puppies also already pointed from the puppy classes.

Von Schwabing

Von Schwabing Rottweilers at Warwick, Rhode Island, have been doing some excellent winning with their recently finished Champion Finnberg's Erna von Schwabing, C.D. who at age 11 months went Best Puppy in Match in August 1983 under well-known breeder-judge Catherine Thompson.

Two months later, at 13 months, Erna completed her C.D. degree in one weekend. And at age 23 months she completed her A.K.C. championship. The kennel is owned by Roy D. and Fran J. Hiltermann.

Erna is by American and Canadian Champion Birch Hill's Governor, C.D., TT ex Canadian Champion Finnberg's Anneli (Arras vom Koehlerwald, SchH 3, Germany,—Sonja vom Heidenmoor, Finland).

A very promising new importation has recently arrived at Von Schwabing for whom hopes are high. So do be watching for Nixe vom Bayernland who seems destined for future winning.

Von Siegerhaus

Von Siegerhaus Rottweilers are owned by Thomas and Carol Woodward at Corning, California. Carol Woodward has loved the breed since 1963; but it was not until she had married Thom that they became involved showing and in ownership. That was in 1972.

The first von Siegerhaus litter was born in 1979. Since then this kennel has had a dog qualified for the *Canine Chronicle* Top 10 list almost every year. The Woodwards have always owner-handled, which both of them enjoy. In 1982 *Kennel Review* listed two of their bitches as tied for third place among Top Producers, the only West Coast breeders to be so recognized. In 1983 one of their bitches ranked third.

The kennel's foundation bitch, Champion Kyna vom Odenwald, C.D., has the remarkable record of producing 16 title holders. Even more noteworthy is the fact that only one of the 16 was professionally handled. A third of these dogs are dual or triple titled.

Champion Kyna vom Odenwald, C.D., qualified as a Top Producer in both the *Canine Chronicle* and the *Kennel Review* systems. She also qualified for the Medallion Rottweiler Club's Hall of Fame and the American Rottweiler Club's Silver Production Award. She was Top Ten in Obedience, American Rottweiler Club, in 1977. At nine years old, she is still her owners' favorite around the ranch when help is needed in moving cattle.

The Woodwards are now working with their third Rottweiler generation.

Dogs now at von Siegerhaus, in addition to Kyna, include American and Canadian Champion Elka von Siegerhaus, C.D., by Champion Bratiana's Gus de Michaela ex Kirsten's Dandy Brandy, who ranked No. 7 in 1983, American Rottweiler Club System, and in *Canine Chronicle* as of May 1983.

American and Canadian Champion Nemisis von Siegerhaus, by American and Canadian

Champion Trollegen's Frodo ex Champion Kyna vom Odenwald, C.D., was 1985's Best of Opposite Sex winner at Golden Gate Kennel Club in an entry of 151 Rotties, breeder-owner handled.

American and Canadian Champion Quick von Siegerhaus, by Champion Birch Hill's Hasso Manteuffel, C.D.X., T.D., from Champion Meid von Siegerhaus finished both titles by 15 months' age, always breeder-owner handled and almost entirely shown in the Bred-by Exhibitor Class.

Champion Siegen vom Odenwald, C.D., by American and Canadian Champion Uwe vom Kursaal ex Champion Maxi vom Kursaal finished championship at age 16 months; now spayed.

American and Canadian Champion Wotan Zwei von Sonnenhaus, C.D., by Champion Wotan vom Kastanienbaum ex Champion Vala v Kursaal was No. 9 ranked in *Canine Chronicle* in 1981—a multi-Group placer who had both titles by 15 months old was, sadly, stolen from the Woodwards in October 1983.

The titled offspring of Champion Kyna vom Odenwald, C.D. are listed below. Kyna herself is of German parentage, both her sire, Nowak von der Wigg, and her dam, American and Canadian Champion Kitty vom Jursaal, being imports from there. In addition to the aforementioned Nemisis, her "kids" include Champion Laadie Drayea von Siegerhaus; American and Canadian Champion Nicholas von Siegerhaus, C.D.; American and Canadian Champion Lord Samuel von Siegerhaus, C.D.; Nacht Music von Siegerhaus, C.D.; Champion Meid von Siegerhaus; Mahadev von Siegerhaus, C.D.X.; Kora von Siegerhaus, C.D.; Kioki von Siegerhaus, C.D.; Nolan von Siegerhaus, C.D.X. (holder of the Irene McKenzie Memorial Trophy offered at the Golden Gate Kennel Club Show for 1983 and 1984, owned by Robert Nolan and Joyce Szalka, Concord, California); Medeah's Nadia von Siegerhaus, C.D.; Reich von Siegerhaus, C.D.; Mandy von Siegerhaus, C.D.; Kerry von Siegerhaus, C.D. (also major pointed); Niyah von Siegerhaus, C.D. (also close to Canadian and American championships); and although not yet titled as we write, Luger von Siegerhaus who is major pointed.

Then there is Schotzie of Siegerhaus, a well-known Rottweiler celebrity, owned by Marge Connolly, who has become famous in dog circles as "The Banking Rott," making bank deposits for her owner who runs an answering service. Schotzie makes daily visits to the bank, standing in line with the bag in her mouth, moving along with the line until her turn comes at the window; then she reaches her front paws up to the counter and drops the bag for the teller. Needless to say, she is quite an "attention getter," and has been widely written up in Rottweiler and general dog publications.

Von Stolzenfels

Rottweilers von Stolzenfels are bred for both nobility and utility by Jack P. and Dr. Evelyn Ellman at their noted kennel in Augusta, Michigan. The Rottweilers and their owners here enjoy living the pastoral life on a 250 acre estate of meadow, woodlands, and ponds bordering the banks of the Kalamazoo River.

It was in 1964 that Dr. Ellman, a former citizen of Germany who has been associated with the breed since childhood, imported her first puppy. This Rottweiler was Nello vom Silahop, C.D., a son of Bundessieger Blitz vom Schloss Westerwinkel, SchH III and Queen von der Solitude. Viking, as the Ellmans called him, was probably the first Rottweiler trained for Schutzhund in the United States. The Ellmans, who are founding members of the Detroit Kynological Society, trained Viking under the able guidance of Dr. William Fuller of Detroit. This Society put on the first Schutzhund demonstration and trial in the United States. Unfortunately, the Ellmans lost Viking before he could sire a litter for them.

They next imported two daughters of Bundessieger Igor vom Hause Henseler, SchH. I. Both bitches were of magnificent temperament and conformation, but unfortunately were unsuitable for breeding owing to hip dysplasia. Both lived out their lives as beloved pets, Christel reaching 12 years' age, Freya, her litter sister, living to 13½ years old.

The arrival of yet another import, Champion Cosi vom Steigstrassle, was the beginning of the von Stolzenfels' strain in the

United States. Cosi had a terrific temperament, was extremely stable, loving, alert, and very protective of "her" property. In 1980 she was named No. 1 Top Producer by *Kennel Review* among Rottweiler bitches, and she qualified for the Medallion Rottweiler Club's Honor Roll as a producer. Additionally she earned the American Rottweiler Club Silver Award for her producing record. She died at age 12 years, leaving behind a legacy of many worthy champions and working titlists.

Cosi's famous offspring include Champion El Torro von Stolzenfels, who, from the open class, is a Group placing dog over specials; also Champion Etzel von Stolzenfels, campaigned in stern competition on the West Coast. Champion Erda von Stolzenfels, after a little practice in the puppy classes, finished her championship title with five majors in just seven shows. Three of Cosi's very special offspring are Champion Gandolf von Stolzenfels, Champion Imor von Stolzenfels, C.D., and Champion Czarina von Stolzenfels, C.D.

Gandolf finished with three majors, two of which were five-pointers. In 1979 he won the 6-to 9-month puppy class at both the Colonial and the Medallion Rottweiler Club Specialties. He then followed through in 1979 with first in Sweepstakes at the Colonial which he followed up by taking Winners Dog, the latter from the American-bred Class under renowned German judge and breed warden, Heinz Eberz. Gandolf was sired by top winning Champion Centurians Che von der Barr owned by Joe and Donnal Hedl of Chicago.

Imor, also a Che son, finished his championship in a hurry with four majors, three of which were for five points. He also went from the classes to Best of Breed while competing for his title. He, too, has sired champions and obedience titled dogs, including Champion Quaesar von Stolzenfels, a multiple Group placing dog from the open class while working for his title.

Champion Czarina von Stolzenfels, C.D., is the Cosi offspring in whom the Ellmans take most pride. This outstanding homebred bitch is a prototype of the breed. She was sired by Champion Kavon Mr. Murphy, American and Canadian C.D., and a *Dog World Award* winner in obedience. Already as a puppy her quality was obvious, and, owner-handled except for her final points, she piled up an impressive assortment of honors. Twice consecutively she went Best of Opposite Sex at the prestigious Detroit Kennel Club Show, first under well-known international breeder judge Mrs. Bernard Freeman, and the following year under the equally highly esteemed breeder judge Mrs. Barbara Hoard Dillon of Panamint. Additionally she was Best of Opposite Sex two years consecutively at the Medallion Rottweiler Club Specialties. Twice she made the "Ten Best Awards" of the American Rottweiler Club, first in 1978 and again in 1979. Very nice going for a bitch campaigned so sparingly!

Czarina is qualified for the American Rottweiler Club Hall of Fame. Presently her son, Maxwell von Stolzenfels, has been owner handled to three majors, finishing with a fourth in tough competition.

Returning to Cosi and her progeny, one must pause to pay tribute to Ikon, U.D.T., owned by tracking judge Ron Greenberg of Oklahoma City; and Centa, American and Canadian T.D., owned by Walter Wernig of Middleton, MA. Centa might just be the first Rottweiler bitch to have earned both tracking titles at barely two years of age.

Lilly-Marlene von Stolzenfels, owned by Doug Weil, earned her T.D. at the Golden State Specialty. Heiko von Stolzenfels, C.D., surprised both his breeders as well as his owner, Stan Horn of Battle Creek, Michigan, when he received his first leg after only about six weeks of training and finished in short order in three consecutive shows. Not bad for the total greenhorns in obedience!

Next, a new foundation bitch joined the Ellman kennel, procured for them by Friedrich Berger, the past president of ADRK. This was Gunda von Ingenhof, AD. Upon Mr. Berger's advice, Gunda was bred by the Ellmans to German Youth Best Dog, Adrian von Dammerwald, before being shipped to the United States. Adrian was a well-known working dog and producer, owned by Rottweiler judge Ingeborg Lyons. From this litter resulted the outstanding Champion Bandetta von Stolzenfels, U.F.T., owned by Gerald and Kay Watson of Pride, Louisiana. Unfortunately she died just prior to taking her

Schutzhund test. Her owners greatly regret having lost her before she had the opportunity to attain her Schutzhund title towards which they had worked so hard as she was truly a spirited Rottweiler. It was additional sadness that they had not at the time had a litter from her.

Bandetta's litter brother, Bruiser von Stolzenfels, was owned by Mr. Woodard of Chicago, the former president of the American Rottweiler Club. Bruiser earned his T.D. degree. Bandetta, like Czarina, qualified for the Medallion Rottweiler Club Hall of Fame.

The imported Gunda's second litter was sired by Champion Kavon Mr. Murphy, American and Canadian C.D. This produced two excellent champions, the male Champion Dolf Fuller von Stolzenfels, C.D., who finished his championship at age 18 months with four majors, always going on to Best of Winners or Best of Breed. His sister is Champion Darra Michaela von Stolzenfels, C.D., who also finished her title with ease. If Cosi was the most charming personality the Ellmans have known, Darra was by far the smartest Rottweiler they have ever come across. If Czarina was the Marilyn Monroe of Rottweilers in the Ellmans' book, Darra definitely to them was the Einstein of Rottweilerdom. Evelyn Ellman comments, "Darra's vocabulary comprehension was simply outstanding. One could, for example, tell her to go down to the garage and get Jack up here for lunch and off she would trot to the garage, some 400 feet from the house, and soon you would see Jack entering the house being led by Darra." Champion Darra, who finished championship at age 16 months, is also qualified for the Medallion Rottweiler Club Honor Roll.

For her first litter, Darra was bred to the Hedls' Champion Centurion Che von der Barr, producing Champion Kuger who was owned by Tim Mix of Battle Creek, Michigan; and Champion Kundri, C.D., owned by Mike Baker in Arizona. Kundri was trained for C.D. by Mike and obtained it in three consecutive shows at just over one year of age.

The bitch whom Evelyn Ellman describes as having really inherited Darra's "smarts" is Kava von Stolzenfels, C.D.X., owned by Kay

and Bob Willmarth of Kalamazoo, Michigan, and trained by Kay. At ten months of age Kava went High in Trial at a match in Elkhart, Indiana, and her C.D. title was gained quickly with many high scores. Like her owners, Kava is an avid football fan of the University of Michigan Wolverines, and often delights the fans by parading around at the games wearing her U of M muffler and baseball cap.

Kondor von Stolzenfels, owned by the O'Briens of Springfield, Illinois, took first in the puppy class under German judge Heinz Eberz at the 1979 Medallion Rottweiler Club Specialty. Kondor is pointed, has a VB, C.D., and T.D. title, and it is hoped will gain his C.D.X. and Schutzhund titles shortly.

Quincy von Stolzenfels is owned by Bob Edwards of South Carolina, and was one of only two Rottweilers who qualified for the T.D.X. at the 1984 Medallion Rottweiler Club Specialty. His litter brother, Champion Quaesar von Stolzenfels, has multi-Group placements from the open class. Nicholas von Stolzenfels, owned by avid tracking enthusiast Doug Weil, sports a T.D. title. There are several others as well with obedience titles.

Darra is qualified for the Medallion Rottweiler Club Honor Roll and a Bronze Production Award, which she earned from the American Rottweiler Club. Gunda, her dam, also earned these honors, and was retired early to enjoy the life of a house dog to age 12 years.

Recently Dr. Ellman returned from a visit to Germany with an eight-week-old puppy named Ute vom Mummler. This is a daughter from the last litter sired by International Champion Ives Eulenspiegel, SchH III, Gekoert EzA, bred by the well-known German judge and former head breed warden of ADRK, Marianne Bruns. Ute is co-owned with Kay and Gerald Watson of Pride, Louisiana, and quickly gained championship, C.D. and T.D. honors. She is now working on C.D.X. and U.D. titles. Her pups by Klubsieger Champion Mirko von Steinkopf, IPO, SchH I should soon make their debuts in the ring.

Definitely the brightest star on the von Stolzenfels' horizon is Champion Ursus von Stolzenfels, proudly owned and immediately loved by Mr. Haidar Beqaj and his wife, Erika, of Queens, New York. This young dog, ably handled by Walter Kuberski, has already done some exciting winning under extremely knowledgeable judges, so great things are hoped for in his future. Dr. Ellman is quick to say that she does, indeed, consider Bulli, as Ursus is called, the best dog ever bred to date at von Stolzenfels.

Bulli's litter sister, Ursula, is owned by Terry O'Krogley of Summit Hills, Pennsylvania.

Champion Tara von Stolzenfels, owned by the Albert Wackers of Tecumseh, Michigan, also deserves special mention, having taken a Best of Breed from the puppy class over well-known specials and finished by taking a major at the Detroit Kennel Club Show in 1984.

Even though the Ellmans refer to their Rottweiler ownership as a kennel, all their dogs always have lived with them in their home. Dr. Ellman feels that if you devote a good deal of time to your pups, giving them lots of attention and gentle discipline and teaching them what is and what is not acceptable, you will find that having as many as eight Rottweilers in your home at one time is not much more work than owning one who is spoiled.

Von Walber's

Von Walber's Rottweilers at Dexter, Michigan, are owned by Sue Wales and her son Robert Barber, who have been raising the breed since 1982. Their first Rottie was acquired in July 1978, Gunda von Brawn, or "Sara" to her friends. She was bred to Barbara Hooper's Champion Hintz Von Michelsberg, and now Sue Wales takes pride in three generations of their family. Champion Hintz is gone now, but "Sara" is still the well beloved house dog.

From the first breeding of "Sara" to Champion Hintz, Barbara Hooper took two. The dog puppy she chose as pick of litter turned out to be Champion Atom Smasher, who Sue Wales purchased back at age eight months along with some of the older dogs, including Champion Hintz and Chesara Dark Zenda. Her line now is based on Sara, Hintz and Zenda. Speaking of her enjoyment of them, Sue notes, "what wonderful old dogs Hintz

and Zenda were. Beautiful, intelligent, sweet and gentle." Having been warned when she acquired them that these dogs were guard trained and could be dangerous, she found that really all they needed was to be loved in order to be happy.

Well-known professional handler Jim Berger showed Atom Smasher to his championship which was completed at two years old. Then Bob has been showing some of the puppies. Sue comments on the fun it has been temperament testing the last few litters, and how they have come through with flying colors.

Champion Hintz Von Michelsberg became a Top Producer. Chesara Dark Zenda has five champion offspring with another almost finished. Sara will probably be a Top Producer based on her large litters of much quality.

Waxel's

Waxel's Rottweilers are at Irmo, South Carolina, where they are owned by Dr. and Mrs. Richard Wayburn.

The Wayburns have had Rottweilers since about 1974, having prior to that been Boxer breeders for more than 25 years. When the last of their Boxers died, the Wayburns were unable to get the one they really wanted; and so decided that, rather than settle for second choice they switch to another breed. The Rottweiler attracted them as they had always enjoyed living with dogs of working breed temperament, plus the Rotties had the extra appeal of not requiring ear cropping. And so Ms. Franchinstein, C.D.X. joined the family. "Franchi" quickly made a name for herself as the "tree climbing Rottweiler"—from whom no squirrel was safe! She quickly became very, very special to her owners, whom I am sure never have for one moment regretted their change of breed.

When Franchi was a year old. the Wayburns acquired their first Rottie dog who became Champion Rodsden's Adam b Brabant. Also a delightful bitch they were able to breed twice, Champion Wakefield Donka C.D. Their present bitch, Champion Luna vom Stuffelkopf, is a German import who came to the Wayburns at age eight months.

Luna had three litters. At the American Rottweiler Club Specialty in May 1985 one of

CAPTIONS FOR PLATES 65-80:

Plate 65
Ch. Artus vom Adelshof, SchH. III, noted winner, owned by Alan P. Kruse, Howell, Mich.

Plate 66
1. A lovely photo of the great Fetz vom Oelberg owned by Paul and Norma Harris of Kulhwald Kennels, Florida. Photo courtesy of Mrs. Dorit S. Rogers, Bergluft Kennels.

2. Ch. Donnaj Vt. Yankee of Paulus, C.D.X., TT with two of his sons, Ch. Donnaj Crusader *(center)* and Ch. Donnaj Eagle. Jan Marshall, Donnaj Kennels, Woodstock, Vt., is the owner of this imposing trio.

3. Ch. Kokas K's Degen von Burga, C.D., T.D. (April 4, 1973— September 10, 1982) owned by Mary and Dorothy Stringer, Hidden Valley, Burlington, N.J.

4. Ch. Doroh's Janus Erdelied, C.D., multiple Best of Breed and Group placing son of Am. and Can. Ch. Rodsden's Elko Kastanienbaum, C.D.X., T.D. ex Ch. Doroh's Grand Escapade. Breeder, Dorothy Wade. Owned and handled by Surely Rawlings, Coral Gables, Fla.

5. A von Stolzenfels puppy, brother to Ch. Holly's Pimora von Stolzenfels, C.D. Owned by Dr. Evelyn M. Ellman, Augusta, Mich.

6. Ch. Ute vom Mummler, C.D., T.D., outstanding Rottweiler owned by Jack P. and Dr. Evelyn Ellman and Gerald and Kay Watson, Pride, La.

Plate 67
1. Ch. Green Mts. Flora, handled by Bill Burrell at K.C. of Northern N.J. in 1982 for owner Frank Fiorella, Little Flower Rottweilers, Boxford, Mass.

2. Catsa vom Loisachtal, imported daughter of BSG Neno vom Schloss Rietheim, winning Best of Breed from the classes. Owned by von Morgen Carroll Rottweilers, Ontario, Calif.

3. Am. and Can. Ch. Tramonte's Baby Face Nelson taking Best of Winners at Dayton K.C. in 1979. Owned by Jack S. Tramonte, Akron, Ohio.

4. Ch. Srigo's Viking Spirit, by Ch. Panamint Seneca Chief ex Srigo's Honeybun, finished in six shows and was Best of Breed at Westminster Kennel Club, plus numerous Group placements. Also Best of Breed at the Colonial Rottweiler Specialty under Barbara Dillon and at Baltimore County K.C. under Germany's Head Breed Warden, Frederick Berger. Felicia Luburich, Srigo Rottweilers, East Brunswick, N.J.

5. Brimstone's Baron Von Otto, TT, C.D., VB, SchH 1, is the star of the Colonial Rottweiler Club video "The Danish Mental Test." Owned by Windwalker Kennels, James and Roxanna McGovern, Port Crane, N.Y.

6. Am. and Can. Ch. Fritz vom Schyder Haus owned by Edith Alphin, Altar Kennels, Fayetteville, N.C.

7. Ch. Srigo's Billet Doux taking Winners Bitch at Wilmington K.C. in 1978. Owner-handled by Felicia Luburich.

8. Am. and Can. Ch. Hasso Vom Steigstrassle, C.D., finishing his Canadian championship in 1984. Dick McKenny handling for owner Michael R. Helmann, Arlington Heights, Ill.

Plate 68
1. Seren's Chorus of Caesar taking Winners Dog at age six and a half months was bred by Peter and Marilyn Piusz and is owned by Klaus and Erika Beckman, the latter handling.

2. Ch. Donar v d Hoeve Cor Unum, C.D. Imported from Holland, this dog has become a famous winner and sire. Owned by Powderhorn/Wencrest Rottweilers, Hollywood, Calif.

3. Ch. Doroh's Janus Erdelied, C.D. is the winner of multiple Bests of Breed and Group placements. Owned and handled by Surely Rawlings, Coral Gables, Fla.

4. Ch. Tula's A Golden Nugget taking Best of Opposite Sex at Beverly Hills in 1985. Handled by Mike Shea for Tula Demas, San Bernardino, Calif.

Plate 69
1. Ch. Daverick's Albert V Hasenkamp gaining points towards the title at Westbury in 1983. From Daverick Rottweilers' three-champion "A" litter, owned by G. George Rogers and Richard and Ricki Rogers Gordon, Cinnaminson, N.J.

2. Ch. Donnaj Herr I Am, C.D., TT, in August 1982. By Ch. Donnaj Vt. Yankee of Paulus, C.D.X., TT ex Landry's Fraulein v Kristian, he is currently owned by Jan Marshall and Bob Hogan.

3. Ch. Castor von Palisaden winning Best of Breed at South County in 1984. Robert S. Forsyth, judge. Kathleen Kilcoyne handling for owner Glenn Goreski, Dschungel Rottweilers, Wallington, N.J. Castor went on to win the Working Group that day.

4. Rowehaus A. Erwin Rommel, by Ch. Adi von der Lowenau ex Ada vom Platz, was born September 14, 1980, bred by Timothy Platz. Pictured with handler, Sidney Lamont, taking Best of Winners at Hockamock K.C., 1985, for owner Douglas K. Loving, Trezilians Rottweilers, Richmond, Va.

5. Cujo Dustief v Raugust, by Hans Hissong v Raugust ex Bear Are Wishful Thought, born April 23, 1984, bred by Donald Beals. Ron and Charles Carter, owners, Mahogany, Honolulu, Hawaii.

6. Ch. Baron Elko von Dealcrest finishing his title at Northeastern Indiana Kennel Club in Feb. 1985 by taking Best of Winners. By Am. and Can. Ch. Rodsden's Elko Kastanienbaum, C.D.X., T.D., Canadian C.D. ex Ch. Michelob von Appleget. Owned by Larry and Alice Lee, Franklin, Ind.

Plate 70
1. Ch. Pandemonium's Balzac v Bautzlen, TT, and Ch. Pandemonium's Ciastus, C.D., TT, "Smooch" and "Cisco" *(right to left)* here are winning Best Working Dog Brace at Eastern Dog Club, December 1981. Valerie J. Cade, owner, Pandemonium Rotties, Goldens Bridge, N.Y.

2. Ch. Brash Baer von Pioneer, C.D. and Ch. Pioneer's Brute Force, C.D. One of the few Rottweiler Braces to have won Best Brace in Show, handled to this win at North Shore Kennel Club by co-owner Ted Galotti. Bred by Pioneer Kennels, Virginia Aceti and Sheryl Hedrick. Owned by Ted and Kandy Galotti and Sheryl Hedrick.

3. Ch. X-Thedora von Gruenerwald taking Best of Winners at the Westminster Kennel Club in 1981. Judge, Kenneth Peterson. Owner, Dorothea Gruenerwald, Colorado Springs, Col.

4. Noblehaus Behexen, TT, gaining points towards championship at Windham County, November 1984. Mark and Patricia Schwartz, owners, West Nyack, N.Y.

5. Srigo's Joy To The World at the Colonial Rottweiler Club Specialty May 1979. Owner-handled by Felicia M. Luburich, East Brunswick, N.J. One of the many outstanding Rotties who helped make this breeder and this kennel so famous.

6. Ch. Srigo's Incredible Is The Word, magnificent littermate to

Ch. Srigo's Imitation of Life and Srigo's I Am Invincible, the Srigo "I" litter by Ch. Kokas K's Degan v Burge, C.D., T.D., ex Ch. Srigo's Zoom v Kurtz, C.D.

Plate 71

1. Marlo's Sohn v Axel, C.D., T.D. winning Best of Breed at Golden Gate, February 1985. Owned by Terry and Penny Dodds, Novato, Calif. Breeders, Robert and Marlene Lore, Marlo's Rottweilers, Citrus Heights, Calif.

2. Ch. Srigo's Flim Flam Man at Staten Island in 1978. From Srigo Kennels. Felicia Luburich, East Brunswick, N.J.

3. Chism von Gruenerwald at 14 months of age. Owned by Dorothea Gruenerwald, Colorado Springs, Col.

4. Am. and Can. Ch. Srigo's Flight of The Eagle, Am. and Can. C.D., winning the breed under Mrs. Margaret Walton of Lyn Mar Acres fame. Owned by Arthur J. Rihel, Butler, Pa.

Plate 72

1. Koolau's Heavenly Angel owned by Thomas C. Furtado, Hawaii. She is a daughter of the two Australian imports, Heatherglen Amazon and Heatherglen Ecstacy. Pictured taking Best of Opposite Sex in 1982.

2. Ch. Radio Ranch's Circuit Breaker, TT, going Best of Breed from the Open Class at Schooley's Mountain K.C. 1982, owner-handled by Betty Walker, Centereach, N.Y.

3. Am. and Can. Ch. Groll vom Haus Schottroy, Am. and Can. C.D., born in 1975. Pictured at 22 months. Bred by Theo Oymann, West Germany. Owned by Mrs. Bernard Freeman, Freeger Kennels, New York, N.Y.

4. Ch. Dann v Arktus, C.D. in 1982, age eight years. Owned by Judith H. Hassed, Colorado Springs, Col.

5. Ch. Robil Marta von Donnaj, by Am. and Can. Ch. Donnaj Vt. Yankee of Paulus, C.D.X., TT ex Donnaj Touch of Class, is the foundation bitch at Pioneer Kennels. An American Rottweiler Club Producer of Merit, and dam of Pioneer's highly successful "B" litter which includes the first all-breed Best in Show Rottie bitch. Handled by Bill Burrell for owners Virginia Aceti and Sheryl Hedrick.

6. Ch. Dann v Arktos, C.D., by Ch. Nick v Silahopp ex Panamint Dagna v.d. Eichen. Owned by Judith Hassed, Colorado Springs, Col.

7. Ojuara's Boy I'm It von Altree, by Ch. Radio Ranch's Circuit Breaker, TT, ex Ch. Chaka vom Steinkopf, SchH. II. Bred by Betty and Gary Walker, handled by the latter for owners Al D'Anna and Betty and Gary Walker. Taking Best of Winners here at Brookhaven K.C. 1984; judge, Bob Forsyth.

8. Ch. Beabear Von Shadow, by Gibson's Rodsden Von Max ex Ana-Bear Von Stolzenfels, winning the Working Group at Mobile K.C., Sept. 1981. Owner, Donna LaQuatra, Beabear Rottweilers.

Plate 73

1. Am. and Can. Ch. Northwind's Danka, Am. and Can. C.D., 1970-1984. Top Producer in 1979. This magnificent bitch is the dam of 26 champions from only four breedings and is a member of the Medallion Rottweiler Club Hall of Fame as well as winner of the American Rottweiler Club Silver Production Award. By Rodsden's Kluge v d Harque ex Northwind's Tina. Owned by Patricia Hickman Clar, Northwind's Rottweilers, Ottawa, Ontario, Canada.

2. Ch. Simbergs Isis at seven months of age taking a four-point major under judge Lee Reasin at Alberta in 1985. By Am., Can., and Bda. Ch. Northwinds Ingo, C.D., SchH.1 ex Trollegen's Ulla, owned by M. Kanera and Art and Kim Forbes, Canada.

3. Ch. Zulu Talisman, handled by Gary MacDonald, taking Best of Winners under Robert S. Forsyth at K.C. of Buffalo, July 1984. Owner, Elizabeth Miller, Glenmiller Farms, Milverton, Ontario, Canada.

4. Am. Ch. Jessnic Freundlich Iza Rott, by Northwind's Kaiser of Mallam ex Freundlich Nice Gipsy, owned by Pierre and Carole Charbonneau, St. Colomban, Quebec, Canada. Here winning Best Puppy in Group, July 1984.

5. Carado's Satin Sidney taking Winners Bitch en route to her title at Monroe K.C. in 1984. Bred, owned, and handled by Carol Kravets, Carado, Windsor, Ontario.

6. Am. and Can. Ch. Ero von der Mauth, Am. and Can. C.D., TT, 1974-1981, owned by Patricia Hickman Clark.

Plate 74

1. *From left to right,* at nine months, Ch. Zulu Talisman handled by Liz Miller. Ch. Zulu Magic, handled by Jennifer McAuley. Judge, Mr. M. Thorton. Zulu Rottweilers are owned by Elizabeth Miller, Milverton, Ontario, Canada.

2. Can. Ch. Heamac Illo's Baxle, C.D. at age five and a half years in Oct. 1984. In limited showing that year he won six Bests of Breed in Ontario and eight qualifying scores in eight obedience trials. Owner-handled by Mrs. Helen MacPherson, London, Ontario.

3. Gamecard's Ninette, a top winning Canadian bitch who went Best of Breed or Best of Opposite Sex at the Canadian National Specialty three out of four times shown. The only year she didn't win, it was her daughter who beat her. Ninette is owned by Andrea Miles, Hawaii.

4. "Who's that coming?" would seem to be what Abba Gale and Ch. Carado's Mighty Quinn are wondering in this snapshot. Owned by Robert and Peggy Cojocar, Windsor, Ontario.

5. *Left to right:* the Rotties are Can. and Am. Ch. Royson's Diana Glenmiller, handled by Lorry Ross; Can. Ch. Zulu Magic, handled by Liz Miller; and Can. and Am. Ch. Zulu Rockman, handled by Gary MacDonald. Pictured at the Canadian Rottweiler Club Specialty, November 1983. Judge, *far right,* Joan Klem.

6. Helen MacPherson with her handsome Rottie brace at the Thousand Islands Kennel Club Dog Show in 1982. The dogs are Can. Ch. Heamac Illo's Baxle and Can. Ch. Heamac Amy's Brandy. Their wins that day included Best of Breed, Best of Opposite Sex, and Best Brace, truly a clean sweep. The MacPhersons own Heamac Kennels, London, Ontario.

Plate 75

1. Ch. Frolickin Black Hawk, C.D.X., T.T., by Ch. Panamint Nobel v Falkenberg, C.D. ex Ch. Uschi von Haus Henseler, is one of the handsome Rottweilers owned by Pierre and Carole Charbonneau, St. Colomban, Quebec, Canada.

2. *Left to right:* Can. and Am. Ch. Zulu Rockman, Can. and Am. Ch. Royson's Diana Glenmiller, Can. Ch. Talisman (has 2 U.S. majors), Can. Ch. Zulu's Magic (pointed in U.S.). Impressive littermates with their dam, owned by Elizabeth Miller, Milverton, Ontario, Canada.

3. Am. and Can. Ch. Carado's Reaper v Tannenwald, T.T., finishing title at age fifteen months. Bred, owned, and handled by Carol Kravets, Carado Kennels, Windsor, Ontario.

4. Majorhausen's Ever Magic, C.D. at age two years is pointed towards the championship title. Owned by Dr. and Mrs. Tim Steinmetz, Madison, Wis. Bred by Jacques and Pat Major, Canada.

5. Can. and Am. Zulu Rockman *(left)* and Ch. Zulu Talisman, two of Elizabeth Miller's handsome Zulu Rottweilers.

6. Moran Kralicky Sneznik, imported from Czechoslovakia in 1977, pictured at age 22 months. Owned by Marie Kanera, Simeberg Rottweilers, Langley, B.C., Canada.

Plate 76

1. Can. Ch. Simebergs Czarina, by Am. and Can. Ch. Kiros vom Lunsberg ex Can. Ch. Trollegens Gundi, is owned by Marie Kanera, Simeberg Rottweilers, Langley, B.C., Canada.

2. Ch. Majorhausen's Empress Sabrina, TT, homebred from the Majorhausen Rottweilers, Gloucester, Ontario, Canada. A granddaughter of Ch. Radio Ranch's Axel von Notara, being by Am. Ch. Radio Ranch's Xtra Special ex Can. Ch. Northwind's Juno, C.D.X., SchH I, TT.

3. Simebergs Fagan, by Am. and Can. Ch. Trollegens Benjamin ex Am. and Can. Ch. Cito von Simeberg, owned by D. Lory and W. Slonowski, has nine points towards her Canadian championship as we write.

4. Can. Ch. Simebergs Fame and Fortune, by Am. and Can. Ch. Trollegens Benjamin ex Am. and Can. Ch. Cita von Simeberg, is owned by John Foster, Canada. Here taking Best of Winners at age seven months.

5. Am. and Can. Ch. Cita von Simeberg was the No. 1 Rottweiler female in Canada in 1982. By Ch. Kiros vom Lunsberg ex Can. Ch. Trollegens Gundi, C.D. Owned by Marie Kanera, Simeberg Rottweilers.

6. Trollegen's Ulla is one of the outstanding Rottie bitches owned by Marie Kanera.

Plate 77

1. Can. Ch. Northwind's Icon, one of the truly great Rottweilers from Northwind's Kennels, Patricia Hickman Clark. By Igor von Schauer ex Northwind's Danka. Owned by H. and S. Stegmeyer, Ottawa, Ontario, Canada.

2. Ch. Majorhausen's Dynasty, TT, by Am. Ch. Bethel Farm's Apollo ex Can. Ch. Northwind's Juno, C.D.X., SchH.1, TT, is owned by Mr. and Mrs. Wolfgang Floch and Susan J. Suwinski, Cosmos Kennels, Oakville, Ontario, Canada.

3. Ch. Janlyn's Big Mark at about five months of age. Owned by Janlynn Rottweilers, Mr. and Mrs. D.G. Flury, Saskatoon, Sask., Canada.

4. LaVerne MacPherson on lines. Can. Ch. Heamac Amy's Bandy doing what she loved. And Pierre and Joe. Rotties rode on the wagon from 1979 until the MacPhersons' last team in 1983. Yes, Pierre and Joe are pigs. The MacPhersons trained four teams (12 pigs) with always one extra for spare. A team lasted for two summers before growing too large. Heamac Rottweilers, London, Ontario, Canada.

5. Freundlich Satan Beau Buck, C.D., T.T., by Ch. Frolickin Black Hawk, C.D.X., T.T. ex Ch. and OTCH Piasa Abbe v Karman, U.D., T.T., owned by Freundlich Kennel, Pierre and Carole Charbonneau, St. Colomban, Quebec, Canada.

6. Can. Ch. Simebergs Gangster, by Am. and Can. Ch. Trollegens Frodo ex Can. Ch. Simebars Czarina, here is winning

Best Puppy in Show at two months' age. Owned by Bryloukis Rottweilers, Canada.

Plate 78

1. Ch. Janlynn's Bon Adonis, C.D. at age 6½ years. Owned by Janlynn Rottweilers, Saskatoon, Sas., Canada.

2. Pandemonium's Kody at age five months. Handsome "young hopeful" owned by Valerie J. Cade, Goldens Bridge, N.Y.

3. Ch. Simebergs Fame and Fortune at age 18 months. By Am. and Can. Ch. Trollegens Benjamin ex Am. and Can. Ch. Cita von Simeberg. Owner, Marie Kanera, Langley, B.C., Canada.

4. Am. and Can. Ch. Zulu Rockman, owned by Elizabeth Miller, Zulu Kennels, Milverton, Ontario, Canada.

5. A lovely head-study of Ch. Northwind's Tina, 1963-1970, by Darvis vom Weyershof ex Katharina's Adorn of Townview. Owned by Patricia Hickman Clark, Northwind's Rottweilers, Ottawa, Ontario, Canada.

6. Ch. Majorhausen's Countess Cheska, C.D., T.D.X. at age three and a half years in September 1984 with Majorhausen's Famous Pagan, C.D., now pointed at age four months. Owned by Mrs. Minette Barlaug, Prince George, B.C., Canada.

7. Powderhorn's Black Maria, one of the bitches at Powderhorn/Wencrest Rottweilers owned by Mrs. Clara S. Hurley and Michael S. Grossman, Hollywood, Calif.

8. Seven-week-old future Ch. Sunnysides Royal von Meadow grew up to become 1983 No. 6 Rottweiler Bitch in the U.S. and 1984 No. 1 Rottweiler Bitch here. Bred and owned by Donna M. Wormser, Ocala, Fla.

Plate 79

1. Can. and Am. Ch. Royson's Diana Glenmiller. Photo courtesy of Elizabeth Miller, Milverton, Ontario, Canada.

2. Carado's Indiana Jones, age 14 months, went to visit Santa Claus and can't wait for Christmas Day. Owner, Donna Plattner, St. Louis, Mo.

3. Best Brood Bitch at the Canadian National Specialty in 1982 under judge Joan Klem. Can. Ch. Trollegens Gundi with daughters Am. and Can. Ch. Cita von Simeberg, Am. Ch. Simebergs Domino, and Can. Ch. Simebergs Czarina. Owned by Marie Kanera, Langley, B.C., Canada. Mrs. Joan Klem, judge.

Plate 80

1. Aust. Ch. Rotvel Trooper smiles for the camera. Owned by Capt. Craig Bryan, Randwick, N.S.W., Australia.

2. Aust. Ch. Rottser Valeda, C.D. is by Aust. Ch. Top Dog Adam, C.D. ex The Attila Honour, C.D.X. (U.K. import). Mr. S. Lodge, owner, Miller, N.S.W., Australia.

3. Aust. Ch. Rotvel Trooper, owned by Captain C. Bryan, Randwick, N.S.W., Australia.

PLATE 65

Booth

PLATE 66

PLATE 67

1

PLATE 68

PLATE 69

BEST OF
WINNERS
WESTMINSTER
KENNEL CLUB
1981
ASHBEY

WINNERS
WINDHAM COUNTY
KENNEL CLUB
1984
ASHBEY II

PLATE 70

GROUP
FIRST
EASTERN
DOG CLUB
1981
ASHBEY

NORTH SHORE K.C.
BEST IN SHOW

SWEEPSTAKES
TRENTON
KENNEL CLUB
MAY 1979
ASHBEY

SWEEPSTAKES
TRENTON
KENNEL CLUB
MAY 1979
ASHBEY

PLATE 71

PLATE 72

PLATE 73

PLATE 74

1

2

3

4

5

6

PLATE 75

PLATE 76

1

PLATE 77

2

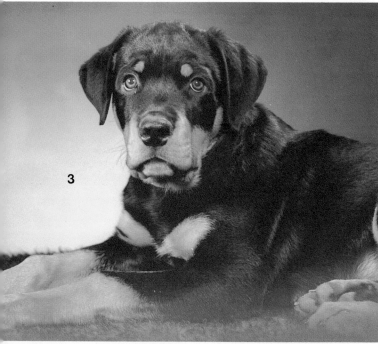

3

4

6

5

PLATE 78

PLATE 79

PLATE 80

her puppies, sired by Mirko, was the Sweepstakes winner, Waxel's Excalibur von Mirko, sired by Mirko and owned by George and Judy Wood of Missouri.

Champion Mirko vom Steinkopf, C.D., SchHIII, IPO III, FH started his claim to fame in Germany. He passed his Zuchtaglikeitspruffen (suitability for breeding test) but left Germany before attempting the Korung (highest court of breeding suitability), which, as Mrs. Wayburn comments, "Assuredly he would have passed." He was judged the ADRK Klubsieger in September 1983 before he was three years of age, and he had already earned every possible working title, as listed following his name.

The Wayburns brought Mirko to the United States before his third birthday. On his arrival here, he quickly became an American Champion in five consecutive shows, going Best of Winners four times and Best of Breed on the fifth, at Baltimore County under a famous Finnish judge, going on to take a Group placement that day.

Since then Mirko has had numerous breed wins and Group placements, along the way gaining his C.D. in three straight trials and becoming a Puerto Rican Champion as well as earning his Championship of the Americas. Mirko has been used sparingly at stud but the quality of his puppies is outstanding as will be noted soon since they are rapidly reaching show age. Jeffrey Brucker handled Mirko in conformation; owner trained and handled in obedience, where he will soon start work on his C.D.X. degree.

At the Colonial Rottweiler Club Specialty in conjunction with Bucks County Kennel Club all-breed Dog Show in May 1985, Mirko really hit it big where prestigious winning is concerned. First by taking Best of Breed in this highly prestigious Specialty Show under Mrs. Muriel Freeman, then proceeded to take a strong Working Group under judge Adrian Aquirre and on to Best in Show all breeds under William L. Kendrick. This occasion marked the biggest all-breed Best in Show numerically ever won by a Rottweiler; and the first time that a Rottie had won his breed Specialty then gone onto Best in Show at the host club event. Surely an occasion to remember and cherish!

Welkerhaus

Welkerhaus Kennels started back in 1974 when Rita Welker, of Oak Ridge, North Carolina, purchased her first of the breed, little dreaming then the impact this puppy would have on her life and on future Rottweilers. This puppy grew up to become Champion Welkerhaus' Rommel, U.D., whose achievements came to include championship at 12 months' age, C.D. degree at 14 months, C.D.X. at 20 months, and Utility Dog five months after that. A Top Producer of 17 champions and 21 obedience titled offspring, he was himself the Top Obedience Rottweiler for 1976 and 1977.

Rommel no longer is with Rita Welker, having died in August 1983 at the age of nine years. But his children, grandchildren, and great-grandchildren are contributing much to this magnificent breed. Sired by Circle ML's Aster (Champion Merrymoore's Iron Duke ex Champion Merrymoore's Gay Spirit) from Wonnemund (Champion Dux vom Hungerbuhl, Sch.H I ex Rodsden's Erde vom Dahl), Rommel in every way lived up to the highest Rottweiler tradition.

The foundation bitch at Welkerhaus was Champion Von Gailingen's Cia, C.D., multi-Best of Breed and Group winner, by Champion Igor von Schauer (Champion Ferdinand v Dachsweil—Champion Erika von Schauer) ex Champion Anka von Gailingen (Champion Dux vom Hungerbuhl, SchH I ex Champion Natascha v Hohenreissach, C.D.). Cia completed her title in three short months, then, her first time out as a special, she went Best of Breed over four top winning specials at only 18 months of age. In 1978 she was No. 3 conformation bitch among Rottweilers in the United States. Her C.D. was also completed in short order in three consecutive trials.

Bred to Rommel for three litters, this combination produced Champion Welkerhaus' Anna von Rommel, C.D., who finished at 15 months owner-handled, won three legs in three consecutive trials, always in the ribbons, to earn her C.D.; Champion Welkerhaus' Amorous Rommel, C.D., who finished at 27 months and is owned by Lyndon and Sue Clark, Greensboro, N.C.; Champion Welkerhaus' Argis von Rommel, C.D., who finished championship at 24 months with two

5-point majors along the way and three obedience legs in three trials, owned by Barry and Linda Collins, Winston-Salem, North Carolina; Champion Welkerhaus' Ace von Rommel, finished with four majors at 15 months and two legs on his C.D., owned by Debbie E. Moss, Archdale, North Carolina; Champion Welkerhaus' Shockoe Ada, finished with four majors, owner, Thomas Motley, Chatham, Virginia; and Welkerhaus' Andar von Rommel, C.D., three legs in three consecutive trials, always in the ribbons, owned by Debbie Biggers, Waxhaw, North Carolina. The above are all from the "A" litter.

The "B" litter included Champion Welkerhaus' Boaz v Bar Ken, C.D., who finished his C.D. at 19 months and his championship at 22 months, owned by Kenneth Dellinger, Nebo, North Carolina; Champion Welkerhaus' Bold Otto, C.D., another to finish both conformation title and obedience degree with ease, owned by Paul and Joyce Bryan, Pittsburgh, North Carolina; and Welkerhaus' Bit-O-Honey, C.D., owned by Nancy Kehrberg and Rita Welker, Tobaccoville, North Carolina, as well as Welkerhaus' Bethany V. Helken, C.D. owned by Vallery Hellmann and Rita Welker, Rostown, Texas and Welkerhaus' Bamf, C.D. owned by Eileen Johnson, Middlesex, North Carolina and Welkerhaus' Bianca of Tulakes owned by C. Laird.

Then from the "D" litter came Champion Welkerhaus' Dreams of Cia, C.D. and Champion Welkerhaus' Dream Come True, as well as the obedience "stars," Welkerhaus' In Diamonds, C.D.X., T.D., Welkerhaus' Drummer Boy, C.D., and Welkerhaus' Dietrich V Clark, C.D.

Cia also produced a litter by Champion Concord's Shar, C.D., which included both conformation and obedience winners.

Wilderness

Wilderness Rottweilers are located at Anchorage, Alaska, where they are owned by Joann H. Turner. The kennel was started during the late 1970's when Joann purchased her first of the breed, a bitch named Lady Ruger, selecting her as a protection dog as she then lived alone in a cabin in northern California. Lady Ruger came to Alaska with her owner, and breezed through her C.D. degree. The breeders she contacted educated Joann about OFA, and Lady Ruger received an "excellent" as did her sire.

The first litter bred at Wilderness was sired by American and Canadian Champion Hasserways Rommel Victor from Lady Ruger. This produced just one female, who was named Chena, and six males. Joann kept the female, who won two majors in Alaska from the puppy classes, then was sent to California to finish as her owner was anxious to "see if she could win in better competition."

Ruger's second litter was born in 1984, sired by Champion Starkheim Duf Morgan Carroll. Several of the four male and five female puppies are looking especially promising.

Meanwhile, Chena's brother, Brand, finished with three 5-point majors to become a champion and had a Group 3rd award along the way. Another brother has ten points, and Kaiser, a third, will be starting his show career during 1985. The Ruger-Rommel litter was a splendid one, even though pedigree-wise it was an "out" breeding. Ruger has her C.D.X. now, too.

In the spring of 1985, Chena was bred to Champion Rodsden's Tristan v Forstwald, C.D., T.D.; the pups are due as we are writing. Joann Turner looked for a long time in her selection of Tristan, who corrects Chena's minor faults, has a solid pedigree, and is a show and working dog.

In 1983 Wilderness Kennel was expanded with the addition of a well-bred male from the East Coast, Xanadu's Bronson Jos v Altar, now with five points; also a bitch from the best obedience Rottweiler of all time bred to a well-known Champion and C.D.X. dog— Way-Mar's Brooks Dawg v Jos. She now has ten points and one C.D. leg. One other addition was a bitch puppy from Srigo Kennels by Champion Bronco von Raiderfels who is very promising at seven months, and is starting out on tracking.

Joann Turner's small Wilderness Kennel has been quite successful during 1984 in Alaska, and the two January shows were a sweep for the kennel, with dogs bred there taking all of the points, Best of Opposite Sex and Best of Breed both days. Joann comments, "I have been very lucky, but I also work on learning more, talking with leading breeders, reading, and most importantly educating the potential puppy buyers."

Wilhelmberg

Wilhelmberg Rottweilers are owned by Brenda C. Grigsby at Jasper, Tennessee. Foundation bitch here is Duchess of Highland Park, who put her owner off to a good start in the breed by producing a litter which included six American Champions and one Canadian Champion, which her owner believes to be a record for the breed.

Duchess and three of her daughters (by two different sires) form the background of the future breeding program at this kennel. The abovementioned litter from Duchess was sired by the late Champion Rodsden's Bruin von Hungerbuhl, C.D.X. The offspring of this litter include American and Canadian Champion O-Haus Master Von Ansel owned by Ruth and Harold O'Brien, Mt. Juliet, Tennessee; Champion Heather's Meadow V Ansel owned by Richard Verbosky, Franklin, Tennessee; Champion Camus Valley Hildagard V Kutz, owned by Dan and Debby Kutz, Springdale, Washington; Champion Pawkit's KD Von Ansel owned by Colleen Hackett, Spokane, Washington; Champion Schon Vormund Tier Heidi owned by Brenda Grigsby; and Champion Camus Valley Kaiser VD Kutz, owned by Debby and Dan Kutz, Springdale, Washington.

Named a Top Producer for both 1983 and 1984, Duchess has received the *Dog World Award of Merit* in the breeding division for 1984, and she has been nominated for the Medallion Rottweiler Club Honor Roll for her producing record.

Incidentally, Duchess' progeny also includes two working police dogs, one in Louisiana and one in Arkansas, plus two daughters in Tennessee ready to begin in the Schutzhund trials.

Brenda Grigsby has been involved with Rottweilers since about 1980, belongs to several of the breed Specialty Clubs, and is a strong supporter of the Medallion Rottweiler Club Code of Ethics.

Windwalker

Windwalker Rottweilers are owned by Roxanna and Jim McGovern of Port Crane, New York, who, although fairly new to Rottweilers, have a very solid background in the Dog Fancy as breeders of German Shorthaired Pointers, their breed in both conformation and field work for some 14 years.

Their first Rottweiler was Brimstone's Baron von Otto, C.D., VB, TT, SchH I, by Champion Chaka Vom Steinkopf, SchH II ex Champion Balalaika of Ho-Rued-Ho. "Otto" was obtained by the McGoverns as an eight-week-old puppy in 1982 and he was, basically, their introduction to the breed as well as their introduction to the sport of Schutzhund.

With the first year of Otto's life devoted to being a puppy and learning the basics of obedience, the next 18 months were devoted to acquiring several impressive titles. In October 1983, Otto passed the American Temperament Test, gaining his first title, "TT." His C.D. was completed in January 1984 with scores of 184½, 190 and 191. In June 1984 Otto travelled with Roxanna to the Medallion Rottweiler Club's first Schutzhund Trial, and earned his VB. A week later, he participated in the Danish Mental Test, conducted by Mr. Aage Christensen, President of the Danish Rottweiler Club and a Test Official in Denmark. A video was made of the entire proceedings, directed by George Chamberlain, and Mr. Christensen said of Otto, "he was an excellent example of how a Rottweiler should behave in this test"—which approximately one out of fifty dogs passes in Europe. Otto has the distinction, at the time of this writing, to be the only Rottweiler in the United States to have completed this test from start to finish.

In October 1984, Otto obtained his Schutzhund I degree at Niagara-On-The-Lake, with Highest Schutzhund I for the day he competed and then for the entire three-day trial. He had a rating of "pronounced courage" for his protection work. During 1985 he is working on adding the C.D.X. and Schutzhund II to his current degrees.

Von Bruka Jaguar was acquired by the McGoverns in November 1983. She is a daughter of Champion Eiko Vom Schwaiger Woppen,

C.D.X. from Bundy Vom Luckshof, whom the McGoverns co-own with Sue Suwinski, Brimstone Rottweilers. "Gretchen," as she is known, has two Reserves from the puppy class, but is now waiting for maturity before competing seriously for her championship. She is not just sitting idly by, however, as she is now ready to compete for her C.D. title.

Rodsden's Lindenwood Here, by Champion Gasto Vom Liebersbacherhof, SchH I C.D.X., TD ex Champion Lindenwood's Anaconda, C.D., came to Windwalker in September 1984 and is just now getting started at match shows and in obedience training.

Strongly believing that the basis of any good breeding program is an outstanding foundation bitch, the McGoverns arranged to lease Champion Rodsden's Heika v Forstwald from Linda and Bill Michels, Lindenwood Kennels, for their first litter. Heika is from the "winningest" breeding in the history of Rottweilers, which has to date produced 12 A.K.C. Champions and eight Specialty winners. She is currently in training for her Schutzhund I, and will be bred to Champion Mirko vom Steinkopf, SchH III, IPO III, FH, C.D., who is by Dingo vom Schwaiger Wappen, SchH III ex Esta vom Steinkopf, Schutzhund I during 1985.

Zornhaus

Zornhaus Rottweilers at Wilton Manors, Florida, are owned by Pamela Zorn Anderson, who is an excellent naturalist artist. She has been "in" Rottweilers since about the mid-1970's, and feels justifiable pride in her dogs and their accomplishments over this short period of time.

Her favorite Rottie is the lovely bitch Champion Katryn the Great Von Ursa who has had a very exciting career. "Katie" earned her C.D. title at 11 months of age with a 1st, 2nd and 3rd placement, her scores averaging 194 in these three shows. She achieved her C.D.X. and breed championship titles on the same day at the age of 18 months. "Katie" placed out of the ribbons only once in her show career, which included four times Best of Winners, twice Best of Opposite Sex, three

times Best of Breed, and a Group 3rd—each time over the males. The dam of three litters to date, "Katie" has chosen the timing of their arrival well. The first puppies were born on Thanksgiving, the second on New Years, and the third on the birthday of her owner's Mother. Pretty neat???

Champion Torburhop's Pattom Von Brawn is another splendid Rottweiler to be found at Zornhaus. Pamela Anderson is a great admirer of American and Canadian Champion Donnaj Vt. Yankee of Paulus, C.D.X., and is pleased at now being able to structure all of her present breedings on his pedigree, to help incorporate the qualities she particularly finds pleasing in the breed.

Rottweilers in Hawaii

The first Rottweiler of which we have heard in Hawaii was Rodsden's Kaiser von der Harque, from the Rodsden's famous "K von der Harque" litter. He was brought to Hawaii in the late 1960's, and then sold to the Brenners on the big Island (Hawaii). Kaiser was shown only twice, on one of which occasions he was Best of Breed and Group 2nd.

Until about 1980, most of the Rottweilers imported to Hawaii were of Australian breeding coming from the Mummerys' Heatherglen Kennel, as well as the Auslese and Rotvel Kennels. More recently there have been some American imports, these from Big Oaks, Bratiana, Donnaj, Goldenwest, Majorhausen, Rodsden, and Trollegens. In between these two periods there were some English imports from Pat Lanz's Borgvaale Kennels. As we understand it, prior to 1985 there were only two males and several bitches being shown there in the breed. Most of the activity has been with the conformation dogs; very few have been active in obedience. Peter Kamakawiwoole did import two from Borgvaale Kennels, putting a C.D. on one and a C.D.X. on the other. Richelle Uyeda of Richmark Rottweilers has two bitches, one from Peter Kamakawiwoole breeding of his two Borgvaale Rotties, this being Konia's Danica von Lanz, C.D., T.D.; the other an American import of Trollegen breeding, Ridgerunner's Rowdy Roma, C.D. Richelle titled both her dogs.

Jill Nakache owns the Rottweilers von Haiem at Kailua, all of her dogs having been imported from the mainland. They came there from as close as California and as far away as Georgia and Florida. Jill comments that so far there just is no real Rottweiler quality being bred in Hawaii, but several fanciers have joined her in working to establish a good gene pool there looking towards the future. She herself has several animals from several different bloodlines with which she is working, all good, yet the lines do overlap each other.

Jill's own first Rottweiler came from the Grass Valley Humane Society in California in 1980. Since age 14 she had been aware of Rottweilers, and wanting one as a pet; but somehow it took more than she could manage to convince her Mom to buy her an eight hundred dollar pet. Until that time she had always owned Dobies and German Shepherds; but she took this male from the pound, who was a coated Rottweiler, had him neutered, named him Saber, and placed him in a good home where he still is living happily.

The first bitch Jill imported from the mainland was Axelite von Meadow, a daughter of the great Champion Radio Ranch's Axel. Her dam and all four grandparents are, like Axel, OFA certified and Champion Top Producers.

At present Jill is greatly excited over a puppy bitch she has who is doing "just beautifully." She is Ronzwyler's Anka von Haiem, who was bred by Ron Fisher of Modesto. She is a daughter of Rodsden's Strawlane Zephyr (by Rodsden's Zarras von Brabant) from a heavily Bratiana line-bred dam. Anka came

into quarantine at 10½ weeks' age. She got out on June 7th, entered her first puppy match June 9th where she won her class, and started in tracking on June 10th at which she is showing tremendous aptitude. Truly a natural tracker who already obviously considers herself an old pro.

Then there is Jill's new puppy, Big Oaks Lasko von Haiem, who was bred by Cat Klass in Georgia. He is sired by the German import Champion Eiko vom Schwaiger Wappen, C.D.X., SchH.III, FH, OFA rated, ex Champion Beaverbrook Brenna von Fable, she a daughter of Champion Trollegen's Fable and Champion Rodsden's Amber vom Brabant.

Another puppy at this busy kennel is Big Oaks Kila von Haiem, sired by Champion Big Oaks Bogart von Brenna. And also there is a male from California who was sired by Rhomarks Paddington Bear ex Champion Marlo's Borgha da Bratiana.

No breed could possibly have a more enthusiastic fancier than Rottweilers have in Jill Nakache! She is the founder of Hawaii's first Rottweiler Club, known as the Hawaii Rottweiler Club, and anyone wishing more information on this organization may address her at 1068 Maunawili Road, Kailua, Hawaii, 96734.

Jill Nakache also belongs to the Western Rottweiler Owners Association, the Medallion Rottweiler Club, and has applications for membership pending in the American Rottweiler Club and the Colonial Rottweiler Club. She was only nine years old when she entered her first dog show.

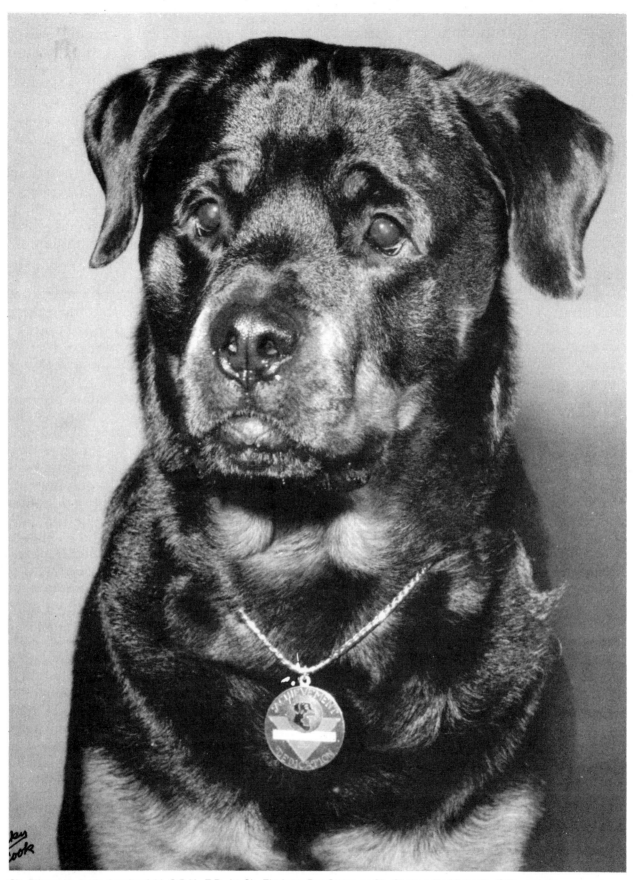

Ch. Rhomarks Axel v Lerchenfeld, C.D.X., T.D., by Ch. Elexi von Der Gaarn ex Ch. Chelsea De Michaele, C.D., wearing his American Rottweiler Club Achievement Dedication Medal in 1984. Axel's proud owners are Ken and Hildegard Griffin, Novato, California.

CHAPTER FOUR

Rottweiler Clubs in the United States

Colonial Rottweiler Specialty, May 1960. C. Ross Hamilton, judge, awards Best of Breed to Ch. Jaro vom Schleidenplatz, handled by John W. Houser for Charles McKelvy.

In the United States there are numerous Specialty Clubs devoted to Rottweilers, all of them doing a good job for the protection and well being of their breed. The one of greatest importance, since it is the Parent Club of the breed, is the American Rottweiler Club which came into being in 1971. There is a somewhat unique story here, for actually the Rottweiler Club of America was chartered by the American Kennel Club back in 1947-1948 to become Parent Club for Rottweilers. As you have read in an earlier chapter, this club was formed in California, was extremely active at the very beginning, then owing to a lack of interest and/or differences of opinion, ceased to exist—leaving Rottweilers temporarily without a Parent Club. At the American Kennel Club's suggestion, a new club for this purpose was formed. However, probably on the "once burned, twice cautious" theory, this undertaking progressed both slowly and methodically.

Then during the summer of 1971, delegates from the various local Rottweiler Clubs already established and functioning smoothly on the East Coast, the West Coast and in the Mid-West, held an informal meeting to discuss the formation of a new National or Parent Club for Rottweilers. The Constitution and By-Laws for the Club which had been recommended by the American Kennel Club were approved and charter memberships became open to interested individuals from all areas of the United States. In 1974, William Stahl, a long-time dedicated Rottie breeder and exhibitor, one of the delegates when formulating plans were made, and founder of the Colonial Rottweiler Club, was elected first President of the American Rottweiler Club which then consisted of 359 charter members.

Among its earliest projects was a Revision of the Breed Standard. Back in 1935 when the breed originally was approved for competition at A.K.C. dog shows, the Breed Standard in use at that period in Germany was partially adopted here for the breed, with one important difference; although over the years frequent revisions were made to their Standard in Germany, no such action was taken in the United States, due, undoubtedly, to the period in which no American Rottweiler Parent Club was functioning. Consequently there was much to be done in this area. Fanciers felt that the breed lacked sufficient definite specifications regarding size, correct gait, temperament, and, possibly most important of all, a listing of the most critical disqualifying faults for the guidance of judges and breeders attempting to evaluate and assess the ideal Rottweiler. It took five years and four revisions, from which a new Standard finally emerged in 1979, and as we are writing this book, work is just winding up on an Illustrated Standard which does a truly excellent job in helping interested parties learn how to correctly evaluate the breed.

The ARC lost no time in getting started on a program of Match Shows, earning the necessary qualifications to hold Specialty Shows. These Match Shows were held in various areas of the country, affording the members a better opportunity to become acquainted with one another and to enjoy participation in Club activities. Then, in the Spring of 1981, the first Independent Specialty of the American Rottweiler Club took place in the Boston, Massachusetts, area—a smashing success in every detail—and since has become an annual event. By the beginning of the 1980's, ARC membership numbered about 750, including members from all of the United States, Canada, Australia, Germany, France, Puerto Rico, Jamaica and El Salvador.

The American Rottweiler Club has earned this writer's deep respect for the excellent educational program it presents. First of all, there is the *Rottweiler Pictorial*, the idea for which was conceived by Mrs. Dorothea Gruenerwald when serving as President of the Club, 1975-1977. So great a success was this one, with its 325 pictures and three generation pedigrees of champion and obedience titleholders, that it was repeated with *Rottweiler Pictorial* No. 2 in 1978, this one featuring 400 or more pictures and pedigrees, plus a section devoted to Producers of Merit and Rottweilers no longer alive who had made major contributions. Then came the No. 3 volume, again by popular demand, again filled with invaluable information. And I understand that Volume No. 4 may well be in the offing for the near future.

The American Rottweiler Club issues a free pamphlet in return for a self-addressed and stamped legal size envelope which is filled with useful information for the prospective Rottie owner. This may be had upon request from Mrs. Doris Baldwin, P.O. Box 23741, Pleasant Hill, California 94523, who will also be glad to provide any additional information requested of her regarding this breed.

The American Rottweiler Club has formulated a Statement of Principles and Practices which is similar in some respects to a Code of Ethics, with the exception that it is not a mandatory Code.

Officers of the American Rottweiler Club at the time of writing are: President, Mrs. Catherine Thompson; Vice-President, Michael Conradt; Secretary, Sophie Dunn; Treasurer, Sandra Swearington. Directors are Jan Marshall, Dorothy Stringer, Marcia Tucker, Dorothea Gruenerwald, and Margareta McIntyre. Ann Maurer is editor of the *Pictorial*.

Another project of ARC is its bi-monthly newsletter, which has grown from a six-page edition to a 60-page or more volume of reference. It has at least twice won awards from the Dog Writers Association of America for excellence in the category of National Club Newsletter, Printed.

Medallion Rottweiler Club
One of the oldest active Rottweiler Specialty Clubs in the United States is the Medallion Rottweiler Club which is based in Illinois. The club was organized at a meeting on July 11, 1959 at which the following Charter Members were in attendance: Dr. and Mrs. James Alexander, Mr. and Mrs. P. Fitterer, Mr. and Mrs. Ludwig Gessner, Mr. Werner Gessner, Mr. and Mrs. Richard Klem, Mr. and Mrs. Franz Liebfried, Mr. and Mrs. Seymour Levine, Col. and Mrs. Leon Mandel, Mr. and Mrs. Perrin Rademacher, Mr. and Mrs. John Refieuna, Mr. and Mrs. Eugene Schoelkopf, and Mr. and Mrs. William Stark.

Medallion held its first Specialty Show in 1969. The Eleventh Annual Specialty Show, in 1979 was the third to have been held as an independent Specialty Show rather than in conjunction with an all-breed event. A very gala event for this club was the Tenth Annual Specialty which was celebrated with a three-day weekend consisting of a Judging Seminar on Friday, the Specialty and Annual Meeting and Dinner the second day, featuring the initial presentation of awards to those Rottweilers elected to the Hall of Fame and Honor Roll, and on Sunday an obedience demonstration.

It was the Medallion Rottweiler Club which, in 1979, introduced Rottweiler Futurity Stakes here in the United States.

Medallion supports with entries and trophies various all-breed events in the Mid-West area. The Club has published a Tenth Anniversary Book and a Twentieth Anniversary Book on these respective occasions, both very interesting and worthwhile. They also issue a bi-monthly newsletter and provide a "New Member Information Kit" which is sent to all new members and includes a membership card and list, Rottweiler Standard chart, AKC Standard, ADRK Standard and breeding rules, Medallion Rottweiler Club's Constitution and By-laws, Dictionary of Dog Terms, and Code of Ethics.

Colonial Rottweiler Club

The Colonial Rottweiler Club was founded in 1956, and held its first Specialty Show in 1959. In May 1980 it celebrated its 21st Specialty in conjunction with the Trenton Kennel Club event. In 1985 it held its 26th Annual Specialty, this time at Bucks County Kennel Club on May 4th.

Colonial also sponsors a very popular and high quality Sweepstakes.

Golden State Rottweiler Club

June 1962 saw the birth of California's Golden State Rottweiler Club, by year's end, the name having been officially adopted, with a total membership of 16.

Rottweilers were scarce in Southern California at this period, making it the goal of the "founding fathers" of this group to build an atmosphere of friendliness among all Rottweiler owners, at the same time working for promotion of a wider public interest and recognition of the breed. The early members were aware as well of the necessity of improving the available breeding stock and providing a source of mutual advice, support, and education not only to its members but to non-members as well. For this purpose the *Golden State Rottweiler Newsletter* was inaugurated, later renamed *The Guardian Newsletter Of The Golden State Rottweiler Club* which is now sent to hundreds of members and subscribers around the world.

Golden State's first Annual Specialty Show took place in 1969, and these shows have been held each year since that time. The previous year had seen adoption of a Club Policy regarding hip dysplasia, and in April 1969 a Code of Ethics was adopted—both for the purpose of helping to improve the physical soundness of the breed.

Among the members whose energies and interest have contributed to Golden State's success in reaching fulfillment of its goals are Mrs. Clara Hurley, who developed a highly useful genetic tool known as the "Biodex" which makes available to breeders information pertinent to the hip dysplasia background of the breeding stock with which they may be working, an invaluable source of knowledge to those breeders who are deeply concerned over this serious problem.

Another hard working member of Golden State is Mrs. Margareta McIntyre, known throughout the Rottweiler world as a judge of great excellence. This is a Club which has served the Rottweiler well in the past and continues to do so at present.

Western Rottweiler Club

Another splendid organization on the Pacific Coast devoted to this breed is the Western Rottweiler Owners, which was founded in October 1962 by a group which included Erna Pinkerton, President; Dorothy Cholet, Corresponding Secretary; Margaret Perry, Recording Secretary; Robert Cholet, Treasurer; Ken Hoard, News Editor; Wright Huntly, Assistant Editor; and Jack Dumas, Membership Chairman.

Western Rottweiler owners work hard to promote their goal of enjoyment, improvement and preservation of the Rottweiler breed. Club President Margaret Teague and Recording Secretary Lucy Ang in 1979 published a booklet compiled by them, *"On Owning A Rottweiler,"* which has been a great success and has done its work well towards the education goal.

Western Rottweiler Owners support the breed entry at the Annual Golden Gate Kennel Club Show in February.

Dogwood Rottweiler Club

One of the newer Rottweiler Clubs is the Dogwood Rottweiler Club in the Atlanta, Georgia area. A very busy organization, this one, with a full program of Working Group matches, all-breed matches, show training classes, and all-breed obedience classes. The feeling among Dogwood members is that their activities should welcome the inclusion of all breeds due to the demand for quality dog related programs in the Atlanta area. The Club's public Obedience Classes were the first hosted by a Rottweiler Club and were very ably taught by a famous and respected trainer. Tracking and Schutzhund work are other interests of the members of this group.

The Greater New York Rottweiler Club

As we are writing this book, the Greater New York Rottweiler Club is the youngest Rottweiler Club. During the short period of time since its inception, it has made tremendous strides, right from the first meeting which was attended by 18 people who had responded to an advertisement in a local publication. Monthly meetings were set up, a constitution and by-laws drawn up, and a code of ethics was agreed upon. The name Long Island Rottweiler Club was chosen originally as the group's identification; however, as the membership grew this seemed inadequate for the club's full membership, and the name was changed in order to better reflect the geographic scope of the membership which has now grown to about 70 persons.

The goals of the Greater New York Rottweiler Club are to improve and preserve all the qualities of the Rottweiler as a total dog, including conformation, working ability and sound temperament. Public education about the drawbacks and virtues of the breed also comes as a high priority item. Just as important is it for the membership to get together and enjoy their dogs.

To help attain the latter goal, three fun matches have been held with all-breed obedience, three American Temperament Testing Society Tests (now an annual event), monthly educational programs, show handling and obedience classes, tatoo clinics, the formation of a Rottweiler rescue squad, a Rottweiler hot line answering calls from the club advertisements in *The New York Times* and *Newsday* (thus providing a much needed source of honest, accurate information on the breed); while on the lighter side, an annual Rottie Olympics is held along with a pig roast and clam bake. Members compete in a variety of events, including a Best Dressed Rottie parade.

Members of this club whose dogs have attained conformation and/or working titles are honored at an annual awards dinner.

The Greater New York Club's most ambitious undertaking to date has been a Rottweiler Symposium given by longtime enthusiast and authority Mrs. Bernard Freeman.

Inquiries and new members are welcome. Karen DiCicco, 10 Ocean View Road, Lynbrook, New York, 11536 is the secretary.

Rottweiler Clubs in Hawaii

In Hawaii there are two Specialty Clubs devoted to the Rottweiler: the Hawaii Rottweiler Club and the Rottweiler Club of Hawaii, both active organizations in support of their breed.

The Hawaii Rottweiler Club held its first Fun Match on March 10, 1985, where Ted Awaya was the judge. Winners were Ridgerunner's Rowdy Roma, owned and handled by Richelle Uyeda, Best of Breed; Buchmar's Apollo Regere, C.D.X., owned and handled by Bruce Mao, Best of Opposite Sex.

The Rottweiler Club of Hawaii, meanwhile, had its first Fun Match announced for May 28, 1985. The judge here was scheduled to be Masaru Nishiki of Honolulu. Officers of Rottweiler Club of Hawaii are: President, Neal O'Connor. Vice-President, Sam Kipapa. Secretary, Kathy Crumpton. Treasurer, Eleanor Hinton.

Jill Nakache is Secretary of the Hawaii Rottweiler Club.

A. R. C. STATEMENT OF PRINCIPLES AND PRACTICES

This **STATEMENT** is established in accordance with the objectives of **THE AMERICAN ROTTWEILER CLUB.** Adherence to these **PRINCIPLES AND PRACTICES** is expected of all members.

Introduction: The Rottweiler is above all a working dog and must exhibit the temperament, intelligence and structure of a working companion. The physical appearance should be as described in the AKC standard.

1. Study and strive to conserve and improve the breed in structure, temperament and working ability, never sacrificing one for the others.

2. Breed only AKC registered dogs and bitches which are either OFA-certified or which have been evaluated and been found to be free of hip dysplasia by two board-certified radiologists at an accredited University Veterinary School. Dogs with a foreign HD-negative status should be re-X-rayed and found to be free of HD as described above before being used for breeding. All dogs should be tattooed in an individual and identifiable manner before having hips X-rayed. Breed only dogs and bitches of stable temperament and with no disqualifying faults according to the AKC Rottweiler Standard (undershot, overshot, missing teeth, long coat, any base color other than black, or a total absence of markings). Do not breed any dog or bitch with any of the following faults: monorchidism, entropion, ectropion.

3. Offer at stud, with a contract, only mature (eighteen months or older), healthy dogs with normal hips, free of communicable diseases, having none of the faults listed above. Refuse stud service to any bitch not meeting the same requirements.

4. Breed only bitches two years of age or older with normal hips, free of communicable diseases, having none of the above faults, to not more than one stud dog at any one season, and not more than two out of three seasons consecutively. Plan all litters with the goal of improving the breed.

5. Maintain the highest possible standards of health, cleanliness and care of breeding stock, with all stock sold guaranteed to be in healthy condition, including adequate protection against known diseases.

6. Choose names of AKC registration which do not use prefixes or kennel names associated with other recognized breeders of Rottweilers in the U.S., Canada, Germany or any other foreign country, unless written permission is obtained from the original user of the name.

7. Sell all dogs with a written contract. Keep and pass on to Buyers accurate health, breeding and registration records and pedigree records of at least four generations. Registration papers may be withheld or breeder's rights retained only by mutual agreement in writing, signed by both parties. Urge that all Rottweilers not purchased as show and breeding stock be made incapable of reproducing, and urge that registration papers be withheld, until a veterinarian's certificate is received as proof of sterilization.

8. Evaluate honestly according to the AKC Standard, and state clearly to the Buyer the quality of any Rottweiler sold. All advertising should be honest and informative and should in no way misrepresent the stock offered. Prices should be based on individual merit.

9. Sell only to responsible persons and refuse to knowingly deal with unethical breeders, pet shops, wholesalers, catalog houses or their commercial sources. Rottweilers should not be given as prizes in contests, nor should the breed be exploited in any detrimental manner.

10. Encourage working titles to retain breeding stock's correct working temperament. Show future breeding stock in the ring, keeping in mind that the purpose of such shows is to improve the breed by objective evaluation of the animals in competition according to the Breed Standard.

11. Observe the highest standards of sportsmanship and good will at breed shows, obedience and schutzhund trials, and at any other event involving Rottweilers. Assist all newcomers to the breed, so that they may be guided in the ways that can best conserve and improve the Rottweiler.

As a member of the American Rottweiler Club, I have read and understand that I shall be expected to abide by the above Statement of Principles and Practices in all ways.

Top: Ch. Alastar's Abbye vom Altar taking Winners Bitch and Best of Opposite Sex for a four-point major, Houston K.C. 1982. Owned by Carole Anderson, Alastar Kennels, Conroe, Texas. **Bottom:** Ch. Welkerhaus' Rommel, U.D. in July 1977 at age three years. Owned by Rita A. Welker, Oak Ridge, North Carolina.

CAPTIONS FOR PLATES 81-96

Plate 81

1. Aust. Ch. Rotvel Skyhigh with owner's nephew, Martyn Windeyer. Capt. Craig Bryan, Randwick, N.S.W., Australia.

2. Aust. Ch. Rottsea Valeda, C.D. owned by Stephen Lodge, Miller, N.S.W., Australia.

3. "The family" belonging to Captain Craig Bryan. From the left, Aust. Ch. Rotvel Trooper, Tarinbeck Camilla, and Aust. Ch. Rotvel Skyhigh, distinguished winners of tremendous merit.

4. Ebshine Zulian Conan, *left,* and Ebshine Zulian Jensen are four-month-old puppies at Ebshine Kennels, Sweetman's Creek, N.S.W., Australia.

5. Nottrott Angelina at six weeks of age. By Powderhorn's Fetz of Wencrest (U.S.A. import) ex Aust. Ch. Pottset Valeda, C.D. Owned by Stephen Lodge.

6. Auslese Freidl, age seven weeks, by Auslese Iago Rabe (U.K. import) ex Echo vom Magderberg (German import) owned by Stephen Lodge.

Plate 82

1. Aust. Ch. Rottsea Valeda, C.D. with friend "Cocky." Stephen Lodge, owner, Miller, N.S.W., Australia.

2. Aust. Ch. Baskina Zoiz Rebel, by Baskina Black Kojak, C.D. ex Borgvaale Sunday Morning (imported U.K.) after winning Best of Breed at Singleton Show Society in November 1984. Owned by Ebshine Kennels, Veeni Hudson, Sweetman's Creek, N.S.W., Australia.

3. Handsome head study of the noted Australian winning bitch, Aust. Ch. Zeldermann Zuleika, by Aust. Ch. Bilpin Cardith, C.D. ex Aust. Ch. Brandlouchin Bessie. Owned by Ebshine Kennels.

4. Cooling off in the water on a hot day. Aust. Ch. Zeldermann Zuleika owned by Ebshine Kennels.

5. Aust. Ch. Zeldermann Zuleika travels to the dog shows in comfort.

6. Hertzog Astro at 15 months. By Aust. Ch. Retohr Regnans ex Aust. Ch. Rotvel Uberbeiten. Owned by Mrs. Cheryl Wakeham, Koonawarra, N.S.W., Australia.

7. Aust. Ch. Rottser Valeda, C.D. with Aust. Ch. Brabantsia Delrego as a puppy. Stephen Lodge, owner.

8. Hertzog Alena at 15 months. By Retohr Regnans ex Rotvel Uberbeiten. Owned by Mrs. C. Wakeham.

Plate 83

1. Kava von Stolzenfels, C.D.X. "Hail to the victor." Owned by Dr. Evelyn M. Ellman, von Stolzenfels, Augusta, Mich.

2. Am. and Can. Ch. Ivan von Gruenerwald, owned by Forrest Wells, practicing with his Frisbee.

3. Ch. Delphi Bitt' Amax with a friend, Mike Spelman, in a photo used to promote Rottweilers as working companions in Florida wildlife magazines. Although Bitt loves to swim and retrieve thrown articles, it is her daughter, Delphi Echo, C.D., who has repeatedly demonstrated the value of a Rottweiler as an ideal retriever both in the water and on land.

4. Oskar von Paulus, U.D., "Buddy", with a friend he met at an obedience demonstration. Owned by Sandy Mejias, Alexandria, Virginia. This handsome Rottie during his lifetime went to nursing homes, worked with a pyschiatrist helping children with dog phobias, was in countless T.V. shows and commer-

cials, and was a faithful friend and protector for his owners and their four children. He was a very special Rottweiler! Photo courtesy of Mary Lou Fiala.

Plate 84

1. Thewina Summer Ferrymaster, C.D.X., now working on his Schutzhund training. Owned by Ravenwood Rottweilers, Linda B. Griswold, Michigan City, Ind.

2. Thewina Summer Ferrymaster, C.D.X. practicing his Schutzhund work. Ravenwood Kennels.

3. Ch. Koskemo Furst Hasso, SchH III, FH, doing protection exercise at the North American Schutzhund III Championship competition. Owned by Pat and Max Kaefer, Maple Ridge, B.C., Canada.

4. Ch. Koskemo Furst Hasso, SchH III, FH, retrieving in North American Schutzhund III Championship Competition. Owned by the Max Kaefers, Vom Frasertal Rottweilers.

5. Ch. Koskemo Furst Hasso, SchH III, FH, demonstrating protection at the North American Schutzhund Championship Competition. Owned by Max and Pat Kaefer, Vom Frasertal Rottweilers.

6. Ch. Koskemo Furst Hasso, SchH III, FH, photographed in action during protection exercise at the North American Schutzhund III Championship. Owned by Max and Pat Kaefer, Vom Frasertal Kennels.

7. Ch. Koskemo Furst Hasso, SchH III, FH, going over the wall at the North American Schutzhund III Championship. Owned by Max and Pat Kaefer, Vom Frasertal Rottweilers.

8. Ch. Koskemo Furst Hasso, SchH III, FH, owned by Max and Pat Kaefer.

Plate 85

1. & 2. The Danish Mental Test is used throughout Europe to certify dogs for breeding. Shown are scenes from the Colonial Rottweiler Club video tape which was made of the entire test. Brimstone's Baron von Otto, C.D., TT, VB, SchH 1 is the "star." Owned by Windwalker Kennels, Port Crane, N.Y.

3. & 4. "V" rated Arko vom Grenzlandring, SchH. III, owned by Alan P, Kruse and Benson Ford, Jr., exhibiting good form taking a jump (3) and obstacle climbing (4).

5. Am. and Can. Ch. Rodsden's Birch Hill Hanna, C.D.X., T.D., owned by Jane Wiedel, Stockton, Ill.

6. Panamint Ideal Impression, C.D.X., T.D.X., SchH 1, showing off her superb tracking form. Owned and trained by Dennis and Margaret Teague, Chutzpah Rottweilers, Newcastle, Calif.

7. Ch. Powderhorn's Abel, C.D., owned by Powderhorn/Wencrest Rottweilers, Mrs. Clara S. Hurley and Mr. Michael S. Grossman, Hollywood, Calif.

8. Ch. Rodsden's Birch Hill Bess, C.D.X., T.D. owned by Jane Wiedel, Birch Hill Rottweilers, Stockton, Ill.

Plate 86

1. "In training." Pioneer's Das Bedazzled, bred and owned by Pioneer Kennels, Virginia Aceti and Sheryl Hedrick.

2. Am. and Bda. Ch. Von Gailingen's Dark Delight, U.D.T., Bda. C.D.X., Can. C.D., the first Rottweiler to complete a C.D.X. degree in Bermuda. Owned and trained by Catherine M. Thompson, Von Gailingen Rottweilers, Freehold, N.J.

3. Ch. Rhomark's Axel v. Lerchenfeld, C.D.X., T.D. completing his C.D. title. On this five-show circuit, in Oregon in 1983, Axel qualified in all of them, was highest scoring Rottweiler in one of the trials, with a score of 193, and in conformation won two Bests of Breed and a Group placement. Owned by Ken and Hildegard Griffin, Novato, Calif.

4. Ch. and OTCH. Piasa Abbe v Karman, U.D., T.T., by Ch. Jack vom Emstal, C.D. ex Ch. Panamint Prise v Rheintal earning a Utility Award. Owned by Pierre and Carole Charbonneau, St. Colomban, Quebec, Canada.

Plate 87

1. Into the water on the retrieve!

2. "Gotcha!" The Rottie heads back through the water with the bird.

3. Coming back to land with her retrieve.

4. "Here it is, boss." The Rottie delivers the duck.

5. Ch. Northwind's Juno, C.D.X., SchH. 1, TT, by Am. and Can. Ch. Ero v.d. Mauth, Am. and Can. C.D. ex Am. and Can. Ch. Northwind's Danka, Am. and Can. C.D. Bred by Patricia Hickman-Clark. This is the foundation bitch at Jacques and Pat Major's Majorhausen Kennels, Orleans, Ontario, Canada.

6. Ch. Marlo's Sohn v Axel, C.D., T.D., earning his Tracking Dog title with his owner-handler Penny Dodds, Novato, Calif.

7. Am. and Can. Ch. Von Gailingen's Dassie Did It, U.D.T., Can. C.D., exhibited the excellent performance which made her so successful in gaining these degrees. Bred, owned, trained, and handled by Catherine M. Thompson, Von Gailingen Rottweilers, Freehold, N.J.

8. Ch. Bandetta von Stolzenfels, U.D.T., dumbbell in mouth, is owned by Rottweilers Pionierhaus, Jerry and Kay Watson, Pride, La.

Plate 88

1. Outstanding obedience dog, Thewina Summer Ferrymaster, owned by Linda B. Griswold, Michigan City, Ind.

2. Thewina Summer Ferrymaster, C.D.X. owned by Ravenwood Rottweilers, Linda B. Griswold.

3. The fantastic obedience dog, Thewina Summer Ferrymaster, C.D.X., one of the English imports at Ravenwood Kennels, Linda B. Griswold.

4. Thewina Summer Ferrymaster, C.D.X., whom his owner says "will jump anything." Linda B. Griswold, Ravenwood Rottweilers.

5. Ch. Rodsden's Heiko V Forstwald, C.D., VB, TT, on lease to Roxanna and Jim McGovern, Port Crane, New York, by Linda and Bill Michels, Brunswick, Ohio.

6. Am. and Can. Ch. Von Gailingen's Dassie Did It, U.D.T., Can. C.D. Bred, owned, trained, and handled by Catherine M. Thompson, Von Gailingen Rottweilers, Freehold, N.J.

7. Ravenwood Rainbow Connection, C.D., by Ch. Ravenwood Phoenix Rising, C.D. ex Thewina Summer Frolic, C.D. Age 16 months here, owned by Ravenwood Rottweilers, Linda B. Griswold.

8. Fraulein Cinder von Fox, C.D., by Ch. Bethel Farm's Apollo ex Demon von Fox, bred by Marvin Fox and owned by Beth and Ronald Cepil. He attained his C.D. at 14 months' age in three consecutive trials.

Plate 89

1. Von Gailingen's the Katz Meow at just six months. By KS/Ch. Condor Zur Klamm, SchH III, FH, ex Am. and Bda. Ch. Von Gailingen's Dark Delight, U.D.T., Bda. C.D.X., Can. C.D. Catherine M. Thompson, owner, Freehold, N.J.

2. Berglufts Gustel at seven weeks. Lovely head and strong bone. Owned by Dorit S. Rogers, Bergluft Kennels, Sewickley, Pa.

3. Profile of a future winner. 14-week-old bitch puppy by Ch. Beaverbrook Eisen v Bruin. Owned by Gary and Laura Brewton, Powell, Tennessee.

4. Hertzog Alena at 9 weeks learning to strike a pretty pose. Mrs. W. Wakeham, owner, Koonawarra, N.S.W., Australia.

5. Berglufts Hasso at age four and a half months. Note the lovely head and strong bone of this puppy for his age. Owned by Dorit S. Rogers, Sewickley, Pa.

6. Ch. Graudstark's Pandemonium, 1977-1985, the foundation of Pandemonium Rottweilers, owned by Valerie J. Cade, Goldens Bridge, N.Y.

7. Loneagle's Bravura v Seren, C.D., T.D., by Ch. Donnaj Vt. Yankee of Paulus, C.D.X. ex Ch. Doroh's Fantastic Serenade, C.D.X., moves along smartly for co-owner Jody Engel during the Rottweiler judging at Greater Miami, January 1985.

8. Note the movement, reach, drive, and solid topline of Ch. Quanto van het Brabantpark owned by Powderhorn/Wencrest Rottweilers, Hollywood, Calif.

Plate 90

1. A future very bright "star," Am. and Can. Ch. Jacqueline Da Bratiana at three months' age winning her first Best of Breed at a local fun match with her owner-handler Marlene Lore. Note how beautifully this puppy stands in the "stacked" position, so important in a mature show dog!

2. Head-study of Ch. Jiggs von Kruse owned by Alan P. Kruse, Howell, Mich.

3. Mrs. Denny Kodner making a judge's examination of Xanadu's Bronson Jos v Altar, owned by Joann H. Turner, Anchorage, Alaska.

4. "Move him straight down and back, please," instructs the judge, Mrs. Denise Kodner, as she judges Xanadu's Bronson Jos v Altar. Owner, Joann H. Turner.

5. Noblehaus Executor at four months of age winning Best Puppy in Match at the Long Island Rottweiler Club Specialty Match in September 1984. Noblehaus Kennels, Mark and Patricia Schwartz, West Nyack, N.Y.

6. Kato von Siegerhaus owned by Chyrel Prather.

Plate 91

1. A little help from one's friend! Here we see one of the Chinese Shar Pei bitches owned by the Frank J. Fiorellas nursing some of Pandora's Rottie pups as though they were her own. Little Flower Kennels, Boxford, Mass.

2. Ch. Katryn the Great Von Ursa, C.D.X. with her puppies. Pamela Anderson, owner, Zornhaus Rottweilers, Wilton Manors, Fla.

3. These handsome seven-week-old puppies are littermates, linebred on Ch. Radio Ranch's Axel v Notara, being by Ch. Radio Ranch's Ebony Gold Bar ex Ch. Radio Ranch's Ten of Goldmoor. These are four puppies from a litter of nine, sev-

eral of which are already winning well. Marge Gold, breeder-owner, Goldmoor, Concord, N.C.

4. "Rub-a-dub-dub, 10 Rotts in a tub." Bath time at von Morgen Carroll for these ten puppies by Ch. Starkheim's Duf Morgen Carroll ex Ch. V.W. Serena of Summerfield. Bill and Betty Carroll, von Morgen Carroll Rottweilers, Ontario, Calif.

5. Ch. Doroh's Janus Erdelied, C.D. pictured at three months. Promising show prospect puppy owned by Surely Rawlings, Coral Gables, Fla.

6. Beaverbrook puppy at five weeks of age, sired by Champion Bronco v Rauberfeld. Owners, Gary and Laura Brewton, Powell, Tenn.

7. "C'mon, Mom, let's play," is what baby Beau's Alotta Dolly, here three weeks old, seems to be saying. Owned by Bob and Judy Beaupre, Aliquippa, Pa.

8. Pfenning von Siegerhaus (Am. and Can. Ch. Lord Samuel von Siegerhaus ex Kirstens Dandy Brandy) must be thinking, "Let me at those ears," while enjoying a game with a Basset friend. Von Siegerhaus Rottweilers, Thom and Carol Woodward, Corning, Calif.

Plate 92

1. The German import, Gina v Kursaal, playing at the pond when 11 weeks old. Owned by Edith Alphin, Altar Kennels, Fayetteville, N.C.

2. This pup is only a couple of days old. An interesting study in size as one compares the puppy to the mother's paw. Owned by LaVerne and Helen MacPherson, Heamac Rottweilers, London, Ontario, Canada.

3. Ch. Alec von Beenen at three months. Owned by Dr. and Mrs. Royal Poel, bred by the Beenens.

4. "In jail." A puppy from the Beenen "A" litter peers wistfully through the bars of his pen. Lin and Don Beenen, Lowell, Mich.

5. Lindenwood's Bouncer at six weeks. Linda P. Michels, owner, Brunswick, Ohio.

6. An appealing youngster from Dschungel Rottweilers owned by Glenn Goreski, Wallington, N.J.

7. Kismet, nine-month-old kitten at Delphi Kennels, snuggles into the whelping box with Ch. Delphi Bitt' Amax and her five-day-old litter. Good friends belonging to Al and Bonnie Wimberly, Havana, Fla.

8. Brina von Beenen at seven weeks. Owned by Kevin and Christine Johnson, bred by Don and Lin Beenen.

Plate 93

1. "Don't try to steal MY bike," warns this young grandson of Ch. Dolf Fuller von Stolzenfels, now owned by a fancier in Puerto Rico. Bred by Dr. Evelyn M. Ellman, von Stolzenfels Rottweilers, Augusta, Mich.

2. Madchen Greta von Fox caught in the act of being a pizza thief! Owned by Ellen and Edward Towarnicki, bred by Marvin Fox, Philadelphia, Pa.

3. Robert Barber with Gunda Von Brawn and a puppy. Von Walber Kennels, Dexter, Mich.

4. Hasso and Hilde von Schwabing, both holders of obedience degrees, just sitting around on a lovely spring day. Two of the splendid Rottweilers owned by Roy and Fran Hiltermann, Von Schwabing Kennels, Warwick, R.I.

5. A litter of dreams and hopes produced by Ch. Rodsden's Ansel von Brabant ex Ch. Delphi Bitt' Amax share a sunny afternoon with Bonnie Wimberly at Delphi Rottweilers.

6. Darth Vader and Grand Moff Tarkin pulling the Frolic'n Acres Fire Department Hose Wagon Replica in front of one of the Seattle Fire Department's aerial ladder trucks. Stephen Johnson, co-owner with Charlotte Johnson and Linda Schuman, is a Fire Lieutenant for Seattle.

7. Recherchez von Siegerhaus dives in as hound friend watches admiringly. Thomas and Carol Woodward, von Siegerhaus Rottweilers, Corning, Calif.

8. Anne Katherine Beenen with her dogs. She is the daughter of Don and Lin Beenen, Lowell, Mich.

Plate 94

1. Am. and Can. Ch. Davericks Alex vom Hasenkamp, C.D. takes time out from dog shows and training to win first prize in the Palmyra, N.J. 1983 Halloween Parade's "Tiny Tots" division. Alex pulled eight-month-old Anne Rogers Gordon two miles while wearing this costume, receiving applause throughout the entire event. The Richard Gordons, Daverick Kennels, Moorestown, N.J., are owners.

2. Arrow of Lone Eagle, C.D.X., T.D., U.C.D. keeps young Curtis Engel company. Note how watchful he is of the baby. Matt and Jody Engel, Loneagle Rottweilers, Miami, Fla.

3. Delphi Rottweilers also raise Arabian horses. Here is Jeepers Treu Argus and several of his equine friends, all belonging to Al and Bonnie Wimberly, Delphi, Havana, Fla.

4. Faustus von Stolzenfels with his young master, Joshua Bo Johnson. Faustus is a son of Ch. Erda v Stolzenfels ex Ch. Dolf Fuller v Stolzenfels, C.D. and is owned by Rev. Charles Arnett, Culver, Indiana, who says he is a terrific baby sitter. Photo courtesy of Evelyn Ellman, owner of von Stolzenfels Rottweilers, the breeder of Faustus.

5. "Santa's helpers." *Left to right,* Seren's Arpeggio, Am. and Can. C.D.; Ch. Doroh's Fantastic Serenade, Am. and Can. C.D.; Stephen Piusz, age 11 months; and Mondberg's Bulger V Beier. Peter and Marilyn Piusz, Johnstown, N.Y.

6. Demon von Fox at 13 months' age with her constant companion Matthew Fox. These two playmates have grown up together and continue to share a loving relationship. Owned by Marvin Fox, Philadelphia, Pa.

7. Am. and Can. Ch. Rodsden's Kato v Donnaj, C.D.X., T.D. The first Rottweiler to win Best in Show in the U.S., handled to all his wins by his owner Jan Marshall, Donnaj Kennels, Woodstock, Vt. He was the grandsire of Ch. Donnaj Vt. Yankee v Paulus. Pictured here with Dale Marshall in 1969 when one year old.

8. Two baby Rottweilers playing "take the shoe," both owned by Edith D. Alphin, Altar Rottweilers, Fayetteville, N.C.

Plate 95

1. Ch. Bergluft's Gunda is owned by Bill and Sandy Fabry, Brea, California. Pictured with breeder, Dorit S. Rogers, handling to Winners at Mahoning Shenango K.C. in 1979.

2. Ch. Erdelied Astraea, C.D., bred by Joanna Sawyer; owned and handled by Surely Rawlings, Coral Gables, Fla. No. 1 Rottweiler Bitch 1980. No. 3 Rottweiler Bitch 1981. Grand Prize Futurity winner and top owner-handled bitch 1980 and 1981. Many Bests of Breed and multiple Group placements.

3. Ch. Meid von Siegerhaus, by Ch. Wotan von Kastanienbaum ex Ch. Kyna vom Odenwald, C.D., handled by Thomas

Woodward. Von Siegerhaus Rottweilers, Thom and Carol Woodward, Corning, Calif.

4. Ch. Srigo's Watch My Smoke, Top Rottweiler Bitch in the U.S.A. for 1973, bred and owned by Felicia Luburich, East Brunswick, N.J.

5. Ch. Green Mountain's Beau Jangles, by Ch. Donnaj Green Mountain Boy, taking a Best of Breed for owner Anthony P. Attalla handled by Carol Petruzzo.

6. Ch. Riegele's Agreta Maid gaining points towards her title. Owned by Ellen B. Walls, Riegele Farms, Hartly, Del.

Plate 96

1. Ch. Frolic'n Sundance Kid, C.D., Am. and Can. T.D., owned by Frolic'n Rottweilers, Charlotte and Stephen Johnson and Linda Schuman, Redmond, Wash. Sired by Am., Can., Bda., Mex., and Int. Ch. Jack vom Emstal, Am. and Can. C.D., PC, SchH1 ex Kandy von der Sandhaufen.

2. Ch. Cora v Frankenberg, SchH.1 owned by Alan P. Kruse, Howell, Mich.

3. Paco von Stolzenfels in the puppy class at eight and a half months. Dr. Evelyn M. Ellman, von Stolzenfels Rottweilers, Augusta, Mich.

4. Ch. Frolic'n Grand Moff Tarkin, C.D. taking a Group placement on the way to his championship at Longview-Kelso in 1982. By Am. and Can. Ch. Panamint Nobel v Falkenberg, C.D. ex Am., Can., and Mex. Ch. Panamint Rani vd Sandhaufen, CD. Owned by Frolic'n Rottweilers, Stephen and Charlotte Johnson and Linda Schuman, Redmond, Wash.

5. Am., Can., Mex. Ch. and 1978 World Siegerin Uschi vom Hause Henseler, C.D., ADRK SchH 1. A Producer of Merit from the Frolic'n Rottweilers, Charlotte and Stephen Johnson, and Linda Schuman.

6. Ch. Arras vom Schloss Stutensee, SchH III, 1PO III, FH, AD, C.D.X., T.D., TT, Gekort EzA in January 1983 on the way to his championship taking points under Rottweiler breeder-judge Barbara Dillon. Owned by Frolic'n Rottweilers, Charlotte and Stephen Johnson and Linda Schuman.

BIRCH HILL ROTTWEILERS
PEDIGREE

WF 337369
Individual Reg. No.

Litter Reg. No. _____

A/C CH. BIRCH HILL'S QUINCY, C.D.T.D.

RO-6213-T (Good)

Registered Name of Dog

Date Whelped ___ June 1, 1982 ___ Sex __ Male __

Breeder ___ Jane F. Wiedel ___ Address 4400 S. Eden Rd., Stockton, IL 61085

Owner ___ Jane F. Wiedel ___ Address __ 815-598-3159 __

PARENTS	GRANDPARENTS	GREAT-GRANDPARENTS	GREAT-GREAT-GRANDPARENTS
SIRE: A/C CH. Rodsden's Elko Kastanienbaum, A/C CD, Amer. CDXTD WD 694350 RO-1448	International CH. Elko vom Kastanienbaum, SchH 1 46 340 HD Free, Utrecht	Elko vom Kaiserberg, 44 352 SchH 1	Hasso vom Oelberg, SchH 3 39 223
			Anni vom Kaiserberg 42 306
		Gitta vom Bucheneck, 44 776 SchH 1 HD Free, Utrecht	Furst vd Villa Daheim, SchH 1 42 204
			Indra v Schloss Westerwinkel, 40 758 SchH 1
	CH. Gundi vom Reichenbachle 48 086 HD Free, Utrecht RO-846	Berno vom Albtal, 42 673 SchH 3, FH	Hasso vom Oelberg, SchH 3 39 223
			Heidi vom Durrbach 38 916
		Antje von der Wegscheide 41 225	Quick vd Solitude, SchH 3, FH 38 608 HD Free, Utrecht
			Anka v d Kurmark 37 832
DAM: CH. Rodsden's Birch Hill Omega, CDTD WE 449505 RO-3024	CH. Rodsden's Bruin v Hungerbuhl, CDX WD 375753 RO-1189	CH. Dux vom Hungerbuhl, SchH 1 WC18804 RO-234	Kuno vom Butzensee, SchH 3 40 415
			Britta vom Schlossberg 39 075
		CH. Rodsden's Frolich Burga, CDTD WC589812 RO-649	CH. Max v d Hobertsburg 44 896 RO-320
			CH. Rodsden's Willa vd Hargue, WB854722 RO-321 UDT
	CH. Rodsden's Gay Lady, TD WC 635810 RO-647	CH. Rodsden's Ikon vd Hargue, CD WC81494 RO-355	CH. Rodsden's Kluge vd Hargue, WA553102 RO-50 CD
			CH. Rodsden's Ericka Deidre Dahl WB703173 RO-157
		CH. Rodsden's Lady Luck, CD WB262642 RO-60	CH. Falk vom Kursaal, SchH 1 40 523
			CH. Afra v Hasenacker, CD, 38 822 SchH 1

PLATE 81

1

2

3

4

5

6

PLATE 82

PLATE 83

PLATE 84

PLATE 85

PLATE 86

PLATE 87

PLATE 88

PLATE 89

PLATE 90

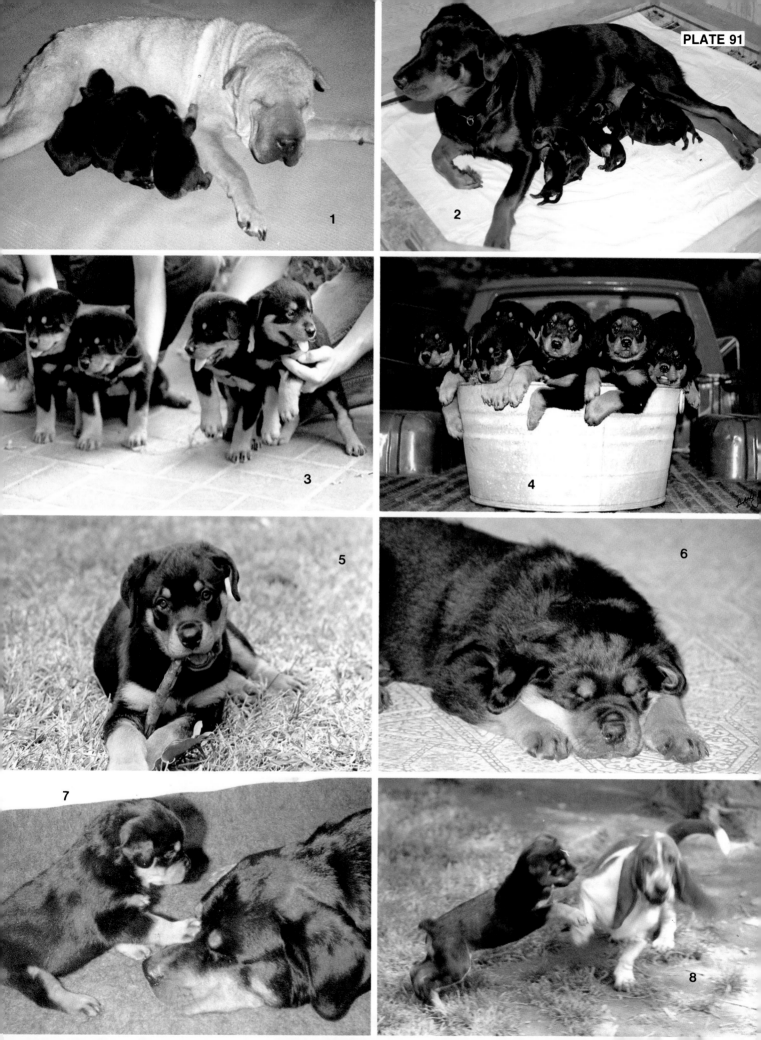

PLATE 91

PLATE 92

PLATE 93

PLATE 94

PLATE 95

PLATE 96

1

2

3

4

GROUP
THIRD
LONGVIEW-
KELSO
KENNEL CLUB
SUMMER 1982

5

6

BEST OF
WINNERS
GOLDEN GATE
KENNEL CLUB
JANUARY 1983
MIKE LOISTER

Top: This handsome English lithograph of Rottweiler puppies has been loaned to us from the collection of Linda B. Griswold, Ravenwood Kennels, Michigan City, Indiana. **Bottom:** Am. and Can. Ch. Elka von Siegerhaus, C.D., owned by Thom and Carol Woodward, Corning, California.

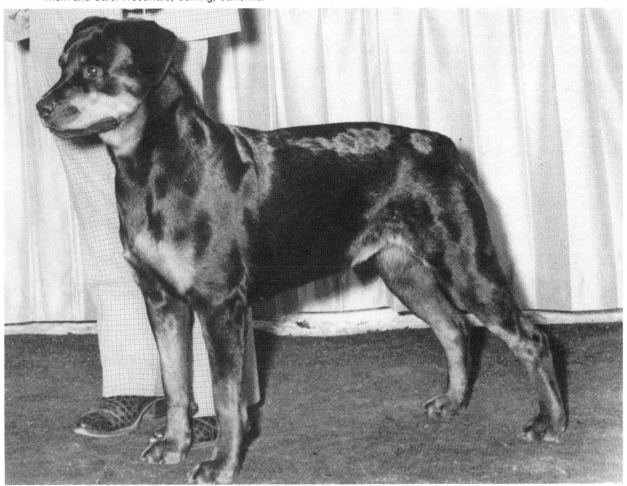

Am., Can., and Bda. Ch. Northwind's Ingo at age seven years at Bucks County K.C. in 1972. By Igor von Schauer ex Northwind's Danka. Owned by Patricia Hickman Clark.

CHAPTER FIVE

Rottweilers in Canada

Ch. Zulu Argus, C.D., SchH I, SV enjoying the winter weather with Brian and Eric Briere, the children of his owner.

The Rottweiler has been a very successful breed in Canada, and there are numerous kennels which are contributing well to the progress of the breed both there and in the United States.

On the following pages we bring you kennel resumes of half dozen or more outstanding Canadian breeders and some of their achievements, writing of the kennels in alphabetical order. The majority of Rottweiler breeders presently active there became so during the 1970's, in some cases having transferred their interest from other breeds. Probably the earliest of the now active Rottie kennels in Canada is Northwinds, whose owner started with the breed during the early 1960's, was a founder and the first President of Canada's parent Specialty Club for Rottweilers.

Many Americans travel to Canada to show their dogs each year, making for keen competition from those who come to visit and the ones raised there as homebreds. The latter, I might remark, hold their own quite impressively.

The first Canadian-bred all-breed Best in Show winning Rottweiler there was Canadian Champion Rintelma the Dragoon, who is also an important Specialty winner. This fine dog was bred and owned at the Winnipeg kennels of Pat Johnson and Jim Schwartz.

Carado

Carado Rottweilers, at Windsor, Ontario, Canada, are owned by Carol Kravets who started out in Dobermans in 1972, but by 1975 she was becoming increasingly interested in the Rotties, and was searching for the best foundation bitch she possibly could find.

This turned out to be a beautiful daughter of Champion Radio Ranch's Axel v Notara, who proved to be an excellent producer. Among her progeny was American and Canadian Champion Carado's Reaper v Tannenwald, T.T., who very promptly finished all three of these titles while still under 15 months of age, entirely owner-handled.

Canadian Champion Carado's Mighty Quinn, owned by Robert and Peggy Cojocar of Windsor, Ontario, also finished in six shows, owner-handled by Carol in the United

211

States, taking Best of Winners and Best of Breed in back to back weekends from the puppy class. Her litter brother, American and Canadian Champion Carado's Commander Cody T.T. owned by Suzanne Stewart of Inkster, Michigan, was No. 3 Rottweiler in Canada for 1984 in 11 shows, owner-handled.

Since Windsor is right on the border of Detroit, Canadian dogs from this area are shown 90% of the time in the United States.

Carado's Satin Sidney has ten points now in the show ring but has been busy, as well, in the whelping box. We will soon be seeing her four puppies in competition. They are Carado's Satin Classic, Road Warrior, Blade Runner, and Onyx Guterzug.

Freundlich

Freundlich Rottweilers are owned by Pierre and Carole Charbonneau at St. Colomban, Quebec, whose breeding program began in 1978 when they acquired an American female who became Canadian Champion and Obedience Trial Champion Piasa Abbe v Karman, U.D., T.T., with a very fine pedigree. Abbe is the daughter of International Champion Jack Vom Emstal and Champion Panamint Prise V. Rheintal. At nine months she completed her Canadian championship with several Bests of Breed to her credit along the way.

In 1981, Abbe was the second Rottweiler in Canada in obedience, and she successfully passed her temperament test. Abbe was bred only once, to her owners' second Rottweiler acquisition, Canadian Champion Frolickin Black Hawk, C.D.X., T.T., by Champion Panamint Nobel V. Falkenburg, C.D. ex Champion Uschi Von Hause Henseler. Hawk was No. 3 Rottweiler in obedience in Canada for 1981.

From this breeding came six puppies, four of which earned obedience titles and presently Freundlich Saran Beau Buck C.D., T.T. has been pointed and is on the verge of finishing championship.

From this litter, one bitch was kept by the Charbonneaus, Freundlich Nice Gipsy, C.D. who has proven to be a very useful brood bitch.

In 1983, Jessnic Freundlich Iza Rott was acquired, a daughter of American and Canadian Champion Northwind's Kaiser of Mallam ex Ch. Beowulf's Gibson Girl. The quality of Damien (Iza Rott) led the Charbonneaus to breed their Gipsy to Kaiser in 1984.

Freundlich is a new kennel whose goal is to protect the breed, respect the standard, and keep the Rottweiler a good working dog and a healthy, wonderful companion.

Heamac

Heamac Rottweilers at London, Ontario, are owned by LaVerne and Helen MacPherson, who selected Rottweilers after serious consideration of several of the herding and working breeds. Living on a farm, they wanted a breed that requires little grooming, is family oriented, and is uncommon. So it was that in 1972 they purchased a bitch from Millerhaus Kennels. Susi was a good-natured bitch who became a champion but was unable to conceive. She taught her owners much about the breed.

The next purchase was a daughter of Champion Phasel Seclusion, Canadian Champion Millerhaus Jolen Amy whom they bred to Illo v Tannenwald (son of Champion Radio Ranch Axel v Notawa) owned by Jim and Judy Burns. This litter produced American and Canadian Champion Heamac Illo's Be-A-Pet, American and Canadian C.D.X.; Canadian Champion Heamac Illo's Baxle, Canadian C.D., and Canadian Champion Heamac Amy's Bandy. Pet is owned by Mary Lou Szabo of Toledo, Ohio. Bandy and Baxle have both produced champions and obedience degree dogs and fine family pets.

From Delbert and the late Mary Kreger the MacPhersons purchased, in 1979, Kreger's Caesar Brandy Gem, C.D. and in 1980 American and Canadian Champion Kreger's Nero Hercules Heamac. Herc is now co-owned by Kevin and Paula Ray and Bill and Judy Stine.

The MacPhersons have worked hard to give people a good introduction to the Rottweiler. Bandy and Baxle have been in many parades and fairs in southern Ontario, where they have attracted considerable attention, especially when accompanying the team of pigs which the MacPhersons made famous riding behind them with their Rotties.

Now that the MacPhersons have left the farm to become city residents, their breeding will of necessity be limited. Nonetheless, they are always interested in talking with people about their well-loved breed, and in helping them when asked. As Helen says, "There is much to learn about this fine breed with which dedicated, diligent breeders have worked hard for years."

Janlynn

The first Rottweiler litter at Janlynn Kennels, owned by Mr. and Mrs. D. C. Flury at Saskatoon, Sask, Canada, was born on November 7, 1975 from their foundation bitch, Champion Veran's Bon Terra, C.D., a daughter of Champion Jaheriss Drummer Boy ex Champion Rodsden's Hera vom Norden. The sire of the puppies was Champion Rintelna of Cork. From this litter two dogs were shown, Janlynn's Conquering Caesar and J's Megan Merrymaid, both of whom became Canadian champions.

Terra's second litter was from the Flurys' Champion Rintelna Kona (Champion Angus vom Haus Kalbus ex Champion Rotvel Cyllene.) Five of these puppies grew up to become Champions Janlynn's Bon Adonis, C.D.; J's Big Mark; J's Bon Katrina; J's Big Shadow of Kona, and J's Bright and Breezy.

Champion J's Megan Merrymaid's first litter produced a female named Janlynn's Countess Natasha, who became a Canadian champion and earned her C.D.X. degree. On March 9, 1980, Countess Natasha produced one of Canada's top winning dogs, Champion Wathaman's Adventurous Griffin, C.D., who is a multiple Best in Show and Group-placing Canadian winner.

For Terra's third litter she was bred to Champion Cantass Wendigo, son of Arras vom Kohlerwald ex Champion Don-Ari's Brigitte, this time producing Champion Janlynn's Dana, C.D., who later produced Champion Janlynn's Jewel, C.D. (from Janlynn's Big Mark). Jewel has since produced Janlynn's Nibi and Neele (pointed) using Griffin as a stud dog.

With four generations of Janlynn bitches and a combination of outcrossing and line-breeding, Janlynn's Rottweiler lines have developed. To date, 19 Canadian Championships, 17 C.D. degrees, two C.D.X., and one Utility Dog have been earned by the Janlynn Rotties in limited showing.

Ch. Janlynn's Minto, C.D. owned by Susan Grandberg went BOS and Janlynn's Nibi, owned by breeders Mr. & Mrs. D. C. Flury went winners dog at the Rottweiler Club of Canada National Specialty on April 18, 1985.

Kyladie

When Aime and Adele Brosseau, owners of Kyladie Rottweilers in Alberta, purchased their first of the breed in 1977, they had little idea that he would grow up to become a famous winner, for they intended him as a pet and family companion. These folks were dog show exhibitors at heart, however, and as the Rottweiler matured, looking increasingly handsome, they decided to try him out in the ring. Luck, and a good dog, were with them! He lost no time in becoming Champion Hallenhof's Gentleman Bayre, C.D., and when the show records were compiled at the end of 1978, he proved to be Canada's No. 2 Rottweiler for that year. Bayre was actually bred in Canada; however, his pedigree is strong in United States owned dogs such as Rodsden's Kluge v d Harque and Harras von Sofienbusch and Rodsden's Goro v Sofienbusch.

A bitch then was purchased and bred to Bayre. This resulted in a litter of which four completed show championships and four earned Obedience degrees.

The puppies from this litter grew up to become Champion Kyladie's Arabasque, a champion at nine months; Champion Kyladie's Avitar the Wiz, C.D., finished at 13 months; Champion Kyladie's Starmaster Antares; Champion Kyladie's Baybe; and Kyladie's Beowulf the Brave, C.D.

Majorhausen

Majorhausen Rottweilers are owned by Jacques and Pat Major, Gloucester, Ontario, Canada, where the foundation of the breeding program is the lovely bitch "Tessa," more formally Canadian Champion Northwind's Juno, C.D.X., Schutzhund I, TT, a daughter of Canadian and American Champion Ero von der Mauth, Canadian and American C.D., TT, ex Canadian and American Champion Northwind's Danka, Canadian and American C.D.

A champion at one year's age, "Tessa" had gained her C.D. six months later with a High in Trial award, and became No. 3 Rottweiler in Obedience in Canada for 1977, adding her C.D.X. in 1979. She was the first Rottweiler bitch in Canada to gain a Schutzhund I degree, which she accomplished in 1978; and in 1980 she became the first TT Rottweiler bitch there.

"Tessa" earned a Medallion Rottweiler Club Honor Roll Award in 1981; an American Rottweiler Club Producer of Merit in 1982; and was admitted to the Medallion Rottweiler Club Hall of Fame in 1984. She is the dam of 12 champions; nine Companion Dog Degree holders; and one each with C.D.X., T.D., T.D.X., and Schutzhund I; plus eight TT Rottweilers. And she is the granddam of a Best in Show winner.

Tessa's death on July 4, 1985 was a very sad one for her family and for her breed. Her litters, on which Majorhausen Rottweilers are based, were by American and Canadian Champion Donnaj Vt. Yankee of Paulus, C.D.X., TT and Champion Bethel Farms Apollo, two litters by each of these great sires. The offspring have kept Majorhausen Kennels among the Top Ten Rottweiler breeders in Canada for a number of years.

Northwind

Northwind Rottweilers, at Ottawa, Canada, are owned by Patricia Hickman Clark, founding President of the Canadian Rottweiler Club and a charter member of the American Rottweiler Club. This very influential and famous kennel came into existence during the spring of 1963, with the purchase of Northwind's Tina, a DerVis vom Weyerhof daughter out of Katharina's Adorn of Townsview from Dr. and Mrs. D. S. Masland of Carlisle, Pennsylvania.

Tina was to become not only the foundation bitch at Northwind but one of the "all time" foundation bitches of the breed in North America thanks to three of her distinguished offspring:—Northwind's Darras, Danka and Donar.

Northwind's Darras (not to be confused with Barras) did for Canada what Barras and Donar did for the United States. Darras provided foundation stock for the famous Canadian kennels, Don-Ari and Fairvalley, as did Donar in the United States for Rodsden. Danka contributed to both sides of the border.

Tina had only four litters during her lifetime, which were born in October 1964, May 1966, February 1968 and July 1970. She died during September 1970 of stomach torsion when her "D" litter was only seven weeks old. From these four litters, she produced four American Champions, three Dual Champions, 14 Canadian Champions and four holders of C.D. obedience degrees. We salute her tremendous contribution to the breed!

Danka, Deena, Della, Darras, and Donar were all kept at Northwind in order to assure that the succeeding foundation Northwind stock would be free of hip-dysplasia. They *all* passed. From this group, Danka and Della took over their dam's former position as the foundation brood bitch in the Northwind's line, and although Della produced only one planned-breeding litter (by Rodsden's Goro von Sofienbusch) before succumbing to cancer, she was the first Canadian-bred bitch to place third in the Working Group, which she did under Mrs. Augustus Riggs. Also, she was the dam of Gage, Gina, and Gino, all of whom completed their Canadian and/or American championships in great style at Specialty Shows in the United States or Canada.

Danka, as her mother had done, produced four litters for Northwind before retiring to the loving care of the Nichols family in 1978 where she and her daughter, Ilsa, had been boarding during the two preceding years while their owner lived abroad. Patricia Hickman-Clark comments, "We feel great appreciation for the expertise and patience of both Jan Marshall and "Kato" (Champion Rodsden's Kato v Donnaj) thanks to which Danka ever became a producer. She was almost four when her litter sired by Kato was born." This was Northwind's "H" litter. The "I" and

"K" litters were from Danka by Igor von Schauer; the "J" litter from Danka by Ero von der Mauth. The total of 29 puppies born in these four litters produced 26 champions (14 Canadian, 12 American, plus one of them had a Bermudian championship as well), nine obedience degree holders, and two with Schutzhund I degrees. Included were a Colonial Rottweiler Club Best of Breed winner, and an all-breed Best in Show winner. This added up to Danka's having been the No. 1 Rottweiler producing bitch and No. 3 among All-Breeds in 1979 in the United States and the *all time* Top Producer in Canada, a record yet to be equalled. Some of Danka's most famous offspring include American and Canadian Champion Northwind's Helga (the dam of Champion Donnaj Green Mountain Boy); Northwind's Ingo; American Champion Northwind's Indigo, Schutzhund I (Winners Bitch at the Colonial Rottweiler Club Specialty in 1977); American Champion Northwind's Just Blew In (No. 6 among Top Ten 1977 who, along with Northwind's Kaiser helped provide foundation stock for Jessnic Kennels in the United States); American and Canadian Champion Northwind's Kaiser (mentioned above, who was Best of Breed at the Colonial Rottweiler Club Specialty in 1982); and American Champion Northwind's Kreimhilde, C.D. (High in Trial, Medallion Rottweiler Club 1979, with 196½ score).

Danka lived to the ripe old age of 14 years with the special care of her adopted family.

Northwind has imported only two Rottweilers from Europe, both of them males. In 1975 the dog who was to become American and Canadian Champion Ero von der Mauth, joined the kennel from Germany, and in 1978 Bergsgarden's Nero came from Sweden as a puppy.

Ero is described as having been "a tribute to the breed in both temperament and conformation, whom being owned by was a rare privilege." Unfortunately, due to cruciate ligament problems he was shown only on a very limited basis, and bred very seldom. He provided foundation stock for Canada's Konigsberg Rottweilers and for Tulakes in the United States. He died in 1981 after going Best of Breed in the Canadian Rottweiler Club Specialty Show in that same year.

Bergsgarden's Nero was brought to Northwind just at the time when the breeding program and kennel activities there fell by the wayside due to family commitments and thus never really had the opportunity to fulfil his potential. In an effort to assure his well-being, Nero was placed in a co-ownership and became unavailable for the limelight it was felt he deserved. He completed his American Championship by taking Winners Dog at the Colonial Rottweiler Club in 1980, after which he never returned to Canada and so far as is known at Northwind never again saw the inside of a show ring. Nor was he used at stud to any extent, although he did produce the Pandemonium "F" litter with the success that Patricia Hickman Clark had envisioned when she bought him in Sweden. He died in 1984.

Northwind's Ilsa, Danka's daughter who was to have become her replacement in the breeding program, also went to a new home in 1978. She was in whelp at the time to Ero von der Mauth and produced some splendid foundation stock for another kennel.

Other kennels who owe their foundation stock to Northwind in addition to those mentioned in the foregoing text, include both Donnaj and Powsell and Green Mountain through Northwind's Helga; Noblehaus through Northwind's Kindred Spirit; Pandemonium through Nero; and in Canada, Heidergruen through Northwind's Jewel and Majorhausen through Northwind's Juno.

Northwind itself was not so lucky following the 1978 crisis, and it was not until 1984, following four years of searching in Europe, the United States and Canada, that Patricia finally located a replacement bitch with whom to carry on her "very limited but very demanding" breeding program. This bitch, of course, is strong in Northwind's linebreeding with two bitches from the "C" on one side and two males from the "D" litter on the other side of her pedigree. An accidental breeding between this bitch and an Ero von der Mauth grandson produced a very lovely litter which as of June 1985 appears to be of the quality for which Northwind is world famous, and which it has so consistently produced in the past. So who knows what accomplishments may be realized during 1986!

Simeberg

Simeberg Rottweilers are the result of their breeder, Marie Kanera of Langley, in British Columbia, Canada, having fallen in love with one back in 1972. Eight years later, with the cooperation of Trollegens Rottweilers, owned by Maureen Wilkinson, a foundation bitch and sire were selected, and started her on her way with the breed.

Canadian Champion Trollegens Gundi, C.D., by American Champion Dux von Hungerbuhl ex Jaheriss Geeda, was mated with American Champion Kiros vom Lunsberg, thus establishing Simeberg Kennels in 1980. This first litter produced four champion daughters. The foundation bitch, Gundi, was Best Brood Bitch at the 8th National Rottweiler Specialty in Calgary, Alberta, in 1982. Her daughters were Canadian and American Champion Cita von Simeberg, No. 1 Rottweiler Bitch in Canada 1982; Canadian Champion Simebergs Czarina, Winners Bitch at Rottweiler Specialty in Calgary; American Champion Simebergs Domino, Reserve Winners Bitch, Rottweiler Specialty, Alberta; and Miss Dominique von Simeberg, Winners Female at National Show in Prague, Czechoslovakia, 1983.

In their turn, the daughters are now producing winners. Canadian and American Champion Cita von Simeberg bred to Champion Trollegens Benjamin produced Simeberg's "F" litter. Of these, Canadian Champion Simebergs Fame and Fortune completed his championship at one year. Simebergs Fabius C.D. completed obedience title at 13 months.

Canadian Champion Simebergs Czarina bred to Canadian and American Champion Trollegens Frodo, C.D., produced the "G" litter. From this, Canadian Champion Simebergs Gangster was Best Puppy in Show at age ten months under judge Glen Fancy, and had completed championship by one year.

Other members of the Simeberg family include the Czechoslovakian import, Moran Kralicky Sneznik, who sired a litter from Canadian and American Champion Van Tieleman's Charly Girl owned by Trollegens Rottweilers. This breeding produced an outstanding litter. One of the offspring, Canadian Champion Trollegens Yanka, is owned by Simeberg Kennels, and finished her championship at one year.

Another Trollegens Rottweiler owned by Simebergs, Trollegens Ulla, is the daughter of the import, Karin Fralicky, from American and Canadian Champion Van Tieleman's Cisco. Ulla and American and Canadian Champion Northwinds Ingo, C.D., Schutzhund I, from the "I" litter, produced Canadian Champion Simebergs Isis, who completed her Canadian title with three majors and two Best Puppy in Breed awards, making her debut at only seven months old.

Vom Frasertal

Vom Frasertal Rottweilers are a relatively new arrival in the world of purebred dogs and Rottweilers. Owned by Max and Pat Kaefer at Maple Ridge, British Columbia, the kennel was registered with the Canadian Kennel Club in October 1981. However, the events leading up to this one had spanned a period of two years prior to that time.

In late September 1979, the Kaefers purchased their first dog, a male Rottweiler puppy. This bundle of fur, claws and teeth went on to become Champion Koskemo Furst Hasso, SchH.III, FH. In the process of obtaining these titles Hasso set a new standard for Rottweilers in North America.

At just over one year of age, Hasso finished his Canadian championship. Two months later, at 14 months, he passed Schutzhund I. At 20 months of age he passed Schutzhund II. On May 10, 1981, at 22 months' age, he became the first Rottweiler and the first dog in Canada to have earned both a Schutzhund III and a bench show championship title. Six weeks later he was the youngest dog and the only Rottweiler to participate at the first North American Schutzhund III Championships. At that meet he tied for highest protection score (96) and obtained the second highest obedience score (87). Approximately one year later, on July 17, 1982, he added the second Rottweiler "first" to his credit by becoming the first Rottweiler in Canada to obtain his FH title. To this day, his passing score of 96 is uncontested by any Rottweiler on Canadian soil, Max Kaefer tells us, and he also is still the only dog in Canada to have a Championship, Schutzhund III and FH title.

In addition, from the point of view of what the Germans call "Wesen" which we translate as "temperament" or "character," Hasso was one of the finest Rottweilers. Unfortunately, Hasso's hips were not good enough for him to pass OFA, and consequently he was never used for breeding. Sad to say, it was that hip disease that brought his life to an untimely end on December 28, 1984.

The Kaefers' second Rottweiler, a German import bitch, arrived at Frasertal in the fall of 1981 as a ten-weeks-old puppy. In an attempt to follow in Hasso's footsteps, she turned into Champion Nancy von Tengen, SchH III. On the journey to Schutzhund III she, like Hasso, set a number of "first" for Rottweilers in North America.

Nancy finished her championship at two years of age, and at approximately the same time obtained her Schutzhund I title. On July 8, 1984 she made history by becoming the first Rottweiler bitch to obtain Schutzhund II in Canada. Six weeks later, on August 18, 1984, she obtained her second "first," the fourth "first" for Vom Frasertal Kennels, by becoming the first Rottweiler bitch to obtain the Schutzhund III title in Canada. To date Nancy's highest Schutzhund III score is 90-86-97.

So far Nancy has produced two litters, in both cases having been bred in Germany to the one and only Clint vom Schwaiger Wappen, Schutzhund III, FH (Gekoert EzA).

In her first litter of three, Nancy produced two very promising puppies, Arko vom Frasertal, soon to make his mark in the show ring and on the Schutzhund field; and Alki von Frasertal. Aries von Frasertal enjoys life as a pet on Vancouver Island.

In her second litter, a one puppy litter, Nancy produced Bron vom Frasertal who is to remain at home with his breeders. Hopefully he will follow in the footsteps of his parents and, as well, continue the quest for excellence where Hasso retired.

Zulu

Glenmiller Farms, in which Zulu Kennels are situated, is an ongoing dairy farm with purebred Holstein cattle. Prior to 1978, the Millers' working farm dogs were Collies and an occasional Bouvier des Flandres, sent in by Glenmiller Farms, a separate kennel wholly owned by Elizabeth Miller's son, William Miller. The Bouviers were sent to the farm to help develop their herding instincts. It is interesting to note that among Elizabeth Miller's guest list are to be found such names in Bouvier fame as American and Canadian Champion Glenmiller Beau Geste and American and Canadian Champion Glenmiller Bandit, outstanding show dogs in 1983 and 1984 respectively.

Nonetheless, after Elizabeth Miller's first encounter with a Rottweiler, at the Kitchener, Ontario, Dog Show, this is the breed which won her heart. She was completely intrigued by the poise and dignity of a Rottweiler puppy bitch she saw there, who turned out to be Champion Fairvalley's Hearty Tanya owned by Solera's Kennel. When the day came to replace their old Collie, Elizabeth purchased a show potential male puppy by the name of Torburhop's Kaiser v Brauen from Barbara Hooper in Detroit. Kaiser met with an early and tragic death when only 16 months of age, leaving Elizabeth Miller resolved never again to be without a Rottie.

Then it was that Zulu's foundation bitch was purchased, 13-months-old American and Canadian Champion Royson Diana Glenmiller. A daughter of the 1979 American Rottweiler Club Specialty Show Best of Breed winner, American and Canadian Champion Sciroco's Nashu'a of Royson ex the bitch who was Best of Opposite Sex to Best of Breed at this same Specialty Show, Canadian Champion Doonesbury's Myria-Angeline. The latter bitch, Myria, when only 17 months of age had received a Working Group 2nd, four Working Group 4th placements, a Puppy Working Group, 41 Bests of Breed, two Bests of Opposite Sex, and Reserve Winners Bitch at the Medallion Specialty, August 1977, with 47 bitches in competition. Anxious that Diana should follow in the paw-prints of her dam, Elizabeth Miller developed Diana to her full potential, showing her to the championship title both in Canada and in the United States. Then Diana was bred to American Champion Bulli von Meyerhoff, and here also she did herself, her heritage, and her owner proud,

Top: Am. and Can. Ch. Northwind's Barras (1966–1976) by Rodsden's Kluge v d Harque ex Northwind's Tina. Owned by M. Romoser, Chicago, Ill. **Bottom:** Am. Ch. Northwind's Bricka, born in 1966, sired by the same parents as Barras. Owned by A. Tice of Connecticut. Photos courtesy of breeder Patricia Hickman Clark, Ottawa, Onatrio, Canada.

with a litter in which four Canadian champions gained title, two American champions, one Schutzhund degree, one S.V., and one Canadian C.D. Certainly a litter in which a breeder can take pride!

One of the above progeny, Champion Zulu Magic, was bred to International and American Champion Bronco vom Rauderfeld SchH.III, F.D. owned by Srigo Kennels in the United States. This breeding has produced a litter of ten, five each of males and females, of obvious and exciting quality.

Zulu is a small, select kennel dedicated to upholding the standard of the Rottweiler, and is owned and operated by Elizabeth Miller, Milverton, Ontario, Canada.

Top left: Ch. Olga von Gruenerwald, by Ch. Donar v.d. Neckarstroom (Dutch import) ex Ch. Jenni von Gruenerwald, was one of the foundation bitches of Alan P. Kruse's Von der Kruse Rottweilers, Howell, Michigan. **Top right:** An informal snapshot of Ch. Ursus von Stolzenfels taken by his owner, Erika Beqaj, Richmond Hill, N.Y. **Bottom:** Carsan's Jumping Jack Flash, by Birch Hill's Governor, C.D. ex Doroh's Hallelujah Tulla, U.D. Co-owned by Mary Lou Fiaua and Sandy and Carlos Meijas, Washington, D.C. Photo by Chris Cavaliere.

Aust. Ch. Brabantsia Delrego, by Guiding Flame (U.K. import) ex Brabantsia Aleta. Owned by Stephen Lodge, New South Wales, Australia.

CHAPTER SIX

Aust. Ch. Zeldermann Zuleika, by Aust. Ch. Bilpin Carrith, C.D. ex Aust. Ch. Brandlouchin Bessie, was 1983 Rottweiler of the Year in New South Wales, Australia. Owned by Ebshine Kennels, Veeni Hudson, Sweetman's Creek, N.S.W.

Rottweilers in Australia

As with so many other breeds in this extremely dog-loving country, Rottweilers have been well received by the Australians and from what we see in photographs, and from what our judging friends who have been there tell us, there are some extremely handsome dogs representing the breed in Australian show rings. Two highly successful Specialty Clubs are the Rottweiler Club of New South Wales, which sponsors many successful events; and the Rottweiler Club of Victoria, of which this is also true.

The Australian breeders always seem to me to be particularly deserving of credit and appreciation for their achievements in the producing of highest quality dogs. It is certainly not easy for them to bring in new stock with which to enhance their own due to the lengthy quarantine period; yet they do so when necessary, making their selections carefully, then using them to best advantage.

Rotties are invariably well represented by splendid specimens at their Specialty Shows; at the Royal Shows; and at other events throughout that vast country.

On the following pages, we tell you of some of the noted Rotties and Rottie owners in Australia. You will note the pride with which they speak of the Rottweilers there; also the number of breed-representatives who gain championship titles and other honors at an early age.

Captain Craig Bryan

Captain Craig Bryan of Randwick, New South Wales, Australia, takes tremendous pride in his very handsome and noted Rottweiler dog, Australian Champion Rotvel Trooper. Bred by one of the forerunners of the Rottweiler in Australia, Miss Jay D. Belles (formerly Pherson), Trooper was born October 26, 1981, a son of Rotvel Zorro from Rotvel Vivian. He gained his Australian title at age 21 months and by May 1985, is still being shown successfully.

Apart from multiple Best of Breed awards, Trooper has six "in Group" awards to his credit. At the Annual Rottweiler Championship Specialty Shows since 1982 he was Opposite Baby Puppy in Show in 1982; Best Junior in Show in 1983; Best Intermediate,

Reserve Challenge in 1984; and Best Open in Show 1985. At the Spring Fair he was Best Intermediate and Reserve Challenge in 1983; at the Winter Classic Best Puppy in Breed 1982; Best Junior in Breed 1983. At Sydney Royal Easter Show, Best Open, Challenge, and Runner-up to Best of Breed 1984. At the Ribbon Parade, Best Intermediate and Best Exhibit in 1983. Best Champion Exhibit in 1984. And he was the Rottweiler Score Point Champion in 1983/84.

Ebshine

The start of Ebshine Kennels at Sweetman's Creek, New South Wales, Australia, came about when in 1976 Miss Veeni Hudson and her family purchased their first Rottweiler dog, Cardwell Adelwin, known affectionately as "Mauser." Never before had they known a dog to be so affectionate and loyal to his family as this one. At age 13 months, although not disobedient with his owners around the house, he became unruly when walking on the street. So he was taken to obedience school where Miss Hudson started training him there with other dogs. Eight months later she decided to trial him. He went through all his exercises with ease, and became the first Rottweiler to earn a C.D. title in New South Wales, at the same time making his 16-year-old owner-handler the youngest handler there to accomplish this achievement with her dog. Mauser finished his degree in three trials within one month's time.

After moving to a country property, Veeni Hudson acquired her first bitch in 1978, Klusenhayn Charney, "Carla" to her owners. While not the world's greatest show bitch, her owner loved her dearly and she is sadly missed now having been put to sleep following a lengthy illness in 1985. During her lifetime, Carla produced a lovely litter of eight puppies by Baskina Black Kojak, C.D., owned and bred by Joan Bull, Baskina Rottweilers. These puppies are now producing their own heirs to this bloodline.

In 1979 Miss Hudson purchased another bitch, age two years, Ravenspur Ariadane, or "Elsa." She was shown, gaining her Australian Championship in eight months' time. She and Carla worked well together in herding

cattle and livestock. "Elsa" produced Ebshine's very first litter, sired by "Mauser," which was really exciting, with 11 puppies.

Then in 1981, Zeldermenn Zuleika came. Purchased as a show bitch she proved to be one of the best, starting to win at the very tender age of four months. She is now a multiple "in Group" and "in Show" all breeds winner, and gained her Australian title when only 12 months of age. She won Challenge Bitch in 1983's Rottweiler Club of New South Wales Championship Show, and also best gaited bitch and best colored bitch. She was the 1982 and 1983 New South Wales Rottweiler of the Year. She has won classes at Sydney's Royal Easter Show and is still showing her style even now.

After watching the up-and-coming offspring of Baskina Black Kojak, C.D., Miss Hudson bought a dog puppy of his from an English import bitch, Borgvaale Sunday Morning. This puppy, Baskina Zoiz Rebel, shaped up to be yet another Australian Champion for Ebshine Kennels. "Centurian" is his masterful call name, and he is now producing some truly excellent puppies.

From Centurian and Zuleika came a small but very special litter in December 1984, three puppies known as Ebshine's Zulian Conan (dog) and Ebshine Julian Jenjen and Ebshine Zulian Celica (bitches). The latter, Celica, is in Roseville (far North Queensland) and the other two have been kept at Ebshine.

At present Ebshine's Rottweiler family consists also of Cesardepasaj Kramskoja, "Cameo," who is half way through to title at age eight months. Rottsunvale Helvetia, "Haley," still a pup but shaping up well, owned in partnership with Rob Miller and Jeff Hart of Rottsunvale Rottweilers, is a granddaughter of Australia's great show dog and sire, Australian Champion Lanzeon Vaughn. Then there are two more of Centurian's daughters, Janeolla Foegarty and Janeolla Desma, who are litter sisters.

As yet there are no true Ebshine champions, but this is basically due to Miss Hudson's only ever having bred four litters from this prefix. However, a dog called Ebshine Gross Mute, from Mauser and Else, sired a champion bitch called Windswept Paper

Roses. There is also Ebshine True Commander, who is well on his way to the title, and offspring of Centurian who are also in the ring and winning points towards their titles.

The future of Ebshine Kennels lies with these dogs. It is a small but thriving kennel that is expanding, and 1986 and 1987 should prove to be rather a special period as these youngsters will prove as they mature.

Hertzog

Robert and Cheryl Wakeham, of Koonawarra, N.S.W., Australia, bought their first dog, Retohr Regnans (by Australian Champion Lanzeon Vaughan ex Tooraweena Heidi) from Peter and Rhonda Foster as a show prospect in 1979. His first show, Rottweiler Club of New South Wales, Easter 1980, saw him go up as Baby in Show under Mr. B. Dryburgh. Since then "Kane" has achieved an amazing degree of success.

This splendid Rottweiler, at 13 months' age, completed his championship from a challenge line-up that included his sire, and since then has won Reserve Challenge at the prestigious Sydney Royal; Challenge and Best of Breed at another Sydney Royal, Best in Show at Rottweiler Club of New South Wales Championship Show, Australian-bred in Show Rottweiler Club of New South Wales Specialty Show, numerous Challenges, Best of Breed and in Group Awards at major shows under international judges, culminating in Open Dog and Reserve Challenge under Herr Willi Fausner at the Rottweiler Club of Victoria Specialty in 1984.

Cheryl's eye for a good dog held up with her selection of Rotvel Uberbeiten (Rotvel Inca ex Rotvel Nadjia) from a litter bred by Joy Belles of "Rotvel" fame. "Hope" has had a varying degree of success, and is considered a very typey bitch with a good Rottweiler temperament. She was purchased as a prospective brood bitch because of her excellent pedigree, and has lived up to this in the production of her first "A" litter which is now 15 months old. These pups are successful in the show ring. Hertzog Alena looks extremely promising and Hertzog Astro is shaping up as a nice young dog. He has had some good wins as a Baby Dog and was recently awarded Reserve Challenge Dog under breed specialist

Ms. Nina Bondarenko at the Rottweiler Club of New South Wales Specialty for 1985.

At the moment of writing, May 1985, the Wakeham's "B" litter, by Rotvel Alpine Atom ex Rotvel Uberbeiten, is still in the nest but showing very exciting promise even at so early an age. Feeling that the true indication of just how successful a stud dog and the breeder are lies in the attitude that people have towards him and his progeny. If the reaction that has been generated by "Kane" and "Hope" is any indication, they have certainly been highly successful representatives for their breed.

Cheryl Wakeham gives much credit for the kindness and help she has received from Joy Belles in furthering her own interest in and success with the breed. Joy Belles has been raising top quality Rottweilers in Australia for 15 years or more, and her handsome Rotvel dogs are to be found in most of the leading lines there. She is a dedicated breeder of true working type Rottweilers who is only too happy to assist sincere newcomers striving to do likewise.

A young bitch, Retohr Daring Gem, by Rotvel Ives ex Retohr Brave Kai, is being watched with special interest at the time of writing, having lately taken Best Baby in Show at the 1985 Rottweiler Club of New South Wales Specialty.

As for "Kane": he rules supreme as a beloved family pet, a success in the show ring, and an ambassador of good will for his breed. We understand that he has qualified to be placed on the Honor Roll of the Rottweiler Club of New South Wales as a dog worthy of recognition in years to come.

Stephen Lodge's Rottweilers

The first Rottweiler owned by Mr. Stephen Lodge at Miller in New South Wales, Australia, was the puppy who grew up to become Australian Champion Rottser Valeda, C.D. This excellent bitch has done very well for Mr. Lodge, having won Best of Breed at Winter Classics in 1983 and 1984, the first time from the puppy class at age nine months. She also was Challenge Certificate winning bitch at the Spring Fair in 1983 under Mr. Robert Forsyth from the U.S.A., and at Canberra Royal in 1983 under Mr. K.

BREED:	ROTTWEILER

SEX	FEMALE

DATE OF BIRTH: 1ST JUNE 1981

BRED BY: MISS. P. MOTT

NAME: CH. ZELDERMENN ZULEIKA	Reg. No. (N) 621154
COLOUR and MARKINGS: BLACK AND TAN	
OWNED BY: V. HUDSON	

PARENTS	GRANDPARENTS	GREAT-GRANDPARENTS	GREAT-GREAT-GRANDPARENTS
SIRE: CH. BILPIN GARRITH C.D. No. 494919 Owned by: Mr. Q. Rogers	SIRE: ROTVEL ULYSSEUS 21.V.74	S. CH. HEATHERGLEN FRITZ 4.V.73 D. ROTVEL ECHO 9.V.71	HEATHERGLEN RUDI S. 4.V.66 CHESARA DARK WISHFUL (IMP. U.K.) D. 145316/71 CH. AUSLESE POMMERY S. 7.V.70 HEATHERGLEN MARLO D. 3.V.69
	DAM: ISOLA PHAEDRA 69.V.76	S. KOROBEIT HUD (IMP. N.Z.) 9469/75 D. MURRALGAH ADELLE 23.V.74	UPEND GALLANT ALF (IMP. U.K.) S. 142431/72 N.Z. CH. ATTILA BATHSHEBA D. 143488/73 (IMP. U.K.) HEATHERGLEN RUDI S. 4.V.66 KOROBEIT GIDGET D. 11.2.72
DAM: CH. BRANDLOUCHIN BESSIE No. V.14495 Owned by: MISS P. MOTT	SIRE: CHESARA DARK BORIS (IMP. U.K.) A78826A12	S. TORRO TRIOFACTOR FROM CHESARA 59633/75 (IMP. HOLLAND) D. CHESARA DARK OLGA 182490/73	BRUTUS VOM GEORGSHOF S. A.D.R.K. 43287 FACHATRIOMFACTOR D. 406890 CH. CHESARA KRUGER S. 2173BE CHESARA DARK WANDERER D. 145317/771
	DAM: RYDAVLON BRANDI 50.V.75.	S. HEATHERGLEN GINALDUS 11.V.74 D. HEATHERGLEN TEANA 25.V.74	HEATHERGLEN RUDI S. 4.V.66 CHESARA DARK WISHFUL (IMP. U.K.) D. 145316/71 CHESARA DARK NOBLEMAN S. 158145/71 HEATHERGLEN JUNO D. 9.V.72.

I hereby certify that the above information is correct to the best of my knowledge and belief.

SIGNED: _____   DATE: _____

224

Hertzog Alena and Hertzog Astro at 15 months of age. Littermates by Retohr Regnans ex Rotvel Uberbeiten. Owned by Mrs. C. Wakeham, New South Wales, Australia.

Brown, New Zealand, and was Reserve Challenge at the Sydney Royal in 1984 and 1985. Valeda completed her championship title at 10½ months of age, a record for the breed in Australia, Mr. Lodge points out.

In obedience Valeda earned Highest Scoring Novice at an all-breed trial to complete her C.D. degree; then at the 1985 Rottweiler Club of New South Wales Obedience Trial she was in Open for her first time and took High in Trial there.

Valeda was expecting her second litter as this was written. One of the bitches from her first litter, at six months and three days old, has already been awarded her first Challenge Certificate.

The second Rottweiler at Mr. Lodge's kennel is Australian Champion Brabantsea Delrego. Unfortunately three days after the Lodges received him at eight and a half weeks' age he came down with parvo and was quite awhile recovering from this dread disease. He did so, though, and at 20 months of age has had Best of Breed at Canberra Royal in 1984 and Best Minor in Group; then in 1985 he returned to again take Best of Breed at Canberra Royal and runner-up in Group under judges Mr. Crowley, from Victoria, and Mr. R. Norris, from West Australia.

The third of the Lodges' Rottweilers is the puppy they kept from Valeda's first litter, sired by Powderhorn's Fetz of Wencrest (U.S. import). This one is now eight months old, and the fourth of the breed has lately joined the family at 11 weeks of age from Australian Champion Auslese Iago Rabe (U.K. import) and Echo vom Magdeberg (German import).

Janbicca The Craftsman, a promising six-week-old puppy from Janbicca Kennels, Mr. K. and Mrs. J. M. Bloom, Ringmer, East Sussex, England.

CHAPTER SEVEN

The Rottweiler in Great Britain

Eng. Ch. Ablaze of Janbicca, winner of eight Challenge Certificates, is an outstanding Rottweiler owned in England by Janbicca Kennels, Mr. K. and Mrs. J. M. Bloom. Photo by Frank Garwood and reproduced courtesy of the owner. Janbicca Kennels are at Ringmer, East Sussex.

The first appearance in public by a Rottweiler in Great Britain was in 1937 when the great "dog lady" who has been associated with so many breeds, Mrs. Thelma Gray, whose Rosavel Kennels are world famous, entered Crufts' with Rozavel Arnolf v.d. Eichener Ruine. He was one of two Rotties owned at the time by Mrs. Gray; and with his kennel-mate, International Champion Rozavel Vefa v Kohlerwald, attracted much attention and admiration on the part of the British public. A third Rottweiler belonging to Mrs. Gray, an English-born homebred named Anna, helped create the good impression made by her breed when she became known for outstanding performance in obedience trials. Probably had it not been for the advent of World War II, the breed would then have enjoyed a notable popularity rise. But as it was, no outstanding activity took place for these dogs in Great Britain until 1954.

Several importations then were brought in. Mrs. Chadwick's Quinta Eulanspiegel of Mallion and Captain Roy-Smith's Ajax v Fuhrenhamp, turned up among the entries at Crufts'

1955, with five of them the following year, including at least one who was a British homebred. Since then interest and representation have been steady.

Mrs. Chadwick also imported the handsome German-bred Rudi Eulanspiegel from Marianne Bruns in Germany. These Eulanspiegel Rottweilers were of tremendous importance to the breed in England, representing finest German type and quality which was passed on to their descendants.

There are numerous excellent Rottweiler kennels currently active in Great Britain. Among them are Mrs. Pat Lanz's Borgvaale establishment, at Hempstead, Herts, which specializes in both Pulis and Rottweilers. Although she is unable to show her Rottweilers as extensively as previously, Mrs. Lanz has owned and/or bred many champions and consistent winners in this breed. Her present winners include Borgvaale Enchanted Shadow, by Irish Champion Borgvaale Christian ex Borgvaale Black Orchid.

House of Herburger, Rosalie and Peter Hughes, owners, at Boston, Lincolnshire, owns Herburger's Blanes Max, a Junior Warrant winner, also with Reserve C.C. and Best of Breed wins to his credit. "Lenz" was Best Puppy in Show at the Rottweiler Club Championship Show in 1983. Numerous other awards and wins have come to this dog as well, including an "excellent" grading in TT. Sired by Powderhorn Fetz of Wencrest, now in Australia, this dog has behind him the top German and Dutch bloodlines of International Champion Oscar van het Brabantpark, International Champion Farro v het Brabantpark, and International Champion Erno v Wellesweiler.

Another member of this kennel is the import, Herburger Arno von Ross, linebred to International Champion Dux vom Hungerbuhl; and Arno's son, the Best of Breed and Reserve Best in Show winner, Herburger Rio Grande, from Champion Natasha, also belongs to the Hughes.

Mrs. B. Butler, Newport, Shropshire, owns Champion Upend Gallant Gairbert, Champion Ausscot Franzell from Upend, and Champion Upend Gay Quilla. Her Upend Gallant Theodoric, a Junior Warrant winner, started out a good show career with half a dozen Best Puppy in Breed awards. He is a son of Champion Caprido Minstrel of Potterspride ex Upend Gay Jenny, C.D.

Tellimar Rottweilers, Barry and Lynne Mitchell, owners, Arnold, Notts, own Kim of Churchlea from Tallimar, a Challenge Certificate and Reserve C.C. winner; also Chaymaie Louisianna from Tellimar and her son, Tellimar's Hero, the latter sired by Champion Rottsann's Classic Crusader of Vormund.

Heranmine Rottweilers belong to Mr. and Mrs. W. Brownley, Underwood, Notts, the owners of the famous Rottsann Classic Centurian, whose story has particular interest, this lovely dog having come from a pet home. Very quickly following acquisition by the Brownleys he started to make his presence felt in the show ring, highlighted by his win of the Challenge Certificate, Best of Breed, and Best in Show in more than 300 entries at the Midland Rottweiler Club Championship Show. Also at Heranmine are to be found other such famous Rotties as Champion Karla of Heranmine and Champion Herburger

Count Ferro. Karla has an especially imposing show record as the winner of ten Challenge Certificates, six Reserve Challenge Certificates, and three Bests in Show.

Champion Rottsann Classic Crusader of Vormund, one of England's most respected Rottweilers, is owned by John and Jennie Dunhill, Vormund Kennels, Sandygate, Sheffield, England. This is a son of Chesara Dark Herod ex Porrot Fantasia.

Other of their Rotties include Dolly Daydream of Potterspride, Junior Warrant and Challenge Certificate winner, by Champion Caprido Minstrel at Potterspride ex Tara Treenaire; also Yorlander Grecian Girl of Vormund, by Chesara Dark Hunter's Dawn from Yorlander.

Jane and Michael Heath, Quinton, Birmingham, are owners of another well-known name in British Rottweilers, Champion Harburger Touch of Brilliance from Vauhirsch.

Janbicca

Janbicca Kennels, located at Ringmer, East Sussex, England, feature Rottweilers and Pugs and are owned by Mr. K. and Mrs. J. M. Bloom.

The Blooms are justifiably proud of their Rottweilers, having produced three champions and been responsible for several others. They have also exported winning dogs to a number of countries, including the holder of a Working Certificate in Australia, Janbicca Supersonic.

Champion Janbicca the Superman was a record-holding dog of his time, winner of 14 Challenge Certificates, a Junior Warrant holder, and Stud Dog of the Year 1980, the only dog in the breed to date to hold all three titles during his lifetime in Great Britain. He is the sire of four champions, Ablaze of Janbicca, Fryerns Advocator (from the same litter), Iseala the Saxon (Reserve Working Group, Crufts 1983), and Jagen Blue Aria. Superman himself was Best of Breed at Crufts in 1976 and Best of Opposite Sex in 1977.

Champion Ablaze of Janbicca, Superman's daughter, has won eight Challenge Certificates. Although she herself has not yet produced a champion, she is the granddam of an important young dog, Janbicca Perseus, based in Ireland and the winner of his class at

Crufts in 1985. In addition he is already the holder of a Reserve Challenge Certificate. Dear Deception of Janbicca was one of a team from this kennel featured in a BBC television program.

BRITISH STANDARD

• **General appearance**—The Rottweiler is an above-average-sized stalwart dog. His correctly proportioned, compact and powerful form permits of great strength, manoeuverability and endurance. His bearing displays boldness and courage; his tranquil gaze manifests good nature and devotion.

• **Head and skull**—The head is of medium length; the skull between the ears is broad. The forehead line is moderately arched as seen from the side. Occipital bone well developed but not conspicuous. Cheeks well muscled but not prominent, with the zygomatic arch well formed. The skin on the head should not be loose although it is allowed to form moderate wrinkle when the dog is attentive. Muzzle fairly deep with topline level and length not longer than the length from stop to occiput.

• **Nose**—The nose is well developed with proportionately large nostrils and is always black.

• **Eyes**—The eyes should be of medium size, almond shaped and dark brown in colour; eyelids close lying.

• **Ears**—The ears are pendant, small in proportion rather than large, set high and wide apart on the head, lying flat and close to the cheek.

• **Mouth**—The teeth are strong and the incisors of the lower jaw must touch the inner surface of the upper incisors. The flews are black and firm; they fall gradually away towards the corners of the mouth, which do not protrude excessively.

• **Neck**—The neck should be of fair length, strong, round and very muscular. It should be slightly arched and free from throatiness.

• **Forequarters**—The shoulders should be well placed on the body, long and sloping with the elbows well let down, but not loose. The legs should be muscular with plenty of bone and substance. The pasterns should be bent slightly forward and not completely vertical. The front legs seen from all sides must be straight and not placed too closely to one another.

• **Body**—The chest should be roomy, broad and deep with the ribs well sprung. The depth of brisket will not be more, and not much less than 50% of the shoulder height. The back should be straight, strong and not too long; ratio of shoulder height to length of body should be as 9 is to 10; the loins short, strong and deep, the flanks should not be tucked up. The croup should be broad, of proportionate length, and very slightly sloping.

• **Hindquarters**—The upper thigh not too short, broad and strongly muscled. The lower thigh well muscled at the top and strong and sinewy lower down. Stifles fairly well bent. Hocks well angulated without exaggeration and not completely vertical.

• **Feet**—The feet should be strong, round and compact with the toes well arched. The hind feet are somewhat longer than the front. The pads should be very hard and the toenails short, dark and strong. Rear dewclaws removed.

• **Gait**—In movement the Rottweiler should convey an impression of supple strength, endurance and purpose. While the back remains firm and stable there is a powerful hind thrust and good stride. First and foremost, movement should be harmonious, positive and unrestricted.

• **Tail**—Carried horizontally. It is short, strong and not set too low. It should be docked at the first joint.

• **Coat**—The coat, which consists of top coat and undercoat, should be of medium length, coarse and flat. The undercoat, which is essential on the neck and thighs, should not show through the outer coat. The hair may also be a little longer on the back of the forelegs and breachings.

• **Colour**—The colour is black with clearly defined markings on the cheeks, muzzle, chest and legs, as well as over both eyes and the area beneath the tail. Colour of markings ranges from rich tan to mahogany brown.

• **Size**—For males the height at the shoulder should be between 25 and 27 inches and for females between 23 and 25 inches. However, height should always be considered in relation to the general appearance of the dog.

• **Faults**—The following faults are noted for the clarification of the Standard: (1) Too lightly or too heavily built. (2) Sway backed or roach backed. (3) Cow hocked, bow hocked, or weak hocked. (4) Long or excessively wavy coat. (5) Any white markings. (6) Nervousness and viciousness are highly undesirable.

NOTE—Male animals should have two apparently normal testicles fully descended into the scrotum.

Am. and Can. Ch. Marksman von Turick, owned by Lee Whittier, Woodstock, Vermont, here is taking Best of Winners at Mohawk Valley in 1982.

CHAPTER EIGHT

The *Illustrated* Standard

Sponsored and produced
by the
American Rottweiler Club

Ch. Rodsden's Duke Du Trier, owned by Mr. and Mrs. Olson and handled by Richard Orseno, taking one of his Best in Show victories at Illinois Valley K.C. in 1971.

The Rottweiler, as we know the breed today (1980's) is still a reflection of the dog used in the 18th and 19th Century—a large, robust, and powerful dog with the character and structure associated with other working breeds.

The first Standard for the breed appeared in Germany in the early 1900's. The general type outlined at that time has not changed substantially, nor has the dog's character.

We shall leave the documentation of their origin to others, with only a comment that very few species of domestic canines can authentically be traced back more than several hundred years. The purposes and functions for which the Rottweiler was bred and developed are no longer applicable. Rarely is he required to walk with the butcher, pull milk carts or protect and herd cattle.

In this century we have found the Rottweiler to be functional in different capacities—in guarding home, family and property, and in police work. Here is a breed that is devoted, loyal and of medium temperament. He is bold, fearless, but very patient and never loses his nerve. His nature is hard, his movements and emotions controlled. He reacts slowly to the unusual. He is a dog which thrives in learning situations, be it obedience, tracking or rescue work.

The Rottweiler is not a dog to be chained or constantly kenneled. His short coat makes him easy to groom. His urge to exercise is not pronounced. He is a versatile dog, possessed of great intelligence, stamina and a relatively calm disposition.

The qualities we find in the breed today have not been lost over the centuries. The attributes of temperament, structure and function are the primary responsibility of breeders, exhibitors and judges and must be preserved.

The purpose of this Illustrated Standard is to detail reasons for breeding correct structure, correct type and correct movement. Certain anatomical parts of the dog must be correctly structured in order to preserve soundness, whether it be of movement, topline, fronts or rears. The whole is the sum of the various parts.

231

During the past ten years, there have been subtle changes in the structure and type of Rottweilers bred and exhibited in the U.S. With the population explosion in the breed, there is even less consistency in type than before. Why?

One obvious reason is that with the influx of newcomers to the breed, scant attention has been given to the Standard. Details such as almond-shaped eyes, correct markings and broad chests matched with broad heads have been neglected in breeding programs. The natural substance of the cart-dog has been replaced with a more refined, elegant specimen which does not reflect the heavy-duty dog of earlier times. A Rottweiler should not have a houndy head, should not appear weedy, leggy or fine-boned. He should exemplify sturdiness, stoutness and substance, without being "fat" or overpowering. The Rottweiler is an agile, noble dog of substance, resembling neither a Mastiff nor a Doberman. Refinement in both dogs and bitches is incorrect if we are to adhere to the Standard.

This Illustrated Standard has been prepared with the thought that breeders, exhibitors and judges will gain better insight into the basic purpose of the Rottweiler, past and present. Our utilization of the dog has been modified because of changing requirements, but the basic structure, the basic character and deportment should remain typical of the Cart Dog.

OFFICIAL STANDARD

The Board of Directors of the American Kennel Club has approved the following revised Standard for Rottweilers:
• *General Appearance—The ideal Rottweiler is a large, robust and powerful dog, black with clearly defined rust markings. His compact build denotes great strength, agility and endurance. Males are characteristically larger, heavier boned and more masculine in appearance.*
• *Size—Males, 24" to 27"; Females, 22" to 25". Proportion should always be considered rather than height alone. The length of the body from the breast bone (sternum) to the rear edge of the pelvis (ischium) is slightly longer than the height of the dog at the withers, the most desirable proportion being as 10 to 9. Depth of chest should be fifty percent of the height.* SERIOUS

FAULTS—*Lack of proportion, undersize, oversize.*
• *Head—Of medium length, broad between the ears; forehead line seen in profile is moderately arched. Cheekbones and stop well developed; length of muzzle should not exceed distance between stop and occiput. Skull is preferred dry, however some wrinkling may occur when dog is alert.*
• *Muzzle—Bridge is straight, broad at base with slight tapering towards tip. Nose is broad rather than round, with black nostrils.*
• *Lips—Always black; corners tightly closed. Inner mouth pigment is dark. A pink mouth is to be penalized.*
• *Teeth—42 in number (20 upper and 22 lower); strong, correctly placed, meeting in a scissors bite—lower incisors touching inside of upper incisors.* SERIOUS FAULTS: *Any missing tooth, level bite.* DISQUALIFICATIONS: *Undershot, overshot, four or more missing teeth.*
• *Eyes—Of medium size, moderately deep set, almond shaped with well-fitting lids. Iris of uniform color, from medium to dark brown—the darker shade is always preferred.* SERIOUS FAULTS: *Yellow (bird of prey) eyes; eyes not of same color; eyes unequal in size or shape. Hairless lid.*
• *Ears—Pendant, proportionately small, triangular in shape; set well apart and placed on skull so as to make it appear broader when the dog is alert. Ear terminates at approximate mid-cheek level. Correctly held, the inner edge will lie tightly against cheek.*
• *Neck—Powerful, well muscled, moderately long with slight arch and without loose skin.*
• *Body—Topline is firm and level, extending in straight line from withers to croup.*
• *Brisket—Deep, reaching to elbow.*
• *Chest—Roomy, broad with well-pronounced forechest.*
• *Ribs—Well sprung.*
• *Loin—Short, deep and well muscled.*
• *Croup—Broad, medium length, slightly sloping.*
• *Tail—Normally carried in horizontal position—giving impression of an elongation of top line. Carried slightly above horizontal when dog is excited. Some dogs are born without a tail, or a very short stub. Tail is normally docked short close to the body. The set of the tail is more important than length.*

• **Forequarters**—SHOULDER BLADE—*Long, well laid back at 45 degree angle. Elbows tight, well under body. Distance from withers to elbow and elbow to ground is equal.* LEGS—*Strongly developed with straight, heavy bone. Not set closely together.* PASTERNS—*Strong, springy and almost perpendicular to ground.* FEET—*Round, compact, well arched toes, turning neither in nor out. Pads thick and hard; nails short, strong and black. Dewclaws may be removed.*

• **Hindquarters**—*Angulation of hindquarters balances that of forequarters.* UPPER THIGH—*Fairly long, broad and well muscled.* STIFLE JOINT—*Moderately angulated.* LOWER THIGH—*Long, powerful, extensively muscled leading into a strong hock joint; metatarsus nearly perpendicular to ground. Viewed from rear, hind legs are straight and wide enough apart to fit in with a properly built body.* FEET—*Somewhat longer than front feet, well arched toes turning neither in nor out. Dewclaws must be removed if present.*

• **Coat**—*Outer coat is straight, coarse, dense, medium length, lying flat. Undercoat must be present on neck and thighs, but should not show through the outer coat. The Rottweiler should be exhibited in a natural condition without trimming, except to remove whiskers, if desired.* FAULT—*Wavy coat.* SERIOUS FAULTS—*Excessively short coat, curly or open coat, lack of undercoat.* DISQUALIFICATION—*Long coat.*

• **Color**—*Always black with rust to mahogany markings. The borderline between black and rust should be clearly defined. The markings should be located as follows: a spot over each eye; on cheeks, as a strip around each side of the muzzle, but not on the bridge of nose; on throat; triangular mark on either side of breastbone; on forelegs from carpus downward to toes; on inside of rear legs showing down the front of stifle and broadening out to front of rear legs from hock to toes; but not completely eliminating black from back of legs; under tail. Black penciling markings on toes. The undercoat is gray or black. Quantity and location of rust markings is important and should not exceed ten percent of body color. Insufficient or excessive markings should be penalized.* SERIOUS FAULTS—*Excessive markings; white markings any place on dog (a few white hairs do not constitute a marking); light-colored markings.* DISQUALIFICATIONS: *Any base color other than black; total absence of markings.*

• **Gait**—*The Rottweiler is a trotter. The motion is harmonious, sure, powerful and unhindered, with a strong fore-reach and a powerful rear drive. Front and rear legs are thrown neither in nor out, as the imprint of hind feet should touch that of forefeet. In a trot, the forequarters and hindquarters are mutually co-ordinated while the back remains firm; as speed is increased legs will converge under body towards a center line.*

• **Character**—*The Rottweiler should possess a fearless expression with a self-assured aloofness that does not lend itself to immediate and indiscriminate friendships. He has an inherent desire to protect home and family and is an intelligent dog of extreme hardness and adaptability with a strong willingness to work. A judge shall dismiss from the ring any shy or vicious Rottweiler.*

• **Shyness**—*A dog shall be judged fundamentally shy if, refusing to stand for examination, it shrinks away from the judge; if it fears an approach from the rear; if it shies at sudden or unusual noises to a marked degree.*

• **Viciousness**—*A dog that attacks or attempts to attack either the judge or its handler is definitely vicious. An aggressive or belligerent attitude towards other dogs shall not be deemed viciousness.*

• **Faults**—*The foregoing is a description of the ideal Rottweiler. Any structural fault that detracts from the above-described working dog must be penalized to the extent of the deviation.*

• **Disqualifications** — *Undershot, overshot, four or more missing teeth. Long coat. Any base color other than black; total absence of markings.*

COMMENTARY

• **General Appearance**

The ideal Rottweiler is a large, robust and powerful dog, black with clearly defined rust markings. His compact build denotes great strength, agility and endurance. Males are characteristically larger, heavier boned and more masculine in appearance.

COMMENTARY—The well-conditioned Rottweiler is comparable to the heavy-weight boxer in fighting form—sturdy, muscled, yet agile: *therefore carrying no excess weight.* A distinction must be drawn between male and female. The male is larger, heavier boned and reflects masculinity in his bearing and expression. The female is somewhat smaller, and

General Appearance

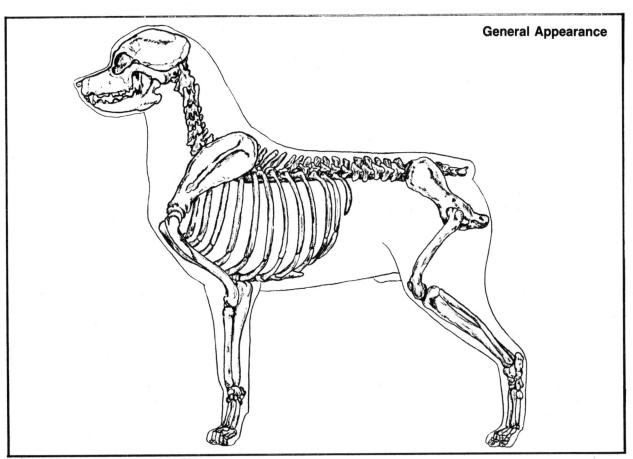

Size

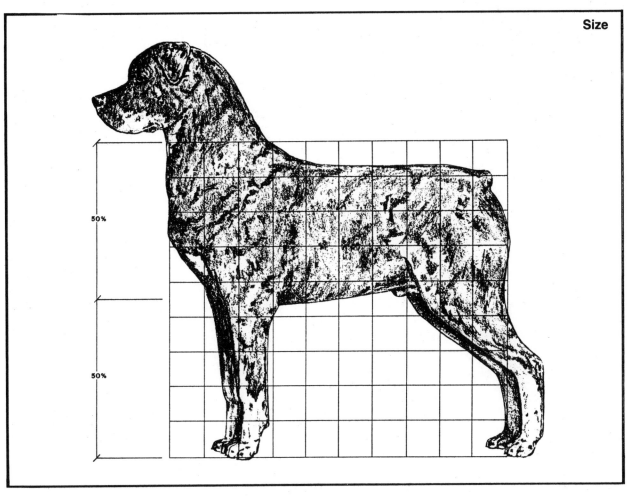

50%

50%

Head

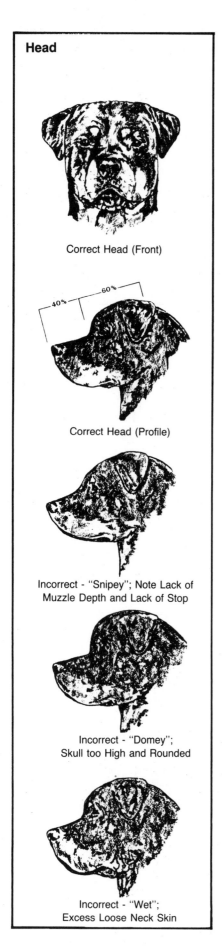

Correct Head (Front)

Correct Head (Profile)

Incorrect - "Snipey"; Note Lack of Muzzle Depth and Lack of Stop

Incorrect - "Domey"; Skull too High and Rounded

Incorrect - "Wet"; Excess Loose Neck Skin

Muzzle
Lips
Teeth

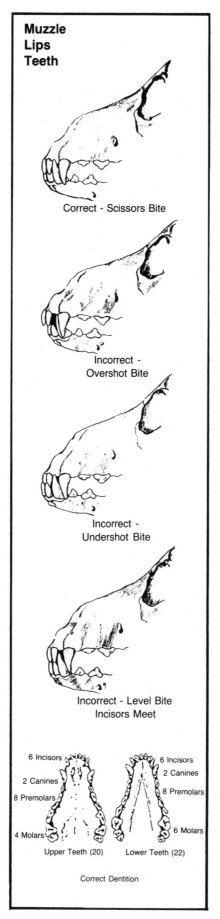

Correct - Scissors Bite

Incorrect - Overshot Bite

Incorrect - Undershot Bite

Incorrect - Level Bite Incisors Meet

6 Incisors
2 Canines
8 Premolars
4 Molars
Upper Teeth (20)

6 Incisors
2 Canines
8 Premolars
6 Molars
Lower Teeth (22)

Correct Dentition

Eyes

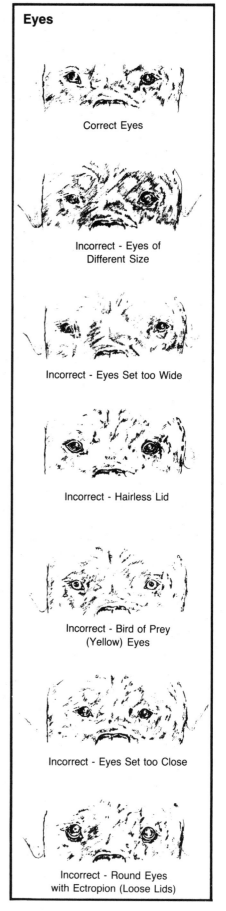

Correct Eyes

Incorrect - Eyes of Different Size

Incorrect - Eyes Set too Wide

Incorrect - Hairless Lid

Incorrect - Bird of Prey (Yellow) Eyes

Incorrect - Eyes Set too Close

Incorrect - Round Eyes with Ectropion (Loose Lids)

should be distinctly feminine in her expression and demeanor.

• **Size**

Males, 24" to 27"; Females, 22" to 25". Proportion should always be considered rather than height alone. The length of the body from the breast bone (sternum) to the rear edge of the pelvis (ischium) is slightly longer than the height of the dog at the withers, the most desirable proportion being as 10 to 9. Depth of chest should be fifty percent of the height. SERIOUS FAULTS—*Lack of proportion, undersize, oversize.*

COMMENTARY—There is a lack of size uniformity among Rottweilers throughout the U.S. Height and length are important, because a working dog cannot perform properly if he is not correctly balanced. A square dog is as faulty as a long-bodied dog. Unfortunately, there is a tendency to place the largest Rottweiler, regardless of balance and body type, high in the ribbons. This is not correct. Preference should be given to the most balanced dog within the stated range.

• **Head**

Of medium length, broad between the ears; forehead line seen in profile is moderately arched. Cheekbones and stop well developed; length of muzzle should not exceed distance between stop and occiput. Skull is preferred dry, however some wrinkling may occur when dog is alert.

COMMENTARY—Correctly, the proportion of skull to foreface is approximately as 3 is to 2, with an average overall head length of 9 to 10 inches in males, and 8½ to 9 inches in bitches.

The skull must be broad and deep to match the muzzle. The stop is definite, more pronounced in males which contributes to their masculine expression.

• **Muzzle**

Bridge is straight, broad at base with slight tapering towards tip. Nose is broad rather than round, with black nostrils.

COMMENTARY—The bridge of the muzzle is straight when viewed from the side and broad when viewed from the front. There should be a strong chin to maintain the depth and breadth of muzzle.

• **Lips**

Always black; corners tightly closed. Inner mouth pigment is dark. A pink mouth is to be penalized.

COMMENTARY—A pink mouth on a black dog is not pleasing to the eye. It is also felt that this will lead to lack of pigmentation in other areas.

• **Teeth**

42 in number (20 upper and 22 lower); strong, correctly placed, meeting in a scissors bite—lower incisors touching inside of upper incisors. SERIOUS FAULTS—*Any missing tooth, level bite.* DISQUALIFICATIONS—*Undershot, overshot, four or more missing teeth.*

COMMENTARY—It is preferred that the Rottweiler have 42 correctly placed teeth—and correct scissors bite. ANY missing tooth should be considered a serious enough fault to lower the placement, as should a level or wry (unaligned) bite.

• **Eyes**

Of medium size, moderately deep set, almond shaped with well-fitting lids. Iris of uniform color, from medium to dark brown—the darker shade always preferred. SERIOUS FAULTS—*Yellow (bird of prey) eyes; eyes not of same color; eyes unequal in size or shape. Hairless lid.*

COMMENTARY—It is a serious fault to have eyes that are yellow or light amber in color. Eye expression should be alert, intelligent and animated, not staring, dull or piercing. Too round an eye; eyes set too far apart or too close together, or a hairless eye *rim* all detract from the noble expression of the dog.

• **Ears**

Pendant, proportionately small, triangular in shape; set well apart and placed on skull so as to make it appear broader when the dog is alert. Ear terminates at approximate mid-cheek level. Correctly held, the inner edge will lie tightly against cheek.

COMMENTARY—Too long or too large ears give the Rottweiler a "houndy" look, as do ears set too low. Ears set too high give a terrier look. Many Rottweiler puppies, during the teething stage, will hold their ears incorrectly—either manifesting a "rose ear" or an incorrect crease in the ear. It is particularly true of puppies with smaller ears. Breeders and owners may tape a puppy's ears during teething to aid in correct carriage. Properly set and carried ears are essential to true Rottweiler expression and deviations should be penalized.

• Neck

Powerful, well muscled, moderately long with slight arch and without loose skin.

COMMENTARY—Proper length of neck is related to correct shoulder layback. A dog with a short "bull" neck will often have upright shoulders. A "throaty" appearance is undesirable, but judges should determine whether this is excess skin or the collar displacing skin on the neck.

• Body

Topline is firm and level, extending in straight line from withers to croup.

COMMENTARY—There should be no dip or roach, either standing or moving, as the back must serve to transmit the power generated by the rear quarters for follow through to the forequarters. Rottweilers which display either a sloping or high-in-rear topline are incorrect.

• Brisket

Deep, reaching to elbow.

COMMENTARY—Leggy dogs are not in good proportion, the legs being longer than the distance from elbow to withers. Conversely, a dog whose legs are too short also lacks correct body proportion. The brisket must reach the elbow.

• Chest

Roomy, broad with well-pronounced forechest.

COMMENTARY—The forechest should extend forward beyond the junction of the upper arm and the shoulder blade. Correct forechest is usually found in those dogs with well-set shoulders.

• Ribs

Well sprung.

COMMENTARY—The rib cage should be well sprung, neither flat (slab-sided) nor round (barrel-shaped).

• Loin

Short, deep and well muscled.

COMMENTARY—The strength and shortness of loin is further enhanced by the Rottweiler's nearly level underline (which is almost parallel to the topline). A moderate "tuck-up" is evident on puppies—a level underline appears on the adults.

• Croup

Broad, medium length, slightly sloping.

COMMENTARY—With a properly set-on tail, the croup will never be too sloping. Such tail placement helps give the desired level topline.

• Tail

Normally carried in horizontal position—giving impression of an elongation of top line. Carried slightly above horizontal when dog is excited. Some dogs are born without a tail or have a very short stub. Tail is normally docked short close to the body. The set of the tail is more important than length.

COMMENTARY—The placement of the tail is more important than the length, as it is indicative of the set of the croup. Tails held vertically are incorrect. The tail should be docked fairly close to the body (1 to 1½ joints).

• Forequarters

Shoulder Blade—long, well laid back at 45 degree angle. Elbows tight, well under body. Distance from withers to elbow and elbow to ground is equal.

COMMENTARY—The shoulder layback is important to the Rottweiler's correct movement. He should have sufficient width between the front legs (enough for a man's hand). Elbows should be tight. Common causes of loose elbows are loaded shoulders or incorrect shoulder angulation. Again, correct angulation and proportion are important; withers to elbow and elbow to ground 50-50.

• Legs

Strongly developed with straight, heavy bone. Not set closely together.

COMMENTARY—Viewed from the side, the front foot should be directly under the center of the shoulder blade. Viewed from the front, the legs should be straight and far enough apart to allow for correct width of chest.

• Pasterns

Strong, springy and almost perpendicular to ground.

COMMENTARY—A *slightly* bent pastern is desired to act as a shock absorber for the forequarter assembly when the dog is in motion.

• Feet

Round, compact, well arched toes, turning neither in nor out. Pads thick and hard; nails short, strong and black. Dewclaws may be removed.

COMMENTARY—Flat, hare or splayed feet are incorrect, as are feet which turn outward "east-west." Thick and hard pads give cushion and resist tearing. Front dewclaws are *not* removed in Europe but can be here in the U.S. at the option of the breeder.

Ears	Neck	Body

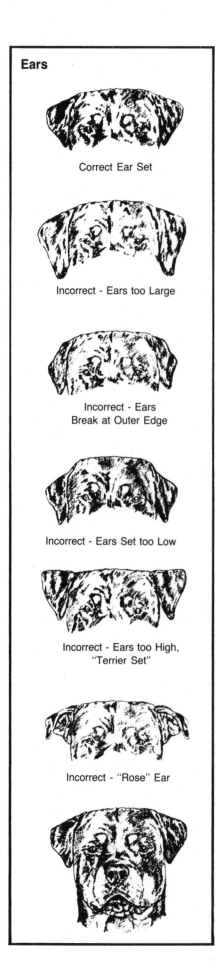

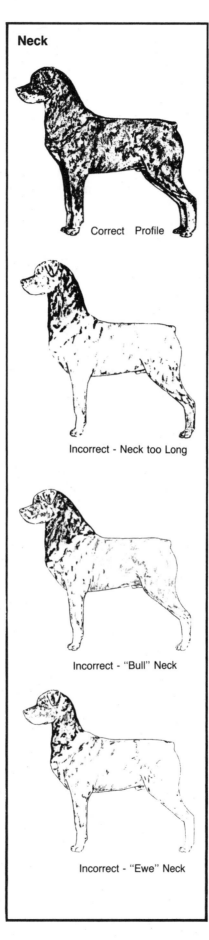

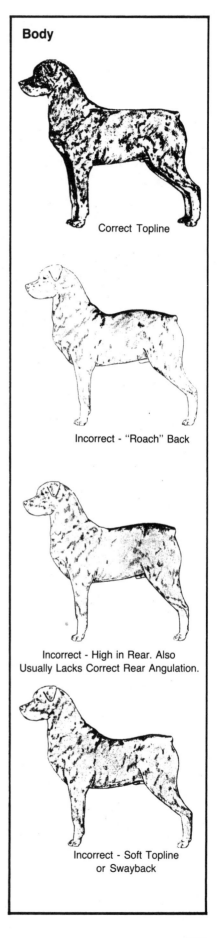

Ears

Correct Ear Set

Incorrect - Ears too Large

Incorrect - Ears
Break at Outer Edge

Incorrect - Ears Set too Low

Incorrect - Ears too High,
"Terrier Set"

Incorrect - "Rose" Ear

Neck

Correct Profile

Incorrect - Neck too Long

Incorrect - "Bull" Neck

Incorrect - "Ewe" Neck

Body

Correct Topline

Incorrect - "Roach" Back

Incorrect - High in Rear. Also
Usually Lacks Correct Rear Angulation.

Incorrect - Soft Topline
or Swayback

Brisket
Chest
Ribs

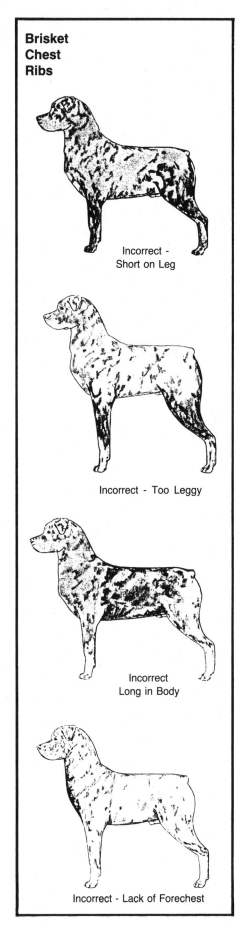

Incorrect -
Short on Leg

Incorrect - Too Leggy

Incorrect
Long in Body

Incorrect - Lack of Forechest

Loin
Croup
Tail

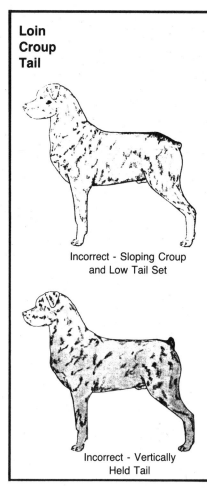

Incorrect - Sloping Croup
and Low Tail Set

Incorrect - Vertically
Held Tail

Pasterns
Feet (front)

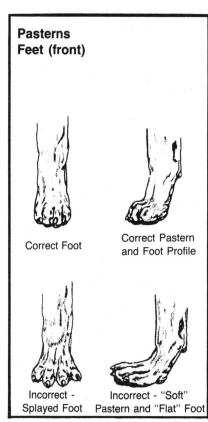

Correct Foot

Correct Pastern
and Foot Profile

Incorrect -
Splayed Foot

Incorrect - "Soft"
Pastern and "Flat" Foot

Forequarters
Legs

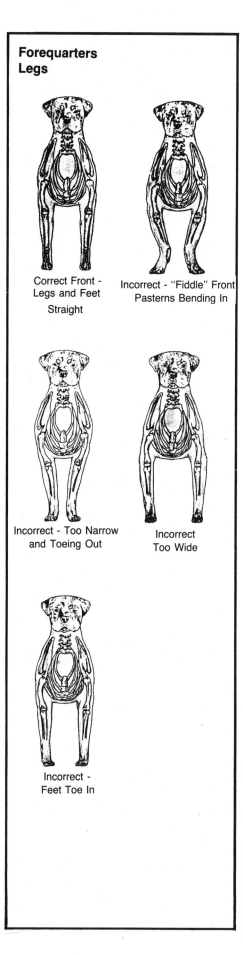

Correct Front -
Legs and Feet
Straight

Incorrect - "Fiddle" Front
Pasterns Bending In

Incorrect - Too Narrow
and Toeing Out

Incorrect
Too Wide

Incorrect -
Feet Toe In

• Hindquarters

Angulation of hindquarters balances that of forequarters.

COMMENTARY—The degree of angulation of forequarters and hindquarters must be compatible to achieve balance and correct movement.

• Upper Thigh

Fairly long, broad and well muscled.

COMMENTARY—Prominent muscling of the inner and outer thighs should be visible when viewed from the rear.

• Stifle Joint

Moderately angulated.

COMMENTARY—A correctly angulated (bent) stifle contributes to good movement, i.e., rear drive and length of stride. The Rottweiler should not appear as straight in stifle as a Mastiff nor as angulated as a German Shepherd Dog. The rear angulation should balance that of the front.

• Lower Thigh

Long, powerful, extensively muscled leading into a strong hock joint; metatarsus nearly perpendicular to ground. Viewed from rear, hind legs are straight and wide enough apart to fit in with a properly built body.

COMMENTARY—Viewed from the side, the lower thigh should be long and have substantial breadth and depth. A Rottweiler should hock neither in nor out.

• Feet

Somewhat longer than front feet, well arched, toes turning neither in nor out. Dewclaws must be removed if present.

COMMENTARY—Rear feet should be as described for front feet, but are slightly longer overall. Dewclaws, if present on the rear legs, should be removed approximately three to four days after whelping.

• Coat

Outer coat is straight, coarse, dense, medium length, lying flat. Undercoat must be present on neck and thighs but should not show through the outer coat. The Rottweiler should be exhibited in a natural condition without trimming, except to remove whiskers, if desired. FAULT—*Wavy coat.* SERIOUS FAULTS—*Excessively short coat, curly or open coat, lack of undercoat.* DISQUALIFICATION—*Long coat.*

COMMENTARY—The correct texture and length of coat (slightly longer than a Doberman coat) requires no trimming; therefore, the Rottweiler should be shown in his natural state. The amount of undercoat will vary with climatic conditions.

Incorrect coats detract from the appearance of the dog. Wavy, soft, wiry, open or curly coats and a very short (Doberman) coat should be penalized, as should a visible undercoat.

Whiskers are sensory organs, and it is strongly recommended that they never be cut. Awards should be withheld if there is any doubt as to alteration of coat or color. NOTE: AKC Rules Applying to Registration and Dog Shows, Chapter 15, Sec. 9 states in part: "A dog . . . which has been changed in appearance by artificial means . . . will be disqualified." Sec. 9-B further states: "If in the judge's opinion any substance has been used to alter or change the natural color or shade of natural color or natural markings of a dog, then in such event the judge shall withhold any and all awards from such dog. . . ."

• Color

Always black with rust to mahogany markings. The borderline between black and rust should be clearly defined. The markings should be located as follows: a spot over each eye; on cheeks, as a strip around each side of the muzzle, but not on the bridge of nose; on throat; triangular mark on either side of breastbone; on forelegs from carpus downward to toes; on inside of rear legs showing down the front of stifle and broadening out to front of rear legs from hock to toes; but not completely eliminating black from back of legs; under tail. Black penciling markings on toes. The undercoat is gray or black.

Quantity and location of rust markings is important and should not exceed ten percent of body color. Insufficient or excessive markings should be penalized. SERIOUS FAULTS—*Excessive markings; white markings any place on dog (a few white hairs do not constitute a marking); light-colored markings.* DISQUALIFICATIONS—*Any base color other than black; total absence of markings.*

COMMENTARY—Base color must be black, with dark rust-colored markings, as described. The darker shades are preferable. Excessively large markings in any location are undesirable, as are sooty or light-colored (tan) markings. Markings can sometimes be too small (or non-existent) on some or all areas. This is also incorrect.

Hindquarters
Upper Thigh

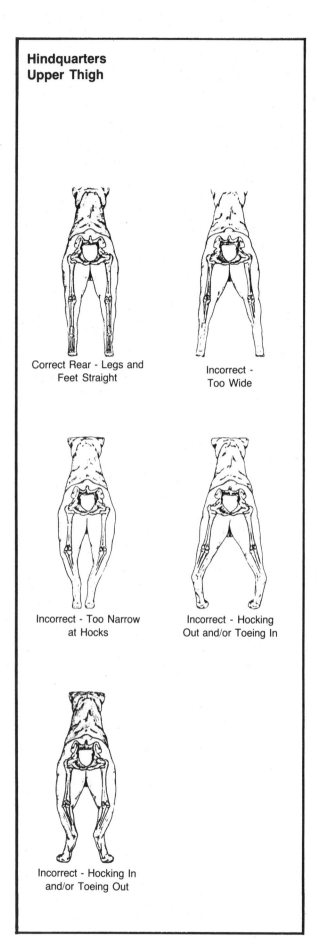

Correct Rear - Legs and
Feet Straight

Incorrect -
Too Wide

Incorrect - Too Narrow
at Hocks

Incorrect - Hocking
Out and/or Toeing In

Incorrect - Hocking In
and/or Toeing Out

Stifle Joint
Lower Thigh

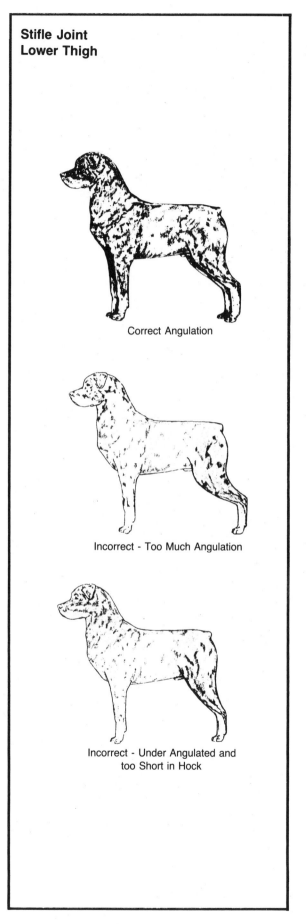

Correct Angulation

Incorrect - Too Much Angulation

Incorrect - Under Angulated and
too Short in Hock

• Gait

The Rottweiler is a trotter. The motion is harmonious, sure, powerful and unhindered, with a strong fore-reach and a powerful rear drive. Front and rear legs are thrown neither in nor out, as the imprint of hind feet should touch that of forefeet. In a trot, the forequarters and hindquarters are mutually co-ordinated while the back remains firm; as speed is increased legs will converge under body towards a center line.

COMMENTARY—As a working dog, requiring both agility and endurance, the Rottweiler should move in a straight line (without crabbing), exhibiting a smooth, rhythmical gait. The reach of the foreleg should be of good length, and the rear drive to conform requires proper flexion of the hock and stifle joints. When viewed from the side, the back should be firm with no give, and there should be no "rolling" of the body.

• Character

The Rottweiler should possess a fearless expression with a self-assured aloofness that does not lend itself to immediate and indiscriminate friendships. He has an inherent desire to protect home and family, and he is an intelligent dog of extreme hardness and adaptability with a strong willingness to work.

A judge shall dismiss from the ring any shy or vicious Rottweiler. SHYNESS—*A dog shall be judged fundamentally shy if, refusing to stand for examination, it shrinks away from the judge; if*

it fears an approach from the rear; if it shies at sudden or unusual noises to a marked degree. VICIOUSNESS—*A dog that attacks either the judge or its handler is definitely vicious. An aggressive or belligerent attitude towards other dogs shall not be deemed viciousness.*

COMMENTARY—The behavior of the Rottweiler in the show ring should be that of a controlled animal, willing and adaptable and trained to submit to examination of mouth, testicles, etc. However, an aloof or reserved dog should not be penalized, as this reflects the accepted character of the breed.

• Faults

The foregoing is a description of the ideal Rottweiler. Any structural fault that detracts from the above-described working dog must be penalized to the extent of the deviation.

• Disqualifications

Undershot, overshot, four or more missing teeth. Long coat. Any base color other than black; total absence of markings.

STANDARD APPROVED BY AKC, 9/11/79

• Conclusion

It is hoped that these illustrations and commentaries will help breeders, exhibitors and judges better understand correct and incorrect features of the total Rottweiler, thereby achieving greater uniformity and consistency of type. If breeders conscientiously strive to breed to the Standard, and judges judge according to the Standard, we can preserve the noble dog named ROTTWEILER.

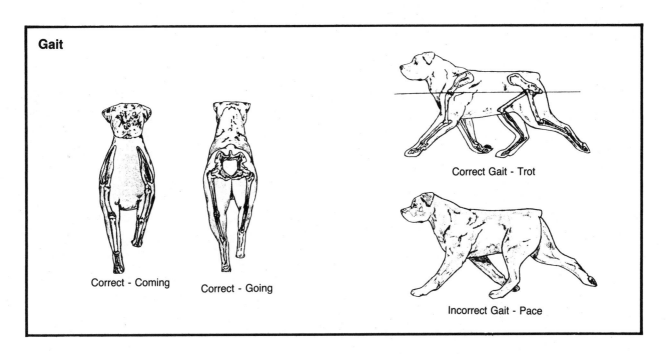

Gait

Correct - Coming

Correct - Going

Correct Gait - Trot

Incorrect Gait - Pace

Razdy's A Second Chance, left, and Ch. Razdy's Akemo-Grande, right, (the latter co-owned by breeder Judith Uggiano and by D. Hendershot) are flower girl and ring bearer at the wedding of Dorothy Hendershot and Bill Smith. There can be no doubt that these two Rotties are devoted to their owners!

CHAPTER NINE

Should *You* Own a Rottweiler?

Cora v Hartumer Busch literally "flies through the air with the greatest of ease." Owned by Powderhorn/Wencrest Rottweilers, Mrs. Clara Hurley and Michael Grossman, Hollywood, California.

The acquisition of a Rottweiler should not be taken lightly; nor should it be rushed into with the thought that these wonderful dogs are suitable for any and all people. This very definitely is *not* the case. If the breed is right for you, and you for it, the relationship will be long and rewarding. But if it is not, unhappiness and disaster may well be the result. So please do not buy in haste, then perhaps repent at leisure. It simply is not fair to you or to the Rottweiler.

The first consideration before purchase of your Rottweiler is your reason for wanting one. Are you the sort of person who truly enjoys the company of your dog, and who intends to share generously in spending time with it? The Rottweiler is among the most devoted and loyal of all breeds, developing strong attachment to its owner. While making them natural protectors, these traits also make them demanding of your time and attention. Being with you is a genuine need with such a dog, even to the extent of following you from place to place around the house,

"dogging" your footsteps, so to speak. Mutual companionship and association are essential between a Rottweiler and its person. Without it the dog will not be at its best, nor develop the true personality which makes the breed so special to those who understand and appreciate these dogs.

Rottweilers vary considerably in temperament, ranging from the reserved "one man dog" to the quite outgoing, affectionate one who loves almost everyone. Truly they seem to have an inborn sense of humor, making them fun animals—and many a Rottweiler owner has a whole series of stories proving this fact about his canine friend!

Socialization is the key word where your Rottweiler's temperament is concerned. From the very beginning, as early as young puppyhood, these dogs should be played with, loved and cuddled by people—their owners, the family and friends. As the dog matures, the more time the two of you spend together, or the entire family spends with the dog, the better adjusted, more satisfactory and happier companion he or she will become. It is nothing short of cruel to keep a Rottweiler shut off by himself, or living exclusively in a kennel. If you acquire a Rottweiler, do so with this thought in mind! Being permitted to share his or her owner's life is the ideal circumstance under which this breed should live. Even if you have a kennel, arrange a routine by which your dogs each get to spend a fair share of their time with you in the house. If possible, all of it! The more time a member of this breed spends with the family, the better adjusted, more satisfactory companion it will become. In short, if you want a dog whom you will see only occasionally, do *not* get a Rottweiler!

The size and power of a Rottweiler also must be taken into consideration, for their strong muscular development makes them true powerhouses for their size. It is no exaggeration to say that a fully grown Rottweiler can quite easily and quite unintentionally knock a person to the ground, which makes the breed unsuitable for the elderly or infirm or for small children, unless reared with the child from puppyhood.

Again, due to its size and power, obedience training is a *must* for all Rottweilers, and should be started by you at home when the animal is just a few months old. Join a training class with your dog. Follow the advice of the person from whom the dog was purchased as to locating a good one. Remember that too rough or heavy-handed a trainer should be avoided. Dogs as intelligent as Rottweilers can generally be controlled through verbal reprimands as they are anxious to please those they love. While upon some occasions there may be a need for physical correction, this should not be done in an overly rough or brutal manner. The dog should obey your commands out of a desire to earn your pleasure, not out of fear! Patience, time, and realization of the dog's intelligence and sensitivity should bring about the desired results.

As with any breed of dog, some Rottweilers are suitable for small children (and vice-versa)—others are not. It is of particular importance in this breed that my remarks in another chapter regarding teaching your children that dogs are not toys, and are to be treated with respect and kindness be heeded. Many Rottweilers love children (note the great number of illustrations in this book featuring this fact) and would protect them with their very lives, and these are especially valuable guardians for your youngster due to the breed's intelligent awareness of danger. But others resent the rough handling sometimes inflicted on dogs or puppies by a child who does not realize that his roughness or teasing may be hurting the pet. The danger here, of course, is the fact that due to the dog's size and strength should his patience be tried beyond endurance considerable damage can be inflicted on the child; it is not that Rottweilers are less patient with children than are other breeds.

With regard to other pets in your home, again it depends greatly on the individuals concerned. Rottweiler puppies are usually the easiest to introduce where an older, established pet is already "in residence," as the baby is less likely to be resented than a more mature dog.

The introduction of a grown dog into a household where other Rottweilers are already "in command" can and frequently does lead to a problem. This matter depends on the background, bloodlines and rearing of the individual dogs, and is surely not exclusive only to Rottweilers; but, again, their size and power make it sometimes a potentially dangerous situation. If you attempt it, do so only when the dogs are under strict supervision. Do not leave them alone together until you are certain they are completely adjusted to one another; and do nothing to create jealousy or resentment on the part of either dog. Remember that *you* are the center of your established Rottie's life, and his possessive nature will make him react, possibly with violence, towards any dog he considers to be a threat to that relationship.

All Rottweilers are aggressive to some degree, especially where their own property and territory are concerned. They lose no time in developing a strong sense of their "territorial rights," and feel it their duty to defend this place or area, which is one of the reasons they are so highly esteemed as guard dogs. It is also one of the things which you, the owner, must realize and be prepared to handle if a Rottweiler joins your family.

Top left: Perfect trust between the tiny Papillon and the mighty Rottweiler! Powderhorn Koch of Wencrest is obviously quite happy at having his four-month-old friend perched on his head. Both are owned by Thomas and Doris Baldwin, Pleasant Hill, California. **Top right:** Jeanette McGovern with Otto, Brimstone's Baron Von Otto, in August 1982. Windwalker Kennels, Jim and Roxanna McGovern, Port Crane, N.Y. **Bottom:** Ch. Altar's Gandolf vom Axel exchanges greetings with equine friend. David W. Lauster owns this handsome Rottweiler in Naples, Florida.

Top: Charlotte Johnson, co-owner of Frolic'n Rottweilers, with Ch. Frolic'n Darth Vader, C.D.X., T.D., TT at the 1985 Dogs On Camera Exhibit for the American Kennel Club Museum. Owned by the Johnsons and Linda Schuman, Redmond, Washington. **Bottom left:** A "therapy" puppy from von Dorow Kennels at the Terrace West Nursing Home, Midland, Texas. Ms. Estes has several photos of her puppies taken during visits to Terrace West, and the happy faces on the patients as they hold or play with these dogs speak eloquently of the pleasure Rotties bring. **Bottom right:** Gatstuberget's Troll, C.D. in the Christmas Parade, December 1968. Powderhorn/Wencrest Rottweilers, Mrs. Clara S. Hurley and Mr. Michael S. Grossman, Hollywood, California.

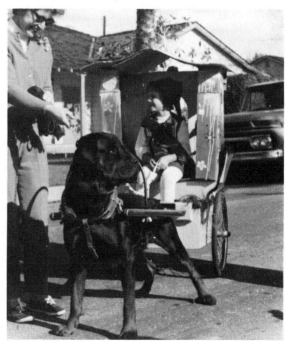

This breed is not a "nervous biter" inclined to bite without what it views to be sound provocation. However, never forget that for hundreds of generations Rotties have worked as guard dogs, an instinct which is always present and must be carefully channelled or you will find yourself with problems.

The Rottweiler usually works not only by preventing an intruder from entering the property, but also by making it impossible for that person to leave. When one considers that this "intruder," in the Rottweiler's eyes, may be the postman, a delivery-man, the gardener, the meter reader, or a friend of yours stopping by to call, it is not difficult to picture the embarrassing situations which can, and unless guarded against *do*, result. An incident involving anyone being cornered by one of these dogs in your absence will soon find you stopping at the post office to pick up your formerly cheerfully delivered mail; your home being avoided by UPS and others making package deliveries (let's hope your neighbors do not mind the role of "middleman" in these transactions), mowing your own lawn and doing the meter reading for the utility company, and becoming far less popular than formerly with the "droppers in" among your friends!

Careful obedience training will help to alleviate this situation, however, as the dog learns to be under control of your voice. All regular visitors to your home should be carefully "introduced" to the dog while you are making it clear that *you* consider this person a friend and welcome on your property, familiarizing the dog with them and so that he learns *also* to regard them as friends. It doesn't take long, as the dog's sensitivity to your attitude and feeling in the matter will be reflected in his own.

The American Rottweiler Club in its excellent pamphlet, *Introducing The Rottweiler*, makes the following statements:—

"Aggressiveness varies with the individual to some degree, although all Rottweilers have a strong territorial instinct and if socialized properly as a puppy will defend their master's home, car, and property from intruders. Rottweilers have also been known to bully or bluff their owners or other family members, a trait that is most disconcerting, but which can be prevented through early obedience training.

"Many families have purchased a Rottweiler for its protective instinct, only to discover later that it brings with it a considerable moral and legal responsibility. Problems can arise quickly; strangers must never come into your home or yard unannounced; the dog doesn't know the difference between a burglar or your brother. Your Rottweiler must be carefully schooled to accept your friends into your home, but physical contact or roughhousing should be approached carefully until the dog realizes it's all in fun. People expected to be in contact with the dog while the owners are absent should be thoroughly familiar to the dog. Although they usually do not bite without provocation, even being cornered and held by one is a very unnerving experience."

We hope that the foregoing has succeeded in alerting you to the fact that in acquiring a Rottweiler you are acquiring a responsibility. It is very much to the credit of the Rottweiler Specialty Clubs and the dedicated breeders that they make every effort to avoid dogs of this breed becoming involved in unsuitable situations. They do not want you to buy a Rottweiler and *then* learn the facts about the breed; they want you to enter into Rottweiler ownership with a full understanding of exactly what it entails because you are aware and appreciate the fact that to the true dog lover the pleasures of belonging to such a dog more than make up for the responsibilities. You will find this statement substantiated in many kennel stories and other sections of this book.

Cared for properly, by an owner wanting a dog for the pleasure of its company, the Rottweiler owner is richly rewarded by the companionship of one of the most remarkably responsive and intelligent of all dogs.

Ch. Altar's Gandolf vom Axel snapped informally with handler Wendy Wolforth. David W. Lauster, von Balingen Rottweilers, Naples, Florida, owner.

CHAPTER TEN

What It's Like to Own a Rottweiler

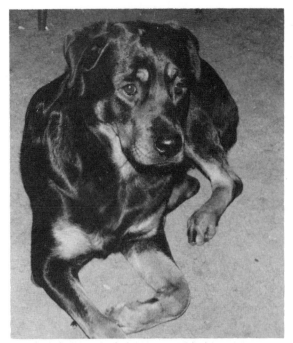

Gunda Von Brawn, the "Sara" in Sue Wales's story.

Sue Wales, of Von Walber's Rottweilers, puts it into words so well that we are going to include them here; she speaks with the same enthusiasm one hears from almost everyone who has grown to know this breed well.

Says Sue:—"I have been loved by several different dogs of a variety of breeds over the years, but my Rottweiler is the most special of all. Rotts think on a different level.

"If you buy a cuddly puppy, it will be at least three years before you meet the dog that will be upon maturity. By age four, it's hard to remember all the things your young dog did. Things like chewing holes in the wall big enough to push a basketball through, chewing the heels off all my high heel shoes, breaking windows, and shredding the trash. Murder crossed my mind more than once while Sara was growing up. Now that she has grown, I wouldn't change her for the world.

"I will someday have to replace her. I'm not looking forward to it, but I know I'll always own a Rottweiler, and I will never change breeds again. I know when Sara greets me at the door that no one is lurking behind the door except the kids. I'll never wake up to find a strange man in my room. And I know the kids are safe in their beds because Sara checks every room during the night as well as during the day.

"When I look into her eyes, I know that I am loved."

Norma Dikeman and Her Rottweiler, Scharf

Norma Dikeman lives at Westfield, New York, and is a Rottweiler owner. She also has emphysema, so must work more slowly than most trainers with her Rottweilers. Norma takes great pleasure in working with Scharf, and is proud of the fact that he works WITH her, despite the way she must walk. Another example of the wonderful companionship and understanding between a Rottweiler and his person! Needless to say, Norma is proud of Scharf's accomplishments.

Scharf is Norma's first Rottweiler who certainly provided her with a wonderful introduction to the breed. His winning personality, intelligence and charisma make him a delightful companion, and wherever he goes he makes friends.

The Dikemans also have a second Rottweiler now, co-owned with Linda Michels. She is a daughter of Champion Gasto vom Leibersfached ex Champion Heiko vom Forstwald.

Scharf has a special friend, a pig. We understand that the two spend much time playing together, and that their antics are always amusing. One of many examples of the fact that Rottweilers make friends easily with other species as well as their own!

Your Rottweiler as a Retriever

We all are accustomed to thinking of Rottweilers as dogs of many talents, but it has taken some sportsmen from Florida to point out to us the fact that they make excellent dogs for those who enjoy hunting, and can take their place quite neatly with the retrieving breeds.

Al and Bonnie Wimberly, owners of Delphi Kennels who raise Rotties and Arabian horses in Havana, Florida, have sent us a photo of one of their dogs, Champion Delphi Bitt Amex, posing with a friend, Mike Spelman, to be used in Florida wildlife publications as a promotion on Rottweilers as working companions in the field. Mr. Spelman and his wife, Gayle, own a daughter of this bitch, Delphi Echo, C.D., who is a working retriever, and to prove it they have sent the accompanying photos of her doing exactly that, which we hereby share with you.

Echo was just 11 months of age when she retrieved her first ducks opening day of the 1983 hunting season on Lake Jackson at Tallahassee. They have found her to work equally well on land or in water, and she has had numerous successful dove and quail hunts to her credit.

So, if you like to hunt and own a Rottweiler, why not try out your Rottie as a hunting companion? You may find doing so extremely rewarding, for this truly IS an all-purpose dog in one package!

Rottweilers and Their People

This is the story of Champion Ursus Von Stolzenfels, called "Bulli," and of how he came to live in the Beqaj household. "Bulli" came there as a family pet following the death of a ten year old German Shepherd. For two years the family was without a dog, missing their beloved lost friend. Then suddenly one day Erika Beqaj realized that she was afraid to go to their country home along with her two then-very-young sons now that there was no longer a canine protector to guard their safety; and she knew that the time had come to look for another large dog.

They did not want a Shepherd this time, as the loss of the old one was still strongly felt and they knew that they would keep making unfair comparisons. So a change of breed was also in order, and after all the appropriate studying of various breeds, it was decided that this time they would try a Rottweiler, the reasons being his "fierce appearance and his air of self-assured intelligence." As Mrs. Beqaj says, "He seemed to combine the power of the Mastiff with the agility of the Doberman and the hardiness of the all-American mutt."

After making several phone calls, this family was recommended to some breeders whom they contacted. All of them very kindly answered any and all questions, but one in particular stood out as she asked these prospective Rottweiler owners just as many questions as they asked her. Only later did they realize that they were being investigated as a proper home for this breed. They waited a little more than a year for the ideal puppy to be born, and since that time their home has never been the same.

The first week with their new pup was nothing more than rushing him out the door to attend to personal matters, although he made it quite clear after the first two days that by then he knew exactly where he was expected to go. They played with him, fed him, and took him along everywhere for socializing; a very important part of correctly raising a Rottweiler, they had been told repeatedly. They found the next couple of months being devoted almost exclusively to the puppy and to his needs, of which he had sufficient number to keep the entire family occupied. The whole family participated, and it is interesting that as a result the puppy developed an entirely different relationship with each of its members. Mr. Beqaj had to impress the puppy with the fact that he was the leader of the pack, and did so. Mrs. Beqaj was the one attending to his basic needs such as breakfast, lunch and dinner, and the teenage sons became his playmates, always ready for some ball chasing, wrestling, the usual boy stuff.

In between, and very informally, there was a little obedience training which he grasped very quickly with hardly any need for repetition so it was always fun—but it also became a necessity as he started to mature. One cannot rely entirely on physical control of these very powerful beasts—the control must also be verbal. It was also discovered that the bond that is formed during obedience work also helps in establishing a very solid relationship of trust. As more serious obedience training started at age six months, Bulli was found to become slightly resistant, and whatever training they had used successfully with their Shepherds was not succeeding with this dog. The advice of the breeder was to take formal obedience training where the presence of other dogs would also be helpful, as, indeed, proved to be the case.

At the classes, Bulli's owners met other Rottweiler owners, who gradually gravitated to each other. Next thing they knew, they were entering Bulli in a match show, which they found to be fun, sociable and encouraging. Then along came a conformation match, which they also tried. Bulli took Best in Match, and again Mr. and Mrs. Beqaj met nice people with whom they have become close friends. There were other match shows where this good young dog continued to do well. Then came the *big* step—entry at the Colonial Rottweiler Club Specialty Match, where, in October 1983, Bulli won first in his class. Slightly more than six months later, he finished his championship at just 19½ months of age with a five point major at a prestigious Rottweiler Specialty, this one the point show of the Colonial Rottweiler Club. A period of excitement and happiness for his family and for himself!

This story should be of interest to all new and prospective Rottweiler owners for several reasons. First, please note the fact that this was accomplished by amateur owners of just one dog which is as well a house pet—all negative conditions in the usual thinking of what it takes to own a winner. This dog made a very satisfactory record in keenest show ring competition and is a pet whose owners say of him, "He's an absolute pleasure to live with. Every day is a fun-filled day with Bulli. There is never a dull moment in our home, and Bulli has become friend, companion, entertainer, and by pure nature of his genes, the protector of our home. We always thought of Rottweilers as 'ugly' brutes; but we soon found the 'ugly' to be only skin deep. They are a dignified breed, arrogant, willful, determined, intelligent, loyal, courageous, and are comedians at heart. We can only hope that the exploding popularity of this breed does not 'change' it the way it has other breeds."

After gaining his successes in the conformation ring, Bulli has returned to obedience. His owners found that he had remembered all he had been taught a year earlier, and that now he is far more eager to work, doing so with enthusiasm. It is hoped that he will gain his C.D. title and also to have some time to go out tracking. He will continue to be shown on a limited basis as a special.

And there you have one family's experience with their first Rottweiler! Could there possibly be a dog bringing more complete pleasure and companionship in more ways than this one?

Rottweilers are wonderful with children, both as protectors and as companions. Am. and Can. Ch. Von Gailingen's Dassie Did It, U.D.T., Can. C.D. and her friend Katy Nicholson are testimony to that fact. Dassie is owned by Catherine Thompson, Von Gailingen, Freehold, N.J.

CHAPTER ELEVEN

Selection of a Rottweiler

Kato von Siegerhaus, known to friends as "Kato the Clown," is owned by Chyrel Prather.

Once you have made the decision that this is the breed of dog you wish to own, the next important step for you is to determine the right individual dog to best satisfy your needs. Do you prefer to start out with a puppy, with an adult dog, or with one partially mature? Do you prefer a male or a female? What type of dog do you wish—one for show or for competition in obedience? Are you looking for one for breeding, possibly as the foundation for a kennel? Do you simply want one for companionship, to be a family pet?

A decision should be reached about these matters prior to your contacting breeders; then you can accurately describe your requirements and the breeder can offer you the most suitable dog for your purposes. Remember that with any breed of dog, as with any other major purchase, the more care and forethought you invest when planning, the greater the pleasure and satisfaction likely to result.

Referring to a dog as a "major investment" may possibly seem strange to you; however, it is an accurate description. Generally speaking, a sizable sum of money is involved, and you are assuming responsibility for a living creature, taking on all the moral obligations this involves. Assuming that everything goes well, your choice will be a member of your family for a dozen or more years, sharing your home, your daily routine, and your interests. The happiness and success of these years depend largely on the knowledge and intelligence with which you start the relationship.

Certain ground rules apply to the purchase of a dog, regardless of your intentions for its future. Foremost among these is the fact that no matter what you will be doing with the dog, the best and most acceptable place at which to purchase this dog is a kennel specializing in that breed. Even though pet shops occasionally have puppies for sale, they are primarily concerned with *pet* stock, puppies without pedigrees. When you buy from a breeder you are getting a dog that has been the result of parents very carefully selected as individuals and as to pedigree and ancestry. For such a breeding, a dog and a bitch are chosen from whom the breeder hopes to achieve show type dogs that upgrade both his own kennel's quality and that of the breed generally. Much thought has been given to the conformation and temperament likely to result from the combination of parents and bloodlines involved, for the breeder wants to produce sound, outstanding dogs that will further the respect with which he is regarded in the Dog Fancy world. A specialist of this sort is interested in raising *better* dogs. Since it is seldom possible to keep all the puppies from every litter, fine young stock becomes available for sale. These puppies have flaws so slight in appearance as to be unrecognizable as such by other than the trained eye of a judge or a specialist on this breed. These flaws in no way affect the strength or future good health of these dogs; they simply preclude success in the show ring. The conscientious breeder will point them out to you when explaining why the puppy is being offered for sale at "pet price." When you buy a dog like this, from a knowledgeable, reliable breeder, you get all the advantages of good bloodlines with proper temperament, careful rearing, and the happy, well-adjusted environment needed by puppies who are to become satisfactory, enjoyable adults. Although you are not buying a show dog or show prospect, puppies raised in the same manner have all the odds in their favor to become dogs of excellence in the home and in obedience.

If you are looking for a show dog, obviously everything that has been said about buying only from a specialized breeder applies with even greater emphasis. Show-type dogs are bred from show-type dogs of proven producing lines and are the result of serious study, thought, and planning. They do *not* just happen.

Throughout the pages of this book are the names and locations of dozens of reliable breeders. Should it so happen that no one has puppies or young stock available to go at the moment you inquire, it would be far wiser to place your name on the waiting list and see what happens when the next litter is born than to rush off and buy a puppy from some less desirable source. After all, you do not want to repent at leisure.

Another source of information regarding recognized breeders of a particular breed is the American Kennel Club, 51 Madison Avenue, New York, NY 10010. A note or phone call will bring you a list of breeders in your area.

Information can also be obtained from professional handlers. They have many contacts and might be able to put you in touch with a breeder and/or help you choose a dog.

The moment you even start to think about purchasing a dog, it makes sense to look at, observe, and study as many members of the breed as possible prior to taking the step. Acquaint yourself with correct type, soundness, and beauty before making any commitments. Since you are reading this book, you have already started on that route. Now add to your learning by visiting some dog shows if you can. Even if you are not looking for a show dog, it never hurts to become aware of how such a dog appears and behaves. Perhaps at the shows you will meet some breeders from your area with whom you can discuss the breed and whom you can visit.

If you wish this dog to be a family dog, the most satisfactory choice often is a bitch (female). Females make gentle, delightful companions and usually are quieter and more inclined not to roam than males. Often, too, they make neater house dogs, being easier to train. And they are of at least equal intelligence to the males. In the eyes of many pet owners, the principal objection to having a bitch is the periodic "coming in season." Sprays and chlorophyll tablets that can help to cut down on the nuisance of visiting canine swains stampeding your front door are available; and, of course, advocated is the spaying of bitches who will not be used for show or breeding, with even the bitches who are shown or bred being spayed when their careers in competition or in the whelping box have come to a close. Bitches who have been spayed, preferably before four years old, remain in better health later on in life, because spaying almost entirely eliminates the dangers of breast cancer. Spaying also eliminates the messiness of spotting on rugs and furniture, which can be considerable during her periods with a member of a medium-sized or large breed and which is annoying in a household companion.

To many, however, a dog (male) is preferable. The males do seem to be more strongly endowed with true breed character. But do consider the advantages and disadvantages of both males and females prior to deciding which to purchase.

If you are buying one as a pet, a puppy is usually preferable, as you can teach it right from the beginning the ways of your household and your own schedule. Two months is an ideal age at which to introduce the puppy into your home. Older puppies may already have established habits of which you will not approve and which you may find difficult to change. Besides, puppies are such fun that it is great to share and enjoy every possible moment of their process of growing up.

When you are ready to buy, make appointments with as many breeders of this breed as you have been able to locate in your area for the purpose of seeing what they have available and discussing the breed with them. This is a marvelous learning experience, and you will find the majority of breeders are willing and happy to spend time with you, provided that you have arranged the visit in advance. Kennel owners are busy folks with full schedules, so do be considerate about this courtesy and call on the telephone before you appear.

If you have a choice of more than one kennel where you can go to see the dogs, take advantage of that opportunity instead of just settling for and buying the first puppy you see. You may return to your first choice in the long run, but you will do so with greater satisfaction and authority if you have seen the others before making the selection. When you look at puppies, be aware that the one you buy should look sturdy and big-boned, bright-eyed and alert, with an inquisitive, friendly attitude. The puppy's coat should look clean and glossy. Do not buy a puppy that seems listless or dull, is strangely hyperactive, or looks half sick. The condition of the premises where the puppies are raised is also important as you want your puppy to be free of parasites; don't buy a puppy whose surroundings are dirty and ill kept.

One of the advantages of buying at a kennel you can visit is that you are thereby afforded the opportunity of seeing the dam of the puppies and possibly also the sire, if he, too, belongs to the breeder. Sometimes you can even see one or more of the grandparents. Be sure to note the temperament of these dogs as well as their conformation.

If there are no breeders within your travelling range, or if you have not liked what you have seen at those you've visited, do not hesitate to contact other breeders who are recommended to you even if their kennels are at a distance and to purchase from one of them if you are favorably impressed with what is offered. Shipping dogs is done with regularity nowadays and is reasonably safe, so this should not present a problem. If you are contacting a well-known, recognized breeder, the puppy should be fairly described and represented to you. Breeders of this caliber want you to be satisfied, both for the puppy's sake and for yours. They take pride in their kennel's reputation, and they make every effort to see that their customers are pleased. In this way you are deprived of the opportunity of seeing your dog's parents, but even so you can buy with confidence when dealing with a specialized breeder.

Every word about careful selection of your pet puppy and where it should be purchased applies twofold when you set out to select a show dog or the foundation stock for a breeding kennel of your own. You look for all the things already mentioned but on a far more sophisticated level, with many more factors to be taken into consideration. The standard of the breed must now become your guide, and it is essential that you know and understand not only the words of this standard but also their application to actual dogs before you are in a position to make a wise selection. Even then, if this is your first venture with a show-type dog, listen well and heed the advice of the breeder. If you have clearly and honestly stated your ambitions and plans for the dog, you will find that the breeders will cooperate by offering you something with which you will be successful.

There are several different degrees of show dog quality. There are dogs that should become top-flight winners which can be campaigned for Specials (Best of Breed competition) and with which you can hope to attain

Working Group placements and possibly even hit the heights with a Best in Show win. There are dogs of championship quality which should gain their titles for you but are lacking in that "extra something" to make them potential Specials. There are dogs that perhaps may never finish their championships but which should do a bit of winning for you in the classes: a blue ribbon here and there, perhaps Winners or Reserve occasionally, but probably nothing truly spectacular. Obviously the hardest to obtain, and the most expensive, are dogs in the first category, the truly top-grade dogs. These are never plentiful as they are what most breeders are working to produce for their own kennels and personal enjoyment and with which they are loathe to part.

A dog of championship quality is easier to find and less expensive, although it still will bring a good price. The least difficult to obtain is a fair show dog that may pick up some points here and there but will mostly remain in class placements. Incidentally, one of the reasons that breeders are sometimes reluctant to part with a truly excellent show prospect is that in the past people have bought this type of dog with the promise it will be shown, but then the buyer has changed his mind after owning the dog awhile, and thus the dog becomes lost to the breed. It is really not fair to a breeder to buy a dog with the understanding that it will be shown and then renege on the agreement. Please, if you select a dog that is available only to a show home, think it over carefully prior to making a decision; then buy the dog only if you will be willing to give it the opportunity to prove itself in the show ring as the breeder expects.

If you want a show dog, obviously you are a person in the habit of attending dog shows. Now this becomes a form of schooling rather than just a pleasant pastime. Much can be learned at the ringside if one truly concentrates on what one sees. Become acquainted with the various winning exhibitors. Thoughtfully watch the judging. Try to understand what it is that causes some dogs to win and others to lose. Note well the attributes of the dogs, deciding for yourself which ones you like, giving full attention to attitude and temperament as well as conformation.

Close your ears to the ringside "know-it-alls" who have only derogatory remarks to make about each animal in the ring and all that takes place there. You need to develop independent thinking at this stage and should not be influenced by the often entirely uneducated comment of the ringside spoilsports. Especially make careful note of which exhibitors are campaigning winning homebreds—not just an occasional "star" but a series of consistent quality dogs. All this takes time and patience. This is the period to "make haste slowly"; mistakes can be expensive, and the more you have studied the breed, the better equipped you will be to avoid them.

As you make inquiries among various breeders regarding the purchase of a show dog or a show prospect, keep these things in mind. Show-prospect puppies are less expensive than fully mature show dogs. The reason for this is that with a puppy there is the element of chance, for one never can be absolutely certain exactly how the puppy will develop, while the mature dog stands before you as the finished product—"what you see is what you get"—all set to step out and win.

There is always the risk factor involved with the purchase of a show-type puppy. Sometimes all goes well and that is great. But many a swan has turned into an ugly duckling as time passes, and it is far less likely that the opposite will occur. So weigh this well and balance all the odds before you decide whether a puppy or a mature dog would be your better buy. There are times, of course, when one actually has no choice in the matter; no mature show dogs may be available for sale. Then one must either wait awhile or gamble on a puppy, but please *be aware that gambling is what you are doing.*

If you do take a show-prospect puppy, be guided by the breeder's advice when choosing from among what is offered. The person used to working with a bloodline has the best chance of predicting how the puppies will develop. Do not trust your own guess on this; rely on the experience of the breeder. For your own protection, it is best to buy puppies whose parents' eyes have been certified clear and who have been O.F.A.-certified free of hip dysplasia.

Although initially more expensive, a grown show dog in the long run often proves to be the far better bargain. His appearance is unlikely to change beyond weight and condition, which depend on the care you give him. Also to your advantage, if you are a novice about to become an exhibitor, is that a grown dog of show quality almost certainly will have been trained for the ring; thus, an inexperienced handler will find such a dog easier to present properly and in winning form in the ring.

If you plan to have your dog campaigned by a professional handler, have the handler help you locate and select a future winner. Through their numerous clients, handlers usually have access to a variety of interesting show dogs; and the usual arrangement is that the handler buys the dog, resells it to you for the price he paid, and at the same time makes a contract with you that the dog shall be campaigned by this handler throughout the dog's career.

If the foundation of a future kennel is what you have in mind as you contemplate the purchase of a dog, concentrate on one or two really excellent bitches, not necessarily top show bitches but those representing the finest producing lines. A proven matron who has already produced show-type puppies is, of course, the ideal answer here; but, as with a mature show dog, a proven matron is more difficult to obtain and more expensive since no one really wants to part with so valuable an asset. You just might strike it lucky, though, in which case you will be off to a flying start. If you do not find such a matron available, do the next best thing and select a young bitch of outstanding background representing a noted producing strain, one that is herself of excellent type and free of glaring faults.

Great attention should be paid to the background of the bitch from whom you intend to breed. If the information is not already known to you, find out all you can about the temperament, character, and conformation of the sire and dam, plus eye and hip rating. A person just starting in dogs is wise to concentrate on a fine collection of bitches and to raise a few litters sired by leading *producing* studs. The practice of buying a stud dog and then breeding everything you have to that dog does not always work out. It is better to take advantage of the availability of splendid stud dogs for your first few litters.

In summation, if you want a family dog, buy it young and raise it to the habits of your household. If you are buying a show dog, the more mature it is the more certain you can be of the future. If you are buying foundation stock for a breeding program, bitches are better than dogs, but they must be from the finest *producing* bloodlines.

Regarding price, you should expect to pay up to a few hundred dollars for a healthy pet puppy and more than that for a show-type puppy with the price rising accordingly as the dog gets older. A grown show dog can run well into four figures if of finest quality, and a proven brood matron will be priced according to the owner's valuation and can also run into four figures.

When you buy a purebred dog or puppy that you are told is eligible for registration with the American Kennel Club, you are entitled to receive, from the seller, an application form that will enable you to register your dog. If the seller cannot give you the application, you should demand and receive an identification of your dog consisting of the breed, the registered names and numbers of the sire and dam, the name of the breeder, and the dog's date of birth. If the litter of which your dog is part has been recorded with the American Kennel Club, then the litter number is sufficient identification.

Do not accept a verbal promise that registration papers will be mailed to you. Demand a registration application form or proper identification. If neither is supplied, do not buy the dog. These words are to be especially heeded if you are buying show dogs or breeding stock.

Panamint One More Time, C.D., T.D.X., SchH I, AD at age eight weeks. Owned and trained by Dennis and Margaret Teague, Chutzpah Rottweilers, Newcastle, California.

CHAPTER TWELVE

Caring for a Rottweiler Puppy

Puppies at Von Beabear grow up loving children! Sabrina LaQuatra, here four years old, enjoys one of the outstanding puppies owned by her mother, Donna LaQuatra. Sired by Ch. Kaiserelli Puko Von Schleper ex Ch. Delphi's Thetis Von Beabear.

Ownership of a dog entails a great deal of responsibility. You must be willing and prepared to provide your pet with shelter, food, training, and affection. With proper attention and care, your pet will become a loving member of the family and a sociable companion to be enjoyed for many years to come.

Advance Preparation

The moment you decide to become the owner of a puppy is not one second too soon to start planning for the new family member in order to make the transition period more pleasant for yourself, your household, and the puppy.

The first step in preparation is a bed for that puppy and a place where you can pen him up for rest periods. Every dog should have a crate of its own right from the very beginning. This will fill both of the previously mentioned requirements, and the puppy will come to know and love this crate as his special haven. Crates are ideal, for when you want the puppy to be free, the crate door stays open. At other times, you securely latch it and know the puppy is safe from harm,

comfortable, and out of mischief. If you plan to travel with your dog, his crate comes along in the car; and, of course, to travel by plane, the dog must be put in a crate. If you show your dog, or take him to obedience trials, what better place to keep him when you are not working with him than in his crate? No matter how you look at it, a crate is a very sensible, sound investment in your puppy's comfort, well being, and safety—not to mention your own peace of mind.

Preferred are the sturdy wooden crates with removable side panels. These wooden crates are excellent for cold weather, with the panels in place, and they work equally well for hot weather when the solid panels are removed, leaving just the wire sides for better ventilation. Crates made entirely of wire are all right in the summer, but they provide no protection from drafts or winter chills. Solid aluminum crates are not suggested due to the manner in which aluminum reflects surrounding temperatures. If it is cold, so is the metal of the crate. If it is hot, that too is reflected, sometimes to the point that one's fingers can be burnt when handling it.

When you choose the puppy's crate, be certain that it is roomy enough not to be outgrown as your dog matures. He should have sufficient height in which to stand up comfortably and sufficient area to stretch out full length when relaxed. When the puppy is young, give him shredded newspapers as his first bed. In time, the newspapers can be replaced with a mat or turkish towels. Carpet remnants are great for the bottom of the crate as they are inexpensive and in case of accidents can be easily replaced. Once the dog has matured past the chewing stage, a pillow or a blanket for something soft and comfortable is an appreciated luxury in the crate.

Sharing importance with the crate is a safe area where the puppy can exercise and play. If you are an apartment-dweller, a baby's playpen works well for a young puppy and a portable exercise pen (which will come in handy if you show your dog) is good for a mature dog. If you have a yard of your own, then the fenced area in which he can stay outdoors safely should be ready and waiting upon his arrival. It does not need to be a vast area, but it should have shade and be secure. Do have the fenced area planned and installed *before* bringing the puppy home if you possibly can do so; this is far more sensible than putting it off until a tragedy occurs. If you have close neighbors, stockade fencing works out well, as then the neighbors are less aware of the dog and the dog cannot see and bark at everything that passes near the area. If you live in the country, then regular chain-link fencing is fine. To eliminate the possibility of the dog jumping the fence when he matures, the fence should be six feet high. As an absolute guarantee that a dog cannot dig his way out under the fence, an edging of cinder blocks tight against the inside bottom of it is very practical protection. If there is an outside gate, a key and padlock are a *must* and should be *used at all times*. You do not want to have the puppy or dog set free in your absence either purposely or through carelessness. People have been known to go through a fence and then just leave the gate ajar. So for safety's sake, keep the gate locked so that only someone responsible has access to its opening.

The ultimate convenience, of course, is if there is a door in your house situated so that the fence can be installed around it, thereby doing away with the necessity for an outside gate. This arrangement is ideal, because then you need never be worried about the gate being left unlatched. This arrangement will be particularly appreciated during bad weather when, instead of escorting the dog to wherever his fenced yard is, you simply open the house door and he exits directly into his safe yard.

If you have only one dog, however, do not feel that he will get sufficient exercise in the fenced area; most dogs just sit there when they're alone. Two or more dogs will play and move themselves around; one dog by himself does little more than make a leisurely tour once around the area and then lie down. You must include a daily walk or two in your plans if your puppy is to be rugged and well.

When you go to pick up your dog, you should take a collar and lead with you. Both of these should be appropriate for the breed and age of the dog, and the collar should be one that fits him now, not one he has to grow into. Your new dog also needs a water dish (or two, one for the house and one for outside) and a food dish. These should preferably be made from an unbreakable material. You will have fun shopping at your local pet shop for these things, and probably you will be tempted to add some luxury items of which you will find a fascinating array. For chew things, either Nylabone or real beef bones (leg or knuckle cut to an appropriate size, the latter found as soup bones at most butcher shops or supermarkets) are safe and provide many hours of happy entertainment, at the same time being great exercise during the teething period. Rawhide chews can be safe, too, if made under the proper conditions. There was a problem, however, several years back owing to the chemicals with which some of the rawhide chew products had been treated, so in order to take no chances, avoid them. Also avoid plastic and rubber toys, *particularly* toys with squeakers. If you want to play ball with your dog, select a ball that has been made of very tough construction. Even then do not leave the ball with the puppy alone; take it with you when you finish the

Top left: Eike vom Klosterdiek at 11 weeks of age. Born December 1984, by Falko von der Tente, SchH. III ex Gitte Von Der Bergschmiede, SchH. 1, this is a puppy whose future is eagerly anticipated by owners Larry and Alice Lee, Larran, Franklin, Indiana. **Top right:** Wilderness Murphy, by Starkheim Duf Morgen Carroll ex Lady Ruger, as a puppy. Wilderness Kennels, Joann H. Turner, Anchorage, Alaska. **Bottom:** "Hello out there." Three-week-old Powderhorn's Tank of Wencrest peering through the fence. A very promising "young hopeful" by Falko from Loki at Powderhorn/Wencrest Rottweilers owned by Mrs. Clara S. Hurley and Mr. Michael S. Grossman, Hollywood, California.

game. There are also some nice "tug of war" toys which are fun when you play with the dog. But again, do not go off and leave them to be chewed in privacy.

Too many changes all at once can be difficult for a puppy. Therefore, no matter how you eventually wind up doing it, for the first few days keep him as nearly as you can on the routine to which he is accustomed. Find out what brand of food the breeder used, how frequently and when the puppies were fed, and start out by doing it that way yourself, gradually for a week or two making whatever changes suit you better.

Of utmost precedence in planning for your puppy is the selection of a good veterinarian whom you feel you can trust. Make an appointment to bring the puppy in to be checked over on your way home from the breeder's. Be sure to obtain the puppy's health certificate from the breeder, along with information regarding worming, shots, and so on.

With all of these things in order, you should be nicely prepared for a smooth, happy start when your puppy actually joins the family.

Joining the Family

Remember that as exciting and happy as the occasion may be for you, the puppy's move from his place of birth to your home can be a traumatic experience for him. His mother and littermates will be missed. He will perhaps be slightly frightened or awed by the change of surroundings. The person he trusted and depended on will be gone. Everything, thus, should be planned to make the move easy for him, to give him confidence, to make him realize that yours is a pretty nice place to be after all.

Never bring a puppy home on a holiday. There just is too much going on, with people and gifts and excitement. If he is honoring "an occasion" (a birthday, for example), work it out so that his arrival will be a few days before or, better still, a few days after the big occasion. Then he will be greeted by a normal routine and will have your undivided attention. Try not to bring the puppy home during the evening. Early morning is the ideal time, as then he has the opportunity of getting acquainted, and the first strangeness wears off before bedtime. You will find it a more peaceful night that way, without a doubt. Allow the puppy to investigate his surroundings under your watchful eye. If you already have a pet in the household, carefully watch that things are going smoothly between them, so that the relationship gets off to a friendly start; otherwise, you may quickly have a lasting problem. Be careful not to let your older pet become jealous by paying more attention to the newcomer than to him. You want a friendly start. Much of the future attitude of each toward the other depends on what takes place that first day.

If you have children, again, it is important that the relationship start out well. Should the puppy be their first pet, it is assumed that you have prepared them for it with a firm explanation that puppies are living creatures to be treated with gentle consideration, not playthings to be abused and hurt. One lady raised her children with the household rule that should a dog or puppy belonging to one of the children bite one of the children, the child would be punished, not the dog, as Mother would know that the child had in some way hurt the dog. This strategy worked out very well, as no child was ever bitten in that household and both daughters grew up to remain great animal lovers. Anyway, on whatever terms you do it, please bring your children up not only to *love* but also to *respect* their pet, with the realization that dogs have rights, too. These same ground rules should also apply to visiting children. Youngsters who are fine with their own pets may unmercifully tease and harass pets belonging to other people. Children do not always realize how rough is too rough, and without intending to, they may inflict considerable pain or injury if permitted to ride herd on a puppy.

If you start out by spoiling your new puppy, your puppy will expect and even demand that you continue to spoil it in the future. So think it out carefully before you invite the puppy to come spend its first night at your home in bed with you, unless you wish to continue the practice. What you had considered to be a one-night stand may be accepted as just great and expected for the future. It is better not to start what you may consider to be bad habits which you may find difficult to overcome later. Be firm with the puppy, strike a routine, and stick to it. The puppy will learn more quickly this way, and everyone will be happier as a result.

Socialization and Training

Socialization and training of your new puppy actually starts the second you walk in the door with him, for every move you make should be geared toward teaching the puppy what is expected of him and, at the same time, building up his confidence and feeling of being at home.

The first step is to teach the puppy his name and to come when called by it. No matter how flowery or long or impressive the actual registered name may be, the puppy should also have a short, easily understood "call name" which can be learned quickly and to which he will respond. Start using this call name immediately, and use it in exactly the same way each time that you address the puppy, refraining from the temptation to alternate various forms of endearment, pet names, or substitutes which will only be confusing to him.

Using his name clearly, call the puppy over to you when you see him awake and looking about for something to do. Just a few times of this, with a lot of praise over what a "good dog" he is when he responds, and you will have taught him to come to you when he hears his name; he knows that he will be warmly greeted, petted, and possibly even be given a small snack.

As soon at the puppy has spent a few hours getting acquainted with his new surroundings, you can put a light collar on the puppy's neck, so that he will become accustomed to having it on. He may hardly notice it, or he may make a great fuss at first, rolling over, struggling, and trying to rub it off. Have a tasty tidbit or two on hand with which to divert his attention at this period, or try to divert his attention by playing with him. Soon he no longer will be concerned about that strange new thing around his neck.

The next step in training is to have the puppy become accustomed to the lead. Use a lightweight lead, attached to the collar. Carry him outdoors where there will be things of interest to investigate; then set him down and see what happens. Again, he may appear hardly to notice the lead dangling behind him, or he may make a fuss about it. If the latter occurs, repeat the diversion attempts with food or a toy. As soon as the puppy has accepted the presence of the lead, pick up the end of it and follow after him. He may react by trying to free himself, struggling to slip his head through the collar, or trying to bite at the lead. Coax him, if you can, with kind words and petting. In a few moments, curiosity regarding his surroundings and an interesting smell or two should start diverting him. When this takes place, do not try at first to pull on him or guide his direction. Just be glad that he is walking with the lead on and let him decide where to go. When he no longer seems to resent the lead, try gently to direct him with short little tugs in the direction you would like him to travel. Never jerk him roughly, as then he will become frightened and fight harder; and never pull steadily or attempt to drag him, as this immediately triggers a battle of wills and each of you pulling in an opposite direction. The best method is a short, quick, gentle jerk, which, repeated a few times, should get him started off with you. Of course, continue to talk encouragingly to him and offer him "goodies" until he gets started. Repetition of the command "Come" should accompany all of this.

Once this step has been mastered and walks are taken on the lead pleasantly and companionably, the next step is to teach him to remain on your left-hand side. Use the same process as you used to teach him to respond correctly while on the lead, this time repeating the word "Heel." Of course, all of this is not accomplished in one day; it should be done gradually, with short work periods each time, letting the puppy know when he pleases you. The exact length of time required for each puppy varies and depends on the aptitude of each individual puppy.

Housebreaking a puppy is more easily accomplished by the prevention method than by the cure. Try to avoid "accidents" whenever you can rather than punishing the puppy once they have occurred. Common sense helps a great deal. A puppy will need to be taken out at regularly spaced intervals: first thing in the morning directly from his bed, immediately after meals, after he has napped, or whenever you notice that he is "looking for a spot." Choose roughly the same place outdoors each time that you take the puppy out for this purpose, so that a pattern will be established. If he does not go immediately, do not just return him to the house as chances are that he will go the moment he is back inside. Try to be patient and remain out with him until you get results; then praise him enthusiastically and both of you can return indoors. If you catch the puppy having an "accident," pick him up firmly, sharply say, "No!" and rush him outside. If you do not see the accident occur, there is little point of doing anything beyond cleaning it up, as once it has happened and been forgotten, the puppy will likely not even realize why you are angry with him.

Your puppy should form the habit of spending a certain amount of time each day in his crate, even when you are home. Sometimes the puppy will do this voluntarily, but if not, he should be taught to do so. Lead the puppy by the collar over to the crate, and then gently push him inside firmy saying "Down" or "Stay" as you fasten the door. Whatever command you use, always make it the same word for each act every time. Repetition is the big thing in training, and the dog must learn to associate a specific word or phrase with each different thing he is expected to do. When you mean "Sit," always say exactly that. "Stay" should mean that the dog should remain where he was when you gave the command. "Down" means something else again. Do not confuse the dog by shuffling the commands, as you will create confusion for him and a problem for yourself by having done so.

As soon as he has received his immunization shots, take your puppy with you wherever and whenever possible. Nothing else can equal this close association for building up self-confidence and stability in a young dog. It is extremely important that you spend the time necessary for socialization, particularly if you are planning on the puppy becoming a show dog.

Take your puppy in the car, so that he will learn to enjoy riding without becoming carsick, as can happen to a dog unused to the car's motion. Take him everywhere you go, provided you are certain he will not be unwelcome or create any difficulties by his presence; visiting friends and relatives (if they like dogs and do not have house pets of their own who will consider your puppy an intruder), to busy shopping centers (always keeping him on his lead), just walking around the streets of your town. If someone admires him, as always seems to happen under these circumstances, encourage that person to pet or talk with him; becoming accustomed to people in this manner always seems especially beneficial in instilling self-confidence. You want your puppy to develop a relaxed, happy canine personality and like the world and its inhabitants. The most debilitating thing for a puppy's self-confidence is excessive sheltering and pampering. Keeping a growing puppy always away from strange people and strange dogs may well turn him into a nervous, neurotic dog—surely the last thing anyone can enjoy as a pet.

Make obedience training a game with your puppy while he is extremely young. Try to teach him the meaning of and expected responses to the basic terms such as "Come," "Stay," "Sit," "Down," and "Heel," along with the meaning of "No" even while he is still too young for formal training, and you will be pleased and proud of the good manners that he will exhibit.

Feeding

There was a time when providing good, nourishing food for our dogs involved a far more complicated routine and time-consuming process than people now feel is necessary. The old belief was that the daily rations should consist of fresh beef, vegetables, cereal, egg yolks, and cottage cheese as basics, with such additions as brewer's yeast and other vitamin supplements.

During recent years, however, many attitudes have been changed regarding the necessity, or even the desirability, of this procedure. Eggs, cottage cheese, and supplements

Top: C'mon, let's play." Rottie pup from the Brimstone "A" litter owned by Susan J. Suwinski, Ithaca, N.Y. **Bottom:** "Chow time"! Six-week-old von Stolzenfels puppies pitching in! Dr. Evelyn M. Ellman, owner, von Stolzenfels, Augusta, Michigan.

to the diet are still given, but the basic methods of feeding dogs have changed; and the changes are definitely for the better in the opinion of many an authority. The school of thought now is that you are doing your dogs a definite service when you feed them some of the fine commercially prepared dog foods in preference to your own home-cooked concoctions.

The reasoning behind this new outlook is easy to understand. The production of dog food has grown to be a major industry, participated in by some of the best known, most highly respected names in the dog fancy. These trusted firms do turn out excellent products. People are feeding their dogs these preparations with confidence, and the dogs are thriving, prospering, and keeping in top condition. What more could we want or ask?

There are at least a half dozen absolutely splendid dry foods which can be mixed with water or broth and served to your dog, either "as is" or with the addition of fresh or canned meat. There is a variety of canned meat preparations for your dog, either 100% meat to be mixed with kibble or complete prepared dinners, a combination of both meat and cereal. There are several kinds of "convenience foods," these in packets which you open and dump out into the dog's dish. It is just that simple. The "convenience foods" are neat and easy for you at anytime especially when traveling, but ordinarily feeding a dry food mixed with hot water, to which canned meat is usually added, is preferred. Leftover meat scraps or ground beef are sometimes added instead of the canned meat. Actually the canned meat, with its added fortifiers, is more beneficial to the dogs than the fresh meat. However, the two can be used alternately or, if you prefer and your dogs do well on it, by all means use ground beef.

Dogs enjoy variety in the meat part of their diet, which is easy to provide with the canned meat. The canned meats available include all sorts of beef (chunk, ground, stewed, and so on), lamb, chicken, liver, and numerous concoctions of several of these blended together.

There also is prepared food geared to every age bracket of your dog's life, from puppyhood on through old age, with special additions or modifications to make it especially nourishing and beneficial. The dogs of yesteryear never had it so good during the canine dinner hour because these foods are tasty and geared to meet the dog's gastronomical approval.

Additionally, contents and nutritional values are clearly listed on the labels, and careful instructions for feeding exactly the right amount for the size and weight of each dog are also given.

With the great choice of dog foods available today, the addition of vitamins is not necessary; but if you prefer, there are several highly satisfactory vitamin products available at pet shops. These products serve as tasty treats along with being beneficial.

Of course there is no reason not to cook up something for your dog's dinner if you would feel happier doing so, but it seems superfluous when such truly satisfying rations are available at so much less expense and trouble.

How often you feed is a matter of how a schedule works out best for you and for your dog or dogs. Many owners prefer to feed their dogs once a day. Others feel that twice daily is better for the digestion and more satisfying to the dog, particularly if he is a family member who stands around and watches the preparation of family meals. The important thing is that you *do not overfeed*, as overfeeding can bring on many canine problems.

From the time your puppy is fully weaned until he reaches about twelve weeks of age, he should be fed four times daily. His breakfast and his dinner should consist of about two or two and a half cups of moistened puppy kibble to which about one cup (slightly more if necessary to soften) of hot water or broth has been added, mixed with either a quarter-pound of fresh ground beef or a quarter-can of canned beef (these amounts are approximate as there is no harm in slightly more of the beef and a bit less kibble if you prefer). At noontime and at bedtime the puppy should be given one can of evaporated milk mixed with one can of slightly warmed water.

As the puppy grows older, from three to six months of age, cut back to three meals daily, substituting the milk meals with a meal of meat and kibble. If the puppy cleans his dish with gusto and is not putting on too much weight, you will know the amount of food is

1982 litter by Ch. Starkheim Duf Morgen Carroll ex Ch. V.N. Serena of Summerfield. Owned by Paula A. Cingota, Summerfield Arabians and Rottweilers, Jamul, California. Photo courtesy of Catherine M. Thompson, Von Gailingen. Freehold. N.J.

right for him. If he is starting to look chubby, cut back a bit on the amount; you do not want your puppy to be fat. Too much weight can be overburdening on growing limbs and muscles and can also result in a sagging topline. So do guard against it. If the puppy is eating up everything but looking thin, slightly increase the amount of food, as he may not be getting all he needs. At six months of age, the pup should be fed twice daily, and at twelve months, if you wish, you may cut back to one daily feeding with a biscuit or two morning and evening. If you do feed just once daily, the meal should be given by early afternoon. Don't forget to have the puppy checked regularly for worms and to keep a watchful eye. Each puppy is an individual and needs to be treated as such.

Remember that fresh, cool water should always be available for your dog. This is of utmost importance to his good health throughout his lifetime.

Ch. Cache von Gruenerwald finishing his championship with a Best of Breed win under judge Henry Stoecker at the Amarillo K.C., owner-handled by Dorothea Gruenerwald, Colorado Springs, Colorado.

CHAPTER THIRTEEN

Showing Your Rottweiler

Ch. Doroh's Fantastic Serenade, Am. and Can. C.D.X. and Mondberg's Bulger V Beier, C.D.X., Can. C.D. are owned by Peter and Marilyn Piusz, Seren Rottweilers, Johnstown, N.Y.

The groundwork for showing your dog has been accomplished with your careful selection and purchase of your future show prospect. If it is a puppy, it is assumed that you have gone through all the proper preliminaries of good care, which actually should be the same whether the puppy is a pet or a future show dog, with a few extra precautions in the case of the latter.

General Considerations

Remember that a winning dog must be kept in trim, top condition. You want him neither too fat nor too thin, so do not spoil his figure and his appearance, or his appetite for proper nourishing food, by allowing family members or guests to be constantly feeding him "goodies." The best "treat" of all is a small wad of ground raw beef or one of the packaged dog "goodies." To be avoided are ice cream, potato chips, cookies, cake, candy, and other fattening items which will cause the dog to gain weight. A dog in show condition must never be fat, nor must he be painfully thin to the point of his ribs fairly sticking through the skin.

The importance of temperament and showmanship cannot possibly be overemphasized. These two qualities have put many a mediocre dog across, while lack of them can ruin the career of an otherwise outstanding specimen. So, from the day your dog or puppy arrives home, socialize him. Keep him accustomed to being with people and to being handled by people. Encourage your friends and relatives to "go over" him as the judges will in the ring, so that at the shows this will not be a strange, upsetting experience. Practice showing his "bite" (the manner in which his teeth meet) deftly and quickly. It is quite simple to spread the lips apart with your fingers, and the puppy should be accustomed and willing to accept this from you or from the judge, without struggle. The puppy should also be accustomed to having his jaws opened wide in order for his teeth to be counted, since missing teeth, if other than premolars, is a serious fault. Some judges ask the exhibitors to handle the mouths, showing them bite and jaws, rather than doing it themselves. These are the considerate judges who prefer not to risk spreading any possible virus infections by taking their hands from one dog's mouth to another's; but the old-fashioned judges still persist in doing the latter, so the dog should be prepared for either.

Take your future show dog with you in the car, so that he will love riding and not become carsick when he travels. He should associate going in the car with pleasure and attention. Take him where it is crowded: downtown, shopping malls, or, in fact, anywhere you go where dogs are permitted. Make the expeditions fun for him by frequent petting and words of praise; do not just ignore him as you go about your errands or other business.

Do not overly shelter your future show dog. Instinctively you may want to keep him at home, especially while a young puppy, where he is safe from germs or danger; but this can be foolish on two counts. To begin with, a dog kept away from other dogs or other environments builds up no natural immunity against all the things with which he will come in contact at the dog shows. Actually it is wiser to keep him well up-to-date on all protective "shots" and then allow him to become accustomed to being among other dogs and dog owners. Also, a dog who never goes among people, to strange places, or among strange dogs, may grow up with a timidity of spirit that will cause you deep problems when his show career gets under way.

Keep his coat in immaculate condition with daily grooming (which takes only a few minutes) and baths when they later are necessary. For the latter, use a mild shampoo or whatever the person who bred your puppy may suggest. Several of the "brand name" products do an excellent job, and there are several which are beneficial toward keeping the dog free of fleas. Look for them at your pet supplier's. Be sure to rinse the dog thoroughly, leaving no traces of soap which may cause itching or skin irritation. It is a wise precaution to put a drop of castor oil in each eye to ensure no soap irritation. Use warm water (be sure it is not uncomfortably hot or chillingly cold) and a good spray. An electric hair dryer is a great convenience; use it after first blotting off the excess moisture with a Turkish towel. Do not let water find its way into the ear cavity. A wad of cotton in the ear guards

against this possibility. Toenails also should be watched and trimmed every few weeks. It is important not to let nails grow too long as they can become painful and ruin the appearance of foot and pastern.

Assuming that you will be handling the dog personally, or even if he will be professionally handled, it is important that a few moments of each day be spent practicing dog show routine. Practice "stacking," or "setting him up," as you have seen the exhibitors do at the shows you've attended, and teach him to hold this position once you have him stacked to your satisfaction. Make the learning pleasant by being firm but lavish in your praise when he behaves correctly. Work in front of a mirror for setting up practice; this enables you to see the dog as the judge does and to learn what corrections need to be made by looking at the dog from that angle.

Teach your dog to gait at your side, or moving out ahead of you as his learning progresses, on a loose lead. When you have mastered the basic essentials at home, then look for and join a training class for future work and polishing up your technique. Training classes are sponsored by show-giving clubs in many areas, and their popularity is steadily increasing. If you have no other way of locating one, perhaps your veterinarian may know of one through some of his clients; but if you are sufficiently aware of the dog show world to want a show dog, you will probably be personally acquainted with other fanciers who will share information of this sort with you.

Accustom your show dog to being in a crate (which you should be doing, even if the dog is to be only a pet). He should be kept in the crate "between times" for his own well-being and safety.

A show dog's teeth must be kept clean and free of tartar. Hard dog biscuits can help toward this. If tartar does accumulate, see that it is removed promptly by your veterinarian. Bones are not suitable for show dogs once they have their second teeth as they tend to damage and wear down the tooth enamel (bones are all right for puppies, as they help with the teething process).

Beyond these special considerations, your show-prospect will thrive under the same treatment as accorded any well-cared-for family pet. In fact, most of the foregoing is applicable to a pet dog as well as to a show dog, for what it boils down to is simply keeping the dog at his best.

Match Shows

Your dog's first experience in show ring procedure should be at match show competition. There are several reasons for this. First of all, this type of event is intended as a learning experience for both the puppies and for the exhibitors; thus you will feel no embarrassment if your puppy misbehaves or if your own handling technique is obviously inept. There will be many others in that same position. So take the puppy and go, and the two of you can learn together what it is like actually to compete against other dogs for the approval of the judge.

Another reason for beginning a show career at match shows is the matter of cost. Entries at the point shows nowadays cost over ten dollars. True, there are many clubs who reduce this fee by a few dollars for the Puppy Classes (but by no means do all of them), but even so it is silly to throw this amount away when you know full well your puppy will not yet have the ring presence to hold his own. For the match shows, on the other hand, the entry fee is usually less than five dollars, so using those shows as a learning ground for you and your puppy certainly makes better sense. Another advantage of match shows is that advance entries for them are seldom necessary, and even those clubs having them usually will accept additional entries the morning of the show. If you wake up feeling like taking the puppy for an outing, you can go right ahead. The entries at point shows, however, close about two and a half weeks in advance.

You will find the judges more willing to discuss your puppy with you at a match show than during the day of a full and hectic point show; one of their functions, when officiating at a match, is to help new exhibitors with comments and suggestions. We might wish that we could do so at the point shows; but, generally speaking, our schedules do not permit this time to be taken. Unless you stay until the judge's working day is ended, it is often difficult to get even a few words with

him. The informality of match shows makes it far easier to get a judge's verbal opinion there; and since judges at these events are usually professional handlers or already licensed judges who are working toward applying for additional breeds, the opinions should be knowledgeable and helpful.

As with training classes, information regarding match shows can be obtained from breeders in your area, your local kennel club if there is one, your veterinarian, or, of course, the person in charge of your training class, if you belong to one. The A.K.C. can also furnish this information; and if your local newspaper carries a pet column, announcements of such coming events will almost certainly appear there.

Point Shows

Entries for American Kennel Club licensed or member point shows must be made in advance. This must be done on an official entry blank of the show-giving club and then filed either in person or by mail with the show superintendent (or show secretary) in time to reach the latter's office prior to the published closing date and hour or the filling of the advertised quota. These entries should be written out clearly and carefully, signed by the owner of the dog or his agent (your professional handler), and must be accompanied by the entry fee; otherwise they will not be accepted. Remember, it is not when the entry blank leaves your hands or is postmarked that counts but the time that the entry arrives at its destination. If you are relying on the postal system, bear in mind that it is not always reliable, and waiting until the last moment may cause your entry to arrive too late for acceptance. Leave yourself a bit of leeway by mailing *early*.

A dog must be entered at a dog show in the name of the actual owner at the time of entry closing date for that specific show. If a registered dog has been acquired by a new owner, the dog must be entered in the name of that new owner at any show for which entries close following the date of purchase, regardless of whether or not the new owner has actually received the registration certificate indicating that the dog is registered in the new owner's name. State on the entry form whether or not the transfer application has been mailed to the American Kennel Club, and it goes without saying that the latter should be promptly attended to when you purchase a registered dog.

When you fill out your entry blank, be sure to type, print, or write legibly, paying particular attention to the spelling of names, correct registration numbers, and so on. Sign your name as owner *exactly*—not one time as Jane Doe, another as Jane C. Doe, and another as Mrs. John Doe.

Puppy Classes are for dogs or bitches that are six months of age and under twelve months, who were whelped in the United States, and are not champions. The age of a puppy is calculated up to and inclusive of the first day of a show you are entering. For example, the first day a dog whelped on January 1st is eligible to compete in a Puppy Class at a show is July 1st of the same year; and he may continue competing in Puppy Classes up to and including a show on December 31st of the same year, but he is *not* eligible to compete in a Puppy Class at a show held on or after January 1st of the following year.

The Puppy Class is the first one in which you should enter your puppy, for several reasons. To begin with, a certain allowance for behavior is made in recognition of the fact that they *are* puppies and lack show experience; a puppy who is immature or displays less than perfect ring manners will not be penalized so heavily as would be the case in an adult class such as Open. It is also quite likely that others in the Puppy Class will be suffering from the same puppy problems as your own; all of the puppies will be pretty much on equal footing where age and ring assurance are concerned. A puppy shown in the same class with fully matured individuals who are experienced in the show ring looks all the more young and inexperienced and thus is far less likely to gain the judge's admiration than in a class where the puppy does not seem out of place. There are many good judges who will take a smashing good puppy right from the Puppy Class on through to Winners, but more often than not, this puppy started the day and was "discovered" by the judge right where it belonged, in the Puppy Class. Another bonus of using Puppy Class is the fact that numerous clubs offer a reduced entry fee to those competing in it; this certainly is beneficial because showing dogs is becoming increasingly expensive.

One word of caution on entering the Puppy Class: carefully check the classification, as in some cases it is divided into a 6-9 months old section and a 9-12 months old section; if this is the case you will have to ascertain that your puppy is entered in the correct section for the age he will be on the day of the show.

The Novice Class is for dogs six months of age and over, whelped in the United States or in Canada, who *prior to* the official closing date for entries have *not* won three first prizes in the Novice Class, any first prize at all in the Bred-by-Exhibitor, American-bred, or Open Classes, or one or more points toward championship. The provisions for this class are confusing to many people, which is probably the reason it is so infrequently used. A dog may win any number of first prizes in the Puppy Class and still retain his eligibility for Novice. He may place second, third, or fourth not only in Novice on an unlimited number of occasions but also in Bred-by-Exhibitor, American-bred, or Open and still remain eligible for Novice. But he may no longer be shown in Novice when he has won three blue ribbons in that class, when he has won even one blue ribbon in either Bred-by-Exhibitor, American-bred, or Open, or even a single championship point.

In determining whether or not a dog is eligible for the Novice Class, keep in mind the fact that previous wins are calculated according to the official published date for closing of entries, not by the date on which you may actually have made the entry. So if, in the interim, between the time you made the entry and the official closing date, your dog makes a win causing it to become ineligible for Novice, change your class *immediately* to another for which your entry will be eligible. The Novice Class always seems to have the fewest entries of any class, and therefore it is a splendid "practice ground" for you and your young dog while you both are getting the "feel" of being in the ring.

Bred-by-Exhibitor Class is for dogs whelped in the United States or, if individually registered in the American Kennel Club

Stud Book, for dogs whelped in Canada that are six months of age and over, are not champions, and are owned wholly or in part by the person or the spouse of the person who was the breeder or one of the breeders of record. Dogs entered in this class must be handled *in this class* by an owner or by a member of the immediate family of the owner. Members of an immediate family for this purpose are husband, wife, father, mother, son, daughter, brother, or sister. This is the class which is really the "breeder's showcase," the one which breeders should enter with special pride, to show off their achievements. It is *not necessary* for the winner of Bred-by-Exhibitor to be handled by an owner or a member of the owner's family in the Winners Class, where the dog or bitch *may be handled by whomsoever the exhibitor may choose*, including a professional handler.

The American-bred Class is for all dogs excepting champions, six months of age or older, who were whelped in the United States by reason of a mating which took place in the United States.

The Open Class is for any dog six months of age or older (this is the only restriction for this class). Dogs with championship points compete in it; dogs who are already champions can do so; dogs who are imported can be entered; and, of course, American-bred dogs compete in it. This class is, for some strange reason, the favorite of exhibitors who are "out to win." They rush to enter their pointed dogs in it, under the false impression that by so doing they assure themselves of greater attention from the judges. This really is not so; and it is my feeling that to enter in one of the less competitive classes, with a better chance of winning it and then getting a second crack at gaining the judge's approval by returning to the ring in the Winners Class, can often be a more effective strategy.

One does not enter for the Winners Class. One earns the right to compete in it by winning first prize in Puppy, Novice, Bred-by-Exhibitor, American-bred, or Open. No dog who has been defeated on the same day in one of these classes is eligible to compete in Winners, and every dog who has been a blue-ribbon winner in one of them and not defeated in any of the others *must* do so. Following the selection of the Winners Dog or the Winners Bitch, the dog or bitch receiving that award leaves the ring. Then the dog or bitch who placed second in the class, unless previously defeated by another dog or bitch at the same show, re-enters the ring to compete against the remaining first-prize winners for Reserve. The latter award means that the dog or bitch receiving it is standing by "in reserve" should the one that received Winners be disallowed through any technicality when the awards are checked at the American Kennel Club. In that case, the one that placed Reserve is moved up to Winners, at the same time receiving the appropriate championship points.

Winners Dog and Winners Bitch are the awards which carry points toward championship with them. The points are based on the number of dogs or bitches actually in competitin; and the points are scaled one through five, the latter being the greatest number available to any dog or bitch at any one show. Three-, four-, or five-point wins are considered majors. In order to become a champion, a dog or bitch must win two majors under two different judges, plus at least one point from a third judge, and the additional points necessary to bring the total to fifteen. When your dog has gained fifteen points as described above, a certificate of championship will be issued to you, and your dog's name will be published in the list of new champions which appears monthly in *Pure-Bred Dogs/ American Kennel Gazette*, the official publication of the American Kennel Club.

The scale of championship points for each breed is worked out by the American Kennel Club and reviewed annually, at which time the number required in competition may be either changed (raised or lowered) or remain the same. The scale of points for all breeds is published annually in the May issue of the *Gazette*, and the current ratings for each breed within that area are published in every dog show catalog.

When a dog or a bitch is adjudged Best of Winners, its championship points are, for that show, compiled on the basis of which sex had the greater number of points. If there are two points in dogs and four in bitches and the dog goes Best of Winners, then *both* the dog and the bitch are awarded an equal number of points, in this case four. Should the Winners Dog or the Winners Bitch go on to win Best of Breed, additional points are accorded for the additional representatives of the breed defeated by so doing, provided, of course, that there were entries specifically for Best of Breed competition, or Specials, as these specific entries are generally called. If your dog or bitch takes Best of Opposite Sex after going Winners, points are credited according to the number of the same sex defeated in both the regular classes and Specials competition. Many a one- or two-point class win has grown into a major in this manner.

Moving further along, should your entry win the Working Group from the classes (in other words, if it has taken either Winners Dog or Winners Bitch, Best of Winners, and Best of Breed), you then receive points based on the greatest number of points awarded to any breed included within that Group during that show's competition. Should the dog's winning streak also include Best in Show, the same rule of thumb applies, and he receives points equal to the highest number of points awarded to any other dog of any breed at that event.

Best of Breed competition consists of the Winners Dog and the Winners Bitch, who automatically compete on the strength of those awards, in addition to whatever dogs and bitches have been entered specifically for this class for which champions of record are eligible. Entries who, according to their owner's records, have completed the required number of points for a championship after closing of entries for the show but whose championships are unconfirmed, may be transferred from one of the regular classes to the Best of Breed competition, provided this transfer is made by the show superintendent or show secretary *prior to the start of judging at the show.*

This has proven an extremely popular new rule, as under it a dog can finish on Saturday and then be transferred and compete as a Special on Sunday. It must be emphasized that the change *must* be made a half hour *prior* to the start of the day's judging, which means to the start of *any* judging at the show, not your individual breed.

In the United States, Best of Breed winners are entitled to compete in the Variety Group which includes them. This competition is not mandatory; it is a privilege which exhibitors should value. The dogs winning *first* in each Variety Group *must* compete for Best in Show.

Non-regular classes are sometimes included at the all-breed shows, and they are almost invariably included at Specialty shows. These include Stud Dog Class and Brood Bitch Class, which are judged on the quality of the offspring (usually two) accompanying the sire or dam. The quality of the latter two is beside the point; it is the youngsters that count, and the qualities of *both* are averaged to decide which sire or dam is the best and most consistent producer. Then there is the Brace Class (which, at all-breed shows, moves along to Best Brace in each Variety Group and then Best Brace in Show), which is judged on the similarity and evenness of appearance of the two members of the brace. In other words, they should look like identical twins in size, color, and conformation and should move together almost as a single dog, one person handling with precision and ease. The same applies to the Team competition except that four dogs are involved and, if necessary, two handlers.

The Veterans Class is for the older dog, the minimum age of whom is usually seven years. This class is judged on the quality of the dogs, as the winner competes for Best of Breed, and, on a number of occasions, has been known to win it. So the point is *not* to pick the oldest looking dog, as some seem to think, but the best specimen of the breed, exactly as throughout the regular classes.

Then there are Sweepstakes and Futurity Stakes, sponsored by many Specialty clubs, sometimes as part of their shows and sometimes as separate events. The difference between the two is that Sweepstakes entries usually include dogs and bitches from six to eighteen months of age, and entries are made at the usual time as others for the show, while for a Futurity the entries are bitches nominated when bred and the individual puppies entered at or shortly following their birth.

Junior Showmanship

If there is a youngster in your family between the ages of ten and seventeen, there is

Von Bruka Jaguar photographed by C. H. Brown, Ithaca, N.Y. "Gretchen" was age seven months here and belongs to James and Roxanna McGovern, Port Crane, N.Y.

no better or more rewarding a hobby than having a dog to show in Junior Showmanship competition. This is a marvelous activity for young people. It teaches responsibility, good sportsmanship, the fun of competition where one's own skills are the deciding factor of success, proper care of a pet, and how to socialize with other young folks. Any youngster may experience the thrill of emerging from the ring a winner and the satisfaction of a good job done well.

Entry in Junior Showmanship is open to any boy or girl who is at least ten years old and under seventeen years old on the day of the show. The Novice Junior Showmanship Class is open to youngsters who have not already won, at the time the entries close, three firsts in this class. Youngsters who have won three firsts in Novice may compete in the Open Junior Showmanship Class. Any junior handler who wins his third first-place award in Novice may participate in the Open Class at the same show, provided that the Open Class has at least one other junior handler entered in it. The Novice and Open Classes may be divided into Junior and Senior Classes. Youngsters between the ages of ten and twelve, inclusively, are eligible for the Junior division; and youngsters between thirteen and seventeen, inclusively, are eligible for the Senior division. Any of the foregoing classes may be separated into individual classes for boys and for girls. If such a division is made, it must be indicated on the premium list. The premium list also indicates the prize for Best Junior Handler, if such a prize is being offered at the show. Any youngster who wins a first in any of the regular classes may enter the competition for this prize, provided the youngster has been undefeated in any class at that show.

The high point of each year's Junior Showmanship competition is when those talented juniors who qualify compete in these classes at the Westminster Kennel Club Dog Show in Madison Square Garden in New York City each February. The privilege of doing so is gained by the number of classes won during the preceding year, and the qualifications are explained in detail on the Westminster premium list and entry blank.

Junior Showmanship Classes, unlike regular conformation classes in which the dog's quality is judged, are judged entirely on the skill and ability of the junior handling the dog. Which dog is best is not the point—it is which youngster does the best job with the dog that is under consideration. Eligibility requirements for the dog being shown and other detailed information can be found in *Regulations for Junior Showmanship*, issued by the American Kennel Club.

A junior who has a dog that he or she can enter in both Junior Showmanship and conformation classes has twice the opportunity for success and twice the opportunity to get into the ring and work with the dog. Dogs and juniors work well together, and this combination has often wound up in the winner's circle. There are no age restrictions on a child showing in breed competition, and a youngster may start at any age his parents think suitable. Of course, much depends upon the individual child, and it hardly needs to be pointed out the irresponsibility of turning too young a child, or one not yet able to control it, loose at a dog show with one of *any* of the large, powerful breeds. Too many totally unexpected things could happen.

Pre-Show Preparation
Preparation of the things you will need as an exhibitor should not be left until the last moment. They should be planned and arranged for at least several days before the show in order for you to relax and be calm as the countdown starts.

The importance of the crate has already been discussed, and we assume it is already in use. Of equal importance is the grooming table, which by now you may have already acquired for use at home. You should take it along with you, as your dog will need final touches before entering the ring. If you do not have one yet, a folding table with a rubber top is made specifically for this purpose and can be purchased from the concession booths found at most dog shows. Then you will need a sturdy tack box (also available at the show's concessions) in which to carry your brush, comb, scissors, nail clippers, whatever you use for last minute clean-up jobs, cotton swabs, first-aid equipment, and anything else you are in the habit of using on the dog, such as a leash or two of the type you prefer, some well-cooked and dried-out liver or any of the small packaged "dog treats" your dog likes for use as "bait" in the ring, and a Turkish towel.

Take a large thermos or cooler of ice, the biggest one you can accommodate in your vehicle, for use by "man and beast." Take a jug of water (there are lightweight, inexpensive ones available at all sporting goods shops) and a water dish. If you plan to feed the dog at the show, or if you and the dog will be away from home more than one day, bring food from home so that he will have the type to which he is accustomed.

You may or may not have an exercise pen. This is a *must*, even if you have only one dog. While the shows do provide areas for exercise of the dogs, these are among the best places to come into contact with any illnesses that may be going around, and having a pen of your own for your dog's use is excellent protection. Such a pen can be used in other ways, too, such as a place other than the crate in which to put the dog to relax and a place in which the dog can exercise at rest areas or motels during your travels. A word of caution: never tie a dog to an exercise pen or leave him unattended in it while you wander off, as the pens are not sufficiently secure to keep the dog there should he decide to leave, at least not in most cases. Exercise pens are also available at the dog show concession booths should you not already have yours when you reach the dog's first show. They come in a variety of heights and sizes.

Bring along folding chairs for the members of your party, unless all of you are fond of standing, as these are almost never provided by the show-giving clubs. Have your name stamped on the chairs so there will be no doubt as to whom the chairs belong. Bring whatever you and your family enjoy for drinks or snacks in a picnic basket or cooler, as show food, in general, is expensive and usually not great. You should always have a pair of boots, a raincoat, and a rain hat with you (they should remain permanently in your vehicle if you plan to attend shows regularly), as well as a sweater, a warm coat, and a change of shoes. A smock or big cover-up

apron will assure that you remain tidy as you prepare the dog for the ring. Your overnight case should include a small sewing kit for emergency repairs, headache and indigestion remedies, and any personal products or medications you normally use.

In your car you should always carry maps of the area where you are headed and an assortment of motel directories. Generally speaking, it has been found that Holiday Inns are the friendliest about taking dogs. Some Ramadas and some Howard Johnsons do so cheerfully (the Ramadas indicate on each listing in their directory whether or not pets are welcome). Best Western usually frowns on pets (not all of them but enough to make it necessary to find out which do). Some of the smaller chains welcome pets. The majority of privately owned motels do not.

Have everything prepared the night before the show to expedite your departure. Be sure that the dog's identification and your judging program and other show information are in your purse or briefcase. If you are taking sandwiches, have them ready. Anything that goes into the car the night before will be one thing less to be concerned with in the morning. Decide upon what you will wear and have it out and ready. If there is any question in your mind about what to wear, try on the possibilities before the day of the show; don't risk feeling you may want to change when you see yourself dressed a few moments prior to departure time! In planning your outfit, wear something simple that will make an attractive background for your dog, providing contrast to his color, calling attention to the *dog* rather than to yourself. Sports clothes always seem to look best at a dog show. What you wear on your feet is important, as many types of flooring are slippery, and wet grass, too, can present a hazard as you move the dog. Make it a rule to wear rubber soles and low or flat heels in the ring, so that you can move along smartly.

Your final step in pre-show preparation is to leave yourself plenty of time to reach the show that morning. Traffic can get extremely heavy as one nears the immediate vicinity of the show, finding a parking place can be difficult, and other delays may occur. You'll be in better humor if you can take it all in your stride without the pressure of watching every second because you figured the time too closely.

Day of the Show

From the moment of your arrival at the dog show until after your dog has been judged, keep foremost in your mind the fact that he is your purpose for being there. You will need to arrive in advance of the judging in order to give him a chance to exercise after the trip to the show and take care of personal matters. A dog arriving in the ring and immediately using it for an exercise pen hardly makes a favorable impression on the judge. You will also need time to put the final touches on your dog, making certain that he goes into the ring looking his very best.

When you reach ringside, ask the steward for your arm-card with your dog's entry number on it and anchor it firmly into place on your arm with the elastic provided. Make sure that you are where you should be when your class is called. The fact that you have picked up your arm-card does not guarantee, as some seem to think, that the judge will wait for you more than a minute or two. Judges are expected to keep on schedule, which precludes delaying for the arrival of exhibitors who are tardy.

Even though you may be nervous, assume an air of cool, collected calm. Remember that this is a hobby to be enjoyed, so approach it in that state of mind. The dog will do better, too, as he will be quick to reflect your attitude.

If you make a mistake while presenting the dog, don't worry about it—next time you'll do better. Do not be intimidated by the more expert or experienced exhibitors. After all, they, too, were once newcomers.

Always show your dog with an air of pride. An apologetic attitude on the part of the exhibitor does little to help the dog win, so try to appear self-confident as you gait and set up the dog.

The judging routine usually starts when the judge asks that the dogs be gaited in a circle around the ring. During this period the judge is watching each dog as it moves along, noting style, topline, reach and drive, head and tail carriage, and general balance. This is the time to keep your mind and your eye on your dog, moving him at his most becoming gait and keeping your place in line without coming too close to the dog ahead of you. Always keep your dog on the inside of the circle, between yourself and the judge, so that the judge's view of the dog is unobstructed.

Calmly pose the dog when requested to set up for examination. If you are at the head of the line and many dogs are in the class, do not stop halfway down the end of the ring and begin stacking the dog. Go forward enough so that sufficient space is left for the other dogs. Simple courtesy demands that we be considerate and give others a chance to follow the judge's instructions, too.

Space your dog so that on all sides of the dog the judge will have room in which to make his examination; this means that there must be sufficient room between each of the dogs for the judge to move around. Time is important when you are setting up your dog, so practice in front of a full-length mirror at home, trying to accustom yourself to "getting it all together" correctly in the shortest possible time. When you set him up, you want his forelegs well under the dog, feet directly below the elbows, toes pointing straight ahead, and hindquarters extended *correctly*. Hold the dog's head up with your hand at the back inner corner of the lips, your left hand extending the tail to its proper position. You want the dog to look "all of a piece," head carried proudly on a strong neck, correct topline, hindquarters nicely angulated, the front straight and true, and the dog standing firmly on his feet.

Listen carefully as the judge instructs the manner in which the dog is to be gaited, whether it is straight down and straight back; down the ring, across, and back; or in a triangle. The latter has become the most popular pattern with the majority of judges. "In a triangle" means down the outer side of the ring to the first corner, across that end of the ring to the second corner, and then back to the judge from the second corner, using the center of the ring in a diagonal line. Please learn to do this pattern without breaking at each corner to twirl the dog around you, a senseless maneuver we sometimes have noted.

Ch. Rhomarks Axel v Lerchenfeld, handled by Robert Hanley for Ken and Hildegard Griffin, Novato, California. Winning Best in Show at Two Cities Kennel Club, June 20, 1982.

Judges like to see the dog move in an *uninterrupted* triangle, as they get a better idea of the dog's gait.

It is impossible to overemphasize that the gait at which you move your dog is tremendously important, and considerable thought and study should be given to the matter. At home, have someone move the dog for you at different speeds so that you can tell which shows him off to best advantage.

Do not allow your dog to sidetrack, flop, or weave as you gait him, and do not let him pull so that he appears to lean on the lead as you are gaiting him. He should move in a straight line, proudly, smoothly, and firmly. That is your goal as you work with him on a lead in preparation for his show career. Movement is an important feature of a breed; thus, it is essential that yours displays his movement to full advantage.

Baiting your dog should be done in a manner which does not upset the other dogs in the ring or cause problems for their handlers. A tasty morsel of well-cooked and dried-out liver is fine for keeping your own dog interested, but discarded on the ground or floor, it can throw off the behavior of someone else's dog who may attempt to get it. So please, if you drop liver on the ground, pick it up and take it with you when you have finished.

When the awards have been made, accept yours courteously, no matter how you may actually feel about it. To argue with a judge is unthinkable, and it will certainly not change the decision. Be gracious, congratulate the winners if your dog has been defeated, and try not to show your disappointment. By the same token, please be a gracious winner; this, surprisingly, sometimes seems to be even more difficult.

Medeah's Shane De Michaele, C.D. (1977–1980) was winner of a *Dog World* Award of Canine Distinction (with obedience scores of 196½, 197, and 196½). Winner of the 1979 Western Rottweiler Owners' Irene Mackenzie Memorial Obedience Trophy for the Highest Scoring Dog of the Year (score 199). Associated Obedience Clubs of Northern California Competition—Top Novice Dog 1979 (all breeds) with scores 198, 199, and 198½. California State Obedience Competition Runner-Up Novice Dog 1979 (all breeds). Owned by Von Medeah Rottweilers, Keith and Charlotte Twineham, Union City, California. Breeder, Michelle Quail, Lewisville, Texas.

CHAPTER FOURTEEN

Obedience and the Rottweiler

Am. and Can. Ch. Von Gailingen's Dark Delight, U.D.T., Bda. C.D.X., Can. C.D. Owner, Mrs. Catherine Thompson, Freehold, New Jersey.

Dogs have a well-deserved reputation for great intelligence, loyalty, and service. Properly trained and managed dogs have distinguished themselves not only in the show ring but also in other endeavors. Many, many dogs who are show champions also have earned one or more obedience titles; and many have achieved success in various fields of specialized work, only one of which is described in detail here.

Obedience

For its own protection and safety, every dog should be taught, at the very least, to recognize and respond promptly and correctly to the basic commands "Come," "Heel," "Down," "Sit," and "Stay." Doing so might at sometime save the dog's life and, in less extreme circumstances, will certainly make him a better citizen, more well-behaved and far more pleasant as a companion.

If you are patient and enjoy working with your dog, study some of the excellent books available on the subject of obedience and start at an early age to teach your puppy these basic manners. If you need the stimulus of working with a group, find out where obedience training classes are available (usually your veterinarian, your dog's breeder, or a dog-owning friend can tell you) and you and your dog can join up. If you have difficulty locating such a class, the American Kennel Club will, upon request, provide you with this information.

As an alternative, you could, of course, let someone else do the training by sending your dog to class, but this is far less rewarding as you then lose the opportunity of working with the dog, developing the rapport and closeness which the two of you can enjoy by working together. Since there could hardly be found a more intelligent, easily trainable breed of dog than this breed, it certainly should prove worth your while to attempt the task yourself.

If the latter has been your decision, there are some basic rules which you should follow. You must remain calm and confident in attitude at all times. You must never lose your temper and frighten your dog or punish him unjustly. Never, ever, resort to cruelty. Be quick and lavish with your praise each time a command is correctly followed. Make it fun

Top: Ch. Rhomarks Axel v. Lerchenfeld, C.D.X., T.D. completed his Tracking Degree on March 10, 1985 under judges P. Gail Burnham and Dan Lawer. Owned by Ken and Hildegarde Griffin, Novato, California. **Bottom left:** Am. and Can. Ch. Von Gailingen's Dassie Did It, U.D.T., Can. C.D. here is working with scent articles for utility. **Bottom right:** Gunda von Winterbach, C.D.X., owned by Mrs. Glenn Rowe, is on his way to championship at Huntsville, Alabama, May 1971.

for the dog and he will be eager to please you by responding correctly. Repetition is the keynote, but it should not be continued without recess to the point of tedium. Limit the training sessions to ten- or fifteen-minute periods each time.

Formal obedience training can be followed, and very frequently is, by entering the dog in obedience competition to work toward an obedience degree, or several of them, depending on the dog's aptitude and your own enjoyment. Obedience trials are held in conjunction with the majority of conformation dog shows, both all-breed and Specialty, and as separate events as well. If you are working alone with your dog, you will need to obtain information from someone local, from a Dog Breed Club to which you may belong, or from the American Kennel Club. If you have been working with a training class, you will find information readily available regarding dates and locations of trials.

The goals for which one works in the formal American Kennel Club member or licensed obedience trials are the following titles: C.D. (Companion Dog), C.D.X. (Companion Dog Excellent), and U.D. (Utility Dog). These degrees are earned by receiving three qualifying scores, or "legs," at each level of competition. The degrees must be earned in order, with one completed prior to starting work on the next. For example, a dog must have earned C.D. prior to starting work on C.D.X. Then C.D.X. must be completed before U.D. work begins. The ultimate title possible to attain in obedience work is that of Obedience Trial Champion (O.T.Ch.). In order to qualify for this one, a dog must have received the required number of points by placing first or second in Open or Utility after having earned the Utility Dog rating. There is also a Tracking Dog title (T.D.) to be earned at tracking trials and a new, more difficult-to-attain degree, Tracking Dog Excellent (T.D.X.).

When you see the letters "C.D." following a dog's name, you will know that the dog has satisfactorily completed the following exercises: heel on leash, heel free, stand for examination, recall, long sit, and long stay. "C.D.X." means that tests have been passed in all of the exercises for Companion Dog plus heel free, drop on recall, retrieve over high jump, broad jump, long sit, and long down. "U.D." indicates that the dog has additionally passed tests in scent discrimination (leather article), scent discrimination (metal article), signal exercise, directed retrieve, directed jumping, and group stand for examination.

The letters "T.D." indicate that the dog has been trained for and passed the test to follow the trail of a stranger along a path on which the trail was laid between thirty minutes and two hours previously. Along this track there must be more than two right-angle turns, at least two of which are well out in the open where no fences or other boundaries exist for guidance of the dog or handler. The dog wears a harness and is connected to the handler by a lead twenty to forty feet in length. Inconspicuously dropped at the end of the track is an article to be retrieved, usually a glove or wallet, which the dog is expected to locate and the handler to pick up. The letters "T.D.X." indicate that the dog has passed a more difficult version of the Tracking Dog test, with a longer track and more turns to be successfully worked through.

The owner of a dog holding the U.D. title and the T.D. title may then use the letters "U.D.T." following the dog's name. If the dog has gained his U.D. title and his T.D.X. title, then the letters "U.D.T.X." may follow his name, indicating that he is a Utility Dog and Tracker Excellent.

Many breeds have distinguished themselves admirably in obedience work ever since it first became recognized in the United States. As you read this book, you will note the frequency with which show champions also carry one or more of the obedience titles. Beauty and brains are well combined in this breed, to be sure.

Basko vom Aschafftal, C.D., T.D.X., SchH. II, AD, is a pointed Group placer and has one C.D.X. leg. This dual-purpose Rottweiler is owned and trained by Dennis and Margaret Teague; imported by Barbara Dillon.

CHAPTER FIFTEEN

The Schutzhund Dog

by
Douglas K. Loving
Richmond, Virginia

Thewina Summer Ferrymaster, C.D.X. is "biting the bad guy" during Schutzhund practice. Linda B. Griswold, owner, Ravenwood Kennels, Michigan City, Indiana.

To the uninitiated, the Schutzhund dog might appear a vicious killer. To those of us who participate in the sport, however, quite the opposite is found to be true.

The boxer who fights as though his life depends on the outcome of each bout is often gentle and sensitive outside the ring. For, you see, this fighter is simply doing his job. Just as the sports of football and basketball are rigidly controlled and regulated, so is the Schutzhund sport.

The Schutzhund handler has achieved a level of training and control seldom realized by the average dog owner. He is always striving to realize the full potential of his dog, to honor and preserve this dog's *working* heritage.

Most clubs refuse to help train any dog and handler team that does not participate in all phases of the sport. In the beginning of the protection training, control of the dog is vital. The training level equivalent to an American Kennel Club C.D. degree is often required. The dedication required to achieve this level of training often weeds out the owners who are just looking for a "junk yard" or "attack trained" animal. The latter type dog/handler team without control is dangerous, and there is no room in the Schutzhund sport for such participants.

The handler trains/educates his dog to track, to respond quickly and with self-assurance to obedience commands, and to protect his handler when called upon to do so. The dog's spirited performance is evidence of his willingness to please his handler. Because of this level of training the Schutzhund dog exhibits an air of calmness which comes from the knowledge that he can handle any situation which may arise.

To bring out the protective instincts and responses, the helper brings the dog's prey traits to bear. The dog thinks of his opponent as prey, a darting rabbit for example. By giving these motions to the jute sack, the helper teaches the dog to bite and hold without placing stress on the young dog. In beginning agitation, the dog always wins. The young dog is taught when and how to bite. But, equally important, he is taught when not to bite. Even in young puppies this prey instinct is evident. Watch a puppy as it plays with a chew toy or sock. The side-to-side shaking motion is nature telling your puppy to kill its prey. To deny that such traits exist is to deny your dog his heritage. It is now the responsibility of the trainer to help the dog learn to control his aggression and to channel it into constructive areas without breaking the dog's spirit.

As a house pet the Schutzhund-trained dog is without equal. The Schutzhund dog is a confident but stable pet who is quite capable of protecting his family from harm. The Schutzhund-trained dog who will fearlessly attack an agitator will sit back and watch with amusement as children play-fight a few feet away. He is far less likely to bite when faced with an unfamiliar situation. Remember, the Schutzhund dog has been trained when *not* to bite.

The Schutzhund dog is also at home in the show ring. Who can forget Champion Pio von Kastenienbaum, SchH. II? Or Alan Kruse's Champion Artus vom Adelshof, SchH.III, the Best of Breed winner at the 1985 Westminster Kennel Club Dog Show?

Several hundred exhibitors were on hand to observe Jessica Nichols's American and Canadian Champion Northwinds Kaiser of Mallam perform in the Schutzhund demonstration at the 1984 American Rottweiler Club Specialty Show, then go on to be gaited to first place in the Veteran Dog Class and 4th place in Stud Dog.

In Schutzhund competition, the dog shows his true love for the sport. During his obedience routine, the dog is judged on his enthusiasm. In most cases, the dog's tail never stops wagging, and praise from the handler causes joyous leaps and barks. During the protection phase, the dog receives his ultimate satisfaction. He is able to show his handler that his lessons have been learned well as he protects his best friend from harm. The Schutzhund dog lives for this moment.

To give Schutzhund work a try, contact your local Schutzhund Club, or contact DVG America (Deutsche Verbrand fur de Gebrauchshundsportsverein), 509 Horizon Court, Plano, Texas, 75074.

The Rottweiler Schutzhund

The concept of the Schutzhund trained dog evolved around the beginning of this century in Europe. Although the exercises through the years have changed slightly, basically the sport remains the same, consisting of three phases: tracking; obedience; and protection. The dog must perform all tasks asked of him quickly and with spirit. He must bite hard when required, showing not the slightest hesitation.

The Schutzhund degrees range from Schutzhund I (SchH. I) to Schutzhund II (SchH. II) and then on to Schutzhund III (SchH. III). Each indicates a different plateau of training.

The exercises for the various Schutzhund degrees include the following. In tracking, the dog must follow a person's path which has been previously laid awhile ahead of time, and which includes unmarked turns in several places. The dog must find, and indicate to his handler, several "lost" articles, which must be done regardless of weather conditions.

The obedience exercises include to heel, jump, retrieve, retrieve over a six-foot wall, and walk away from his trainer when ordered to do so, performing these exercises both on and off lead. He must be steady and unintimidated no matter what the distractions, including the sound of gunshot or many strangers milling around the area.

In protection exercises, the dog unassisted by his handler, must respond promptly and properly to critical situations. He must alert his handler to an intruder by barking at a stranger who is standing perfectly still. He must not bite the unmoving person. He must, however, bite hard to stop the intruder from leaving should a move to do so be made, on the dog's assumption that the intruder plans escape or to harm the dog's handler. He must release his hold immediately when the intruder stops struggling, or when commanded to do so by his handler. Even when being threatened by the intruder with a stick, the dog must bite *hard* and *immediately*. He must learn to distinguish between a harmless bystander and a person potentially dangerous, and to handle the situation accordingly. Courage and fighting spirit must be displayed throughout these exercises.

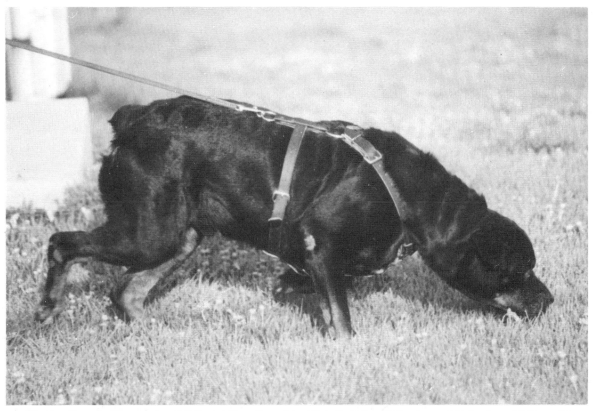

Thewina Summer Ferrymaster, C.D.X., tracking. Owned by Linda B. Griswold, Ravenwood Rottweilers, Michigan City, Indiana.

Various groups are now sponsoring Schutzhund trials and classes in the United States (where it is *not* recognized by the American Kennel Club), but is proving extremely popular with owners of the working breeds. Canada is active, too. And of course Germany has long been a forerunner of this training, with at least several hundred local groups meeting from twice weekly to twice monthly for training. It is not necessary for this training that a dog be a purebred. Any dog that can do Schutzhund work is eligible for it; however, the dogs must have sufficient stamina for the important protection work, and be capable of clearing a hurdle of approximately 30 inches' height, prerequisites which naturally prevent dogs smaller than these from participation. The dogs which most frequently succeed at earning these degrees are German Shepherds, Doberman Pinschers, Rottweilers, Boxers, Hovaworte (in Europe) and Giant Schnauzers.

There are many German titles which keep appearing in pedigrees of dogs there with a background in addition to those of Schutzhund, indicating the dog's proficiency in a specialized field. For example, the FH (Faehrtenhund Degree) is an advanced tracking degree. Then there are two specialized Police Dog Degrees, DPO I and DPO II, similar to advanced Schutzhund degrees.

The AD letters are awarded to dogs who have earned an Endurance Test Degree, abbreviation for the word Ausdauerpruefung. A WH (Wachhund) title indicates the dog's having earned a degree as a Watch Dog.

Then there is the Verkehrssicherer Begleithund which is a dog trained to work as a "Traffic Sure Companion Dog," working in both normal conditions and heavy city traffic. You will see most of these letters appearing in the pedigrees of Rottweilers from Germany.

Schutzhund trials here in the United States are bringing forth some very distinguished workers among the Rottweilers, which certainly comes as no surprise when one considers their heredity!

Ch. Seren's Chantilly Lace, handled by Valerie Cade, taking Winners Bitch at Springfield 1984 for owners Linda Kowalski and Peter and Marilyn Piusz, Johnstown, New York.

CHAPTER SIXTEEN

Breeding Rottweilers

The foundation bitch at Ravenwood Rottweilers, Dagna Von Arktos, C.D., and still going strong at 11 years of age. Owned by Linda B. Griswold, Michigan City, Indiana.

Breeding good dogs requires a lot of hard work. It is not easy to produce dogs who conform as closely as possible to the standard, and it takes years to develop a strain of good and successful dogs. A lot of time and effort must go into choosing the stud dog and brood bitch, and then more time must be spent with the litter once it arrives.

The Stud Dog

Choosing the best stud dog to complement your bitch is not an easy task. The principal factors to be considered are the stud's quality and conformation and his pedigree. The pedigree lists the various bloodlines involved with the ancestry of the dog. If you are a novice in the breed, it is a good idea that you seek advice from some of the more experienced breeders who are old-timers in the fancy and thus would be able to discuss with you some of the various dogs behind the one to which you are planning to breed your bitch. Many times such people accurately recall in minute detail the dogs you need to know about, perhaps even having access to photos of them. And do be sure to carefully study the photos

in this book, as they show representatives of important bloodlines.

It is extremely important that the stud's pedigree be harmonious with that of your bitch. Do not just rush out and breed to a current winner, with no regard for whether or not he can reproduce his quality. Take time to check out the progeny being sired by the dog, or dogs, under your consideration. A dog that has sired nothing of quality for others probably will do no better for you, unless, of course, it is a young stud just starting out; such a stud may not have had the opportunity to produce much of anything, good or bad, thus far. Do you want to waste your bitch's time on an unknown quantity? Wouldn't you prefer to use a dog with a good producing record? You may get a little-known or unproven dog for a less expensive stud fee, but is that really sensible?

Breeding dogs is not a moneymaking proposition. By the time you pay a stud fee, take care of the bitch during gestation, whelp the litter, and raise and care for the puppies (including shots, and food, among other things)

291

until they reach selling age, you will be fortunate if you break even on the cost of the litter. Therefore, it is foolish to skimp on the stud fee. Let nothing influence your selection except that the dog be best suited to your bitch in background and conformation, with the best producing record, regardless of the cost. It is just as expensive to raise mediocre puppies as good ones, and you will certainly fare better financially if you have show-prospect puppies to sell than if you come up with nothing but pets, which you will probably wind up selling for far less than you had intended or you'll end up giving away to get them good homes. Remember, the only excuse for breeding and bringing puppies into the world is an honest effort to improve the breed. So in choosing the stud you use, remember that the best, most suitable one you can find with an impressive producing record will almost certainly be by far the greatest bargain in the long run.

You will have to decide on one of three courses to follow in planning the breeding of your bitch: inbreeding, linebreeding, or outcrossing. Inbreeding is normally considered to be father to daughter, mother to son, or sister to brother. Linebreeding is combining two dogs belonging originally to the same strain or family of dogs, descended from the same ancestors, such as half-brother to half-sister, niece to uncle, granddaughter to grandsire, and so on. Outcross breeding is using a dog and a bitch of completely different bloodlines with no mutual ancestors, or only a few, and these far back, if at all.

Each of these methods has advantages and disadvantages; each has supporters and detractors. Linebreeding is probably the safest, the most generally approved, and the most frequently used with the desired results. Thus it is perfect for the novice breeder because it is the easiest to figure out, especially until one has acquired considerable experience with the breed and the various bloodlines of which it consists.

Inbreeding should be left for the experienced, very sophisticated breeder who knows the line extremely well and thus is in a position to evaluate the probable results. Outcrossing is normally done when you are trying to bring in a specific feature or trait, such as

better movement, better head type, superior bone or substance, or better personality or temperament.

Everyone sincerely interested in breeding dogs wants to develop a line of their own, but this is not accomplished overnight. It takes at least several generations before you can claim to have done so, and during this time the close study of bloodlines and the observation of individual dogs are essential. Getting to know and truthfully evaluate the dogs with which you are working will go a long way in helping you preserve the best in what you have while at the same time remove weaknesses.

As a novice breeder, your wisest bet is to start by acquiring one or two bitches of the finest quality and background you can buy. In the beginning, it is really foolish to own your own stud dog; you will make out better and have a wider range of dogs with which to work if you pay a stud fee for one of the outstanding producing dogs available to service your bitch. In order to be attractive to breeders a stud dog must be well known, must have sired at least one champion (and usually one that has attracted considerable attention in Specials competition), and must have winning progeny in the ring; this represents a large expenditure of time and money before the dog begins to bring in returns on your investment. So start out by paying a stud fee a few times to use such a dog, or dogs, retaining the best bitch out of each of your first few litters and breeding those once or twice before you seriously think of owning your own stud dog. By that time, you will have gained the experience to recognize exactly what sort of dog you need for this purpose.

A future stud dog should be selected with the utmost care and consideration. He must be of very high standard as he may be responsible for siring many puppies each year, and he should not be used unless he clearly has something to contribute to the breed and carries no hereditary disease. Ideally, he should come from a line of excellent dogs on both sides of his pedigree, the latter containing not only *good* dogs but also ones which are *proven successful producers of quality*. The dog himself should be of sufficient quality to hold his own in competition in his breed. He should be robust and virile, a keen stud dog who has proved that he is able to transmit his best qualities to his progeny. Do not use an unsound dog or a dog with a major or outstanding fault. Not all champions seem able to pass along their individual splendid quality and, by the same token, occasionally one finds a dog who never finished but who does sire puppies better than himself *provided that his pedigree is star-studded with top producing dogs and bitches*. Remember, too, that the stud dog cannot do it alone; the bitch must have what it takes too, although some stud dogs, the truly dominant ones, can consistently produce type and quality regardless of the bitch or her background. Great studs like this, however, are few and far between.

If you are the proud owner of a promising young stud dog, one that you have either bred from one of your own bitches or that you have purchased after much serious thought and deliberation, do not permit him to be used for the first time until he is about a year old. The initial breeding should be to a proven matron, experienced in what is expected of her and thus not likely to give the stud a bad time. His first encounter should be pleasant and easy, as he could be put off breeding forever by a maiden bitch who fights and resents his advances. His first breeding should help him develop confidence and assurance. It should be done in quiet surroundings, with only you and one other person (to hold the bitch) present. Do not make a circus of it, as the first time will determine your stud's attitude and feeling about future breeding.

Your young stud dog must allow you to help with the breeding, as later there will be bitches who will not be cooperative and he will need to develop the habit of accepting assistance. If, right from the beginning, you are there helping and praising him, he will expect and accept this as a matter of course whenever it may be necessary.

Before you introduce the dogs, be sure to have some K-Y Jelly at hand (this is the only lubricant that should be used) and either a stocking or a length of gauze with which to muzzle the bitch should it seem necessary, as you do not want either yourself or your stud

dog bitten. Once they are "tied," you will be able to remove the muzzle, but, for the preliminaries, it is best to play it safe by muzzling her.

The stud fee is paid at the time of the breeding. Normally a return service is offered should the bitch fail to produce. Usually one live puppy is considered to be a litter. In order to avoid any misunderstanding regarding the terms of the breeding, it is wise to have a breeding certificate which both the owner of the stud and the owner of the bitch should sign. This should spell out quite specifically all the conditions of the breeding, along with listing the dates of the matings (usually the bitch is bred twice with one day in between, especially if she is a maiden bitch). The owner of the stud should also at this time provide the owner of the bitch with a copy of the stud dog's pedigree, if this has not previously been done.

Sometimes a pick-of-the-litter puppy is taken instead of a stud fee, and this should be noted on the breeding certificate along with such terms as at what age the owner of the stud dog is to select the puppy and whether it is to be a dog puppy, a bitch puppy, or just the "pick" puppy. All of this should be clearly stated to avoid any misunderstandings later on.

In almost every case, the bitch must come to the stud dog for breeding. Once the owner of the bitch decides to what stud dog she will preferably be bred, it is important that the owner of the stud be contacted immediately to discuss the stud fee, terms, approximate time the bitch is due in season, and whether she will be shipped in or brought to the stud owner. Then, as soon as the bitch shows signs of coming into season, another phone call to the stud owner must follow to finalize the arrangements. There have been times when the bitch's owner has waited until a day or two before the bitch should be bred, only to meet with disappointment owing to the dog's absence from home.

It is essential that the stud owner have proper facilities for housing the bitch while she is there. Nothing can be more disheartening than to have a bitch misbred or, still worse, to have her get away and become lost. Unless you can provide safe and proper care for visiting bitches, do not offer your dog at public stud.

Owning a stud dog is no easy road to riches, as some who have not experienced it seem to think; making the dog sufficiently well known is expensive and time-consuming. Be selective in the bitches you permit this dog to service. It takes two to make the puppies; and while some stud dogs do seem almost to achieve miracles, it is a general rule that an inferior bitch from a mediocre background will probably never produce well no matter how dominant and splendid may be the stud to whom she is bred. Remember that these puppies will be advertised and perhaps shown as sired by your dog. You do not want them to be an embarrassment to yourself or to him, so do not accept just any bitch who comes along in order to get the stud fee. It may prove far too expensive in the long run.

A stud fee is generally based on the going price of one show-type puppy and on the sire's record as a producer of winners. Obviously, a stud throwing champions in every litter is worth a greater price than a dog that sires mediocre puppies. Thus a young stud, just starting his career as a sire, is less expensive before proven than a dog with, say, forty or fifty champions already on the record. And a dog that has been used more than a few times but has no winning progeny should, it goes without saying, be avoided no matter how small the fee; he will almost certainly be a waste of your bitch's time.

We need not go into the actual breeding procedure here, as the experienced fancier already knows how it should be handled and the novice should not attempt it for the first time by reading instructions in a book. Plan to have a breeder or handler friend help you until you have become accustomed to handling such matters or, if this is not practical for you, it is very likely your veterinarian can arrange to do it for you or get someone from his staff to preside.

If a complete "tie" is made, that breeding should be all that is actually necessary. However, with a maiden bitch, a bitch who has "missed" (failed to conceive) in the past, or one who has come a long distance, most people like to give a second breeding, allowing one day to elapse in between the two. This second service gives additional insurance that a litter will result; and if the bitch is one with a past record for misses, sometimes even a third mating takes place in an effort to take every precaution.

Once the "tie" has been completed, be sure that the penis goes back completely into its sheath. The dog should be offered a drink of water and a short walk, and then he should be put in his crate or kennel somewhere alone to settle down. Do not permit him to mingle with the other males for a while, as he will carry the odor of the bitch about him and this could result in a fight.

The bitch should not be allowed to urinate for at least an hour. In fact, many people feel that she should be "upended" (held with her rear end above her front) for several minutes following the "tie" in order to permit the sperm to travel deeper. She should then be offered water, crated, and kept quiet.

There are no set rules governing the conditions of a stud service. They are whatever the owner of the stud dog chooses to make them. The stud fee is paid for the act, not for the litter; and if a bitch fails to conceive, this does not automatically call for a return service unless the owner of the stud sees it that way. A return service is a courtesy, not something that can be regarded as a right, particularly as in many cases the failure has been on the part of the bitch, not the stud dog. Owners of a stud in whom they take pride and whom they are anxious to have make records as the sire of numerous champions, however, are usually most generous in this respect; and in no known instances has this courtesy been refused when no puppies resulted from the breeding. Some stud owners insist on the return service being given to the same bitch only, while others will accept a different bitch in her place if the owner wishes, particularly if the original one has a previous record for missing.

When a bitch has been given one return breeding and misses again, the stud owner's responsibility has ended. If the stud dog is one who consistently sires puppies, then obviously the bitch is at fault; and she will quite likely never conceive, no matter how often or to how many different studs she is bred. It is unreasonable for the owner of a bitch to expect a stud's owner to give more than one return service.

The Brood Bitch

One of the most important purchases you will make in dogs is the selection of your foundation brood bitch, or bitches, on whom you plan to base your breeding program. You want marvelous bloodlines representing top producing strains; you want sound bitches of basic quality, free of any hereditary problems. There is no such thing as a "bargain" brood bitch. If you are offered one, be wary and bear in mind that you need the *best* and that the price will be correctly in ratio to the quality.

Conscientious breeders feel quite strongly that the only possible reason for producing puppies is the desire to improve and uphold quality and temperament within the breed, certainly not because one hopes to make a quick cash profit on a mediocre litter, which never works out that way in the long run and can very well wind up adding to the nation's shocking number of unwanted canine waifs. The only reason for breeding a litter is the ambition to produce high-quality puppies of intelligence, show potential, and sound temperament. That is the thought to be kept in mind right from the moment you begin to yearn for puppies.

Your bitch should not be bred until her second period in season; but if she starts her season at an extra early age, say, barely over six months of age and then for the second time just past one year of age, you would be wise to wait until her third heat. Many breeders prefer to wait and finish their bitch's championship and then breed her, as pregnancy can be disastrous to a show coat and getting it back in shape again takes time. The waiting period can be profitably spent carefully watching for the ideal stud to complement her own qualities and be compatible with her background. Keeping this in mind, attend dog shows and watch the males who are winning and, even more important, siring the winners. Subscribe to some of the all-breed magazines and study the pictures and stories accompanying them to familiarize yourself with dogs in other areas of which you

may have not been aware. Be sure to keep in mind that the stud should be strong in the bitch's weak points; carefully note his progeny to see if he passes along the features you want and admire. Make special note of any offspring from bitches with backgrounds similar to your bitch's; then you can get an idea of how well the background fits with his. When you see a stud dog that interests you, discuss your bitch with the owner and request a copy of his dog's pedigree for your study and perusal. You can also discuss the stud dog with other knowledgeable breeders, including the one from whom your bitch was purchased. You may not always get an unbiased opinion (particularly if the person giving it also has an available stud dog), but discussion is a fine teacher. Listen to what they say and consider the value of their comments. As a result, you will be better qualified to reach a knowledgeable and intelligent decision on your own.

When you have made a tentative choice, contact the stud's owner to make the preliminary arrangements regarding the stud fee (whether it will be in cash or a puppy), approximate time the bitch should be ready, and so on. Find out, too, the requirements (such as a copy of your bitch's pedigree, health certificates, and tests) the stud owner has regarding bitches accepted for breeding. If you will be shipping the bitch, find out which airport and airline should be used.

The airlines will probably have special requirements, too, regarding conditions under which they will or will not take dogs. These requirements, which change from time to time, include such things as crate size and type they will accept. Most airlines have their own crates available for sale which may be purchased at a nominal cost, if you do not already have one that they consider suitable. These are made of fiberglass and are the safest type in which to ship a dog. Most airlines also require that the dog be at the airport two hours before the flight is scheduled to depart and that the dog is accompanied by a health certificate from your veterinarian, including information about rabies inoculation. If the airline does not wish to accept the bitch because of extreme temperature changes in the weather but will do so if you sign a waiver stating that she is accustomed to them and should have no problem, think it over carefully before doing so, as you are thus relieving them of any responsibility should the bitch not reach her destination alive or in good condition. And always insure the bitch when you can.

Normally the airline must be notified several days in advance for the bitch's reservation, as only a limited number of dogs can be accommodated on each flight. Plan on shipping the bitch on her eighth or ninth day, but if at all possible arrange it so that she avoids travelling on the weekend when schedules are not always the same and freight offices are likely to be closed.

It is important that whenever possible you ship your bitch on a flight that goes directly to the airport which is her destination. It is not at all unusual, when stopovers are made along the way, for a dog to be removed from the plane with other cargo and either incorrectly loaded for the next leg of the flight or left behind. Take every precaution that you can against human error!

It is simpler if you can plan to bring the bitch to the stud dog. Some people feel that the trauma of the plane trip may cause the bitch not to conceive; others just plain prefer not sending them that way. If you have a choice, you might do better to take the bitch in your own car where she will feel more relaxed and at ease. If you are doing it this way, be sure to allow sufficient time for the drive to get her to her destination at the correct time for the breeding. This usually is any time from the eighth to the fourteenth day, depending on the individual bitch and her cycle. Remember that if you want the bitch bred twice, you must allow a day in between the two services. Do not expect the stud's owner to put you up during the stay. Find a good, nearby motel that accepts dogs, and make a reservation for yourself there.

Just prior to your bitch's season, you should make a visit to your veterinarian with her. Have her checked for worms, make sure that she is up-to-date on all her shots, and attend to any other tests the stud owner may have requested. The bitch may act and be perfectly normal up until her third or fourth week of pregnancy, but it is better for her to have a clean bill of health before the breeding than to bother her after it. If she is overweight, right now is when you should start getting the fat off her; she should be in good hard condition, neither fat nor thin, when bred.

The day you've been waiting for finally arrives, and you notice the swelling of her vulva, followed within a day or two by the appearance of a colored discharge. Immediately call the stud's owner to finalize arrangements, advising whether you will ship her or bring her, the exact day she will arrive, and so on. Then, if she is going by plane, as soon as you know the details, advise the stud owner of the flight number, the time of arrival, and any other pertinent information. If you are shipping the bitch, the check for the stud fee should be mailed now. If the owner of the stud dog charges for his trips to the airport, for picking the bitch up and then returning her, reimbursement for this should either be included with the stud fee or sent as soon as you know the amount of the charge.

If you are going to ship your bitch, do not feed her on the day of the flight; the stud's owner will do so when she arrives. Be sure that she has had access to a drink of water just before you leave her and that she has been exercised prior to being put in her crate. Place several layers of newspapers, topped with some shredded papers, on the bottom of the crate for a good bed. The papers can be discarded and replaced when she reaches her destination prior to the trip home. Rugs and towels are not suitable for bedding material as they may become soiled, necessitating laundering when she reaches her destination. A small towel may be included to make her feel more at home if you wish. Remember to have her at the airport two hours ahead of flight time.

If you are driving, be sure to arrive at a reasonable time of day. If you are coming from a distance and get in late, have a good night's sleep before contacting the stud's owner first thing in the morning. If possible, leave the children and relatives at home; they will not only be in the way, but also most stud owners definitely object to too many people around during the actual breeding.

Once the breeding has been completed, if you wish to sit and visit for a while, that is fine; but do not leave the bitch at loose ends. Take her to her crate in the car where she can be quiet (you should first, of course, ascertain that the temperature is comfortable for her there and that she has proper ventilation). Remember that she should not urinate for at least an hour following the breeding.

If you have not already done so, pay the stud fee now, and be sure that you receive your breeding certificate and a copy of the dog's pedigree if you do not have one.

Now you are all set to await, with happy anticipation, the arrival of the puppies.

Pedigrees

To anyone interested in the breeding of dogs, pedigrees are the basic component with which this is best accomplished. It is not sufficient to just breed two nice looking Rottweilers together, then sit back and await results. Chances are these will be disappointing, as there is no equal to a scientific approach to the breeding of dogs if quality results are the ultimate goal. Those of you who are familiar with the strict requirements of breeding in Germany must be well familiar with this fact!

We have selected for you pedigrees of Rottweiler dogs and bitches representing consistently outstanding producing bloodlines. Some of these dogs are, and have been, so dominant that they have seemed to work out and nick well with almost every strain or bloodline. Others, for best results, need to be carefully linebred. The study of pedigrees and breeding is both a challenge and an exciting occupation.

Even if you are not planning to become a breeder, but are simply interested in owning and exhibiting quality Rottweilers, it is fun to trace back the pedigree of your dog, or dogs, thus learning more about the "family tree." To make it even more interesting, you will find pictures in both this book and my earlier one on the breed, *The Book Of The Rottweiler*, also a T.F.H. publication, which will enable you to pretty much locate the pictures of those dogs and bitches from whom your own Rotties descend, which can be a fascinating project.

Gestation, Whelping, and the Litter

When your bitch has been bred and is back at home, remain ever watchful that no other male gets to her until at least the twenty-second day of her season has passed. Prior to that time, it will still be possible for an undesired breeding to take place, which, at this point, would be catastrophic. Remember, she actually can have two separate litters by two different dogs, so *be alert and take care*.

In all other ways, the bitch should be treated quite normally. It is not necessary for her to have any additives to her diet until she is at least four to five weeks pregnant. It is also unnecessary for her to have additional food. It is better to underfeed the bitch this early in her pregnancy than to overfeed her. A fat bitch is not an easy whelper, so by "feeding her up" during the first few weeks, you may be creating problems for her.

Controlled exercise is good, and necessary, for your pregnant bitch. She should not be permitted to just lie around. At about seven weeks, the exercise should be slowed down to several sedate walks daily, not too long and preferably on the leash.

In the fourth or fifth week of pregnancy, calcium may be added to the diet; and at seven weeks, the one meal a day may be increased to two meals with some nutritional additives in each. Canned milk may be added to her meals at this time.

A week before she is due to whelp, your bitch should be introduced to her whelping box, so that she will have accustomed herself to it and feel at home there by the time the puppies arrive. She should be encouraged to sleep there and be permitted to come and go as she pleases. The box should be roomy enough for her to lie down and stretch out in it; but it should not be too large or the pups will have too much room in which to roam, and they may get chilled if they move too far away from the warmth of their mother. Be sure that there is a "pig rail" for the box, which will prevent the puppies from being crushed against the side of the box. The box should be lined with newspapers, which can easily be changed as they become soiled.

The room where the whelping box is placed, either in the home or in the kennel, should be free from drafts and should be kept at about eighty degrees Fahrenheit. It may be necessary during the cold months to install an infrared lamp in order to maintain sufficient warmth, in which case guard against the lamp being placed too low or too close to the puppies.

Keep a big pile of newspapers near the box. You'll find that you never have enough of these when there is a litter, so start accumulating them ahead of time. A pile of clean towels, a pair of scissors, and a bottle of alcohol should also be close at hand. Have all of these things ready at least a week before the bitch is due to whelp, as you never know exactly when she may start.

The day or night before she is due, the bitch will become restless; she'll be in and out of her box and in and out of the door. She may refuse food, and at this point her temperature will start to drop. She will start to dig and tear up the newspapers in her box, shiver, and generally look uncomfortable. You alone should be with her at this time (or one other person who is an experienced breeder, to give you confidence if this is one of your first litters). The bitch does not need an audience or any extra people around. This is not a sideshow, and several people hovering over the bitch may upset her to the point where she may hurt the puppies. Stay nearby, but do not fuss too much over her. Keep a calm attitude; this will give her confidence. Eventually she will settle down in her box and begin to pant; shortly thereafter she will start to have contractions and soon a puppy will begin to emerge, sliding out with one of the contractions. The mother immediately should open the sac and bite the cord and clean up the puppy. She will also eat the placenta, which you should permit. Once the puppy is cleaned, it should be placed next to the bitch, unless she is showing signs of having another one immediately. The puppy should start looking for a nipple on which to nurse, and you should make certain that it is able to latch on and start doing so at once.

If a puppy is a breech birth (*i.e.*, born feet first), then you must watch carefully that it is delivered as quickly as possible and the sac removed very quickly, so that the puppy does not drown. Sometimes even a normally positioned birth will seem extremely slow in coming. Should either of these events occur, you might take a clean towel and, as the bitch contracts, pull the puppy out, doing so gently and with utmost care. If the bitch does not open the sac and cut the cord, you will have to do so. If the puppy shows little sign of life, make sure the mouth is free of liquid and then, using a Turkish towel or terry cloth, massage the puppy's chest, rubbing back and forth quite briskly. Continue this for about fifteen minutes. It may be necessary to try mouth-to-mouth breathing. Open the puppy's jaws and, using a finger, depress the tongue which may be stuck to the roof of the puppy's mouth. Then blow hard down the puppy's throat. Bubbles may pop out of its nose, but keep on blowing. Rub with the towel again across the chest, and try artificial respiration, pressing the sides of the chest together, slowly and rhythmically, in and out, in and out. Keep trying one method or the other for at least fifteen minutes (actual time—not how long it seems to you) before giving up. You may be rewarded with a live puppy who otherwise would not have made it.

If you are able to revive the puppy, it should not be put with the mother immediately, as it should be kept extra warm for a while. Put it in a cardboard box near a stove, on an electric heating pad, or, if it is the time of year when your heat is running, near a radiator until the rest of the litter has been born. Then it can be put in with the others.

The bitch may go for an hour or more between puppies, which is fine as long as she seems comfortable and is not straining or contracting. She should not be allowed to remain unassisted for more than an hour if she does continue to contract. This is when you should call your veterinarian, whom you should have alerted ahead of time of the possibility so that he will be somewhere within easy reach. He may want the bitch brought in so that he can examine her and perhaps give her a shot of Pituitrin. In some cases, the veterinarian may find that a Caesarean operation is necessary, because a puppy may be lodged in some manner that makes normal delivery impossible. This can occur due to the size of a puppy or may be due to the fact that the puppy is turned wrong. If any of the foregoing occurs, the puppies already born must be kept warm in their cardboard box, which should have been lined with shredded newspapers in advance and which should have a heating pad beneath it.

Assuming that there have been no problems, and the bitch has whelped normally, you should insist that she go outside to exercise, staying just long enough to make herself comfortable. She can be offered a bowl of milk and a biscuit, but then she should settle down with her family. Be sure to clean out the whelping box and change the newspapers so that she will have a fresh bed.

If the mother lacks milk at this point, the puppies will need to be fed by hand, kept very warm, and held against the mother's teats several times a day in order to stimulate and encourage the secretion of her milk, which will probably start shortly.

Unless some problem arises, there is little you need do about the puppies until they become three to four weeks old. Keep the box clean with fresh papers. When the puppies are a couple of days old, the papers should be removed and Turkish towels should be tacked down to the bottom of the box so that the puppies will have traction when they move. This is important.

If the bitch has difficulties with her milk supply, or if you should be so unfortunate as to lose the bitch, then you must be prepared to either hand-feed or tube-feed the puppies if they are to survive. We prefer the tube method as it is so much faster and easier. If the bitch is available, it is better that she continue to clean and care for the puppies in the normal manner, except for the food supplements you will provide. If she is unable to do this, then after every feeding, you must gently rub each puppy's abdomen with wet cotton to induce urination, and the rectum should be gently rubbed to open the bowels.

Newborn puppies must be fed every three or four hours around the clock. The puppies must be kept warm during that time. Have your veterinarian show you how to tube-feed. Once learned it is really quite simple, fast, and efficient.

After a normal whelping, the bitch will require additional food to enable her to produce sufficient milk. She should be fed twice daily now, and some canned milk should be available to her several times during the day.

When the puppies are two weeks old, you should clip their nails, as they are needle-sharp at this point and can hurt or damage the mother's teats and stomach as the pups hold on to nurse.

Between three and four weeks of age, the puppies should begin to be weaned. Scraped beef (prepared by scraping it off slices of raw beef with a spoon, so that none of the muscle or gristle is included) may be offered in very small quantities a couple of times daily for the first few days. If the puppy is reluctant to try it, put a little on your finger and rub it on the puppy's lips; this should get things going. By the third day, you can mix in ground puppy chow with warm water as directed on the package, offering it four times daily. By now the mother should be kept out of the box and away from the puppies for several hours at a time. After the puppies reach five weeks of age, she should be left in with them only overnight. By the time they are six weeks old, the puppies should be entirely weaned and the mother should only check on them with occasional visits.

Most veterinarians recommend a temporary DHL (distemper, hepatitis, leptospirosis) shot when the puppies are six weeks old. This remains effective for about two weeks. Then, at eight weeks, the series of permanent shots begins for the DHL protection. It is a good idea to discuss with your vet the advisability of having your puppies inoculated against the dreaded parvovirus at the same time. Each time the pups go to the vet for shots, you should bring stool samples so that they can be examined for worms. Worms go through various stages of development and may be present in a stool sample even though the sample does not test positive. So do not neglect to keep careful watch on this.

The puppies should be fed four times daily until they are three months old. Then you can cut back to three feedings daily. By the time the puppies are six months old, two meals daily are sufficient. Some people feed their dogs twice daily throughout their lifetime, while others cut back to one meal daily when the puppy reaches one year of age.

The ideal time for puppies to go to their new homes is when they are between eight and twelve weeks old, although some puppies successfully adjust to a new home when they are six weeks of age. Be certain that they go to their future owners accompanied by a description of the diet you've been feeding them and a schedule of the shots they have received and those they still need. These should be included with a registration application and a copy of the pedigree.

Hip Dysplasia

Unquestionably the greatest physical problem to have plagued the Rottweiler over the years has been that of hip dysplasia. Some years back, it was difficult to find a Rottweiler strain or bloodline in which this heartbreaking condition did not exist. Rottweiler breeders determined that something MUST be done about it if their beloved breed was to prosper; and this they have attended to with care and intelligence.

There is a most impressive organization known as the Orthopedic Foundation for Animals, Incorporated, which is affiliated with the School of Veterinary Medicine at the University of Missouri in Columbia, Missouri, 65261, the O.F.A. to which one sees such frequent reference in literature pertaining to the breed. This is a non-profit organization formed for the purposes of collating and disseminating information concerning orthopedic diseases of animals which conducts the Dysplasia Control Registry. Dr. James S. Larsen is Project Director.

The organization advises, encourages, and establishes control programs to lower the incidence of orthopedic diseases; encourages and finances research in orthopedic diseases in animals, and receives funds and makes grants to carry out these objectives.

Orthopedics is the branch of surgery devoted to the prevention and correction of skeletal deformities. As a beginning, the O.F.A. decided to approach canine hip dysplasia, which it was thought could be best handled by forming a Hip Dysplasia Control Registry.

Since dysplasia is an all-encompassing word, and can cover any area where abnormal skeletal structure may exist, X-ray is the only certain way of discovering if, in certain areas of the body, the structure is normal or abnormal. *Hip* dysplasia is a malformation of the hip joint. In order to function smoothly and well, there must of necessity be a good "fit" between the socket (acetabulum) and the ball (femoral head). In some dogs the X-rays have revealed dysplasia so severe that there is no contact whatsoever between ball and joint.

Dysplasia occurs in both sexes, and particularly in the large, fast developing breeds although it has been found upon occasion as well in a very few of the smaller breeds, and somewhere in between the large and the small in the middle-sized breeds.

Dysplastic dogs should, indeed **must** *not be bred.* Never guess because of gait or movement, but make absolutely certain the condition of your Rottweiler's hips by X-ray before he or she is allowed to produce another generation. Circumstances can cause non-appearance of visible symptoms. As an example dogs not required to exert themselves excessively, or who live in dry, warm quarters, may be capable of handling themselves quite well even with some dysplastic hip condition. Thus the only way to be CERTAIN what condition exists is by X-ray, which has now become a popular practice among conscientious breeders of Rottweilers. While it is possible to tell at a few months' age, by use of X-ray, when a particularly poor set of hips exists, many months may pass before the fate of a near-normal set of hips becomes predictable. Therefore the most certain and approved method is to not X-ray before a year of age for a reading upon which you plan to base judgment, and of course the more mature a dog has become, the more reliable a story the X-ray can reveal. O.F.A. will read an X-ray and give a preliminary evaluation under two years of age; but will not issue a number until the dog's second birthday has been passed.

An O.F.A. certification of normal hips means that the X-ray film of that dog, acceptable for certification only after two years' age, has been examined by three Veterinary Radiologists and found to be radiographically free of dysplasia. These examining Radiologists are certified in veterinary radiology by the American Board of Veterinarian Radiology.

If you are planning to breed your Rottweiler, or even if you just own a Rottweiler for the pleasure of its company, you owe it to the breed, in the first instance, and to your individual dog in the second to *have your Rottweiler examined and certified.* If you plan to breed the reasons are obvious. But even if that is the last thing you intend to do, it pays to know the condition of your family dog's hips as well, as much can be done in his living conditions and way of life to make more comfortable and extend his years with you. In other words, the breeder of even one litter MUST know the condition; a pet owner's dog will probably live in greater comfort if the owner is aware should dysplasia exist.

To have a Rottweiler certified, write to O.F.A. for a packet, which is furnished free of charge. In it you will find a 14″ × 17″ film (for a breed this size). If the film is of good quality, properly positioned, and identified, and shows the entire pelvis down to and including the stifle joints, the film will be correct for your size dog.

Also included is a heavy backing sheet for use in returning the film for reading, in the same re-usable envelope in which your packet arrived. A drawing showing how to properly position the film for an acceptable, readable X-ray is included, as is also application card for proper identification of your dog, some of which information will become a permanent part of the X-ray film itself.

Using the envelope and backing sheet in which you received the kit, return the film to O.F.A. with your check for $15.00. All X-rays are retained for their file; therefore if your veterinarian wishes to have one for his file, have him make a duplicate, which can be done by putting two sheets of X-ray film in the cassette.

When your X-ray arrives at the offices in Missouri, it is assigned an application number and if of good diagnostic quality and properly identified and positioned, before being routed to the *three* certified veterinarians for diagnosis.

When the diagnosis is returned to O.F.A., a consensus of opinion report is prepared showing either normal or dysplastic, which is then forwarded to the owner and his veterinarian ONLY. If the consensus is "normal" a certificate and O.F.A. number accompanies the report to the owner.

There are few Rottweilers these days who have not been O.F.A. certified, as reputable breeders and concerned owners have lost no time in taking advantage of the helpfulness to the protection of their breed provided by this means. As I have been working on this book, I have been noticing with interest that the "trailblazer" in this regard was obviously Mrs. Bernard Freeman, as the numbers Ro-1 and Ro-2 were assigned to Rottweilers owned by her, denoting them to be the first of their breed so certified.

By-Laws of the O.F.A. provide for an Advisory Board for Breeders and Owners, which exists for the purpose of maintaining communication and liaison between O.F.A. and the people responsible for the conduct of projects established as supported by O.F.A., thus making the services of O.F.A. and its activities beneficial and available to the widest possible number of interested parties for the greatest effectiveness.

This Advisory Board, with a Chairman to co-ordinate the various participant breeds, keeps in constant contact with the O.F.A. Board to the benefit of the breeder and others working actively in our Dog Fancy.

The O.F.A. is delighted, at any and all times, to welcome breed clubs interested in the study of orthopedic disease in their particular breed, and such groups are cordially invited to advise O.F.A. of this interest and to name a representative. Remember that working TOGETHER with others in the Fancy is the shortest, most direct, route to complete success!

Certificate of Pedigree

VON ANDAN ROTTWEILERS and

VON PAULUS ROTTWEILERS

Mrs. Benjamin C. Tilghman
The Hermitage
RFD 3, Box 191A
Centreville, Maryland 21617
301 - 758-1324

REGISTERED NAME
Andan Freiwillig v Paulus

REGISTERED NUMBER
WF 049355

BREED

DATE OF BIRTH   **SEX**

COLOR   **EYE COLOR**

BREEDERS
Mrs. Benjamin C. Tilghman and
Mrs. Pauline L. Rakowski

This pedigree is certified to be correct to
the best of my knowledge and belief
Signed This _____ Day Of _____, 19___

Mrs. Pauline L. Rakowski
3 Karyn Terrace East
Middletown, N.J. 07748
201-671-9486

SIRE

Amer./Can. C H. Rodsden's
Elko Kantanien-
baum, CDX, TD, Can.
CD, WD694350, RO #1448

Intern'l CH. Elko vom
Sire Kastanienbaum
46 340 SchH 1
HD Free, Utrecht

CH. Gundi vom Reichen-
bachle
48 086
HD Free, Utrecht
RO # 846T

Elko vom Kaiserberg
SchH 1

Gitta vom Bucheneck
SchH 1
HD Free, Utrecht

Berno vom Albtal
SchH 3

Antje von der Wegs-
cheide

Hasso vom Oelberg
SchH 3

Anni vom Kaiserberg

Furst v.d. Villa Da-
heim SchH 1

Indra vom Schloss
Westerwinkel SchH1

Hasso vom Oelberg
SchH 3

Heidi vom Durrbach

Quick v.d. Solitude
SchH 3, Leistungssieg-
er 1966

Anka von der Kurmark

Hasso von Schifferstadt
SchH 1
Dora v d Brotzingergasse

Blitz v Schloss Wester-
winkel SchH 3
Bella v d Paradiesstrasse
SchH 3
Axel vom Simonskaul
SchH 3

Blanka vom Itzelbach SchH 1

Fetz vom Oelberg SchH 2

Dora v Schloss Westerwin-
kel SchH 1
Hasso Von Schifferstadt
SchH 1
Dora v l d Brotzingergasse

Int'l. CH. Lord v Blanken-
horn, SchH 2
Bona v Lopodunum

Droll H v d Brotzingergasse
Soll H v d Solitude
Fanny v d Solitude

Int'l.CH.BS. CH. Harras
vom Sofienbusch SchH 1
Biene v d Felsenquelle

DAM

CH. Andan Vesta v Paulus
Reg No. WD459872
RO # 1297

CH. Rodsden's Ikon
Sire von der Harque, CD
RO # 355

CH. Amsel von Andan,
Dam CD
RO # 300

CH. Rodsden's Kluge
v.d. Harque, CD
RO #50

CH. Rodsden's Ericka
Dierdre Dahl
RO # 157

Amer./Can. CH. Rods-
den's Kato von
Dorma, CDX, TD
RO # 37

Ehrenwache's Andernach
RO #111

Int'l. CH. BS. CH Harras
vom Sofienbusch SchH 1
CH. Quelle v d Solitude

CH. Arco vom Dahl CDX
SchH 3 RO# 73

Rafter M's Randee
RO # 109

Ch. Rodsden's Kluge
v d Harque CD RO #50

CH. Franzi vom Kursaal
RO #37

Fetz vom Oelberg SchH 2
RO #25

Rodsden's Ubermutig
Karla CD

Arno v d Hammerpaote SchH 3
Afra aus den Mayen SchH 1

Droll v d Brotzingergasse
SchH 3
Fanny v d Solitude
Petz vom Oelberg SchH 2

Assy v Borsigplatz

Follow Me's Utz
CH. Rodsden's Nuscha v d

Int'l. CH. BS. Ch. Harras
CH. Quelle v d Solitude

Votan vom Filstalstrand
SchH 2
Assy vom Zipfelbach SchH 1

Hektor v d Solitude
Dora v d Brotgerstrass

CH. Rodsden, CD Kluge v d
Harque, CD RO# 50
CH Afra vom Hasebacker
CD, SchH 1

BERGLUFT ROTTWEILERS, reg.

P. O. BOX 148, SEWICKLEY, PA. 15143

PEDIGREE

NAME _____ *BERGLUFTS GUSTEL* _____

A.K.C. REG. NO. _____ SEX _____ DATE WHELPED *October 8, 1978*

BREEDER _____ *Dorit S. Rogers, P. O. Box 148, Sewickley, Pennsylvania 15143*

SIRE Berglufts Donner AKC WC-626864 OFA	Ch. Kuhlwalds Trakehner AKC WC-845375 OFA RO-315	Ch. Axel vom Schwanenschlag ADRK 44778 AKC WB-753207 OFA RO-166	Furst von der Villa Daheim SchH 1 ADRK 42204
			Cora vom Grevingsberg ADRK 42691
		Ch. Kuhlwalds Little Iodine, C.D. AKC WB-144332 OFA RO-58	Bodo v Stuffelkopf ADRK 40499 OFA RO-28
			Andra von der Vohsbeckshohe ADRK 40769 AKC WA-769700
	Ch. Danka vom Molzberg AKC WB-152977	Cuno vom Kronchen AKC WA-960251	Fetz vom Oelberg SchH 2 OFA-25 ADRK 38416
			Anka vom Siegerland SchH 2 ADRK 37838
		DoJean's Adventurous Miss AKC WA-466562	Victor
			Ch. Gessner's Brenna
DAM Ch. Berglufts Carla AKC WC-379510 OFA RO-538	Ch. Axel vom Schwanenschlag ADRK 44778 AKC 753207 OFA RO-166	Furst v d Villa Daheim SchH 1 ADRK 42204	Axel vom Simonskaul SchH 3 ADRK 39272
			Blanka vom Itzelbach SchH 1 ADRK 39080
		Cora vom Grevingsberg ADRK 42691	Quinn v d Schwarzwiese SchH 1 ADRK 39211
			Britta v d Zuflucht ADRK 40127
	Ch. Drossel vom Molzberg AKC WC-113298 OFA RO-132	Cuno vom Kronchen AKC WA-960251	Fetz vom Oelberg SchH 2 OFA RO-25 ADRK 38416
			Anka vom Siegerland SchH 2 ADRK 37838
		DoJean's Adventurous Miss AKC WA-466562	Victor
			Ch. Gessner's Brenna

DAM

CHAMPION FERDINAND V. DACHSWEIL

CHAMPION LYN MAR ACRES ARRAS V. KINTA

Rodsden's Grosskind

CHAMPION SRIGO'S ZARRAS V. KURTZ, O.F.A.

B.S. CHAMPION ERNO V. WELLESWEILER

CHAMPION SRIGO'S MADCHEN V. KURTZ

CHAMPION SRIGO'S ECONNIE V. LORAC CD

SRIGO'S OF THEE I SING
SRIGO'S ON WITH THE SHOW
SRIGO'S ONLY BY MAGIC

B.S,C.S. FERRO V.D. LOWENAU Sch H 3

AM. BER. CAN. MEX. CH. JACK V. EMSTAL

B.S. DOLLI V. SCHLOSS ICKERN

CHAMPION SRIGO'S ELYSSIAN FIELDS

Troll v. Hook

CHAMPION SRIGO'S XCLUSIVE V. KURTZ

CHAMPION SRIGO'S MADCHEN V. KURTZ

SIRE

CHAMPION FERDINAND V. DACHSWEIL

CHAMPION LYN MAR ACRES ARRAS V. KINTA O.F.A.

Rodsden's Grosskind

CHAMPION KOKAS K'S DEGEN V. BURGA, C.D., O.F.A.

BS,CS FERRO V.D. LOWENAU Sch H 3

Burga v. Isarstrand

Lore v.d. Hobertsburg

AMERICAN, BERMUDIAN, CANADIAN
CHAMPION SRIGO'S THE JIG IS UP, O.F.A.

Grimm v.d. Hobertsburg

A. K. C. S. B. No. _____

Troll v. Hook

Sara v. Hook

CHAMPION SRIGO'S XQUSITE V. KURTZ

BS,CHAMPION ERNO V. WELLESWEILER

CHAMPION SRIGO'S MADCHEN V. KURTZ

CHAMPION SRIGO'S ECONNIE V. LORAC,CD

                                                    CHAMPION FERDINAND V. DACHSWEIL

DAM   CHAMPION LYN MAR ACRES ARRAS V. KINTA

                                                    Rodsden's Grosskind
                 CHAMPION KOKAS K'S DEGEN V. BURGA, C.D.,O.F.A.

                                                    BS,CS FERRO V. D. LAWENAU Sch H 3
                                  Burga v. Isarstrand

                                                    Lore v.d. Hobertsburg

AM. CAN. CHAMPION SRIGO'S FLIGHT OF THE EAGLE, O.F.A.

   A. K. C. S. B. No._____   Grimm v.d. Hobertsburg Sch H 1
                                  Troll v. Hook

                                                    Sara v. Hook

                 CHAMPION SRIGO'S XQUSITE V. KURTZ

                                          B.S.& CHAMPION ERNO V. WELLESWEILER
                                  CHAMPION SRIGO'S MADCHEN V. KURTZ

                                                    CHAMPION SRIGO'S ECONNIE V. LORAC C.D

                                                    CHAMPION JARO V. SCHLEIDENPLATZ

SIRE   CHAMPION FERDINAND V. DACHSWEIL

                                                    Follow Me's Michele

                 CHAMPION LYN MAR ACRES ARRAS V. KINTA

                                                    CHAMPION RODSDEN'S KLUGE V.D. HARQUE
                                  Rodsden's Grosskind

                                                    Bessy v. Stuffelkopf

CHAMPION SRIGO'S ZARRAS V. KURTZ, O.F.A.

AMERICAN ROTTWEILER CLUB AWARD
    BRONZE PRODUCTION OF   B.S. HARRAS V. SOFIENBUSCH Sch H 1
CHAMPIONS & OBEDEINCE TITLES   B.S. CH. ERNO V. WELLESWEILER Sch H

                                                    Alke v. Gommeringen Sch H 2

                 CHAMPION SRIGO'S MADCHEN V. KURTZ

                                                    CHAMPION ARNO V. KAFLUZU
                                  CHAMPION SRIGO'S ECONNIE V. LORAC C.D.

                                                    Srigo's Constance v. Missle.

CERTIFIED PEDIGREE

Name of Dog __CARADOS COMMANDER CODY__ Sex __MALE__ Reg. No. __WF302917__

Breed __ROTTWEILER__ Color __BLACK & RUST__

Date Whelped __JULY 18, 1982__ Breeder __JUDITH M BURNS & CAROL KRAVETS__

```
                                                                    │7  CASAR VOM ZIMMERPLATZ
                                              │3  CH ERO VON DER MAUTH CD          ADRK45322
                                                  WD444951  2-77  (GERMANY)
                                                                    │8  BIENE VON DER MAUTH
Sire-1   CH BULLI VON MEYERHOFF                                         ADRK 45923
         WE360050  4-81
                                                                    │9  CH IGOR VON SCHAUER
                                              │4  NORTHWIND'S INKA        WB678882  11-73
                                                  WD949800      (CANADA)
                                                                    │10 CH NORTHWIND'S DANKA CD
                                                                        WC164450  9-77

                                                                    │11 CH RODSDEN'S NOMAD VD HARQUE
                                              │5  CH RADIO RANCH'S AXEL VON NOTARA  WB619089  12-73
                                                  WC584351  12-78
                                                                    │12 CH KUHLWALDS TARA OF RONLYN
Dam-2    INGA VON TANNENWALD                                            WC014432  12-73
         WD760083  11-80
                                                                    │13 CH LYN-MAR ACRES ATLAS V KINTA
                                              │6  CH RUE DE RENNES         WB070778  3-73
                                                  WC617754  7-76
                                                                    │14 HYLAMAR'S HEIDI
                                                                        WB743427  3-73
```

The Seal of The American Kennel Club affixed hereto certifies that
this pedigree has been compiled from official Stud Book records.

Date Issued __02/10/83__

		Kuno v. Butzensee Sch H 3
SIRE	AM. CH. DUX V. HUNGERBUHL Sch H 1 Gekort	
1978 BUNDESSIEGER GEKORT bis EZA	Britta v. Schlossberg	
BENNO V. ALLGAUER TOR Sch H 3, F.H.		
		Dirk v. Ottenberg Sch H 1
	Evi v. Oberen Argental	
INTERNATIONAL CHAMPION	Dina v. Oberen Argental	
1982 C.S. 3 TIMES BEST IN SHOW ALL BREEDS		
BRONCO V. RAUBERFELD Sch H 3, F.H. ,O.F.A.		
		INT. CH. ALEX V. DOBELTAL Sch H 2
A. K. C. S. B. No. _____	Donar vom Markgraflerland Sch H 3, F.H. Gekort b.EZA	
	Hetta v. Kursaal	
CENTA V. DURSCHTAL Sch H 3 GEKORT bis EZA		
		Cuno v.d. Bonninghardt Sch H 3
	Hexe vom Hiesfeld	
	Carin v. Hiesfeld Sch H 1	

Certificate of Pedigree

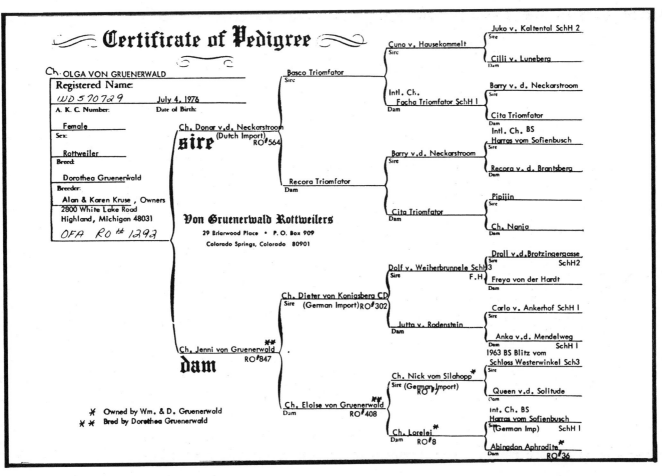

Registered Name: Ch. OLGA VON GRUENERWALD
WD 570729   July 4, 1976
A.K.C. Number: / **Date of Birth:**
Sex: Female
Breed: Rottweiler
Breeder: Dorothea Gruenerwald
Alan & Karen Kruse, Owners
2800 White Lake Road
Highland, Michigan 48031
OFA RO # 1292

Von Gruenerwald Rottweilers
29 Briarwood Place • P.O. Box 909
Colorado Springs, Colorado 80901

sire — Ch. Donar v.d. Neckarstroom (Dutch Import) RO #564
dam — Ch. Jenni von Gruenerwald RO #847

✳ Owned by Wm. & D. Gruenerwald
✳✳ Bred by Dorothea Gruenerwald

- Bosco Triomfator (Sire)
  - Cuno v. Hausekommelt (Sire)
    - Juko v. Kaltental SchH 2 (Sire)
    - Cilli v. Luneberg (Dam)
  - Intl. Ch. Facha Triomfator SchH 1 (Dam)
    - Barry v.d. Neckarstroom (Sire)
    - Cita Triomfator (Dam)
- Recora Triomfator (Dam)
  - Barry v.d. Neckarstroom (Sire)
    - Intl. Ch. BS Harras vom Sofienbusch (Sire)
    - Recora v.d. Brantsberg (Dam)
  - Cita Triomfator (Dam)
    - Pipijin (Sire)
    - Ch. Nania (Dam)
- Ch. Dieter von Konigsberg CD (German Import) RO #302 (Sire)
  - Dolf v. Weiherbrunnele SchH 3 F.H. (Sire)
    - Droll v.d. Brotzingergasse SchH2 (Sire)
    - Freya von der Hardt (Dam)
  - Jutta v. Rodenstein (Dam)
    - Carlo v. Ankerhof SchH 1 (Sire)
    - Anka v.d. Mendelweg SchH 1 (Dam)
- Ch. Eloise von Gruenerwald RO #408 (Dam)
  - Ch. Nick vom Silahopp ✳ (German Import) RO #7 (Sire)
    - 1963 BS Blitz vom Schloss Westerwinkel Sch3 (Sire)
    - Queen v.d. Solitude (Dam)
  - Ch. Lorelei ✳ RO #8 (Dam)
    - Int. Ch. BS Harras vom Sofienbusch (German Imp) SchH 1 (Sire)
    - Abingdon Aphrodita ✳ RO #36 (Dam)

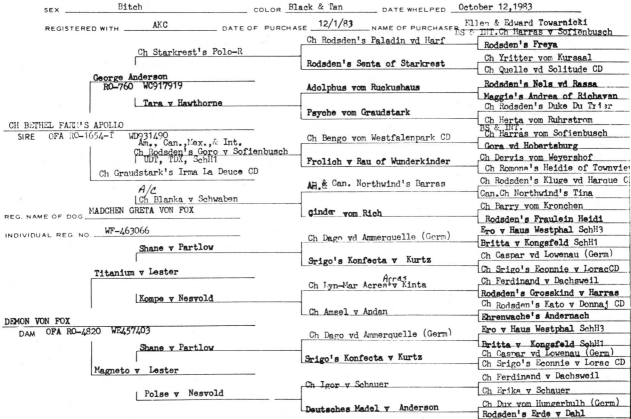

SEX Bitch   **COLOR** Black & Tan   **DATE WHELPED** October 12, 1983
REGISTERED WITH AKC   **DATE OF PURCHASE** 12/1/83   **NAME OF PURCHASER** Ellen & Edward Towarnicki

SIRE: CH BETHEL FAITH'S APOLLO   OFA RO-1654-T   WD931490

- Ch Starkrest's Polo-R
  - Ch Rodsden's Paladin vd Harf
    - BS & INT. Ch Harras v Sofienbusch
    - Rodsden's Freya
  - Rodsden's Senta of Starkrest
    - Ch Yritter vom Kursaal
    - Ch Quelle vd Solitude CD
- George Anderson RO-760 WC917919
  - Tara v Hawthorne
    - Adolphus vom Ruckushaus
      - Rodsden's Nels vd Rassa
      - Maggie's Andrea of Richaven
    - Psyche vom Graudstark
      - Ch Rodsden's Duke Du Trier
      - Ch Herta vom Ruhrstrom
- Am., Can., Mex., & Int. Ch Rodsden's Goro v Sofienbusch UDT, TDX, SchH1
  - Ch Bengo vom Westfalenpark CD
    - BS & INT. Ch Harras vom Sofienbusch
    - Gora vd Hobertsburg
  - Frolich v Rau of Wunderkinder
    - Ch Dervis vom Weyershof
    - Ch Romona's Heidie of Townview
- Ch Graudstark's Irma La Deuce CD
- A/C Ch Blanka v Schwaben
  - Am. & Can. Northwind's Barras
    - Ch Rodsden's Kluge vd Harque C.
    - Can. Ch Northwind's Tina
  - Cinder vom Rich
    - Ch Barry vom Kronchen
    - Rodsden's Fraulein Heidi

DAM: DEMON VON FOX   OFA RO-4820   WE457403
REG. NAME OF DOG: MADCHEN GRETA VON FOX
INDIVIDUAL REG. NO. WF-463066

- Titanium v Lester
  - Shane v Partlow
    - Ch Dago vd Ammerquelle (Germ)
      - Ero v Haus Westphal SchH3
      - Britta v Kongsfeld SchH1
    - Srigo's Konfecta v Kurtz
      - Ch Caspar vd Lowenau (Germ)
      - Ch Srigo's Econnie v Lorac CD
  - Kompe v Nesvold
    - Ch Lyn-Mar Acres Arras v Kinta
      - Ch Ferdinand v Dachsweil
      - Rodsden's Grosskind v Harras
    - Ch Amsel v Andan
      - Ch Rodsden's Kato v Donnaj CD
      - Ehrenwache's Andernach
- Magneto v Lester
  - Shane v Partlow
    - Ch Dago vd Ammerquelle (Germ)
      - Ero v Haus Westphal SchH3
      - Britta v Kongsfeld SchH1
    - Srigo's Konfecta v Kurtz
      - Ch Caspar vd Lowenau (Germ)
      - Ch Srigo's Econnie v Lorac CD
  - Polse v Nesvold
    - Ch Igor v Schauer
      - Ch Ferdinand v Dachsweil
      - Ch Erika v Schauer
    - Deutsches Madel v Anderson
      - Ch Dux vom Hungerbulh (Germ)
      - Rodsden's Erde v Dahl

307

Wilhelmberg Rottweilers
P.O. Box 668   Jasper, TN. 37347

Centurion's Good Buddy
RO-1544

    CH Berglufts Cliff
    RO-548

        CH Axel vom Schwanenschlag
        RO-166

        CH Drossel vom Molzberg
        RO-132

    CH Centurione Alaric of Nordon
    RO-542

        CH Northwind's Donar of Rodsden
        RO-273   (Canada)
        MRC Honor Roll

        CH Rodsden's Ericka Deidre Dahl
        RO-157

DUTCHESS OF HIGHLAND PARK
    RO-2871
    Top Producer 83-84
    DWM Award of Merit 1984
    Dam of only Rottie litter
     to produce six champions,
    (all OFA certified)

    Hart's Beau von Bravo
    HD Normal*

        Bravo von Isarstrand
        RO-494   (Germany)

        Hart's Noel vom Atlas
        HD Normal*

    Tiffany Zest
    HD Normal**

    Eigenschaft's Connie
    HD Normal*

        CH Egon von Lucas, CDX
        RO-278

        CH Suelynn's Asta v Hauslippstadt
        HD Normal*

AMERICAN, DUTCH & LUXEMBOURG CHAMPION

QUANTO V. H. BRABANTPARK

Whelped: October 11, 1974   AKC# WE 464606   O.F.A. #RO-1935-T -- EXCELLENT

Critique from Aachen, Germany - 6th Klubsieger Show - September 5, 1976:

Large, strong, good condition, good bone. Lively, attentive, good natured. Beautiful strong head with well-carried medium sized ears. Medium brown eyes and strong muzzle. Well developed chest and shoulders. Front feet straight and well knuckled. Firm, straight back. Good rear angulation. Coat and color very good, markings on head and chest somewhat unclear. Floating movement. Scissors bite.

Critique from Holland - 's-Gravenhage Show - October 16, 1977:

Beautiful dog, well built with good angulation and level back. Nice head with well-carried ears and brown eyes. Correct coat. Deep colored markings, somewhat sooty. Quiet, good movement. Bite correct.

PARENTS	GRAND-PARENTS	GREAT-GRANDPARENTS	GREAT-GREAT-GRAND-PARENTS
Gerlach v.h. Brabantpark < H.D. Free Utrecht	Moritz v. Silahopp < H.D. Free Utrecht	Brutus v.d. Kurmark <	Bsg. Ch. Harras v. Sofienbusch/I Biene v. Felsenquelle
		Queen v.d. Solitude <	Droll v.d. Brotzingergasse/II Fanny v.d. Solitude
	Ch. Burga v.h. Brabantpark < H.D. Free Utrecht	Fetz v. Oelberg/II < #RO-25 H.D. Free	Hektor v.d. Solitude Dora v.d. Brotzingergasse
		Ch. Rona v.d. Brantsberg <	Duco v.d. Brantsberg Ch. Anka v. Sudpark
Ch. Onsbessy v.d. Brantsberg < H.D. Free Utrecht	Einar v.h. Brabantpark < H.D. Free Utrecht	Axel v. Leitgraben/III <	Mirko v.d. Solitude/II Bsgn. Cora v. Lindeck/I
		Ch. Burga v.h. Brabantpark < H.D. Free Utrecht	Fetz v. Oelberg/II #RO-25 Ch. Rona v.d. Brantsberg
	Capsones v.h. Brabantpark < H.D. Free Utrecht	Ajax v.d. Brantsberg <	Ch. Balder v. Habenichts Nicolette v.d. Brantsberg
		Ch. Rona v.d. Brantsberg <	Duco v.d. Brantsberg Ch. Anka v. Sudpark

308

I L O N A   V O M   H A U S   S C H O T T R O Y

Whelped: October 1, 1976   AKC# WE 299250   O.F.A. #RO-1650

Critique from Germany - Köln, Germany - March 4, 1978 - j. Friedrich Berger:

In the best development, deep & broad, somewhat long. Attentive, spirited & alert. Medium size, good bone, good head, brown eyes-desirable almond-shaped, ears medium heavy. The angulation front and rear correctly placed. Coat and markings very good. Back must still firm up (due to youth). Movement free and far-reaching. (17 months old)   SG 2

Critique from Antelope Valley K.C. - Lancaster, CA - December 9, 1979 - j. Mrs. Mary Macphail, England:

Medium sized compact bitch of excellent type. Good bone and feet. Excellent straight front. Very attractive head and expression. Dark eyes, good ears. Could have a little more reach of neck. Very good angulation. Excellent level top and underlines. Slightly sloping croup. Coat and markings in order. Would not settle down and move.

PARENTS	GRAND-PARENTS	GREAT GRAND-PARENTS	GREAT-GREAT GRAND-PARENTS
		Ch. Erno v. Wellesweiler/I Bsg 65 OFA RO-5	Int.Ch. Harras v.Sofienbusch/I Elke v. Gomaringen
	Int.Ch. Farro v.h. Brabantpark/II HD Free	Ch. Burga v.h. Brabantpark W 64/65 HD Free	Fetz v. Oelberg/II OFA RO-25 Ch. Rona v.d. Brantsberg
Chris v. Wildberger Schloss/II HD Free		Quick v.d. Solitude/III, FH Lsg 66 HD Free	Droll v.d. Brötsingergasse/II Fanny v.d. Solitude
	Centa v. Grünwald/I HD Free	Elke v. Dürrbach	Int.Ch. Lord v. Blankenhorn/II Bona v. Lopodunum
	Jalk v.d. Brantsberg/III, FH HD Lt. Oositive	Arko v.d. Bönninghardt	Erno v. Alt-Hornberg/I Andra v. Tölzer-Hof
Afra vom Haus Schottroy/I HD Lt. Positive Ksgn 73		Burga v.d. Cohorten	Ch. Grimm v.d. Brantsberg W 56 Nora
	Afra v. Wildberger Schloss/II HD Doubtful	Int.Ch. Alex v. Dobeltal/II HD Lt. Positive	Benno v.d. Micheleburg Quinta v.d. Echterdingen
		Centa v. Grünwald/I HD Free	Quick v.d. Solitude/III HD-Free Elke v. Dürrbach

---

SEX __Female__   COLOR __Black & Mahogany__ DATE WHELPED __Dec. 14, 1979__

REGISTERED WITH _____ DATE OF PURCHASE _____ NAME OF PURCHASER _____

	Troll Vom Hook (Germany)	Grimm v.d. Hobertsburg,SchH1	
		Sara vom Hook, SchH1	
Hannibal Von Gruenerwald		CH. NICK VOM SILAHOPP T.P.	
	CH. ELOISE VON GRUENERWALD T.P.	CH. LORELEI T.P.	

CH NERO VON SCHAUER, CD
  SIRE OFA#RO764

	CH. FERDINAND VON DASCHWEIL T.P.	CH JARO VOM SCHLEIDEN-PLATZ	
		Follow Me Michele T.P.	
CH. INGRID VON SCHAUER,CD T.P.		CH. RODSDEN'S KLUGE V D HARQUE, T.P. CD	
	CH. ERIKA VON SCHAUER T.P.	CH. CARA V D CHAUSSEE	

REG. NAME OF DOG TOP PRODUCER, CH. ALASTAR'S ABBYE VOM ALTAR   Carole A.Anderson

INDIVIDUAL REG. NO. __litter co:bred with E.D.Alphin__

AKC#WE485708
OFA#RO3181-T
(Good)

	BSGR.FERRO V.D. LOWENAU,SchH2	Arno V. Stuffelkopf,SchH2	
		Dunja V D Lowenau, SchHI	
INT. CH. JACK VOM EMSTAL, SchH1,CD T.P. (Germany)		Osko V. Silahopp, SchH2	
	BSGRN.DOLLI V. SCHLOSS ICKERN, SchH1	Alma V. Haidgau, SchH1	

Panamint Ever A Lady
  DAM OFA#RO1587-T (Excel)

	CH FALK VOM KURSAAL, SchH3 (Germany) T.P.	Wotan V. Filsalstrand, SchH1	
		BSGRN. ASSY V ZIPFELBACH,SchH1	
CH. PANAMINT SHASTA SAGE T.P.		AM&CAN CH. BULLINO V D NECKARSTROOM	
	CH. PANAMINT CHEYENNE AUTUMN T.P.	AM&CAN CH. PANAMINT RAGNAROK T.P.	

T.P.= Top Producer

I HEREBY CERTIFY THAT TO THE BEST OF MY KNOWLEDGE AND BELIEF THE ABOVE PEDIGREE IS TRUE AND THAT ALL ANCESTORS NAMED ABOVE ARE OF THE SAME BREED.

SIGNED THIS _____ DAY OF _____ 19____

SIGNATURE _Carole Anderson_   ADDRESS _45 Champion Village, Conroe, Tx_

Pedigree of

CH. DOROH'S FANTASTIC SERENADE, A/CCDX RO-1742-T
WD-761312

Date Whelped: May 29, 1977   Sex: Female

Breeder: Dorothy A. Wade, 8421 Poplar Hill Drive, Clinton, Md. 20735

Owner: Peter & Marilyn Piusz, Steerage Rock Road, Brimfield, Ma. 01010

PARENTS	GRANDPARENTS	GREAT-GRANDPARENTS	GREAT-GREAT-GRANDPARENTS
SIRE: Ch. Rodsden's Axel V H Brabant RO-582	Ch. Falco V H Brabantpark RO-286	Int'l Ch, BS, WS, Ch. Erno V Wellesweiler SchH1 RO-5	Int'l Ch, BS, Ch. Harras V Sofienbusch SchH 1
			Alke Von Gomaringen SchH 2
		Dutch Ch. Burga V H Brabantpark HD Free	Fetz Vom Oelberg SchH 2 RO-25
			Dutch Ch. Rona V D Brantsberg
	Ch. Rodsden's Lady Luck CD RO-60	Ch. Falk Vom Kursaal SchH 1	Wotan Vom Filstalstrand SchH 1
			BS, SS Assy V Zipfelbach SchH 2
		Ch. Afra Vom Hasenacker CD SchH 1	Erno Von Alt-Hornberg SchH 1
			Indra Vom Sofienbusch
DAM: Ch. Doroh's Enchantress V Eberle CD RO-867	Casper V Partlow RO-473	Ch. Dago V D Ammerquelle RO-68	Ero V Haus Westphal SchH 3 HD Free
			Britta V Konigsfeld
		Srigo's Konfecta V Kurtz RO-93	Ch. Caspar V D Lowenau
			Ch. Srigo's Econnie V Lorac CD
	Ch. Rodsden's Helsa V Eberle UD RO-380	Ch. Northwind's Donar of Rodsden RO-273	Ch. Rodsden's Kluge V D Harque CD RO 50
			Can Ch. Northwind's Tina
		Rodsden's Gypsy TD RO-54	Ch. Bengo V Westfalenpark CD
			Frolich V Rau of Wunderkinder

```
                              Intl.Ch. Bulli Von Hungerbuhl, SS & Klubsg.71 & 72
                                  Worldsg. 73, gekort EZA

                    Igor Von Kastanienbaum, Sch.3m FH


                              Gitta Von Bhuchaneck, Sch.1

         Ch. Eiko Vom Schwaiger Wappen, CDX, Sch.1 (RO3068)(Germ.)


                              Dack von der Meierei, Sch.3

                    Intl.Ch. Anka Von Lohauserholz, Sch.3, FH Klubsg. & Europesg. 74
                        Bundessg.75, VDH Sg., gehort EZA


                              Tilla vom Kursaal, Sch.2

Ch. Ursus Von Stolzenfels (RO6788)


                         A/C Ch. Northwind's Barras (RO75)

                    Ch. Centurion's Che von der Barr (RO757)


                         Ch. Rodsden's Ericka Diedre Dahl (RO157)

              Kola Von Stolzenfels-Huff (RO2941)


                         Ch. Kavon Mr. Murphy, A/C CD (RO444) Dog World Award Winner

                    Ch. Darra Michaela Von Stolzenfels (RO1221-T)


                    Gunda Von Ingenhof, AD (RO676)(Germ.)
```

Owned by Erika Beqaj, 86-30 104 St., Richmond Hill, NY 11418, Whelped on 9/18/82

Certificate of Pedigree

Registered Name: Rhomarks Axel v. Leichenfeld
Kennel Name: _____
Sex: M
Breed: Rottweiler
A.K.C.S.B. No.: WE 283-248
A.K.C. Litter No.: _____
E.K.C.S.R. No.: _____
C.K.C.S.R. No.: _____
F.D.S.B.: _____
Date of Birth: May 16, 1979
Birthplace: Santa Rosa, Calif.
Breeder: Walter & Ingrid Rhodes
Address: 20 Chelsea Drive
City: Santa Rosa, Calif. 95401

GENERAL DESCRIPTION
Color and Markings: Black & Tan
Weight: _____
Height at Shoulder: _____
Temperament: _____
House-broken?: _____
Field-broken?: _____
Head: _____
Muzzle: _____
Eyes: _____
Ears: _____
Body: _____
Forelegs: _____
Hindlegs: _____
Coat: _____
Tail: _____
Feather: _____
Peculiarities: _____

Sir: (1)

CH. Panamint Otso v. Kraewl U.D.
Sire (3) A.K.C. No. WC 589,767
RO-12b
Owner: H.J. Bev Handler

CH. Bimpse von Der Gaern
Dam (4) A.K.C. No. WB 423,583
Owner: M.E. Bird

Dam: (2)

CH. Elexi von Der Gaern
RO-1583
A.K.C. No. WD 458306
Owner: J. Birch
Address: _____
City: _____

Lord Hannibal De Bretiana
Sire (5) A.K.C. No. WC 562,708
Owner: Elaine M. Overton

Astella von Buehl RO-281
Dam (6) A.K.C. No. WC 739,155
Owner: Michelle Buell

Great Grand Parents:

Black vom Goldenbach
Sire (7) A.K.C. No. WC 520,652
RO-12b German Import

CH. Cilly vom Uhlbachtal
Dam (8) A.K.C. No. WB 575,802

Bodo vom Odenwald
Sire (9) A.K.C. No. WB 16788

Bärbel vom Uhlbachtal
Dam (10) A.K.C. No. WB 723,381
German Import

CH. Fridrich v. Alfabeim
Sire (11) A.K.C. No. WB 227,820
RO-213 Jonathan Bratt (owner)

Catula De Bretiana
Dam (12) A.K.C. No. WA-823,439
RO-219 Mrs. W.W. Bratt (owner)

CH. Dieter v. Königsberg C.D.
Sire (13) A.K.C. No. WB 735,507
RO-302 - German Imp. Barbara Hoard (owner)

Panamint Jodel v.d. Eichen
Dam (14) A.K.C. No. WC 992,077
James E. Buell (owner)

Great Great Grand Parents:

Ero v. Haus Westphal SchH 3 — Sire (15)
Cita vom Rubgarten — Dam (16) Germany
Karol v. Freinhagen SchH 1 — Sire (17) Germany
Carla v. Jakobsbrunnen SchH 1 — Dam (18) Germany
CH. Gocha von Gruenzwald — Sire (19) WA-700922
Panamint Pfeffer — Dam (20)
Arko v. Uhlbachtal SchH 1 — Sire (21) Germany
Quelle von Der Harkt — Dam (22)
Jago vom Kursaal — Sire (23)
Follow Me's Doreen — Dam (24)
CH. Caballero of Rodsden — Sire (25)
Cybele Die Schöne — Dam (26) RO-215
Dolf v. Weiherbrunnerle SchH 3 — Sire (27) Germany
Jutta von Bollenstein — Dam (28)
Troll vom Hook — Sire (29) RO-311
CH. Dotmar v. Kupferdach — Dam (30) RO-157

Great Great Great Grand Parents:

Sire (31) Billo v. Lichtenstein SchH 3
Dam (32) Dina v. Ursushof SchH 3 FH
Sire (33) L.S. Quick v. D. Solitude SchH 3 - FH
Dam (34) Fria v. Durrbach
Sire (35) B.S. Emir v. Freinhagen SchH 3 - FH
Dam (36) Asta v.d. Luneburgerheide
Sire (37) Emir v. Durrbach SchH 1
Dam (38) Solla u. Jakobsbrunnen SchH H2
Sire (39) CH. Wick vom Silahoppe RO-7
Dam (40) CH. Lorelei RO-8
Sire (41) Anton CH. Bullion v.d. Neckarstrom RO-736
Dam (42) Anka CH. Panamint Ragnarok
Sire (43) Emir vom Durrbach SchH
Dam (44) Oadra vom Hohen-Asperg
Sire (45) B.S. Blitz v. Schloss Westerwinkel SchH 3
Dam (46) Mitta vom Jagttal SchH 2
Sire (47) BS. Blitz v. Schloss Westerwinkel SchH 3
Dam (48) Herta vom Kursaal SchH 2
Sire (49) CH. Follow Me's Xerxei
Dam (50) Rita
Sire (51) CH. Arras von Stadthaus
Dam (52) CH. Diedre of Rodsden C.D.
Sire (53) De La Muette Hermes
Dam (54) Carmen von Jubilation of Gerdasse
Sire (55) Droll v.d. Bratingen SchH 2 Jesse
Dam (56) Freya Linden Hardt
Sire (57) Carlo vom Ankerhof SchH 2
Dam (58) Anka von de Mandtweg
Sire (59) Gizmo v. van de Holterburg SchH 1
Dam (60) Sara vom Hook SchH 1
Sire (61) Int'l CH. WS. CH. Erock Willesweiler SchH 2
Dam (62) Bonni vom Muhlbruggrund

I HEREBY CERTIFY that to the best of my knowledge and belief the above Pedigree is true and that all ancestors named above are of the same breed.

Signed this _____ day of 7-4, 19 79.

Signature: Ingrid Rhodes
Address: _____

Certificate of Pedigree

Registered Name: CH. SRIGO'S EAGLE ALL OVER
Kennel Name: BEAUHAVEN KENNEL

Sex: MALE
Breed: ROTTWEILER

A.K.C.S.B. No. WF-203535
A.K.C. Litter No.
E.K.C.S.B. No.
C.K.C.S.B.No.
F.D.S.B. No. RO-6300 (OFA)
Date of Birth: JUNE 8, 1982
Birthplace: U.S.A.
Breeder: SRIGO KENNELS
Address: 1045 ROUTE 18
City: EAST BRUNSWICK, NJ 08816

GENERAL DESCRIPTION:
Color and Markings: BLACK + MAHOGANY
Weight:
Height at Shoulder:
Temperament:
Housebroken?:
Field-broken?:
Head:
Muzzle:
Eyes:
Ears:
Body:
Forelegs:
Hindlegs:
Coat:
Tail:
Feather:
Penchant:

Sire: (1)

CH. EIKO VOM SCHWAIGER
WAPPEN SCH II CDX OFA
A.K.C. No. WE-98350 (6-82)
Owner:
Address:
City:

Dam: (2)

CH. SRIGO'S HEART OF GOLD
A.K.C. No. WD-892313 (6-80)
Owner:
Address:
City:

Grand Parents:

V. IGOR V. KASTANIANBAUM
Sire (3)
A.K.C. No. SCH III F.H. 47541
Owner: CLUB SEIGER

V. ANKA V. LOHAUSERHOLZ
Dam (1)
A.K.C. No. SCH III F.H. H.D. LIGHT +
Owner:

CH. KOKAI'S K'S DEGEN.
Sire (5)
A.K.C. No. VON BURGA CD TD
Owner:

CH. SRIGO'S XQUISITE.
Dam (6)
A.K.C. No. V. KURTZ
Owner:

Great Grand Parents:

INT. CH. BULLI V. HUNGERBUHL
Sire(7)
A.K.C. No. H.D. +/- 42465

GILTA V. BUCHENECK
Dam (8)
A.K.C.N.o. H.D. - 44776

DACK V.D. MEIERI
Sire (9)
A.K.C. No. SCH III

TILLA V. KURSAAL
Dam (10)
A.K.C. No. SCH I

CH. LYN-MAR ACRES ARRAS
Sire (11)
A.K.C. No. V. KINTA

BURGA V. ISARSTRAND
Dam (12)
A.K.C. No.

TROLL V. HOOK
Sire (13)
A.K.C. No.

CH. SRIGO'S MADCHEN.
Dam (14)
A.K.C. No. V. KURTZ

Great Great Grand Parents:

KUNO V. BUTZENSE
Sire (15) SCH III 40415

BRITTA V. SCHLOSSBERG
Dam (16) 39075

FURST V. VILLA
Sire (17) SCH III 42204

INA V. SCHLOSS WESTER
Dam (18) WINKEL SCH I

ALEX V. KLOSTER DISIBOD-
Sire (19) ENBURG SCH II

BARBEL V. GREVINGSBERG
Dam (20) SCH I 42342

ERO V. HAUS WESTPHAL.
Sire (21)

WILMA V. KURSAAL
Dam (22) 39011

CH. FERDINAND V.
Sire (23) BACHSWEIL

RODSDEN'S GROSSKIND
Dam (24) VON HARRAS

B.S. + C.S. FERRO V.D.
Sire (25) LOWENAU

LORE V.D. HOBERTSBURG
Dam (26)

GRIMM V.D. HOBERTSBURG
Sire (27)

SARA V. HOOK SCH I.
Dam (28)

CH.+BS. ERNO V. WELLES
Sire (29) WEILER

CH. SRIGO'S ECONNIE V.
Dam (30) LORAC CD

Great Great Grand Grand Parents:

WOTAN V. FILSTALSTRAND
Sire (31)

EDLE V. DURBACH
Dam (32)

ALEX V. LUDWIGSHOF
Sire (33)

EVI V. KANZACHTAL
Dam (34)

AXEL V.D. SIMONSKAUL
Sire (35)

BLANKA V. ITZELBACH
Dam (36)

FETZ V. OELBERG
Sire (37)

DORA V. SCHLOSS WESTERWINKEL
Dam (38)

ALEX V.D. LUDWIGSHOFEN B.S.
Sire (39)

CORA V.D. NAHE
Dam (40)

QUINN V.D. SCHWARTZWIESE
Sire (41)

BURGA V. ZUFLUCHT
Dam (42)

BILLO V. LICHTENSTEIN
Sire (43)

DINA V. URSUS. HOF
Dam (44)

OSKO V. ECHTERDINGEN
Sire (45)

GERDA V. KURSAAL
Dam (46)

CH. YARO V. SCHLEIDENPLATZ
Sire (47)

FOLLOW ME'S MICHELE
Dam (48)

CH. RODSDEN'S KLUGE (V.A. HARG)
Sire (49)

BESSY V. STUFFELKOPF
Dam (50)

ARNO V. STUFFELKOPF
Sire (51)

DUNJA V.D. LOWENAU
Dam (52)

CARO V. KUPFERDACH
Sire (53)

ADA V. DAHL
Dam (54)

AXEL V.D. KAPPENBERGERHEIDE
Sire (55)

BIENE V. FELSENQUELLE
Dam (56)

FETZ V. OELBERG.
Sire (57)

ASTA V. WEIERBRUNNFELE
Dam (58)

HARRAS V. SOFIENBUSCH
Sire (59)

ALKE V. GOMARINGEN
Dam (60)

CH. ARNO V. KAFLUZU
Sire (61)

CONSTANCE V. MISSLE
Dam (62)

I Hereby Certify that to the best of my knowledge and belief the above
Pedigree is true and that all ancestors named above are of the same breed.

Signed this .... day of .... 19 ....

Address

Madchen Greta von Fox at age 16 months. Owned by Ellen Monica Towarnicki, Philadelphia, Pennsylvania.

CHAPTER SEVENTEEN

Traveling with Your Rottweiler

Going to her new home, traveling safely and comfortably in a crate, is Altar's Lexa von Balingen. Bred by David W. Lauster, von Balingen Rottweilers, Naples, Florida.

When you travel with a dog, you must always remember that everyone does not necessarily share your love of dogs and that those who do not, strange creatures though they may seem, have their rights too. These rights, on which we should not encroach, include not being disturbed, annoyed, or made uncomfortable by the presence and behavior of other people's pets. Since this is an intelligent and easily trained breed, owners should have the dog well schooled in proper canine behavior by the time maturity is reached. Your dog should not jump enthusiastically on strangers, no matter how playful or friendly the dog's intentions. We may love having them do this to us, but it is unlikely that someone else will share our enthusiasm, especially in the case of muddy paws on delicate or light-colored clothes which may be soiled or damaged. A sharp "Down" from you should be promptly obeyed, as should be "Sit," "Stay," and "Come."

If you expect to take your dog on many trips, he should have, for your sake and for his, a crate of appropriate size for him to relax in comfortably. In cases of emergency or accident, a crated dog is far more likely to escape injury. Left in a parked car, a crated dog should have the car windows fully open in hot weather, thus being assured sufficient ventilation. For your own comfort, a dog in a crate does not hang from the car window, climb over you and your passengers, and shed hair on the upholstery. Dogs quickly become accustomed to their crates, especially when started with one, as they should be, from puppyhood. Both you and the dog will have a more enjoyable trip when you provide him with this safeguard.

If you do permit your dog to ride loose in the car, see to it that he does not hang from the windows. He could become overly excited by something he sees and jump out; he could lose his balance and fall out should you stop short or swerve unexpectedly; he could suffer an eye injury induced by the strong wind generated by the moving car. All of these unnecessary risks can so easily be avoided by crating!

Never, ever, under any circumstances, should a dog be permitted to ride uncrated in the back end of an open pick-up truck. Some people do transport their dogs in this manner;

Ch. Pioneer's Beguiled at ten months' age, a famous Best-in-Show-winning bitch bred and owned by Pioneer Rottweilers. Photo by Mark Schwartz.

that is cruel and shocking. How easily such a dog can be thrown out of the car by sudden jolts or an impact! It is certain that many dogs have jumped out at the sight of something exciting along the way, quite possibly into the path of an oncoming car. Some unthinking individuals tie the dog, probably not realizing that if he were to jump under those circumstances, his neck could be broken, he could be dragged alongside the vehicle or get under its wheels, or he could be hit by another vehicle. If you are for any reason taking your dog *anywhere* in an open back truck, *please* have sufficient regard for that dog to provide a crate to protect him. Also please remember that with or without a crate, a dog riding exposed to the sun in hot weather can really suffer and have his life endangered by the heat.

If you are staying in a hotel or motel with your dog, please exercise him somewhere other than in the parking lot, along the walkways, or in the flower beds of the property. People walking to and from their rooms or cars really are not thrilled at "stepping in something" left by your dog and should not be subjected to the annoyance. Should an accident occur, pick it up with tissues or a paper towel and deposit it in a proper receptacle; don't just let it remain there. Usually there are grassy areas on the sides or behind motels where dogs can be exercised with no bother to anyone. Use those places rather than the busy, more conspicuous, carefully tended areas. If you are becoming a dog show enthusiast, you will eventually need an exercise pen to take with you to the show. They are ideal to use when staying at motels, too, as they permit you to limit the dog's roaming space and to pick up after him easily. Should you have two or more dogs, such a convenience is truly a "must!"

Never leave your dog unattended in a room at a motel unless you are absolutely, positively, sure that he will stay quiet and not destroy anything. You do not want a long list of complaints from irate fellow-guests, caused by the annoying barking or whining of a lonesome dog in strange surroundings or an overzealous watch dog barking furiously each time a footstep passes the door. And you certainly do not want to return to torn curtains or bedspreads, soiled rugs, or other embarrassing (and sometimes expensive) evidence of the fact that your dog is not really house-reliable.

If your is a dog accustomed to travelling with you and you are positive that his behavior will be acceptable when left alone, that is fine. But if the slightest uncertainty exists, the wise course is to leave him in the car while you go to dinner or elsewhere and then bring him into the room when you are ready to retire for the night.

When you travel with a dog, it is sometimes simpler to take along his food and water from home rather than to buy food and to look for water while you travel. In this way he will have the rations to which he is accustomed and which you know agree with him, and there will be no problems due to different drinking water. Feeding on the road is quite easy now, at least for short trips, with all the splendid dry prepared foods and high quality canned meats available, not to mention the "just remove it from the packet" convenience foods. And many types of lightweight, refillable water containers can be bought at many types of stores.

If you are going to another country, you will need a health certificate from your veterinarian for each dog you are taking with you, certifying that each has had rabies shots within the required length of time preceding your visit.

Remember that during the summer, the sun's rays can make an inferno of a closed-up car in a matter of minutes, so always leave windows open enough that there is sufficient ventilation for the dog. Again, if your dog is in a crate, this can be done easily and with safety. Remember, too, that leaving the car in a shady spot does not mean that it will remain shaded. The position of the sun changes quickly, and the car you left nicely shaded half an hour earlier may be in the full glare of the sun upon your return. Be alert and be cautious.

When you travel with your dog, be sure to take a lead and use it, unless he is completely and thoroughly obedience trained. Even if the dog is trained, however, using a lead is a wise precaution against his getting lost in strange territory. All of us have seen in the "Lost and Found" columns the sad little messages about dogs who have gotten away or been lost during a trip, so why take chances?

Ch. Siegen vom Odenwald, C.D., handled by Carol Woodward for herself and co-owner Thom Woodward, von Sieger-haus Rottweilers, Corning, California.

CHAPTER EIGHTEEN

Responsibilities of Breeders and Owners

Ojuara's Force Be With You, by Ch. Radio Ranch's Circuit Breaker, TT, ex Arri von der Hembrachbruke, SchH III, FH, at nine weeks old. Owned by Anthony DiCicco and Betty Walker.

Whether you are a one-dog owner, the owner of a show kennel, one involved in obedience, or a breeder, there are definite responsibilities—to your dog or dogs, to your breed, and to the general public—involved which should never be overlooked or taken lightly.

It is inexcusable for anyone to breed dogs promiscuously, producing unneeded litters. The only time a responsible breeder plans a litter is when it is *needed* to carry on a bloodline or to provide dogs for which this breeder has very definite plans, including orders for at least half the number of puppies which will probably be born. Every healthy puppy deserves a good and loving home, assuring its future well-being. No puppy should be born to an uncertain future on someone's assumption that there will be no problem selling or otherwise finding a home for it, as very definitely this is not always easy. Overpopulation is the dog world's most heartbreaking tragedy. Those of us who love dogs should not add to it by carelessly producing more. If you have any reason to feel that the puppies may not be assured of homes, don't breed the bitch; wait for a more propitious time. Certainly no breeder likes the thought of running around frantically trying to find someone who will take puppies off his hands, even if they must be given away. The latter usually is not a good idea anyway, as many people cannot resist saying "yes" to something which costs nothing, regardless of whether or not they really want it. As the dog grows larger and demands more care, their enthusiasm wanes to the point that the dog soon is left to roam the streets where he is subject to all sorts of dangers, and the owner simply could not care less. If one pays for something, one seems to respect it more.

One litter at a time is all that any breeder should produce, making sure that all those puppies are well provided for prior to breeding for another litter. Breeders should do all in their power to ascertain that the home to which each of his puppies goes is a *good* home, one that offers proper care, a fenced in area, and a really enthusiastic owner. There is tremendous respect for those breeders who make it a point to check carefully the credentials of prospective purchasers; all breeders should do likewise on this important point. No breeder wants any puppy to wind up in an animal shelter, in an experimental laboratory, or as a victim of a speeding car. While complete control of such situations may not be possible, it is at least our responsibility to make every effort to turn our puppies over to people who have the same outlook as our own where love of dogs and responsibility toward them are concerned and who realize that the ownership of a dog involves care, not neglect.

It is the breeder's responsibility to sell every puppy with the understanding that should the new owner find it necessary to place the dog elsewhere, you, the breeder, must be contacted immediately and given the opportunity to take back the dog or to help in finding it a new home. Many a dog starting out in what has seemed a good home has, under unforeseen circumstances, been passed along to others, only to wind up in exactly the sort of situation we most want to avoid. Keep in touch with what is happening to your dogs after they are sold.

The final obligation every dog owner shares, be there just one dog or many, is that of leaving detailed and up-to-date instructions in our wills about what is to become of our animals in the event of our death. Far too many of us are apt to procrastinate and leave this matter unattended to, feeling that everything will work out all right or that "someone will see to them." The latter is not too likely to happen, at least not to the benefit of the dogs, unless the owner makes absolutely certain that all will be well for them in the future.

If you have not already done so, please get together with your lawyer and set up a clause in your will specifying what is to be done with each and every dog you own and to whom each will be entrusted (after first ascertaining that this person is willing and able to assume the responsibility); also include details about the location of all registration papers, pedigrees, and kennel records, along with ways of identifying each dog. Just think of the possibilities of what might happen otherwise!

It is not wise to count on family members, unless they share your involvement with the dogs. In many cases our relatives are not the least bit "dog-oriented," perhaps they think we're a trifle crazy for being such enthusiasts, and they might absolutely panic at the thought of suddenly having even *one* dog thrust upon them. They might mean well, and they might try; but it is unfair to them and to the dogs to leave the one stuck with the other!

If you travel a great deal with your dogs, another wise idea is to post prominently in your vehicle and carry in your wallet the name, address, and telephone number of someone to be called to take charge of them in case of an accident. Of course, this should be done by prearrangement with the person named. We have such a friend, and she has a signed check of ours to be used in case of an emergency or accident when we are travelling with our dogs; this check will be used to cover her expenses to come and take over the care of our dogs should anything happen to make it impossible for us to do so.

The registration certificates of all our dogs are enclosed in an envelope with our wills, and the person who will be in charge knows each of them, and one from the other, so there will be no identification problem. These are all points to be considered, for which provision should be made.

Our older dogs are too often disregarded. So many supposedly great dog lovers think nothing of getting an older dog, even though well, happy, and enjoying life, out of the way to make room for younger show prospects or additional puppies. People considered to be genuine dog lovers are the ones who permit their dogs to live out their lives in comfort as loved, respected members of the household or kennel. How quickly some of us seem to forget the pleasures these dogs have brought us with exciting wins and the devotion they have shown to us and our families!

So much for our responsibility to our dogs, but there is also a responsibility to our breed: to keep up its quality and to protect its image. Every breeder should breed only from and for high-grade stock and should guard against the market being flooded with excess puppies. We should display good sportsmanship and concern for the dogs at all times, and we should involve ourselves whenever possible in activities beneficial to the breed.

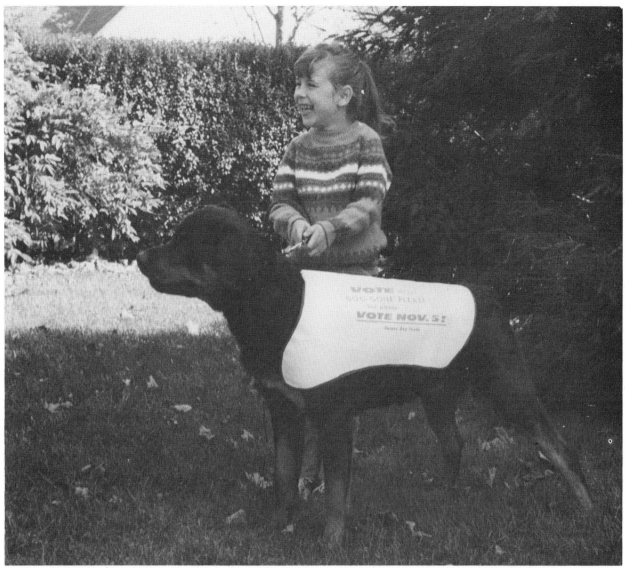

Ch. Freeger's Electra, C.D. Bred by Mrs. Bernard Freeman, co-owner with Mrs. Gisela Nightingale. Pictured campaigning for ERA with Alyssa Nightingale.

To the general public we owe the consideration of good dog ownership. Our dogs should not be permitted to run at large and annoy others. Dogs should not be left barking endlessly, tied outside or closed in the house.

We should pick up after our dogs, as required in most cities, when we exercise them where people must walk. We should, in other words, enjoy our dogs without allowing them to infringe on those who may be less enthusiastic.

Glossary

To the uninitiated, it must seem that fanciers of purebred dogs speak a special language all their own, which in a way we do. The following is a list of terms, abbreviations, and titles which you will run across through our pages which may be unfamiliar to you. We hope that this list will lead to fuller understanding and that it will additionally assist you as you meet and converse with others of similar interests in the world of purebred dogs.

A.K.C. The commonly used abbreviation of American Kennel Club.

Albino. A deficiency of pigmentation causing the nose leather, eye rims, and lips to be pink.

Almond eye. The shape of the tissue surrounding the eye, which creates the almond-shaped appearance required by some breed standards.

American Kennel Club. The official registry for purebred dogs in the United States. Publishes and maintains the Stud Book and handles all litter and individual registrations, transfers of ownership, and so on. Keeps all United States dog show, field trial, and obedience trial records; issues championships and other titles in these areas as they are earned; approves and licenses dog show, obedience trial, and field trial judges; licenses or issues approval to all championship shows, obedience trials, and recognized match shows. Creates and enforces the rules, regulations, and policies by which the breeding, raising, exhibiting, handling, and judging of purebred dogs in the United States are governed. Clubs, not individuals, are members of the American Kennel Club, each of which is represented by a delegate selected from the club's own membership for the purpose of attending the quarterly American Kennel Club meetings as the representative of the member club, to vote on matters discussed at each meeting and to bring back a report to the individual club of any decisions or developments which took place there.

Angulation. The angles formed by the meeting of the bones, generally referring to the shoulder and upper arm in the forequarters and the stifle and hock in the hindquarters.

Apple head. An exaggerated roundness of the top-skull.

Apron. Frill, or longer hair, below the neck.

Bad bite. Can refer to a wryness or malformation of the jaw, or to incorrect dentition.

Bad mouth. One in which the teeth do not meet correctly according to the specifications of the breed standard.

Balance. Symmetry and proportion. A well-balanced dog is one in which all of the parts appear in correct ratio to one another: height to length, head to body, skull to foreface, and neck to head and body.

Beefy. Overmusculation or overdevelopment of the shoulders or hindquarters or both.

Benched Show. Dog show at which the dogs are kept on benches while not being shown in competition.

Best in Show. The dog or bitch chosen as the most representative of any dog in any breed from among the group winners at an all-breed dog show. (The dog or bitch that has won Best of Breed next competes in the group of which its breed is a part. Then the first-prize winner of each group meets in an additional competition from which one is selected the Best in Show.)

Best of Breed. The dog that is adjudged best of any competing in its breed at a dog show.

Best of Opposite Sex. The dog or bitch that is selected as the best of the opposite sex to the Best of Breed when the latter award has been made.

Best of Winners. The dog or bitch selected as the better of the two between Winners Dog and Winners Bitch.

Bitch. A female dog.

Bite. The manner in which the upper and lower jaws meet.

Bloom. The sheen of a coat in healthy, lustrous condition.

Blue-ribbon winner. A dog that has won first prize in the class for which it is entered at a dog show.

Bone. Refers to the girth of a dog's leg bones. A dog called "good in bone" has legs that are correct in girth for its breed and for its own general conformation. Well-rounded bone is round in appearance, flat bone rather flattish. Light bone is very fine and small in diameter, almost spindle-like in appearance; legs are extremely slender. Heavy bone refers to legs that are thick and sturdy.

Brace. Two dogs, or a dog and a bitch, closely similar in size, markings, color, and general appearance, moving together in unison.

Breed. Purebred dogs descended from mutual ancestors refined and developed by man.

Breeder. A person who breeds dogs.

Breeding particulars. Name of the sire and dam, date of breeding, date of birth, number of puppies in the litter, their sex, and name of the breeder and of the owner of the sire.

Brisket. The forepart of the body between the forelegs and beneath the chest.

Brood bitch. A female dog used primarily for breeding.

CACIB. A Challenge Certificate offered by the Federation Cynologique Internationale towards a dog's championship.

Canine teeth. The four sharp pointed teeth at the front of the jaws, two upper and two lower, flanking the incisors; often referred to as fangs.

Canines. Dogs, jackals, wolves, and foxes as a group.

Carpals. Pastern joint bones.

Castrate. To neuter a dog by removal of the testicles.

Cat foot. The short-toed, round tight foot similar to that of a cat.

C.D. An abbreviation of the Companion Dog title.

C.D.X. An abbreviation of the Companion Dog Excellent title.

Ch. Commonly used abbreviation of champion.

Challenge Certificate. A card awarded at dog shows in Great Britain by which championship there is gained. Comparable to our Winners Dog and Winners Bitch awards. To become a British champion a dog must win three of these Challenge Certificates at designated championship dog shows.

Champion. A dog or bitch that has won a total of fifteen points, including two majors, the total number under not less than three judges, two of whom must have awarded the majors at A.K.C. point shows.

Character. Appearance, behavior, and temperament considered correct in an individual breed of dog.

Cheeky. Cheeks which bulge out or are rounded in appearance.

Chest. The part of the body enclosed by the ribs.

Chiseled. Clean-cut below the eyes.

Choke collar. A chain or leather collar that gives maximum control over the dog. Tightened or relaxed by the pressure on the lead caused by either pulling of the dog or tautness with which it is held by the handler.

Chops. Pendulous, loose skin creating jowls.

Cloddy. Thickset or overly heavy or low in build.

Close-coupled. Compact in appearance. Short in the loin.

Coarse. Lacking in refinement or elegance.

Coat. The hair which covers the dog.

Companion Dog. The first obedience degree obtainable.

Companion Dog Excellent. The second obedience degree obtainable.

Condition. General health. A dog said to be in good condition is one carrying exactly the right amount of weight, whose coat looks alive and glossy, and that exhibits a general appearance and demeanor of well-being.

Conformation. The framework of the dog, its form and structure.

Coupling. The section of the body known as the loin. A short-coupled dog is one in which the loin is short.

Cow-hocked. Hocks turned inward at the joint, causing the hock joints to approach one another with the result that the feet toe outward instead of straight ahead.

Crabbing. A dog moving with its body at an angle rather than coming straight at you; otherwise referred to as side-wheeling or si-de-winding.

Crest. The arched portion of the back of the neck.

Crop. Cut the ear leather, usually to cause the ear to stand erect.

Crossing action. A fault in the forequarters caused by loose or poorly knit shoulders.

Croup. The portion of the back directly above the hind legs.

Cryptorchid. An adult dog with testicles not normally descended. A dog with this condition cannot be shown and is subject to disqualification by the judge.

Cynology. A study of canines.

Dam. Female parent of a dog or bitch.

Dentition. Arrangement of the teeth.

Dewclaws. Extra claws on the inside of the legs. Should generally be removed several days following the puppy's birth. Required in some breeds, unimportant in others, and sometimes a disqualification—all according to the individual breed standard.

Dewlap. Excess loose and pendulous skin at the throat.

Diagonals. The right front and left rear leg make up the right diagonal; the left front and right rear leg the left diagonal. The diagonals correctly move in unison as the dog trots.

Dish-faced. The tip of the nose is placed higher than the stop.

Disqualification. A fault or condition which renders a dog ineligible to compete in organized shows, designated by the breed standard or by the American Kennel Club. Judges must withhold all awards at dog shows from dogs having disqualifying faults, noting in the Judges Book the reason for having done so. The owner may appeal this decision, but a disqualified dog cannot again be shown until it has officially been examined and reinstated by the American Kennel Club.

Distemper teeth. Discolored, badly stained, or pitted teeth. A condition so-called due to its early association with dogs having suffered from this disease.

Divergent hocks. Hock joints turn outward, creating the condition directly opposite to cow-hocks. Frequently referred to as bandy legs or barrel hocks.

Dock. Shorten the tail by cutting it.

Dog. A male of the species. Also used to describe male and female canines collectively.

Dog show. A competition in which dogs have been entered for the purpose of evaluation and to receive the opinion of a judge.

Dog show, all-breeds. A dog show in which classification may be provided, and usually is, for every breed of dog recognized by the American Kennel Club.

Dog show, specialty. A dog show featuring only one breed. Specialty shows are generally considered to be the showcases of a breed, and to win at one is a particularly valued honor and achievement, owing to the high type of competition usually encountered at these events.

Domed. A top-skull that is rounded rather than flat.

Double coat. A coat consisting of a hard, weather-resistant, protective outer covering over a soft, short, close underlayer which provides warmth.

Down-faced. A downward inclination of the muzzle toward the tip of the nose.

Down in pastern. A softness or weakness of the pastern causing a pronounced deviation from the vertical.

Drag. A trail having been prepared by drag- ging a bag, generally bearing the strong scent of an animal, along the ground.

Drive. The powerful action of the hindquarters which should equal the degree of reach of the forequarters.

Drop ear. Ears carried drooping or folded forward.

Dry head. One exhibiting no excess wrinkle.

Dry neck. A clean, firm neckline free of throatiness or excess skin.

Dual champion. A dog having gained both bench show and field trial championships.

Dudley nose. Flesh-colored nose.

Elbow. The joint of the forearm and upper arm.

Elbow, out at. Elbow pointing away from the body rather than being held close.

Even bite. Exact meeting of the front teeth, tip to tip with no overlap of the uppers or lowers. Generally considered to be less serviceable than the scissors bite, although equally permissible or preferred in some breeds. Also known as level bite.

Ewe neck. An unattractive, concave curvature of the top area of the neckline.

Expression. The typical expression of the breed as one studies the head. Determined largely by the shape of the eye and its placement.

Eyeteeth. The upper canine teeth.

Faking. The altering of the natural appearance of a dog. A highly frowned upon and unethical practice which must lead, upon recognition by the judge, to instant dismissal from the show ring with a notation in the Judges Book stating the reason.

Fancier. A person actively involved in the sport of purebred dogs.

Fancy. The enthusiasts of a sport or hobby. Dog breeders, exhibitors, judges, and others actively involved with purebred dogs as a group comprise the dog fancy.

Fangs. The canine teeth.

F.C.I. Abbreviation of the Federation Cynologique Internationale.

Feathering. The longer fringes of hair that appear on the ears, tail, chest, and legs.

Federation Cynologique Internationale. A canine authority representing numerous countries, principally European, all of which consent to and agree on certain practices and breed identifications.

Feet east and west. An expression used to describe toes on the forefeet turning outward rather than directly forward.

Fetch. Retrieving of game by a dog, or the command for the dog to do so.

Fiddle front. Caused by elbows protruding from the desired closeness to the body, with the result that the pasterns approach one another too closely and the feet toe outward. Thus, resembling the shape of a violin.

Field champion. A dog that has gained the title field champion has defeated a specified number of dogs in specified competition at a series of American Kennel Club licensed or member field trials.

Field trial. A competition for specified Hound or Sporting breeds where dogs are judged according to their ability and style on following a game trail or on finding and retrieving game.

Finishing a dog. Refers to completing a dog's championship, obedience title, or field trial title.

Flank. The side of the body through the loin area.

Flat bone. Bones of the leg which are not round.

Flat-sided. Ribs that are flat down the side rather than slightly rounded.

Fld. Ch. Abbreviation of field champion, used as a prefix before the dog's name.

Flews. A pendulous condition of the inner corners of the mouth.

Flush. To drive birds from cover. To spring at them. To force them to take flight.

Flyer. An especially exciting or promising young dog.

Flying ears. Ears correctly carried dropped or folded that stand up or tend to "fly" upon occasion.

Flying trot. The speed at which you should *never* move your dog in the show ring. All four feet actually briefly leave the ground during each half stride, making correct evaluation of the dog's normal gait virtually impossible.

Forearm. The front leg from elbow to pastern.

Foreface. The muzzle of the dog.

Front. The forepart of the body viewed head-on. Includes the head, forelegs, shoulders, chest, and feet.

Futurity Stakes. A competition at shows or field trials for dogs who are less than twelve months of age and for which puppies are nominated at or prior to birth. Highly competitive among breeders, usually with a fairly good purse for the winners.

Gait. The manner in which a dog walks or trots.

Gallop. The fastest gait. Never to be used in the show ring.

Game. The animals or wild birds which are hunted.

Gay tail. Tail carried high.

Get. Puppies.

Goose rump. Too sloping (steep) in croup.

Groom. To bathe, brush, comb, and trim your dog.

Groups. Refers to the variety groups in which all breeds of dogs are divided.

Gun dog. One that has been specifically trained to work with man in the field for retrieving game that has been shot and for locating live game.

Guns. The persons who do the shooting during field trials.

Gun-shy. Describes a dog that cringes or shows other signs of fear at the sound or sight of a gun.

Hackney action. High lifting of the forefeet in the manner of a hackney pony.

Ham. Muscular development of the upper hind leg. Also used to describe a dog that loves applause while being shown, really going all out when it occurs.

Handler. A person who shows dogs in competition, either as an amateur (without pay) or as a professional (receiving a fee in payment for the service).

Hard-mouthed. A dog that grasps the game too firmly in retrieving, causing bites and tooth marks.

Hare foot. An elongated paw, like the foot of a hare.

Haw. A third eyelid or excess membrane at the corner of the eye.

Heat. The period during which a bitch can be bred. Also referred to as being "in season."

Heel. A command ordering the dog to follow close to the handler.

Hindquarters. Rear assemblage of the dog.

Hie on. A command used in hunting or field trials, urging the dog to go further.

Hock. The joint between the second thigh and the metatarsus.

Hocks well let down. Expression denoting that the hock joint should be placed quite low to the ground.

Honorable scars. Those incurred as a result of working injuries.

In season. *See* **Heat.**

Incisors. The front teeth between the canines.

Int. Ch. An abbreviation of international champion.

International champion. A dog awarded four CACIB cards at F.C.I. dog shows.

Jowls. Flesh of lips and jaws.

Judge. Person making the decisions at a dog show, obedience trial, or field trial.

Judges residing in the United States must be approved and licensed by the A.K.C. in order to officiate at events where points toward championship titles are awarded; residents of another country whose governing body is recognized by the A.K.C. may be granted special permits to officiate in the United States.

Kennel. The building in which dogs are housed. Also used when referring to a person's collective dogs.

Knee joint. Stifle joint.

Knitting and purling. Crossing and throw- ing of forefeet as dog moves.

Knuckling over. A double-jointed wrist, or pastern, sometimes accompanied by enlarged bone development in the area, causing the joints to double over under the dog's weight.

Layback. 1) Describes correctly angulated shoulders. 2) Describes a short-faced dog whose pushed-in nose placement is accompanied by undershot jaw.

Leather. The ear flap. Also the skin of the actual nose.

Level bite. Another way of describing an even bite, as teeth of both jaws meet exactly.

Level gait. A dog moving smoothly, topline carried level as he does so, is said to be moving in this manner.

Lippy. Lips that are pendulous or do not fit tightly.

Loaded shoulders. Those overburdened with excessive muscular development.

Loin. Area of the sides between the lower ribs and hindquarters.

Lumber. Superfluous flesh.

Lumbering. A clumsy, awkward gait.

Major. A win of either Winners Dog or Winners Bitch carrying with it three, four, or five points toward championship.

Mane. The long hair growing on the top and upper sides of the neck.

Match show. An informal dog show where no championship points are awarded and entries can usually be made upon arrival, although some require pre-entry. Excellent practice area for future show dogs and for novice exhibitors as the entire atmosphere is relaxed and congenial.

Mate. To breed a dog and a bitch to one another. Littermates are dogs which are born in the same litter.

Maturity Stakes. For members of a particular breed who the previous year had been entered in the Futurity Stakes.

Milk teeth. The first baby teeth.

Miscellaneous Class. A class provided at A.K.C. point shows in which specified breeds may compete in the absence of their own breed classification. Dogs of breeds in the process of becoming recognized by A.K.C. may compete in this class prior to the eventual provision of their own individual breed classification.

Molars. Four premolars are located at either side of the upper and lower jaws. Two molars exist on either side of the upper jaw, three on either side below. Lower molars have two roots; upper molars have three roots.

Monorchid. A dog with only one properly descended testicle. This condition disqualifies a dog from competition at A.K.C. dog shows.

Muzzle. 1) The part of the head in front of the eyes. 2) To fasten something over the mouth, usually to prevent biting.

Nick. A successful breeding that results in puppies of excellent quality.

Non-slip retriever. A dog not expected to flush or to find game; one that merely walks at heel, marks the fall, then retrieves upon command.

Nose. Describes the dog's organ of smell, but also refers to his talent at scenting. A dog with a "good nose" is one adept at picking up and following a scent trail.

Obedience trial. A licensed obedience trial is one held under A.K.C. rules at which it is possible to gain a "leg" towards a dog's obedience title or titles.

Obedience trial champion. Denotes that a dog has attained obedience trial championship under A.K.C. regulations by having gained a specified number of points and first place awards.

Oblique shoulders. Shoulders angulated so as to be well laid back.

Occiput. Upper back point of skull.

Occipital protuberance. A prominent occiput noted in some of the Sporting breeds.

O.F.A. Commonly used abbreviation for Orthopedic Foundation for Animals.

Orthopedic Foundation for Animals. This organization is ready to read the hip radiographs of dogs and certify the existence of or freedom from hip dysplasia. Board-certified radiologists read vast numbers of these files each year.

O.T. Ch. An abbreviation of the obedience trial champion title.

Out at elbow. Elbows are held away from the body rather than in close.

Out at shoulder. Shoulder blades set in such a manner that joints are too wide and jut out from body.

Oval chest. Deep with only moderate width.

Overshot. Upper incisors overlap the lower incisors.

Pacing. A gait in which both right legs and both left legs move concurrently, causing a rolling action.

Paddling. Faulty gait in which the front legs swing forward in a stiff upward motion.

Pad. Thick protective covering of the bottom of the foot. Serves as a shock absorber.

Paper foot. Thin pads accompanying a flat foot.

Pastern. The area of the foreleg between the wrist and the foot.

Pedigree. Written record of dog's lineage.

Pigeon chest. A protruding, short breastbone.

Pigeon-toed. Toes point inward, as those of a pigeon.

Pile. Soft hair making a dense undercoat.

Plume. A long fringe of hair on the tail.

Poach. To trespass on private property when hunting.

Pointed. A dog that has won points toward its championship is referred to as "pointed."

Police dog. Any dog that has been trained to do police work.

Put down. To groom and otherwise prepare a dog for the show ring.

Quality. Excellence of type and conformation.

Racy. Lightly built, appearing overly long in leg and lacking substance.

Rangy. Excessive length of body combined with shallowness through the ribs and chest.

Reach. The distance to which the forelegs reach out in gaiting, which should correspond with the strength and drive of the hindquarters.

Register. To record your dog with the American Kennel Club.

Registration Certificate. The paper you receive denoting that your dog's registration has been recorded with the A.K.C., giving the breed, assigned names, names of sire and dam, date of birth, breeder and owner, along with the assigned Stud Book number of the dog.

Reserve Winners Bitch or **Reserve Winners Dog.** After the judging of Winners Bitch and Winners Dog, the remaining first prize dogs (bitches or dogs) remain in the ring where they are joined by the bitch or dog that placed second in the class to the one awarded Winners Bitch or Winners Dog, provided she or he was defeated only by that one bitch or dog. From these a Reserve Winner is selected. Should the Winners Bitch or Winners Dog subsequently be disallowed due to any error or technicality, the Reserve Winner is then moved up automatically to Winners in the A.K.C. records, and the points awarded to the Winners Bitch or Winners Dog then transfer to the one which placed Reserve. This is a safeguard award, for although it seldom happens, should the winner of the championship points be found to have been ineligible to receive them, the Reserve dog keeps the Winners points.

Roach back. A convex curvature of the top- line of the dog.

Rocking horse. An expression used to describe a dog that has been overly extended in forequarters and hindquarters by the handler, *i.e.*, forefeet placed too far forward, hind feet pulled overly far behind, making the dog resemble a child's rocking horse. To be avoided in presenting your dog for judging.

Rolling gait. An aimless, ambling type of action correct in some breeds but to be faulted in others.

Saddle back. Of excessive length with a dip behind the withers.

Scissors bite. The outer tips of the lower incisors touch the inner tips of the upper incisors. Generally considered to be the most serviceable type of jaw formation.

Second thigh. The area of the hindquarters between the hock and the stifle.

Septum. The vertical line between the nostrils.

Set up. To pose your dog in position for examination by the judge. Same as "stack."

Shelly. A body lacking in substance.

Shoulder height. The height of the dog from the ground to the highest point of the withers.

Sire. The male parent.

Skully. An expression used to describe a coarse or overly massive skull.

Slab sides. Flat sides with little spring of rib.

Soundness. Mental and physical stability. Sometimes used as well to denote the manner in which the dog gaits.

Spay. To neuter a bitch by surgery. Once this operation has been performed, the bitch is no longer eligible for entry in regular classes or in the Veterans Class at A.K.C. shows.

Special. A dog or bitch entered only for Best of Breed competition at a dog show.

Specialty club. An organization devoted to sponsoring an individual breed of dog.

Specialty dog show. *See* **Dog show, specialty.**

Stack. *See* **Set up.**

Stake. A class in field trial competition.

Stance. The natural position a dog assumes in standing.

Standard. The official description of the ideal specimen of a breed. The Standard of Perfection is drawn up by the parent specialty club (usually by a special committee to whom the task is assigned), is approved by the membership and by the American Kennel Club, and then serves as a guide to breeders and to judges in decisions regarding the merit, or lack of it, in evaluating individual dogs.

Stifle. The joint of the hind leg corresponding to a person's knee.

Stilted. The somewhat choppy gait of a dog lacking correct angulation.

Stop. The step-up from nose to skull; the indentation at the juncture of the skull and foreface.

Straight behind. Lacking angulation in the hindquarters.

Straight-shouldered. Lacking angulation of the shoulder blades.

Stud. A male dog that is used for breeding.

Stud book. The official record kept on the breeding particulars of recognized breeds of dogs.

Substance. Degree of bone size.

Swayback. Weakness, or downward curvature, in the topline between the withers and the hipbones.

Sweepstakes. Competition at shows for young dogs, usually up to twelve or eighteen months of age; unlike Futurity, no advance nomination is required.

Tail set. Manner in which the tail is placed on the rump.

T.D. An abbreviation of the Tracking Dog. title.

T.D.X. An abbreviation of the Tracking Dog Excellent title.

Team. Generally consists of four dogs.

Thigh. Hindquarters from the stifle to the hip.

Throatiness. Excessive loose skin at the throat.

Topline. The dog's back from withers to tail set.

Tracking Dog. A title awarded dogs who have fulfilled the A.K.C. requirements at licensed or member club tracking tests.

Tracking Dog Excellent. An advanced tracking degree.

Trail. Hunt by following a trail scent.

Trot. The gait at which the dog moves in a rhythmic two-beat action, right front and left hind foot and left front and right hind foot each striking the ground together.

Tuck-up. A natural shallowness of the body at the loin creating a small-waisted appearance.

Type. The combination of features which makes a breed unique, distinguishing it from all others.

U.D. An abbreviation of the Utility Dog title.

U.D.T. An abbreviation of the Utility Dog Tracker title.

U.D.T.X. An abbreviation of the Utility Dog and Tracker Excellent titles.

Unbenched show. Dog show at which dogs must arrive in time for judging and may leave anytime thereafter.

Undershot. The front teeth of the lower jaw reach beyond the front teeth of the upper jaw.

Upper arm. The foreleg between the forearm and the shoulder blade.

Utility Dog. Another level of obedience degree awarded after the completion of the C.D. and C.D.X. titles.

Utility Dog and Tracker. A double title indicating a dog that has gained both utility and tracking degrees. Also known as Utility Dog Tracking.

Utility Dog and Tracker Excellent. A double title indicating a dog that has gained both utility and advanced tracking degrees.

Walk. The gait in which three feet support the body, each lifting in regular sequence, one at a time, off the ground.

Walleye. A blue eye, fish eye, or pearl eye caused by a whitish appearance of the iris.

W.C. An abbreviation of Working Certificate.

Weedy. Lacking in sufficient bone and substance.

Well let down. Short hocks, hock joint placed low to the ground.

Wet neck. Dewlap, or superfluous skin.

Wheel back. Roached back with topline considerably arched over the loin.

Winners Bitch or Winners Dog. The awards which are accompanied by championship points, based on the number of dogs defeated, at A.K.C. member or licensed dog shows.

Withers. The highest point of the shoulders, right behind the neck.

Working Certificate. An award earned by dogs who have proven their hunting ability and who are not gun-shy.

Wry mouth. Lower jaw is twisted and does not correctly align with the upper jaw.

Index

This index is composed of three parts: a general index, an index of kennels, and an index of people mentioned in the text.

General Index

Index of Kennels

Index of People